'/01 $7.00

Brave New Families

BRAVE NEW FAMILIES

Stories of Domestic Upheaval in Late-Twentieth-Century America

With a New Preface

JUDITH STACEY

University of California Press

Berkeley   Los Angeles   London

University of California Press
Berkeley and Los Angeles, California

University of California Press, Ltd.
London, England

First Paperback Printing 1998

©1990 by Basic Books, Inc.
Preface © 1998 by Judith Stacey

Library of Congress Cataloging-in-Publication Data
Stacey, Judith.
    Brave new families : stories of domestic upheaval in late-
twentieth-century America / Judith Stacey : with a new preface.
        p.   cm.
    Originally published: New York : Basic Books, c1990.
    Includes bibliographical references and index.
    ISBN 0-520-21400-5 (pbk. : alk. paper)
    1. Family–California–Santa Clara County–Case studies.
2. Working class families–California–Santa Clara County–Case
studies.   I. Title.
HQ536.15.S26S73 1998
306.85'09794'73–dc21   97-49328
                                                    CIP

Printed in the United States of America
9 8 7 6 5 4 3 2 1

For my mother, Sandie Tuschak,
and the memory of my father, Robert Gisser,
and my grandmother,
Esther Shapiro

Contents

Preface to the 1998 Edition

I confess to experiencing somewhat mixed emotions over the reissue of *Brave New Families*. Whatever personal gratification I might take from the fact of its continuing relevance to understanding contemporary family life in the United States is tempered by my political awareness that the book would have been somewhat dated by now had its underlying social vision prevailed.

In the summer of 1984, when I began to study the families whose lives I portray in this book, the backlash, "profamily" movement of the New Right was in its prime. Buoyed by the ardent, strategic support of profamily activists, President Reagan was on the brink of winning his landslide reelection to a second term in office. At that time the rhetoric and politics of family values were the province of an explicitly right-wing, religious, antifeminist, and antigay social movement. Among the diverse impulses motivating my research was a desire to understand the nature of the growing mass appeal of this campaign. I set out to probe beneath superficial media stereotypes by directly observing the family practices and values of the sort of "ordinary" working people that the press was then characterizing as socially conservative "Reagan Democrats."

By the time *Brave New Families* was first published in 1990, the Reagan-Bush era was on the wane. Although this prospect by no means provided the exclusive conceptual framework I employed in the book, it was also one I had no objection to abetting. Constructing these narratives about working-class families, evangelical Christians, and twentysomething "postfeminists," I sought to shatter some of the stereotypes that were impeding public understanding and support for family diversity and democracy. I hoped that a textured rendering and analysis of the dense complexities of actual postindustrial families might help to challenge the dogmatic moralism of right-wing family politics, on the one hand, and to reinvigorate a more pluralist, feminist family politics, on the other.

And, indeed, soon after the first paperback edition of *Brave New Families* appeared late in 1991, there seemed good reason to expect that national political events would rapidly hasten the book's journey to the archives, where it might serve as an ethnographic document of a quaint, anomalous period in the history of U.S. family life and politics. For during the 1992 electoral season, family-values forces committed a series of extravagant media faux pas that seemed to place their agenda on the defensive. For example, in a televised political spectacle of the sort that is rather unique to the U.S., "Murphy Brown," a TV-sitcom-heroine single mother had resoundingly rebuked the public assault on her character's family values made by Vice President Dan Quayle. Likewise, the 1992 Republican presidential nominating convention had indulged in televised excesses of family-values fervor that had backfired in the polls. By then the Clinton campaign for the presidency was gaining momentum, and it certainly looked as though his "it's the economy, stupid," strategy would soon consign the political rhetoric of family values to history's dustbin.

Indeed, I predicted just that outcome during a 1992 election-eve symposium in which I participated. Had I been right, the ethnographic portrait that *Brave New Families* draws of families negotiating what I termed the postmodern family condition might still have social resonance today, but the book's political message would not. By now our society and culture would have acclimated to the irreversibility of family diversity and transcended the politics of nostalgia. We would have begun to confront the urgent challenges of revamping the basic premises that govern the structure of work, our social institutions, and public policies in ways that might enable families of many shapes and structures to thrive.

I was not right, however. Indeed, I consider it to be as sad a fact for the fate of our families and polity as it may prove good for the fate of this book that I could hardly have been more wrong, or more taken aback by what transpired instead. Although Clinton and the Democrats did prevail in the polling booths the next day, their victory did nothing to extinguish the politics of family values. Instead, family-values rhetoric soon scored a remarkable rebound in our public culture as well as in Congress. A mere few months after Clinton took office, even the once-liberal *Atlantic* magazine featured a cover story lamenting the declining state of family values, titled "Dan Quayle Was Right," and it took less than a year in office for President Clinton himself to convert to this credo.[1]

What was most personally surprising about this unanticipated, and unwelcome, turn of political events was its paradoxical impact on the subsequent career of *Brave New Families* and its author. Even before Clinton's first inauguration, both were drawn into the fray. Late in December 1992, the *New York Times* published an op-ed, "The Controversial Truth: The Two-Parent Family Is Better," by a sociologist who quoted from the conclusion to this book as an example of softheaded denial of the costs of family "decline."[2] Soon other family-values crusaders followed suit, identifying my approach to family change as a laissez-faire form of "family optimism, since it stresses that changes in the contemporary family are really nothing to worry about."[3] The unexpected timing and nature of this revival of interest in *Brave New Families* caught my attention and led me to engage more directly in public debate over the sources and effects of family change. While I had anticipated (and previously received) ideological opposition to my book from right-wing profamily advocates, I did not identify mainstream social science with this perspective. The belated assaults on my book by several social scientists alerted me to the emergence of a distinctively different campaign for family values. Appealing to secular rather than religious authority, the new crusade claims the mantle and rhetoric of social science in support of its belief in the superiority of conventional nuclear family structure and values. Avowedly centrist and "nonpartisan," rather than right-wing, its most visible advocates, like William Galston, David Blankenhorn, Barbara Dafoe Whitehead, and Amitai Etzioni, tend to be immersed more in Democratic than in Republican political networks and initiatives. Postfeminist rather than antifeminist, the new family-values crusade appeals to women's weariness with the double burden of their postindustrial lives, targeting "deadbeat dads" along with careerist moms.

Paradoxically, and poignantly, therefore, the political implications of *Brave New Families* are perhaps even more pertinent today than when I began writing the book a decade ago. Now that the politics of family values have become so much more mainstream and influential, they are also, in my view, more destructive. In the name of the family (as I titled a subsequent book)[4] politicians have been enacting policies that not only fail to promote their avowed goal but inflict tangible harm on too many real families, like the families portrayed in these pages. The preamble to the 1996 Personal Responsibility bill justifying the dismantling of welfare, which most social scientists project will inflict dire consequences on millions of poor families, actually identifies family breakdown as one of the consequences of "welfare dependency" that it seeks to redress. Opening with the assertion that "marriage is the foundation of a successful society," the bill declares, for example, that "the negative consequences of an out-of-wedlock birth on the mother, the child, the family, and society are *well documented* [my emphasis]."[5] Similarly, the Orwellian-named Defense of Marriage Act, which does nothing to strengthen the families of heterosexuals, only undermines the families of gays and lesbians by denying them legal protection for their relationships and depriving them of social respect.

Ironically, in fact, one of the lessons of *Brave New Families* is that most policies promoted by the campaign for family values ultimately do more to increase than to deter family diversity. Take the current popularity of the backlash against no-fault divorce, for example, which fueled the recent passage of a bill in Louisiana to allow engaged couples to enter into a "covenant marriage." In its wish to "slow down the hemorrhaging of the American family through the no-fault divorce system," the Louisiana legislature voted with near unanimity in July 1997 to provide heterosexual couples the option of voluntarily entering a "covenant marriage" that would be far more binding than ordinary marriage contracts. The legislators believed, as the bill's sponsor explained, that this "will prevent potentially weak marriages in some cases," by forcing couples to reflect more seriously on their level of commitment and compatibility.[6] Whether or not the covenant marriage option ultimately serves to strengthen marriage as an institution—an outcome I personally find unlikely—in adopting a two-tier system of marriage and divorce, the Louisiana legislature unwittingly proliferates family diversity. Compelling couples to choose between "no-fault" and "covenant" marriage expands the range of legitimate family structures and fosters greater self-consciousness about our culture's pluralist family values. Moreover, the advent of covenant marriage is likely to diminish further the social status, and perhaps the seriousness, of non-covenant marriage vows. *Brave New Families* depicts a wedding ceremony that one (already legally married) couple held to celebrate their decision to enter a voluntary "covenant marriage," precisely because they viewed their contractual marital bonds as insufficiently meaningful.

The fact that social science has supplanted religion as the principal authority for contemporary backlash family politics provides another reason why *Brave New Families* may enjoy even greater bearing on current politics than it did on the campaign that was dominant when it first appeared. Today the politics of family values involves a veritable industry of "virtual social science" that tirelessly disseminates misleading representations of selective correlations from aggregate data about family life. This sort of virtual social science reduces the messy complexity of family relationships, and of social science research, to simplistic, polarizing, journalistic sound bytes, such as the claim that "the two-parent family is better," or that "fatherlessness is the engine driving our most urgent social problems," or that "illegitimacy is the single most important social problem of our time."[7] But real social science, like any real family, is much more complex and contradictory. *Brave New Families* tries to honor and convey some of that complexity. An in-depth study of a small number of families conducted in the critical sociological tradition of C. Wright Mills, it places their "personal troubles" and triumphs—like an individual's divorce, layoff, religious conversion, remarriage, pregnancy, abortion, or job promotion—in the context of the "public issues" and institutions in which they occur: the employment practices (and malpractices) of the electronics industry, the institutional effects of the tax revolt, the vagaries of social-service opportunities, encounters with feminist ideology and activists and with the local bodies of evangelical religion. This brand of social science yields no sound-byte conclusions, nor does this book, save, perhaps, for the sage closing line uttered by Pam, one of its central figures: "You could never capture me."

Likewise, I believe that most hostile reviewers of this book, like the late historian Christopher Lasch and the contemporary family-values warriors I quoted above, failed to capture it or me.[8] In my view, even a cursory reading should establish how far from sanguine I felt about the state or fate of most of the "domestic upheavals in late-twentieth-century America" that the book portrays. Rather, there are at least two more profound differences between my views about postmodern family life and theirs. First, we assign nearly opposite portions of culpability to the social and individual sources of postmodern family instability. I portray many religious people in *Brave New Families*, but few saints. However, even the worst sinners I studied constantly struggled, some of them rather heroically, to cope with social sins that were not of their own making and were beyond their power to exorcise—from corporate downsizing to escalating real-estate prices, from punishing work schedules and hazardous working environments to deteriorating schools and an absence of health insurance. Thus, where moralistic observers like Lasch perceived the selfish, irresponsible, negligent, hedonistic excesses of morally rudderless parents and youth, I more quickly saw the toll on families exacted by the levels of corporate greed, public neglect, and social irresponsibility permitted by a morally rudderless society.

Second, what the book's critics seem to have badly misconstrued as my "family optimism" is instead my continuing, perhaps utopian, commitment to transcend my political pessimism by working to realize more of the democratic potential of family diversity than we now enjoy. I was by no means optimistic about the prospects for achieving much of this when I wrote *Brave New Families* nearly a decade ago, and certainly I am far less so now than when it first appeared in 1990. However, I also still stubbornly refuse to abandon that ideal. In fact, recently I joined with other family researchers and practitioners to form the Council on Contemporary Families, an organization committed to drawing upon our collective knowledge of and experience with family change to help move the national conversation about family values in a more rational, humane, and democratic direction.[9] Rereading the tales of spirit and spunk displayed in the face of adversity by the brave new families depicted in the pages that follow continually inspires my renewed commitment to this project. I can only hope that with the reissue of this book, my imperfect rendering of their stories of domestic upheaval will encourage others to embrace an expansive vision of family and social values.

Judith Stacey
August 1997

Notes

1. Barbara Dafoe Whitehead, "Dan Quayle Was Right," *The Atlantic* 271, no. 4 (April 1993): 47–84.

2. David Popenoe, "The Controversial Truth: The Two-Parent Family Is Better," *New York Times* (December 26, 1992):13.

3. James Q. Wilson, "The Family-Values Debate," *Commentary* 95, no. 4 (1993): 24.

4. Judith Stacey, *In the Name of The Family: Rethinking Family Values in the Postmodern Age* (Boston: Beacon Press, 1996).

5. Section 3503, "Legislative Accountability," Personal Responsibility Act of 1996, U.S. Congress.

6. Quoted in Kevin Sack, "Louisiana Approves Measure to Tighten Marriage Bonds," *New York Times* (June 24, 1997): A1, 13.

7. Popenoe, op cit; David Blankenhorn, *Fatherless America: Confronting Our Most Urgent Social Problem* (New York: Basic Books, 1995): 2; Charles Murray, "The Time Has Come to Put a Stigma Back on Illegitimacy," *Wall Street Journal* (October 29, 1993), Forum.

8. Christopher Lasch, "Misreading the Facts About Families," *Commonweal* (February 22, 1991):136.

9. For information about the Council on Contemporary Families, see the web site: http://www.slip.net/~ccf/.

Acknowledgments

In 1984 I faced the jitters many authors experience when they begin to contemplate a second book project. Political and intellectual passions motivated my first book about family and revolution in China, but they languished in the years of lonely library research that followed. Choosing my next major research project, I was eager for a "hands-on" engagement in the field. Unschooled in fieldwork research as I was, I did not anticipate the depth or the complexity of the emotional experiences I was about to undergo. My heart, much more than my hands, has been engaged with the people portrayed in this book who so generously agreed to subject their family lives to my impertinent sociological scrutiny. To them I owe my first and greatest debt, as well as my apologies for whatever "domestic upheavals" my intrusive study introduced into their lives.

My second debt is to my own family and friends who sustained me through a personal domestic upheaval which coincided with the onest of this project. Their unstinting love, support, and, especially, their salty humor rescued me countless times from the self-doubt that is an author's bane. Special thanks to: Herb Schreier who has been there strongest and truest "for better and for worse;" our son, Jake, the most creative morale booster and jacket design consultant I know; Sandie Tuschak, my mother and extravagant fan club; Debby Rosenfelt, Linda Collins, and Anne Farrar, my not-so-fictive kin and friends for all seasons; Carole Joffe, Barrie Thorne, Wini Breines, Danny Walkowitz, Judy Walkowitz, Nancy lander, Steve Portugese, Anna Yeatman, Darlaine Gardetto, Ruth Milkman, and Rayna Rapp, who have honed the craft of long-distance friendship and colleagiality into a high art form; and to newer prized friends who counseled and supported me through thorny writing patches: Lillian Rubin, Judy Newton, Evelyn Fox Keller, Carol Stack, and Otto Will.

Two people deserve more gratitude than it is seemly to express. Susie Gerard, my research assistant, chief colleague, enthusiast, and critic, made intellectual, practical, and personal contributions to this book too numerous to recount. She also co-authored an article with me on post-feminist evangelicalism, portions of which appear in chapter 6. Jeff Escoffier, freelance editor and writing therapist extraordinaire, played intellectual midwife to this book. I cannot imagine how I could have endured the labor pains without his wise counsel and inspiring encouragement at every stage.

I am not yet so much of a post-Marxist to forget the material basis of intellectual production. Financial support from an American Council of Learned Societies/Ford Fellowship funded portions of my fieldwork research. Faculty Research Grants from the University of California, Davis, provided crucial research and technical support. A fellowship term at the Humanities Research Institute of the University of California, Davis, and a "Changing Gender Roles" grant from the Rockefeller Foundation funded the release time from teaching that enabled me to write this book. Maureen Goldston handled the daunting administrative burdens of all these privileges with her incomparable competence and cheer. Lenny Siegel, Director of the Pacific Studies Center in Mountain View, California, directed me to crucial contacts, data, and resources in the Silicon Valley, the site of this research. Deirdre Kelly, Marco Orru, Jane McKendry, and Kristin Reller helped me pursue these leads.

Friends and colleagues who read individual chapters attempted, not always successfully, to curb my worst substantive errors and rhetorical excesses. For this I am grateful to: Fred Block, Wini Breines, Karen Halttunen, Susan Krieger, Bev Lozano, Roland Marchand, Aihwa Ong, Ben Orlove, Ilene Philipson, Debby Rosenfelt, Lillian Rubin, Naomi Schneider, Carol Stack, Barrie Thorne, Anna Yeatman, and members of the 1988–89 Interdisciplinary Seminar at the UCD Humanities Research Institute. Steve Fraser, my editor at Basic Books, also paid me the compliment of candor. His swift, rigorous responses to every draft and detail of this book mark him as a paragon of a vanishing editorial breed.

I also imposed the burden of the entire manuscript on Linda Collins, Erica Crowell, and repeatedly on Herb Schreier. All responded with intelligence, wit, and encouragement while freeing me to write by assuming many of my child-care responsibilities. Rare is the book that deserves such generosity; rarer still is one written without it.

Oakland, California
January 1990

The stories in this book are true, and Santa Clara County, California, is the actual location of the study. However, all names and places of residence and work, as well as other identifying details, have been fictionalized in order to protect the privacy of the subjects of this study.

Prologue

It was the day after the World Series Earthquake stunned the San Francisco Bay region in October 1989. Public authorities beseeched us not to burden the overtaxed circuits with unnecessary calls, but few could resist the compulsion to reassure ourselves of the welfare of those we cared about or to obsessively swap our survivors' tales. I was not among those few. I had not spoken with Pamela Gama or Dotty Lewison in more than a month. Relieved to learn that the cataclysm had spared both women's families, as it had mine, its more brutal punishments, I promised to visit each again soon. I would bring my tape recorder, I offered, if they would like to record their responses to this manuscript.

In the interval since we had spoken last, Pam and Dotty both had been reading drafts of the chapters I had written about their respective families. Neither was entirely pleased with what she had read. Dotty wished that I had not portrayed her family's plight in such disheartening terms. It was a depressing story, she agreed, but she would have given it a "more Pollyannaish" cast. However, Dotty observed, "It's your book, not mine." Pam had a comparable response. She had not yet finished reading all of the chapters, in part because she was finding doing so such an uncomfortable experience. Pam had detected a number of minor factual errors in my portrait of her family, but what she found most unsettling was the instrumental account I had given of her reborn religious faith. Perhaps, Pam theorized, she had presented her faith to me this way in response to my own deep feminist secularity. Like Dotty, however, Pam had concluded that my textual errors were not her business. "After all," she reminded me, the book "is really not my baby; it's yours."

In the interval since my prior contact with these astute critics, I had been fretfully grooming this "baby" for its public debut. Selecting the proper garments for the book's two opening chapters—those that would introduce the ethnographic chapters about Pamela's and Dotty's postmodern kinship relationships—troubled me most. My narrative impulse was immediately to introduce my readers to the central characters whose stories, or at least my flawed rendering of these, comprise most, and perhaps the most engaging portions, of this book. But my sociological reflexes pulsed to a more orderly beat. How would prospective readers know what this book is "about" or situate its intellectual bearings, my academic voice chanted, if I neglected to set the stories in the context of the social issues about gender, class, and kinship that moved me to narrate them? Capitulate to your disciplinary proclivities, the narrative voice rejoined, and you might fail to engross many readers who might otherwise find interest and value in the stories whose social meanings you wish to define.

The earthquake and my subsequent conversations with Dotty and Pam quelled this internal dispute—chastening reminders both of the humbling limits of human authority. Just as Pam and Dotty and their kin shaped, but failed to control, my reading of their lives, so too I cannot control your reading of this book. Succumbing less to my academic pretensions, I hope, than to this recognition, I decided to leave the stories dressed in the sociological outfits in which I had already clothed them. Reading the book thus, my tactful new student assistant claimed to be more captivated by the ethnographic tales than by the more formal first two chapters. Readers who, like her, find people's stories fascinating and enjoy imposing their own sense on them might prefer to read chapters 3 through 10 before the first two chapters. Dotty and Pam will reappear in the epilogue to underscore the temerity of my sociological reading of, and intervention into, their families' lives.

October 1989

INTRODUCTIONS

I

The Making and Unmaking of Modern Families

On a spring afternoon half a century from today, the Joneses are gathering to sing "Happy Birthday" to Junior.

There's Dad and his third wife, Mom and her second husband, Junior's two half brothers from his father's first marriage, his six stepsisters from his mother's spouse's previous unions, 100-year-old Great-Grandpa, all eight of Junior's current "grand-parents," assorted aunts, uncles-in-law and stepcousins.

While one robot scoops up the gift wrappings and another blows out the candles, Junior makes a wish—that he didn't have so many relatives.

The family tree by the year 2033 will be rooted as deeply as ever in America's social landscape, but it will be sprouting some odd branches.

—U.S. News & World Report[1]

In the summer of 1986 I attended a wedding ceremony in a small Christian pentecostal church in the Silicon Valley. The service celebrated the same "traditional" family patterns and values that two years earlier had inspired a "profamily" movement to assist Ronald Reagan's landslide reelection to the presidency of the United States. At the same time, however, the pastor's rhetoric displayed substantial sympathy with feminist criticisms of patriarchal marriage. "A ring is not a shackle, and marriage is not a relationship of domination," he instructed the groom. Moreover, complex patterns of divorce, remarriage, and stepkinship linked the members of the wedding party and their guests. The group bore far greater resemblance to the postmodern family of the imaginary

3

twenty-first-century Joneses than it did to the image of "traditional" family life that arouses the nostalgic fantasies so widespread among critics of contemporary family practices.

In the final decades before the twenty-first century, passionate contests over changing family life in the United States have polarized vast numbers of citizens. Outside the Supreme Court of the United States, righteous, placard-carrying Right-to-Lifers square off against feminists and civil libertarians demonstrating their anguish over the steady dismantling of women's reproductive freedom. On the same day in July 1989 when New York's highest court expanded the legal definition of a family to extend rent-control protection to gay couples, a coalition of conservative clergymen in San Francisco blocked implementation of their city's new "domestic partners" ordinance. "It is the totality of the relationship," proclaimed the New York judge, "As evidenced by the dedication, caring and self-sacrifice of the parties which should, in the final analysis, control" the definition of family.[2] But just this concept of family is anathema to "profamily" activists. Declaring that the attempt by the San Francisco Board of Supervisors to grant legal status to unmarried heterosexual and homosexual couples "arbitrarily redefined the time-honored and hallowed nature of the family," the clergymen's petition was signed by sufficient citizens to force the ordinance into a referendum battle.[3] The reckoning came in November 1989, when the electorate of the city many consider to be the national capital of family change narrowly defeated the domestic partners law.

Most popular, as well as many scholarly, assessments of family change anxiously and misguidedly debate whether "the family" will survive the twentieth century at all.[4] Anxieties like these are far from new. "For at least 150 years," historian Linda Gordon writes, "there have been periods of fear that 'the family'—meaning a popular image of what families were supposed to be like, by no means a correct recollection of any actual 'traditional' family—was in decline; and these fears have tended to escalate in periods of social stress."[5] The actual subject of this recurring, fretful discourse is a historically specific form and concept of family life, one that most historians identify as the "modern" family. Students in a course I teach called "The Making and Unmaking of Modern Families" helped me realize that many of us who write and teach about American family life have not abetted public understanding of family change with our counterintuitive use of the concept, the "modern" family. The "modern" family of sociological theory and historical convention designates a form no longer prevalent in the United States—an intact nuclear household unit composed of a male breadwinner, his full-time homemaker wife, and their dependent children. This is precisely the form of family life that many mistake for an ancient, essential, and now-endangered institution.

"How many of you grew up in a modern family?" I used to ask my students at the beginning of each term. I expected the proportion of raised hands to decline, like the modern family, with the years. It baffled me at first to receive precisely the inverse response. Just when demographers were reporting that twice as many American households were headed by divorced, separated, and never-married individuals as were occupied by "modern" families, increasing numbers of my students claimed to have grown up in "modern" ones. This seemingly anomalous finding was the product, of course, of my poorly conceived survey question. Just as I had anticipated, over the years fewer and fewer of my students were coming of age in Ozzie and Harriet families. Quite sensibly, however, unlike me, they did not regard such families as "modern"; to them they were archaic "traditional" ones. Those contemporary family relationships that my students took to be modern comprise the "postmodern" family terrain that is the central subject of this book.

This is a book about the unpredictable, often incongruous, and contested character of contemporary family practices in the postindustrial United States. It is written by a feminist who has learned to respect and understand some of the social appeals of widespread nostalgia for eroding family forms even though I oppose the conservative gender, class, and sexual politics of the profamily movement. I gained this respect in the course of my ethnographic study of two extended kinship networks of primarily white "working-class"* people who live, love, work, and worry in California's famous, and infamous, Silicon Valley. Most of this book, as its subtitle promises, tells stories about the gender, kinship, and class relationships I observed and learned about while studying members of

---

*I place this term in quotation marks to signal its current problematic, transitory status. No single conventional social class category adequately describes the families in this study. "Working class" works best as a shorthand code to evoke the social prejudices that informed this study's original, but soon-discarded, research design.

kin groups I refer to as "Pamela's kin" and "the Lewisons"*—family relationships, that is, that I came to characterize as postmodern. Book I of the ethnography, "Feminism, Fundamentalism, and a Postmodern Extended Family," portrays the creative strategies through which Pamela Gama, the bride at the Christian wedding, and her relatives have responded to postindustrial and postfeminist conditions, while the more troubled history of the Lewisons appears in Book II, "High-Tech Visions and Battered Dreams."

Before I introduce Pamela Gama, Dotty Lewison, and their kin, here I set their family biographies in the broad historical context of the rise and fall of the modern nuclear family system in the United States. I hope thereby to suggest that revolutionary changes and struggles over the definition and meaning of family life have a long and continuing history in this country. Central to these struggles are irreconcilable visions of desirable arrangements between the sexes. For "family," as anthropologists have taken pains to demonstrate, is a locus not of residence but of meaning and relationships.[6] Thus, the question for futurologists is not whether "the family" will survive at all, but how our heirs will be arranging and talking about their gender and kinship relationships when postmodern Junior and his stepsisters celebrate their birthdays less than half a century from today. Through an iconoclastic exploration of family life during this crucial transitional period, this book attempts to enhance those conversations.

THE EPHEMERAL MODERN FAMILY

Now that the "modern" family system has almost exited from its historical stage, we can perceive how peculiar, ephemeral, and internally contradictory was this once-revolutionary gender and kinship order. Historians place the emergence of the modern American family among white middle-class people in the late eighteenth century; they depict its flowering in the nineteenth century and chart its decline in the second half of the twentieth.[7] Thus, for white Americans, the history of modern families

---

*To protect the privacy of participants in this study, I follow the convention of fictionalizing their names, their places of residence and work, and other descriptive details. Santa Clara County, California, however, is the actual general location of this study.

traverses the same historical trajectory as that of modern industrial society.* What was modern about upper-middle-class family life in the half century after the American Revolution was the appearance of social arrangements governing gender and kinship relationships that contrasted sharply with those of "traditional," or premodern, patriarchal corporate units.

The premodern family among white Colonial Americans, an institution some scholars characterize as "the Godly family,"[8] was the constitutive element of Colonial society. This integrated economic, social, and political unit explicitly subordinated individual to corporate family interests, and women and children to the authority of the household's patriarchal head. Decisions regarding the timing and crafting of premodern marriages served not the emotional needs of individuals but the economic, religious, and social purposes of larger kin groups, as these were interpreted by patriarchs who controlled access to land, property, and craft skills. Nostalgic images of "traditional" families rarely recall their instability or diversity. Death visited Colonial homes so frequently that second marriages and blended households composed of stepkin were commonplace. With female submission thought to be divinely prescribed, conjugal love was a fortuitous bonus, not a prerequisite of such marriages. Similarly the doctrine of innate depravity demanded authoritarian parenting to break the will and save the souls of obstinate children, a project that required extensive paternal involvement in child rearing. Few boundaries between family and work impeded such patriarchal supervision, or segregated the sexes who labored at their arduous and interdependent tasks in close proximity. Boundaries between public and private life were equally permeable. Communities regulated proper family conduct, intervening actively to enforce disciplinary codes, and parents exchanged their children as apprentices and servants.

*The family histories of subjugated, "nonwhite" populations in the United States—Native Americans, African-Americans, Mexican-Americans, and Asian-Americans—are also intertwined with that of industrial capitalist development. Yet cultural differences and systemic racial-ethnic subordination produce major differences in the substance and timing of each group's process of family change. I portray the history of the ideal-typical family order of the dominant white population because, until recently, it represented this nation's culturally mandated gender and kinship system. This family regime has been denied to most members of racial and ethnic minorities, and their diverse family arrangements frequently have been judged and found wanting when compared with it. For more comprehensive and comparative texts that treat a broad range of American families, see Mintz and Kellogg, *Domestic Revolutions;* Evans, *Born for Liberty;* Baca-Zinn and Eitzen, *Diversity in American Families;* and Coontz, *Social Origins of Private Life.*

Four radical innovations differentiate modern from premodern family life among white Americans: (1) Family work and productive work became separated, rendering women's work invisible as they and their children became economically dependent on the earnings of men. (2) Love and companionship became the ideal purposes of marriages that were to be freely contracted by individuals. (3) A doctrine of privacy emerged that attempted to withdraw middle-class family relationships from public scrutiny. (4) Women devoted increased attention to nurturing fewer and fewer children as mothering came to be exalted as both a natural and demanding vocation.

The rise of the modern American family accompanied the rise of industrial capitalist society, with its revolutionary social, spatial, and temporal reorganization of work and domestic life. The core premises and practices of the new family regime were far more contradictory than those of the premodern family order. Coding work as masculine and home as feminine, modern economic arrangements deepened the segregation of the sexes by extracting men from, and consigning white married women to, an increasingly privatized domestic domain. The institutionalized subordination of these wives to their husbands persisted; indeed, as factory production supplanted domestic industry, wives became increasingly dependent on their spouse's earnings. The doctrine of separate gender spheres governing the modern family order in the nineteenth century was so potent that few married women among even the poorest of native white families dared to venture outside their homes in search of income.[9]

The proper sphere of working-class married white women also was confined to the home. Yet few working-class families approximated the modern family ideal before well into the twentieth century. Enduring conditions of poverty, squalor, disease, and duress rivaling those in industrializing England,[10] most immigrant and native white working-class families in nineteenth-century America depended on supplementary income. Income from women's out work, child labor, lodgers, and the earnings of employed unmarried sons and daughters supplemented the meager and unreliable wages paid to working men. Not until the post–World War II era did substantial numbers of working-class households achieve the "modern family" pattern.[11]

If the doctrine of separate, and unequal, gender spheres limited women's domain and rendered their work invisible, it also enhanced their capacity to formulate potent moral and political challenges to patriarchy.

Men ceded the domains of child rearing and virtue to "moral" mothers who made these responsibilities the basis for expanding their social influence and political rights. This and the radical ideologies of individualism, democracy, and conjugal love, which infused modern family culture, would lead ultimately to its undoing. It is no accident, historians suggest, that the first wave of American feminism accompanied the rise of the modern family.[12]

With rearview vision one glimpses the structural fragility of the modern family system, particularly its premise of enduring voluntary commitment. For modern marriages, unlike their predecessors, were properly affairs not of the purse but of the the heart. A romantic "until death do us part" commitment volunteered by two young adults acting largely independent of the needs, interests, or wishes of their kin was the vulnerable linchpin of the modern family order. It seems rather remarkable, looking back, that during the first century of the modern family's cultural ascendancy, death did part the vast majority of married couples. But an ideology of conjugal love and companionship implies access to divorce as a safety valve for failures of youthful judgment or the vagaries of adult affective development. Thus, a statistical omen of the internal instability of this form of marriage lies in the unprecedented rise of divorce rates that accompanied the spread of the modern family. Despite severe legal and social restrictions, divorce rates began to climb at least as early as the 1840s. They have continued their ascent ever since, until by the middle of the 1970s divorce outstripped death as a source of marital dissolution.[13] A crucial component of the modern family system, divorce would ultimately prove to be its Achilles' heel.

For a century, as the cultural significance of the modern family grew, the productive and even the reproductive work performed within its domain contracted. By the end of the "modern" industrial era in the 1950s, virtually all productive work had left the home. While advances in longevity stretched enduring marriages to unprecedented lengths, the full-time homemaker's province had been pared to the chores of housework, consumption, and the cultivation of a declining number of progeny during a shortened span of years.[14]

Those Americans, like myself, who came of age at that historic moment were encouraged to absorb a particularly distorted impression of the normalcy and timelessness of the modern family system. The decade between the late 1940s and the late 1950s represents an aberrant period in the history of this aberrant form of family life. Fueled in part, as historian Elaine May has suggested, by the apocalyptic Cold War sensibilities of the post–World War II nuclear age, the nation indulged in what would prove to be a last-gasp orgy of modern nuclear family domesticity.[15] Three-fifths of American households conformed to the celebrated breadwinner–full-time homemaker modern form in 1950, as substantial sectors of working-class men began at long last to secure access to a family wage.[16] A few years later Walt Disney opened the nation's first family theme park in southern California, designed to please and profit from the socially conservative fantasies of such increasingly prosperous families.[17]

The aberrant fifties temporarily reversed the century's steady decline in birth rates. The average age of first-time visitors to the conjugal altar also dropped to record lows.[18] Higher percentages of Americans were marrying than ever before or since, and even the majority of white working-class families achieved coveted homeownership status.[19] It was during this time that Talcott Parsons provided family sociology with its most influential theoretical elaboration of the modern American family, of how its nuclear household structure and complementary division of roles into female "expressive" and male "instrumental" domains was sociologically adaptive to the functional demands of an industrial society.[20] Rare are the generations, or even the sociologists, who perceive the historical idiosyncrasies of the normal cultural arrangements of their time.[21]

The postwar baby boom was to make the behaviors and beliefs of that decade's offspring disproportionately significant for the rest of their lives. The media, the market, and all social and political institutions would follow their development with heightened interest. Thus, a peculiar period in U.S. family history came to set the terms for the waves of rebellion against, and nostalgia for, the passing modern family and gender order that have become such prominent and disruptive features of the American political landscape. The world's first generation of childhood television viewers grew up, as I did, inundated by such weekly paeans to the male breadwinner nuclear household and modern family ideology as *Father Knows Best, Leave It to Beaver,* and *Ozzie and Harriet.* Because unusual numbers of us later pushed women's biological "clock" to its reproductive limits, many now find ourselves parenting (or choosing not to) in the less innocent age of *Thirtysomething, Kate and Allie,* and *Who's the Boss?*[22]

For beneath the sentimental gloss that the fifties enameled onto its domestic customs, forces undermining the modern family of the 1950s accelerated while those sustaining it eroded. In the midst of profamily pageantry, nonfamily households proliferated.[23] As the decade drew to a close, the nation entered what C. Wright Mills, with characteristic prescience, termed its "postmodern period."[24] The emergent postindustrial economy shifted employment from heavy industries to nonunionized clerical, service, and new industrial sectors. Employers found themselves irresistibly attracted to the nonunionized, cheaper labor of women and, thus, increasingly to that of married women and mothers.

One glimpses the ironies of class and gender history here. For decades industrial unions struggled heroically for a socially recognized male breadwinner wage that would allow the working class to participate in the modern gender order. These struggles, however, contributed to the cheapening of female labor that helped gradually to undermine the modern family regime.[25] Escalating consumption standards, the expansion of mass collegiate coeducation, and the persistence of high divorce rates then gave more and more women ample cause to invest a portion of their identities in the "instrumental" sphere of paid labor.[26] Thus, middle-class women began to abandon their confinement in the modern family just as working-class women were approaching its access ramps. The former did so, however, only after the wives of working-class men had pioneered the twentieth-century revolution in women's paid work. Entering employment during the catastrophic 1930s, participating in defense industries in the 1940s, and raising their family incomes to middle-class standards by returning to the labor force rapidly after child rearing in the 1950s, working-class women quietly modeled and normalized the postmodern family standard of employment for married mothers. Whereas in 1950 the less a man earned, the more likely his wife was to be employed, by 1968 wives of middle-income men were the most likely to be in the labor force.[27]

Thus, the apotheosis of the modern family only temporarily concealed its imminent decline. Breadwinners as well as homemakers were renegotiating the terms and tempos of their conjugal commitments. Cultural constraints that tethered women and men to lifelong vows continued to loosen. Writing about the origins of "the virgin and the state," anthropologist Sherry Ortner once theorized that the domestication of men represented a major social evolutionary watershed, which was achieved at considerable cost to the sexuality and autonomy of women.[28] If this is

11

correct, the historic bargain came apart during the sexual revolution of the 1960s. Even in the familistic fifties, as social critic Barbara Ehrenreich has suggested, beats and playboys rebelled against the monogamous breadwinner mold for culturally mandated masculinity.[29] Advances in contraception paved the path for revolutionary changes in women's sexual behavior during the 1960s, changes that feminists alternately depict as the feminization or the masculinization of sex.[30]

The aberrant and contradictory features of fifties' familial culture prepared the ground for the family revolution of the 1960s and 1970s from whose shock effects American society has not yet recovered. The gap between dominant cultural ideology and discordant behaviors generated radical challenges to the modern family. A social movement for gay liberation coincided with the legalization of abortion. Both posed the ultimate challenges to the cultural bond between sexuality and procreation. Particularly important for the fate of the modern family, a massive and militant movement for the liberation of women also revived in those years. And this "second wave" of American feminism[31] made family politics central to its project.

FEMINISM AS MIDWIFE TO POSTINDUSTRIAL SOCIETY

Feminists intentionally accelerated the modern family's demise. *The Feminine Mystique*, Betty Friedan's best-selling critique of "the problem that has no name," inspired the awakening women's movement to launch a full-scale attack on the exploitative and stultifying effects of women's confinement and dependency as homemaker. Soon feminist scholars were warning women that "in truth, being a housewife makes women sick."[32] This backward-looking critique of a declining institution and culture, one that I personally embraced wholeheartedly and helped to disseminate, colluded unwittingly in postindustrial processes, and at considerable political cost to the feminist movement. Although we intended the institutions of domesticity and their male beneficiaries to be the targets of our critique, we placed housewives on the defensive just when sizable numbers of working-class women were attaining this long-denied status. Feminists provided ideological support for divorce and for the soaring rates of female-headed households. Feminist enthusiasm for female autonomy encouraged women's massive entry into the postindustrial labor market. This, in turn, abetted the corporate deunionization strategies that have accompanied the reorganization of the U.S. economy.

Millions of women like myself, derived enormous, tangible benefits from the changes in postindustrial home and work life and from the ways in which feminist ideology encouraged us to initiate and cope with such changes.[33] The lioness's share of these benefits, however, fell to privileged women. As postindustrial society became entrenched, many women, perhaps the majority, found their economic and personal conditions worsening. While unionized occupations and real wages began to decline, women were becoming the postindustrial "proletariat," performing most of the nation's low-skilled, poorly paid jobs. As the overall percentage of jobs that were secure and well paying declined, particularly within blue-collar occupations, increasing numbers of even white men swelled the ranks of the under- and unemployed. Nonetheless, most white male workers still labored at jobs that were skilled and comparatively well paid.[34] The devastating economic effects on women and children of endemic marital instability became widely known. Increasing percentages of women were rearing children by themselves, generally with minimal economic contributions from former husbands and fathers.[35] Yet rising numbers of single mothers who worked full time, year-round, were not earning wages sufficient to lift their families above the official poverty line.[36]

Even as marriage bonds lost their adhesive, they came to serve as a major axis of economic and social stratification. Increasingly, families required two incomes to sustain a middle-class way of life. The married female "secondary" wage earner can lift a former working-class or middle-class family into relative affluence, while the loss or lack of access to a male income drove millions of women and children into poverty.[37] In short, the drastic increase in women's paid employment in the postindustrial period yielded lots more work for mother, but with very unevenly distributed economic benefits and only modest improvements in relative earnings between women and men.[38]

In the context of these developments, many women (and men) became susceptible to the profamily appeals of an antifeminist backlash. Because of our powerful and highly visible critique of the modern family, and because of the sensationalized way by which the media disseminated this critique, feminists received much of the blame for family and social crises that attended the transition from an industrial to a postindustrial order in the United States. "Feminist ideology told women how foolish and exploited they were to be wives and mothers," turning them into "a vicious cartoon," wrote Connaught Marshner, "chairman" of the National Pro-Family Coalition, in her manifesto for the profamily movement, *The New Traditional Woman*.[39]

Had white feminists identified earlier with the plight of the Black "matriarch," we might have been forewarned of our fate. In 1965 Daniel Patrick Moynihan's explosive report, *The Negro Family: The Case for National Action*,[40] blamed Black "matriarchs" for much of the "tangle of pathology" he found in the nation's African-American households. The Moynihan report ignited an acrimonious and deeply sexist debate over the crisis in African-American families, which eventually derailed a planned White House conference on Black families and rights.[41] Debates over feminism and the crisis in white families later caused President Jimmy Carter to scuttle plans for a White House Conference on the Family in the late 1970s. Raging political contests over emergent gender and family arrangements splintered the intended unified conference on "the family" into deeply polarized regional forums on "famil*ies*." In this pluralist definition, liberals and feminists may have won one of the last of our rhetorical victories in the family wars, while the profamily movement of the New Right began to rehearse the antifeminist script that helped to fuel the Reagan revolution of the 1980s.

Ronald Reagan was an undeserving beneficiary of the profamily reaction, as humorist Delia Ephron observes in a book review of Maureen Reagan's dutiful memoir: "It is funny and a bit pathetic that Ronald and Nancy Reagan keep finding out their family secrets by reading their children's books. It is also ironic that this couple who symbolized a return to hearth, home and 1950's innocence should, in reality, be candidates for a very 1980s study on the troubled family."[42] The former president's less dutiful daughter, Patti Davis, agrees: "Anyone who hasn't been living in a coma for the past eight years knows that we're not a close-knit family."[43] It seems an astonishing testimony to Reagan's acclaimed media magic, therefore, that despite his own divorce and his own far-from-happily blended family, he and his *second* lady managed to serve so effectively as the symbolic figureheads of a profamily agenda, which his economic and social policies helped to further undermine.

The demographic record demonstrates that postmodern gender and kinship changes proceeded unabated throughout the Reagan era. The proportion of American households headed by single mothers grew by 21 percent, while rates of employment by mothers of young children continued their decades of ascent. When "profamily" forces helped elect Reagan to his first term in 1980, 20 percent of American children lived with a single parent, and 41 percent of mothers with children under the age of three had joined the paid labor force. When Reagan completed his second term eight years later, these figures had climbed to 24 and 54 percent respectively.[44] The year of Reagan's landslide reelection, 1984, was the first year that more working mothers placed their children in public group child care than in family day care.[45] Reaganites too hastily applauded a modest decline in divorce rates during the 1980s—to a level at which more than half of first marriages still were expected to dissolve before death. But demographers who studied marital separations as well as divorce found the years from 1980 to 1985 to show "the highest level of marital disruption yet recorded for the U.S."[46] Likewise, birth rates remained low, marriage rates fell, and homeownership rates, which had been rising for decades, declined throughout the Reagan years.[47]

Moreover, changes in African-American family patterns that Moynihan's report had treated as pathology, particularly unmarried childbearing and single motherhood, escalated in the Reagan era among whites as well as Blacks.[48] By the time that profamily administration left office, single-parent households were far more numerous than modern families.[49] Little wonder that the profamily movement misrepresented those modern families as "traditional" ones. The Reagan period was indeed the time when the once-modern familial and social order had become the past.

As the modern family order exited, the debate over the meaning of its passing shifted decidedly to the right. Nostalgia for the modern family, and even for premodern patriarchal kinship patterns, generated a backlash literature within feminism as well as elsewhere.[50] Although the antifeminist, profamily movement failed to halt the disintegration of the modern family, it placed feminists and liberals on the defensive and achieved major political gains. So visible and politically effective has been this counterwomen's movement that it has obscured the fact that feminist sympathies and support for changing family life continued among all major age and social groups of Americans throughout the Reagan era. Many feminists ourselves were surprised when a poll conducted by *The New York Times* six months after Reagan left office found that more than

15

BLOOM COUNTY   by Berke Breathed

two-thirds of the women and even a majority of the men agreed that the United States still needs a strong women's movement.[51]

RECOMBINANT FAMILY LIFE

Indeed, as this book illustrates, women and men have been creatively remaking American family life during the past three decades of postindustrial upheaval. Out of the ashes and residue of the modern family, they have drawn on a diverse, often incongruous array of cultural, political, economic, and ideological resources, fashioning these resources into new gender and kinship strategies to cope with postindustrial challenges, burdens, and opportunities. In this book, for example, we observe people turning divorce into a kinship resource rather than a rupture, creating complex, divorce-extended families like those gathered to celebrate Junior's not-so-futuristic birthday. Depicted too are religious "traditionalists" who draw on biblical and human potential movement precepts to form communal households that join married and single members of an evangelical ministry.

And as Americans have been remaking family life, the vast majority, even those seemingly hostile to feminism, have been selectively appropriating feminist principles and practices and fusing these, patchwork style, with old and new gender, kinship, and cultural patterns. In the chapters that follow, as in our society, married women struggle to involve reluctant spouses in housework and child care; unmarried white women choose to have children on their own; homosexual couples exchange marriage vows and share child-rearing commitments; evangelical ministers counsel Christian husbands to learn to communicate with their wives and advise battered women to leave their abusive mates.

I call the fruits of these diverse efforts to remake contemporary family life "the postmodern family." I do this, despite my reservations about employing such a fashionable and elusive cultural concept, to signal the contested, ambivalent, and undecided character of contemporary gender and kinship arrangements. "What is the post-modern?" art historian Clive Dilnot asks rhetorically in the title of a detailed discussion of literature on postmodern culture, and his answers apply readily to the domain of present family conditions in the United States.[52] The postmodern, he maintains, "is first, an uncertainty, an insecurity, a doubt." Most of the "post-" words provoke uneasiness, because they imply simultaneously "both the end, or at least the radical transformation of, a familiar pattern of activity or group of ideas" and the emergence of "new fields of cultural activity whose contours are still unclear and whose meanings and implications . . . cannot yet be fathomed." The postmodern, moreover, is "characterized by the process of the linking up of areas and the crossing of the boundaries of what are conventionally considered to be disparate realms of practice."[53]

Like postmodern culture, contemporary family arrangements are diverse, fluid, and unresolved. Postindustrial social transformations have opened up such a diverse range of gender and kinship relationships as to undermine the claim in the memorable opening line from Tolstoy's *Anna Karenina:* "All happy families are alike, but every unhappy family is unhappy after its own fashion."[54] Today even happy families no longer are all alike! No longer is there a single culturally dominant family pattern to which the majority of Americans conform and most of the rest aspire. Instead, Americans today have crafted a multiplicity of family and household arrangements that we inhabit uneasily and reconstitute frequently in response to changing personal and occupational circumstances.

It is for this reason that I risk the hubris of employing the definite article *the* postmodern family in a book that portrays the gender and kinship strategies of only two white, "working-class" kin networks. The families depicted in this book do not represent the new culturally dominant familial ideal, nor even all of its statistically normative experiences. Under postmodern conditions no such families exist, because no singular family structure or ideology has arisen to supplant the modern family.

We are living, I believe, through a transitional and contested period of family history, a period *after* the modern family order, but before what we cannot foretell. Precisely because it is not possible to characterize with a single term the competing sets of family cultures that coexist at present, I identify this family regime as postmodern. *The* postmodern family is not a new model of family life, not the next stage in an orderly progression of family history, but the stage when the belief in a logical progression of stages breaks down.[55] Rupturing evolutionary models of family history and incorporating both experimental and nostalgic elements, "the" postmodern family lurches forward and backward into an uncertain future.

Analogous features of contemporary economic arrangements generated the concept of postindustrial society. "This is a strange period in the history of the United States," economic sociologist Fred Block explains, "because people lack a shared understanding of the kind of society in which they live. For generations, the U.S. was understood as an industrial society, but that definition of reality is no longer compelling. Yet in its absence, no compelling alternative has emerged." Postindustrial society, therefore, designates "that historical period that begins when the concept of industrial society ceases to provide an adequate account of actual social developments."[56] Under postindustrial conditions more people work in clerical, sales, and services than produce goods, and computer-based automation drastically revises the organization, experience, and distribution of work. While in 1959, 60 percent of total employment in the United States was in goods production and 40 percent in services, by 1985 a dramatic reversal had occurred, with 74 percent of employment in services and only 26 percent in the production of goods. Economists continue to debate the long-term implications, but evidence is mounting that this shift is shrinking middle-income employment and polarizing the occupational structure into a "two-tier workforce" of "good" and "bad" jobs.[57]

While all of the "post-" words are controversial, it is my use of the third of these, postfeminism, that has generated the most spirited objections. The term offends many of my feminist friends who believe the media coined it to sound a premature death knell for the women's liberation movement and "to give sexism a subtler name."[58] Whatever the motives of the media, I regard postfeminism as distinct from sexism or antifeminism. Postfeminism, I believe, is a useful way to characterize this contested period in the history of gender relationships. It can be used as a historical concept, as historian Barbara Bardes notes, to suggest that "the feminist movement is accepted, and to ask, 'Where do you go in the post-feminist age?' "[59] To use it this way, however, understates the continuing need for feminist political efforts as well as the ongoing grassroots struggles for gender justice that can be found throughout our society and the globe. The term postfeminism serves better, I believe, to describe the gender consciousness and strategies of vast numbers of contemporary women and men—those legions of subscribers to the doctrine, "I'm not a women's libber, but. . . ." While they hold their distance from feminist identity or politics, they have been profoundly influenced by feminist ideology. Feminism, antifeminism, and postfeminism coexist uneasily in the current period, and the last of these has altered and complicated the political challenges that advocates of the first must confront.[60]

In short, a debate about feminism and postmodern gender arrangements lies at the core of today's deeply polarized discourse on American family life. This book attempts to intervene constructively in that fractious conversation. It presents stories by and about members of two kin networks of people who have been remaking their family lives in Santa Clara County, California, the "Silicon Valley." It is to that extraordinary setting and to these "ordinary people" that we now turn.

2

Land of Dreams and Disasters:
Postindustrial Living in the Silicon Valley

When I moved here, there were orchards all around, and now there are integrated-circuit manufacturing plants all around. . . . that's been the thrill, because I've been part of it, and it's the most exciting time in the history of the world, I think. And the center of it is here in Silicon Valley.
—Female engineer at Hewlett-Packard, quoted
in *San Jose Mercury News*, 19 February 1985

You know what San Jose reminds me of? It's kind of a cow town in my estimation; it cracks me up that there's all this big stuff going on, this big industry, and Silicon Valley and everything. I mean, when I was a kid and my grandparents lived in Santa Cruz and we drove through San Jose, this was like a dust spot, you know, you got dust on your windshield when you drove through this valley. My uncle was an apricot and almond orchard man around here, and there wasn't anything in San Jose. San Jose was a town south of Oakland, south of the city; it was this little spot over there, and you passed it when you went to Santa Cruz or went down South.
—"Jan," interviewed August 1984

As the seedbed and international headquarters of the electronics industry, the Silicon Valley has been in the vanguard of postindustrial social transformations. Few could have been more astonished by this development than working people who inhabited the region before its technological makeover. In the 1950s, those who occupied Santa Clara County, a

20

sprawling, fertile plain along the southern shore line of San Francisco Bay, inhabited a sparsely populated agribusiness area, one of the world's major prune and apricot suppliers, then known locally with pride, as "the garden of heart's delight." Most likely they worked on farms or in the canneries and food-processing plants that supplied the county's scant eight thousand manufacturing jobs. In 1955 they might have garnered a small share of benefits from the county's peak orchard production year without ever suspecting that local fruit groves were about to disappear even more precipitously than the modern families that tended or admired them.[1]

Residents in the 1950s could not have known that the northern portion of their county was about to become the "Silicon Valley." During the next three decades, the developing electronics industry would convert the garden of heart's delight into a world-renowned high-tech center, regarded alternatively as the solution to American economic malaise or as the prophecy of its decline, a "valley of toxic fright."[2] With ample defense contract funding, Stanford University, located in Palo Alto along the northwest county border, spawned the prolific seeds of scientific industry in this hitherto bucolic valley. Between 1950 and 1980 silicon replaced noncitrus fruit as the region's principal product, the local population grew by more than 400 percent—from nearly 300,000 to more than 1.29 million people—and the region's economy, ecology, and social structure were unrecognizably transformed.[3]

During the 1960s and 1970s, while many urban industrial areas in the United States began to decline, Santa Clara County enjoyed spectacular economic growth. Between 1960 and 1975 county employment grew by 156 percent, three times the national rate, as local manufacturing jobs increased to 130,000 and auxiliary employment in construction and services expanded apace.[4] The electronics industry provided jobs for almost one of every three county workers, and it generated most of the construction and service needs that employed the majority of the rest.[5] In those heady days, the media and even some scholars portrayed the Silicon Valley as a true-life American fairy tale, and few were the voices raised, or heard, in dissent. The Mecca of the new technological entrepreneurs, its worshippers proclaimed, was a sunny land where factories resembled college campuses, where skilled, safe, and challenging work was replacing the monotonous, degrading, dangerous labors of the now-declining in-

21

dustries, and where American technical know-how and entrepreneurial spirit once again would rescue the flagging U.S. economy and better the lives of all.[6]

An unusually high proportion (25 percent) of the electronics industry did consist of the most highly educated and highly paid salaried employees in any U.S. industry—engineers and professionals employed in research and design. Along with those heralded health clubs and fitness tracks, they were offered exceptional challenges and economic opportunities. As in "traditional" industries, however, the vast majority of these most privileged employees were white men (89 percent males, 89 percent non-Hispanic whites). During those start-up years in the 1950s and 1960s the industry also employed white men in most of its production jobs where they too enjoyed unusual opportunities. Even those with very limited schooling could advance into technical ranks, particularly those whom the military had first trained in mechanics before depositing them conveniently in nearby bases.[7]

But as the electronics industry matured, it feminized (and minoritized) its work force, turning increasingly to female, ethnic minority, and recent migrant workers to fill production positions that offered far fewer advancement opportunities. By the late 1970s the industry's occupational structure was crudely stratified by gender as well as by race and ethnicity. White men were at the top, white women and ethnic minorities at the bottom. Almost half the employees were assembly workers and operatives; three-fourths of these were women, and 40 percent were minorities. Two groups of workers made up the middle: the moderately well-paid technicians and craft workers, also primarily Anglo males but into whose ranks women and Asians were making some inroads, and the clerical work force composed overwhelmingly of Anglo women. These middle-income jobs were declining, however; in Silicon Valley as elsewhere in postindustrial America, growth of new jobs is at the top and the bottom.[8] The preferred labor pool for the bottom continued to grow here during the 1980s as the proportion of nonwhite county residents increased dramatically.[9]

The popular media image of egalitarian and innovative work relations symbolized by engineers in blue jeans working at computers in open cubicles masks the startlingly unequal, far-from-innovative working conditions with which the industry's production workers contend. Electronics remains the only nonunionized major industry in the United States, and its production workers earn lower wages and endure greater risks and hardships than do their counterparts in most "traditional" industries. In 1981, for example, electronics workers earned an average wage only 57 percent of that paid to auto and steel workers, despite the mandatory wage concessions extracted from the latter.[10] Ironically, the "clean rooms" in which many electronics workers toil are filled with highly toxic solvents. Almost half of the occupational illness cases reported among semiconductor workers involve systemic poisoning from toxic materials, and the rate of occupational illness in electronics production in California is three times as great as in other manufacturing occupations.[11] Many electronics firms operate around the clock and require production workers to accept night and weekend shifts as well as long and highly irregular schedules. Yet they offer workers no job security and subject them to frequent, sudden layoffs and forced vacations.

In 1974 the first major slump in the electronics industry signaled its inherent volatility. Dependent on defense contracts and highly turbulent global market conditions, the industry's boom-bust cycle and the high failure rate of firms promised recurrent unemployment. Corporate strategists began to ship many production jobs to cheaper labor areas in the United States and abroad and to replace "permanent" workers with a flexible fleet of what soon became the highest concentration of "temporary" workers in the nation—workers, that is, who lack all employee benefits.[12]

By the time I began this study in 1984, "Silicon Valley fever" had begun to subside as most county residents directly or indirectly suffered ill effects of the electronics industry's previously concealed "downside." Increasing numbers of residents were out of work, and the entry-level work available promised few prospects for a family wage. Local unemployment rates rose in the 1980s, escalating sharply during the industry's severe prolonged slump in 1984 and 1985. Even after that recession had bottomed out, untrained, entry-level workers found that their best employment prospects were not in the electronics industry but as hotel housekeepers and security guards.[13]

Employed and unemployed alike suffered from the industry's destruction of their once-bucolic environment. As cancer rates and birth defects in the county rose alarmingly, outraged residents discovered that their water supplies had been contaminated by more than one hundred industrial chemicals that were known or suspected to be carcinogens, mutagens, or teratogens.[14] Air pollution and nightmarish traffic, predictable products of the region's decades of untrammeled, unplanned development, destroyed the celebrated quality of life that had once enticed so many to the fabled region. And yet the cost of living rose as sharply as the quality of life declined. This was not an anomaly; rather, as urban analyst Annalee Saxenian has demonstrated, it is a case of chickens fed by the industry's stratified employment policies now come home to roost. The skewed salaries that the industry paid its sizable professional and managerial elite raised local housing costs to among the highest in the nation, beyond the reach of its underpaid, often underemployed production workers.[15] The local media began to treat its audiences to the embarrassing spectacle of mounting homelessness in the land of affluence. Most of the new homeless, moreover, were family units.[16]

Local and national media became more consistently preoccupied with the escalating narcotics problems of the postindustrial era, and here too the Silicon Valley gave cause for grave alarm. Illegal drug use in the county seat cost its residents $500 million annually, and the region gained an unenviable reputation as the state capital for the use of PCP, a potent animal tranquilizer that induces behavior so violent that local police identify it as "the single highest cause of officer injury in this department."[17] The federal Drug Enforcement Agency identified Silicon Valley as "one of the biggest cocaine users in the United States."[18] Drug dealing offered an irresistible occupational alternative to mounting legions of unemployed youth. Indeed the electronics industry offered many workers on-the-job training in drug dependency, as foremen and coworkers distributed drugs to sustain workers through the monotony and stress of lengthy shifts and speedups. More than 35 percent of the electronics employees surveyed by the *San Jose Mercury News* in 1985 acknowledged using illicit drugs on the job.[19] In 1988 the county Board of Supervisors and the San Jose City Council approved higher bail and longer jail sentences for dealers as they passed a resolution introduced by a coalition of local church groups stating that "drugs represent a severe health epidemic which is destroying the lives of our families and the future of our community."[20]

Such regional maladies may have failed to shake the faith of some high-tech devotees, like the female engineer at Hewlett-Packard quoted at the beginning of this chapter, but in the 1980s more people declared themselves eager to leave than to enter the South Bay futureland. Population

24

growth in Santa Clara County slowed considerably after 1980, falling below California rates. As the decade neared its close, a Bay area poll found the once-glorified Silicon Valley to be the least popular county in the region. Almost half the county residents queried claimed they would prefer to live somewhere else.[21] It was a twist of cruel irony, therefore, when in 1989 Hewlett-Packard—the area's preeminent high-tech firm, credited by many with creating the Silicon Valley—cited the region's spiraling cost of living as the basis for its decision to move 10 percent of its computer manufacturing operations to a less-populated California valley.[22]

While the changing character of work in the Silicon Valley commanded global attention, most outside observers overlooked concurrent gender and family changes that preoccupied many residents. In earlier, self-congratulatory days, before the national political climate made feminism seem a derogatory term, local public officials liked to describe San Jose, the county seat, as a feminist capital. The city elected a feminist mayor and hosted the statewide National Organization of Women convention in 1974. Santa Clara soon became one of the few counties in the nation that could boast of having elected a female majority to its Board of Supervisors. In 1981 high levels of feminist activism made San Jose the site of the nation's first successful strike for a comparable worth standard of pay for city employees. And, according to sociologist Karen Hossfeld, young working-class women who vehemently rejected a feminist identity took for granted women's rights to political and economic equality and to control their own sexuality.[23]

It should come as no surprise, therefore, that during these postindustrializing decades the Silicon Valley has also been the site of a significant degree of family turbulence. Much of the data on local family changes represent an exaggeration of the national trends described in the last chapter. For example, while the national divorce rate was doubling after 1960, in Santa Clara County it nearly tripled. By 1977 more county residents filed divorce papers than registered marriages. By 1980 the divorce rate in the county seat ranked ninth among U.S. metropolitan areas, higher than Los Angeles or San Francisco. Likewise the percentage of "nonfamily households" grew faster in the Silicon Valley than in the nation, and abortion rates were one and one-half times the national figures. And although the percentage of single-parent households was not quite as high as it was in the nation as a whole, the rate of increase was

25

more rapid.[24] The high marriage casualty rate among workaholic engineers was dubbed "the silicon syndrome."[25] County social workers and residents with whom I spoke in the mid-1980s shared an alarmist view of the fate of family life in their locale summarized in the opening lines of a feature article in a local university magazine: "There is an endangered species in Silicon Valley, one so precious that when it disappears Silicon Valley will die with it. This endangered species is the family. And sometimes it seems as if every institution in this valley—political, corporate, and social—is hellbent on driving it into extinction."[26]

These concurrent changes in occupational, gender, and family patterns make the Silicon Valley a propitious site for exploring the ways in which "ordinary" working people have been remaking their families in the wake of postindustrial and feminist challenges. The Silicon Valley is by no means a typical or "representative" U.S. location, but precisely because national postindustrial work and family transformations were more condensed, rapid, and exaggerated there than elsewhere, they should be easier to perceive. Yet most popular and scholarly literature about white working-class people portrays them as the most traditional, as the last bastion, that is, of the modern family. Relatively privileged members of the white working class are widely regarded as the bulwark of the Reagan revolution and the constituency least sympathetic to feminism and family reforms.[27] Those whose hold on the accoutrements of the American Dream is so recent and tenuous, it is thought, have the strongest incentives to defend it. Curiously, however, few scholars have published book-length, in-depth studies of such families in recent years.[28]

Conventional images of progressive, middle-class families embracing egalitarian changes in gender and work patterns that "traditional"—that is to say, "modern"—working-class families resentfully resist fail to recognize the complexity, fluidity, and unresolved character of contemporary gender, class, and family arrangements. Only ethnographic research, I have come to believe, can capture this complexity sufficiently to dispel distortions in the popular clichés. Based on such research, *Brave New Families* narrates stories about working-class gender relations and kinship strategies that are as creative, flexible, and postmodern as those found among the most innovative strata of the middle classes. Indeed, working people, this book argues, have served as the unrecognized pioneers of the postmodern family revolution.

26

AN ACCIDENTAL ETHNOGRAPHY

This book is the product of unplanned ethnographic research, however, of a research plan gone awry. Like an unintentional pregnancy, the field-work on which the book is based seemed to happen to me and to determine its own path of growth. Because the serendipity in this process is a more common and valuable research method than is often acknowledged, it seems worth recounting the seemingly chance events that lie behind my study.

In 1984 a colleague persuaded me to join in conducting a qualitative study of working-class family change in the Silicon Valley during the decades since the electronics industry developed there. After a prelimi-nary period of background study on the region and the industry, sup-plemented by interviews with public officials and local activists, we arrived at a very careful definition of our target sample. We decided to interview Anglo and Chicano members of the population from which the electronics industry drew its production-level work force. Recognizing the gender stratification and the transient nature of employment in the in-dustry, we defined the population to include past and present electronics production workers as well as women and men who were or had been married to, or engaged in intimate emotional and sexual relationships with, such workers. Because we presumed that most would be recent migrants to the region, and we wished to chart changes in the local working class over the several decades of the electronics industry's de-velopment, we planned to supplement these interviews by recording oral histories from "community elders," people who had been adult residents in Santa Clara County since the 1950s.

Intending to conduct interviews on family and work history with at least 150 individuals, we set out in July 1984 on an exploratory phase to identify the major patterns and themes we would pursue more method-ically later on. From July to September 1984 we interviewed thirty-two volunteers drawn from an "opportunity sample" of clients enrolled in employment skills training classes at a major antipoverty agency in Santa Clara County. We were astonished to discover that twenty-nine members of this arbitrary sample qualified for study under the stringent criteria of our original definition. They were indeed members of families from which the electronics industry had recruited production workers. After

27

we had exhausted this supply of volunteers, the study reached a crucial methodological juncture. Although our exploratory interviews confirmed our preliminary sense of family turbulence within the Silicon Valley working class, this could well have been an effect of the built-in bias of our sample. Because the agency had a Job Training Partnership Act (JTPA) youth quota, a target population of female heads of households, and a disproportionately Latina clientele, the majority of our interviewees were young, unmarried, Latina mothers. We felt the need to compensate for these biases of family structure and ethnicity by seeking Anglo interviewees with intact marriages and current employment.

At this point my collaborator, whose interest in the project had waned, left to pursue other research. Feeling anxious and directionless, I set out alone to locate Anglo workers whose marriages had survived employment in the electronics industry. Here serendipity, that undervalued research resource, intervened. The chance juxtaposition of two fieldwork experiences permanently derailed the original research plan and prompted me to pursue instead an open-ended, ethnographic approach to the study of Silicon Valley family life.

The first of these experiences was particularly unsettling. What I had expected to be a fairly casual lunch date with Pamela Gama, an administrator at the antipoverty agency, turned into several hours of revealing personal testimony from Pam, the substance of which surprised, challenged, and threatened me. Prior to that fateful lunch in November 1984, Pam and I had had numerous informal lunches and conversations as well as more formal interviews in which I had treated Pam as an "expert" informant on matters relating to the agency and its clientele. I had had ample opportunity to observe Pam's egalitarian relations with staff and clients and to note her feminist and progressive views on a range of social issues. Before the 1984 election she made many scornful remarks about Reagan, Reaganomics, and the military buildup. I had learned that Pam had been divorced fifteen years earlier from an electronics industry engineer who had risen from the ranks of technicians, and I had pegged her as a slightly cynical feminist who came to feminist consciousness through divorce and a women's reentry program at a local community college. I was taken aback, therefore, during that lunch four months after we had met to learn that Pam was now married to a construction worker with whom she earlier had cohabited and that both were recent converts

28

to Christian evangelicalism who were participating in Christian marriage counseling to improve their relationship. I recorded in my journal at the time:

> This interview blew my mind. Pam's conversion to fundamentalism was completely unexpected. As a feminist I find it deeply troubling, threatening somehow. And yet I'm also fascinated by Pam's account of her turn to this religion and her interpretation of its patriarchal doctrine and its salutary effects on her relationship with Al. Most likely most fundamentalist women don't see things this way, but I don't think Pam's perspective is just idiosyncratic or insignificant.

Exactly one week after receiving this unexpected and not entirely welcome oral history from Pam, I had an analogous, but rather reverse, field experience during my first lengthy visit at the home of the Lewisons. I had come to interview Dotty Lewison, a neighbor of someone who had been helping me locate married interviewees. My contact had told me that Dotty once had been an electronics assembly worker and that she still lived with her husband of thirty years who was retired from an electronics career. Dotty's heavily tattooed husband, Lou, let me into their modest and cluttered tract house where Dotty appeared in time to accept a package from a delivery boy. I watched as Dot unpacked Christmas stocking hangers and a new, gilded Bible. My social prejudices, reinforced by my reading of sociological literature on the working class, cued me to expect her to hold somewhat conservative and antifeminist views, but I was soon to be surprised again. Dotty too had taken feminist courses in a community college women's reentry program, and she reported a broad history of community and feminist activism, including extensive work in the antibattering movement. Her husband, who monitored the interview for accuracy from his position in front of the television in the adjacent living room, confirmed and seemed to approve of Dotty's feminist proclivities. She told me that she no longer was active in political causes, however, but with Lou was attending a metaphysical church and taking classes to develop her gifts for healing and seeing.

Transcribing the tapes from this "fascinating, thoroughly enjoyable" visit with the Lewisons, whose challenge to my preconceptions I found more pleasing than the recent one by Pam, I noted two parallel issues concerning the recent history of gender and class relationships in the

Silicon Valley embedded in both narratives. Although Dotty's retreat from feminism seemed less pronounced than Pam's, and her spiritual quest far less traditional, she too seemed to have shifted her priorities from political activism to religion and her marriage. I noted too that I could not assign class labels to either of these families although many members of both qualified for inclusion in my original "working-class" sample. Pam had been a housewife married to an engineer, then a welfare mother, now a social service worker married to a construction worker. One of her two daughters had done electronics assembly work, another was a drafter, and many other relatives of Pam's and Al's were or had been involved in varying levels of electronics employment. Similarly Dotty, who had alternated homemaking and community activism with a wide array of full- and part-time paid work, had had a two-year stint as an electronics assembly worker before Lou had begun to succeed as an electronics industry line maintenance mechanic and engineer. Four of their five adult children also had past or current employment in the electronics industry at jobs ranging from assembly up to lower-level management. At least among whites, the same families were supplying the electronics industry with workers who occupied very different income and status positions. A given household at any moment was likely to be composed of individuals with diverse employment, income, and mobility histories. Sex, age, and family status structured some of these variations, and the complexity and fluidity of class positions appeared to reflect the marital and occupational instability endemic to the area.

These observations fed my belief that there were important connections to explore between changes in family and gender relationships in the Valley and the devolution of its traditional working class. The aesthetic appeal of the inverse surprises in these two fieldwork events, my desire to engage in much greater depth the issues they raised for me, and my personal attraction to Pam and Dotty prompted me to abandon my original research design and to follow my untrained nose into an uncharted form of ethnographic research. Only two years later did I recognize that events in my personal life also fueled my attraction to Pam and Dotty and the ethnographic quest.

For the previous seven years I had been living in a postmodern family of my own—a joint, semi-collective household I had formed with a woman friend and my longtime male partner. Influenced by feminist criticisms of the modern nuclear family, we had attempted to craft an intentional alternative family form. We were largely successful during our first several years, but as the sociological literature might have predicted, the addition of children disrupted our prior harmony. Gradually our household split along its couple-single fault line, and the major trembler hit the week I interviewed Pam and Dotty. The first six months of this field study coincided with the demise of my antimodern family. This was no random coincident. I switched from conventional interviews to a do-it-yourself ethnographic—that is, to a voyeuristic exploration of contemporary family change—I now believe, to cushion and contemplate unsettling family changes of my own.

Starting with Pam and Dotty, I began to evolve a case-study method of family research. To claim that I began by securing "informed consent" from Pam and Dotty to serve as key informants for intensive field research on their respective kinship networks would gravely misrepresent my level of initiative and direction at the time. Although both women did agree to subject themselves and their kin to my prolonged sociological gaze, it felt as if my first two ethnographic subjects had chosen me, at least as much as the other way around. Pam seduced me, however unwittingly, at first by generously facilitating my access to clients and staff at the agency where she worked, later by offering tantalizing snippets of her personal history as a feminist divorcée of an electronics industry engineer, and finally by her surprising revelation about her religious conversion. And while I first sought out Dotty, I anticipated only one interview. Dotty's infectious warmth, her loquaciousness, and the complex history of the large Lewison family made a second visit both irresistible and necessary. The second visit led to a third, and then a fourth. There was no clear moment of decision to make the Lewisons the subjects of a case study; nor do I believe the decision was more mine than Dotty's.

The method of study that I came to adopt also was mutually determined. The character of Pam's and Dotty's work and family situations and of my own, and major changes in these during the two and one-half-year period of my active but intermittent fieldwork on this project (July 1984–April 1987), structured the locations, timing, frequency, and the character of our ensuing contact. Pam, a social service program director during the first year of this case study, then had considerable control over her work conditions. Able and willing to meet for lengthy lunch dates and to schedule interview time in her private office where I could tape portions of her oral history, Pam also welcomed my participation in agency programs. Until she left the agency in December 1985, I ran errands, attended banquets and conferences that her program sponsored, gave a guest lecture to clients and staff, and spent considerable time observing and visiting Pam and her coworkers on the job. Her new position in a branch of city government was more constraining. Pam no longer had a private office, nor as much authority or autonomy. Consequently, I no longer spent time with her at work, and we supplemented our somewhat shorter lunch dates with other social occasions outside the workplace.

Dotty, a part-time clerical worker in a small insurance office most of the first year of this study, had no time to meet for lunch and very little flexibility in her nine-to-two work schedule. That year we met instead at her home in the late afternoons, at first under retired Lou's watchful eye and with his occasional participation. Soon Lou agreed to be interviewed alone, and I developed the habit of arriving early to visit with him before Dotty returned from work. Occasionally Dotty and I would go for dinner or drinks alone at local restaurants, coffee shops, or cocktail lounges, or I would accompany her on household errands. When she was fired from her job in August 1985 and the Lewisons' youngest daughter with her husband and their three young children moved in with the Lewisons, after being evicted from an apartment, Dotty appreciated long lunch dates outside the home. But after Dotty accepted a full-time job on the front desk of a cable television service office, our meeting times were restricted primarily to evenings and weekends.

My own family life, meanwhile, took place fifty miles removed from these "research sites," and my university employment seventy miles farther beyond. These commitments dictated the commuter character of the fieldwork I could conduct and the seasons of its fluctuating degrees of intensity. During summers and while on leave from teaching, I traveled to the Valley two or three times weekly and responded with some spontaneity to invitations, crises, and other ethnographic "opportunities." My involvement was constrained, however, by my conflicts of interest over the sacrifices this family fieldwork demanded of my own family time. During teaching terms, when the axis of my commuter life shifted to the opposite direction, my visits to the Valley decreased sharply, and I relied on lengthy telephone conversations to maintain contact.

In essence, the field method I employed was to enter gradually into a set of personal relationships with Pam and Dotty and various members of their kinship networks. Through the means just described I came to meet or was introduced to an ever-expanding network of their relatives and friends. As I met or became aware of each additional "significant other" in their lives, I would request permission to meet privately to collect a relatively formal oral history. All but two of the thirty individuals I sought to interview formally agreed to participate. Most of these formal interviews involved at least two meetings of two to three hours each, generally in homes or in coffee shops. And through these visits I entered into ongoing relationships with two additional individuals, one from each kin set, and more casual relationships with numerous others. I accompanied family members to church services and on shopping excursions, hospital visits, and missionary work. I attended a variety of family gatherings and events, occasionally celebratory ones to honor marriages, births, job promotions, or anniversaries. Far more often, however, I found myself witnessing or commiserating over family crises and tragedies including deaths, severe illnesses, layoffs, evictions, suicide attempts, infidelities, and problems with drugs, alcohol, physical abuse, and the law.

At some imprecise moment during the second year of this ethnographic odyssey, I abandoned my intention to expand my "sample" by applying its evolving case-study method to two Chicano family networks. Intellectual and practical considerations entered here. First, to insert the complexities of ethnicity into the study in this manner struck me as ill conceived. Selecting new cases on an ethnic basis would introduce an implicitly comparative framework into a sample far too small to sustain one. It would be impossible to make meaningful ethnic comparisons based on only four extended kin networks; yet to avoid such comparisons would risk falsely universalizing relationships of gender and class. Moreover, there was the danger that my first two cases, the nonminority families, would unavoidably become my standard for comparison. But more mundane considerations may have been more decisive. After eighteen months, I did not feel that I had yet come close to completing the fieldwork on my first two case studies, or that I was socially or physically capable of concurrently entering into and sustaining additional relationships of this sort. I resigned myself to the limitations of a study based on what some social scientists might disparáge as an N of two. As with most ethnographies, depth would have to substitute for breadth in my treatment of

33

family change. By forfeiting the generalizing advantages of a larger sample, I gained the opportunity to study actual systems of gender and kinship relationships *in situ,* to contextualize their multiple and interacting voices rather than simply to accrue more studied and contrived accounts from individuals abstracted from their social milieus.

I justified the far-from-scientific selection of the particular two family networks I found myself studying on multiple grounds. As indicated earlier, many members in each network qualified for study under both sets of formal criteria contained in the more methodical original research design. These were "Anglo" families from which the electronics industry had drawn production workers, and they were families whose residence in the county spanned the history of Silicon Valley. Strikingly, this very small sample also encompassed all the relational and household variations we had targeted for inclusion in the proposal for the larger study: "adults living in households with and without children present . . . people who currently are living in settled family situations and those who are not . . . at least some women and men who presently are participating in marriages or primary relationships that have lasted at least five years."[29] The sample also included a full range of the prominent categories and features of the contemporary family landscape—marriage, separation, divorce, remarriage, serial monogamy, adultery, homosexuality, cohabitation, abortion, unwed childbearing, single parenthood, coparenthood, blended households, and shared households of varying descriptions. Moreover, members of four generations of each family were present in the county, and I had access to a few former spouses, lovers, and some of their new mates as well.

Despite this elaborate attempt to justify my selection of these families for case study, many readers may find good cause to question the legitimacy of treating Pamela's family as working class. Although Pamela is married to a construction worker, and most of her children and their spouses have blue-collar histories, her current occupational status as well as the cultural ambiance and occupational status of her natal and first marital families are indeed middle class. Conversely, while the cultural markings and the economic resources of the Lewisons are more conventionally working class, Lou and one of his daughters achieved middle-class occupational status and income. There is an important implication of the ambiguous class character of these two cases: So fluid and complex are the occupational, economic, and social statuses of white working families in postindustrial society that few can be captured by a single social class category.

Far more important than the formal criteria the two cases satisfied or the structural variety they encompassed is the evocative way in which the histories of these two networks of families illustrate many of the central gender, family, and work issues posed for white "working-class" people in the Silicon Valley over the past quarter century. Both networks originated in the modern families of women whose husbands had benefited from the unusual occupational opportunities offered by the electronics industry to white working-class men during the 1960s and 1970s. Later, postindustrial and feminist challenges disrupted both families and instigated their diverse postmodern responses.

I make no pretense to having located Silicon Valley families that could be construed as representative in any statistical sense of the term. And although the question preoccupied me for a time, I never did, nor do I now believe one ever could, decide whether I had happened onto "ordinary" or extraordinary people. The first year of study I tried hard to believe the former, imagining that the sociological legitimacy of my endeavor rested on the typicality of my subjects. How shaken I was, therefore, when, operating on the same premise, the woman who first had directed me to the Lewisons challenged my decision to study them. Dotty was someone who always lived on the edge of disaster, she accurately informed me, and thus the Lewisons were not a typical family and were not a good case study.

It now seems likely to me that this critic was correct in her judgment that the disaster-prone Lewisons are not "ordinary people." And Pamela Gama may be even more unusual than they. But I am convinced that they and all their kin whom I studied have been negotiating the new, ordinary conditions of social life in the Silicon Valley, negotiating, that is, the set of extraordinary challenges and opportunities contained in the emerging postindustrial order. Indeed I came to view my critic's objection to my study of the Lewisons as evidence instead of its social significance. She felt, I believe, a need to distance herself from the threat of a calamity culture that is far from extraordinary in the Silicon Valley, many of whose ingredients had already affected her own family history as well.

ON FACT, FICTION, AND FATE

The families whose "lived experiences" comprise the field data for this book are representative only in the now-fashionable "discursive" sense of the term. I have constructed narratives from their stories about those experiences that I believe to be culturally meaningful. While elements of fictionalization are intrinsic to ethnographic storytelling, I have attempted to keep the fictions in this book as faithful to factual events and recounted memories as concerns for the protection of human subjects will allow. To say this is to position myself within a complex discourse among anthropologists about the nature of ethnographic "author"-ity.

"Modernist" and "postmodern" anthropologists have challenged the realist theory of knowledge that underlies the narrative strategies of conventional ethnographies in ways I find at once powerful, persuasive, and paralyzing.[30] (Such challenges, feminists justly complain, often build upon and fail to credit comparable feminist criticisms of social science research.[31]) Conventional realist ethnographies, critics charge, unreflexively, and thus dishonestly, assume the voice of an omniscient, invisible author who neutrally reports the objective reality of an exotic "other." This masks the inescapable power relations and the dialogic character of the enthographic research process as well as the proto-fictional character of ethnographic writing. Ethnographers who pretend to discover and report data misunderstand and misrepresent the interactive and subjective character of ethnographic knowledge. Ethnographies are never factual records, but texts structured by the interests, privileges, commitments, quirks, and rhetorical strategies of their authors. Ethnographers, therefore, this view maintains, should self-reflexively assume authorial responsibility for their textual products while abandoning claims to transcendental truth. Doing so requires the insertion of the multiple voices and cultural dialogues of anthropological research into the written ethnography.

While I accept a good deal of this approach, I also perceive dangers. A thoroughly reflexive and dialogic narrative strategy can become too relativistic or solipsistic. Moreover, such a strategy encumbers the writing process beyond the limits of my patience or agility, just as it might unduly strain the forbearance of readers. In the reflexive spirit, therefore, I wish to alert readers of this ethnography to my representational convictions. I share the view that ethnographic "subjects" and authors forge their realities through subjective and dialogic processes. However, I also believe that they do so within the constraints of a relatively objective, albeit always interpreted, set of social arrangements.

As a result, in this text I adopt a dual set of narrative strategies. In the ethnographic chapters I attempt to employ a self-reflexive voice. I am actively present as I was during my fieldwork—participating, interrogating, reacting, learning, interpreting, erring. Still too present, perhaps, to fully suit my editor, the protagonist of a crucial stage of dialogue in the publication process that, by curious convention, rarely receives more than a ceremonial mention in an author's formal acknowledgments. In the ethnographic chapters I also severely curtail my use of the more abstract sociological voice, once again rejecting responsible editorial counsel. "The material is rich indeed, and you write about it well," my editor cajoled me. "But to the degree that readers and reviewers are being asked to go from the introduction through the rest of the text until the conclusion without benefiting from your insights into the larger meaning of all this for understanding the complexly recombinant nature of post-modern family life, to that degree I think you may be taxing their patience beyond reason."

My stubborn hope for indulgence from my readers rests upon a post-modern conviction that many of them, like me, have lost confidence in the objective grand narratives of sociology, a quintessential "modern" Enlightenment science.[32] There are fundamental limits, this research convinced me, to any discipline's ability to make satisfactory sense of individual and social fate. Tension between the sociological quest for generalizable knowledge and inexplicable dimensions of fate dogged all my research and writing—from the accidental origins of my field research to the series of tragic accidents that prompted me to terminate it. By revealing the ways in which crucial aspects of my identity conspired with accidental components of the research process to yield the "rich material" depicted in this ethnography, I equip my readers to evaluate the unavoidably subjective sociological generalizations I derived from this research. In the more analytical, contextualizing chapters that frame the ethnography, however, I risk the less reflexive, realist voice of the conventional, interpretive sociologist that I am not now willing, or able, to disown.

The chapters that follow present stories about the family and work experiences of Pamela's kindred and the Lewisons as cultural representations of the transformations of gender, kinship, and class that have accompanied and, to a large extent, comprise the making of postindustrial society in the Silicon Valley. I believe that the subjects in this book bear a relationship to recent white working-class family history in the area analogous to the one between the Silicon Valley's recent history and the emergence of postindustrial social life in the United States as a whole. If their personal stories and strategies represent somewhat exaggerated, perhaps skewed versions of that collective experience, they do so in ways I take to be deeply revealing of contemporary collective concerns. In the sociological tradition of C. Wright Mills, I view their considerable "personal troubles" as well as their personal triumphs as windows onto significant "public issues" of our times. I do not try, however, to shade these windows from alternative points of view.

I

PAMELA'S KIN: FEMINISM, FUNDAMENTALISM, AND A POSTMODERN EXTENDED FAMILY

3

Pam's Revelation and Mine

While the globe is still full of cultural differences, it is also true that most possibil-
ities are known, or at least have been considered, and that all other cultural worlds
have been penetrated by aspects of modern life. What matters, then, is not ideal life
elsewhere, or in another time, but the discovery of new recombinant possibilities and
meanings in the process of daily living anywhere.
    —George Marcus and Michael Fischer, *Anthropology as Cultural Critique*

I cannot recall the first time I met Pamela Gama. Perhaps it was in the
spring of 1983 when, exploring my interest in the collaborative research
project described earlier, I accompanied a colleague to Social Opportunities and Services (SOS), the social service agency in Santa Clara
County where Pamela was a program director. Perhaps it was not until
July 1984 when we returned to SOS to launch that project formally. I
do remember, however, that Pam's welcoming and supportive response
to the intrusions of our exploratory research relieved much of the stage-
fright I was feeling as a neophyte interviewer. Pam was enthusiastic about
our research, and she provided us with private interviewing spaces and
generous introductions to staff and clients. The first notes about Pam I
recorded transcribed an interview conducted on August 1, 1984. After
spending two weeks interviewing client volunteers, we asked Pam if we
could interview her about SOS, its structure, programs, and clientele.
She readily agreed and invited Jan, her assistant director, to participate.

Most of the interview, and my attention at the time, focused on the contents, goals, funding sources, and the constituencies of the various programs Pam and Jan administered. But, of course, at the same time that we gathered and exchanged information, we all were forming personal impressions of each other. I remember that my impressions of the women were highly favorable and sympathetic. Pam, a very thin, sandy-haired, pretty woman in her mid-forties who, like almost everyone else in the Valley I would come to know, chain-smoked her way through the meeting, had a manner that was warm, responsive, and engaging, yet intense and mildly sarcastic at the same time. Dark-haired, clear-eyed Jan made a striking contrast. Perhaps a decade younger, her strong features were complemented by an appearance of physical strength and confidence, and while Jan shared Pam's friendliness and ironic sense of humor, she was more businesslike than Pam, much more reserved about her personal history.

In the course of that taped discussion, Pam expressed a variety of feminist and other progressive political sentiments, characterized by keen sensitivity to the plight of the regions' laid-off workers and low-income women. Her pithy response to my question about the most visible changes in the family lives of working people in the Silicon Valley was "I think one of the biggest things I see is that women are entering all the shit jobs, getting paid all the shit wages."* And she bemoaned the fate of electronics assembly workers who had made the transition from the canneries only to be laid off in the sudden recession: "You have this whole group of people that aren't working at the canneries any more, and it looks like their boat came in, and it's sinking now."

It was readily apparent that Pam identified quite directly with the needs of the low-income women served by the programs she administered. Throughout the interview she made unsolicited allusions to her personal history to illustrate difficulties and injustices confronting women in the Silicon Valley, allusions that implied that she had traveled much the same road as they. At one point Pam referred to marital stresses she had experienced when her husband, a construction worker, was unemployed,

---

*Direct quotations included in this text derive either from transcripts of tape-recorded sessions with the speakers or from field notes I recorded immediately after the conversations took place. All quotations of more than a sentence or two were recorded. I have edited some selections slightly to remove conversational stammers and the like that are not significant for my interpretive and illustrative uses.

the county unemployment rate for construction workers was 35 percent, and "scab labor increased during that time . . . and took over what few jobs were available." When asked to describe changes in family life she had observed during her twenty-one years of residence in the Valley, Pam volunteered that in 1970 she and Doreen, another SOS staff member, had participated in the county's first reentry program for women at East Valley, a local community college, "so, I think I was changing along with the rest of the people."

Pam went on to describe a rather astonishing pattern to the collective history of the twenty-five women who had participated in the inaugural East Valley reentry group. She claimed that almost all had entered as "happily married" housewives who "had been active in the community . . . and were trying to get some academic credentials for what they had been doing without any," but that only two or three of those marriages still survived. As the women's friendships had proven more resilient, they had had the opportunity to talk a great deal about their generous contributions to the local divorce statistics. Pam reported their conclusion: "Somewhere along the line we took a different look at our relationships and decided that they had problems from the beginning, and we created some new options for ourselves, so that gave us the freedom to think of leaving." The new criterion that fueled the "different look" was easy to characterize: "self-respect; it's real easy." Pam attributed the intoxicating new sense of self-esteem she and her schoolmates had experienced to the supportive relationships with other women that developed in the classroom, and she sought to foster a comparably supportive environment for female clients at SOS.

My preliminary impression was that Pam and her staff presented their clients just such a model of supportive female bonds. Pam and Jan appeared to have a strong friendship and mutual respect, and I was discovering that staff relations generally were interwoven with a number of long-term friendships, such as the one between Pam and Doreen. The atmosphere among the multiracial, multiethnic, and almost exclusively female staff seemed relaxed, good-humored, and tolerant whether the topic of discussion was Geraldine Ferraro's vice-presidential campaign, the ethics of surrogate motherhood contracts, or membership in a Rosicrucian society.

I participated in a great many such conversations before I realized I had embarked upon a study of Pamela's extended family. At the time I stored my spotty field notes on these conversations in a separate file, which I regarded as auxiliary to my primary research data. One of the earliest of these entries records a freewheeling discussion about adoption and surrogate parenting that took place among Pam, Doreen, Jan, myself, and Lorraine, a tall, dashiki-clad Black counselor I had met for the first time that day. Lorraine's comments revealed that she too was a long-term friend of Pam's and another member of that first East Valley reentry program cohort. In the course of the discussion, Lorraine confirmed and embellished Pam's description of the group's collective marital history, adding details that increased my interest in Pam.

Because Lorraine was Black she was outside the definition of the sample I had set out to study, I was not to identify her as kin to Pamela, to interview her formally, or to refile my early notes about her for another two years. However, as I groped my way through that transitional stage of the study, I was sufficiently intrigued by what I began to think of as the East Valley pattern to pursue the matter further by interviewing Doreen. A gregarious, high-spirited woman in her late forties, Doreen was the third to tell me her version of what I came to regard as a paradigmatic tale. A high-school dropout, at eighteen Doreen married Ed, a sailor who had trained as a technician in the navy. She stayed home with the three children they had right away, and in 1957 the family moved to Santa Clara County for Ed to study engineering at a state university while working as an electronics technician. By 1970 he was a successful design engineer who had job-hopped his way to an "upper middle class" annual income of $25,000. Both Doreen and Ed were very much affected by the social movements of the 1960s, and Doreen became active in community struggles for multiethnic education and in the anti-war movement. A Chicana friend from the school campaign encouraged Doreen to join the new reentry program for women at East Valley, which was to have a profound, and unanticipated, effect on her marriage and life course.

By 1970 Doreen and her husband both were politically exhausted and depressed. Deeply discouraged by the assassinations and electoral defeats of all the political leaders they supported, they were suffering as well from right-wing attacks on them personally for their involvement in local struggles. The East Valley experience truly liberated Doreen who became "high on education and began to heal." This seemed to exacerbate her husband's depression, however, as Ed "couldn't handle me being stronger or happier" and began to criticize and blame Doreen "for everything" and to seek his own intoxication at the company's wet bar.

Doreen claims she deeply loved Ed and tried desperately, but unsuccessfully, to save the marriage. Soon, however, Ed met, married, and started a new family with a secretary at the company, a woman a decade younger than Doreen. While the second wife quit work to become a full-time homemaker, as Ed preferred, Doreen continued her schooling and began a career in counseling. An internship at a community Women's Center led to Doreen's first full-time paid job in 1977, a CETA-funded counseling position at SOS.

Doreen and her three children suffered a period of acute downward mobility, from upper middle class to "downright poor," immediately after the marriage dissolved. The comparatively generous monthly support payments of $525 they received (which represented less than one-fourth of Ed's gross salary at the time) were inadequate to support them.[1] Determined to complete her college degree, Doreen relied on student assistance and part-time employment to make ends meet. She was justly proud that, while struggling under these conditions, she had succeeded in earning her B.A., completed the course work for a master's degree, and received consistent promotions and raises during her seven years at SOS. Nonetheless, when I interviewed Doreen in October 1984, she had no prospects of approaching the level of income her husband had been earning at the time of their separation fourteen years earlier.

The "East Valley story" that Pamela, Lorraine, and Doreen shared was a history of paradoxical status and income mobility generated by the widespread national shifts in contemporary women's family and work patterns. East Valley had served these brides of the 1950s as a trapdoor out of the security and constraints of domesticity. Heady with new ideas, skills, self-esteem, and goals, each had begun a journey up the ladder of educational and occupational status, a journey that paradoxically hurtled each woman and her children precipitously down the economic pyramid. Although each was to increase her earning power over time, none would recover the level of material attainment she had enjoyed as an engineer's wife and homemaker before attending East Valley or that her former husband's new wife enjoyed. Downward economic mobility appeared to be one of the ironic consequences of increased educational and career achievement among many housewives. Women like Pam, Lorraine, and Doreen, whose social class once had been determined by the men to whom they were related, now were determining their class positions by themselves, and the results were ambiguous and contradictory. Feminism, particularly the strand popular in the early 1970s that criticized female dependence and encouraged career ambitions, had proven to be incompatible with millions of marriages forged on 1950s' premises. This appeared to be the hidden spring that had released the unsuspected trap.

The collective history of the East Valley circle I had stumbled upon seemed to condense most of the significant social, demographic, economic, and political transformations that had taken place in Santa Clara County over the past several decades. Most notable among these were the rise of the electronics industry, the escalation of female employment and divorce, the demise of the family wage system in the working class, and the rise and decline of grass-roots feminism. Recognizing this, I flirted with the notion that a case study of the original East Valley reentry cohort would be an ideal medium for exploring in greater depth the relationships between these changes as well as their contemporary implications. And that was what led me to my "revelation" interview with Pam.

ALONG THE EAST VALLEY TRAIL

Precisely one week after Ronald Reagan's landslide reelection to the U.S. presidency and four months after I had begun interviewing clients at SOS, I happened onto what would prove to be the single most significant field experience of this study. The lengthy interview with Pamela Gama that I conducted that afternoon was an unscheduled one. I had planned instead to interview a former housewife and electronics assembly worker named Dotty Lewison, but when Dotty canceled at the last minute, I wandered down to SOS hoping not to waste a valuable day of fieldwork time. Jan greeted me warmly and offered to let me tag along on her lunch date with the director of a local home for troubled youth. Just before the appointed time, however, I ran into Pamela, who was enthusiastic about my interest in the East Valley circle and offered to donate her lunchtime to an interview that very day. Begging off lunch with Jan, I explained my interest in Pam's East Valley group and jokingly apologized about treating Jan as a second stringer for what I did not realize would be the first of several times.

Pamela and I took bag lunches into her spacious office overlooking the parking lot of a nuclear weapons factory. I set up my tape recorder expecting to record her chronicle of the journey from fifties' domesticity through seventies' feminism and to clear up my confusion about her former husband's employment history. I had alternately heard him described as an unemployed carpenter and a successful engineer. And for the better part of the next three hours that is largely what I did record. (Later as I transcribed the tape and listened to it through the wiser ears of "hind-sound," I realized that I had ignored the existence of cues to an alternative narrative from the start.)

Pamela began by recounting the family roots of her progressive political sentiments. She reported with pride that "my family was very community-oriented, a strong Democratic family." Pam's parents, now spending their senior years in a local trailer park, were New Deal Democrats with a long history of political engagement. The couple met during the 1930s, organizing destitute farm laborers in Texas. Indeed, Pam blames her mother's impoverished roots and poor nutrition for the difficult births that left Pam mildly, and her younger brother severely, afflicted with cerebral palsy. Pam's father, Fred Porter, became a popular local politician, serving for many years on the city council and the planning commission of the southern California town where Pam and her two siblings grew up. Nonetheless, the family was "pretty poor," Pam claimed, because "my dad could do a lot of things real well, except earn a living." Fred held a host of jobs like electroplater, insurance salesman, and fishing rod salesman in between such failed small business ventures as a feed store and chicken hatchery. Consequently, the family had relied heavily on the income Pam's mother, Martha, earned as an elementary school teacher.

In 1959 Pam graduated from high school and began to attend a local community college. But six months later, at the age of eighteen, Pam married her best friend's brother, Don Franklin. Don was working for a phone company, receiving on-the-job training as a drafter, and because the newlyweds wanted additional income, Pam quit school to work at various office and department store sales clerk jobs. After a gynecological infection raised the specter of potential infertility, Pam tried to become pregnant right away, and her first daughter, Lanny, was born in 1960. Two years later her second daughter, Katie, was born.

The department store where Pam worked had fired her as soon as her pregnancy began to show, and so she had become a homemaker. But as money was tight, Pam supplemented the family income with baby-sitting and sewing jobs. "I was queen of the unskilled jobs," Pam remarked, then laughed sympathetically when I pointed out the cultural devaluation of women's work her remark implied. She claimed to remember that period of her marriage to Don in rosy terms, but inadvertently injected a note of discord as well. "Oh, everything was wonderful. I mean, it was just terrific. I was totally in love. And money was always a big problem. He was working as a drafter at that point, but he's always had a very big need to purchase—cars, cameras, electronic things. He would discuss the purchases, but he could manipulate me just totally. Until I went to East Valley, I really believed that any problems there were in that relationship were because I didn't measure up."

In 1963 when a former supervisor recruited Don for a drafting job at an electronics firm in the developing Silicon Valley, the Franklins realized the dream popular among southern Californians by moving north. There Don began working his way into a successful career in engineering, which enabled the couple to purchase their first house in a new tract development "in the boonies" in 1965. Still primarily a homemaker, Pamela continued her participation in the 'intermediate economy' and made occasional forays into the world of part-time employment as well, but always, she says, in the face of Don's opposition and ridicule. "My husband hated it when I worked," Pam recalled. "He hated it. He always would make fun of it and the kind of wages I'd get. I think he just didn't like me earning money, even though we were always broke, the kind of broke where you have to worry about the PG&E [Pacific Gas & Electric] being turned off. It boils down to control."

Throughout the 1960s, Pam remained primarily a housewife while honoring her family's tradition of community activism. Through her involvement in a Methodist church and in an ecumenical women's group, Pam became active "in community things, social action things," such as a summer school for migrant children, a Headstart program, and a multicultural education program for the public schools.

When Lorraine and her family bought a house across the street from the Franklins, they were the first Blacks to move into the neighborhood.

Pamela was the first to welcome them and to integrate Lorraine into the circle of neighborhood women. A strong friendship developed quickly between the two and deepened in 1967 when each gave birth to her last child. Pam and Lorraine raised Jimmy and Corinne as virtual siblings, fostering a relationship of affection and intimacy between their children that survives today. They also colluded in covert operations to earn independent funds without their husbands' knowledge. Pam had begun to pick up a few housecleaning jobs, and Lorraine would baby-sit for her when she was working. Pam says she enjoyed her clandestine career as a domestic worker, and when she began receiving more job offers than she wanted, she convinced Lorraine to take a few despite her husband's determined opposition to his wife's employment. "She had to hide it from her husband because he had this terrible thing about the Black men and they didn't want their women working, and especially doing housework."

Although, like most couples, Pam and Don had their conflicts, Pam still defined her marriage as a good one and considered herself happily married. Thus in 1970 when Lorraine suggested that she and Pam enroll together in a new reentry program for women at East Valley, Pam "wasn't red hot about it, one way or the other. I thought, well, I'll go, I'll see what it's like." But Pam's attitudes about the program and about her marriage seemed to metamorphose instantaneously. "It's like the minute I got into it, I got totally consumed by it. . . . And it was almost overnight that I became really clear that I wasn't happy."

The East Valley program opened an entirely new world to Pam and her classmates, sending shock waves through their households that few of their fifties' marriages could withstand. There Pam "was exposed to different kinds of folks with different kinds of attitudes," and she opened herself to new experiences and ideas. She went to bars, learned to dance, learned to flirt, learned that married people had affairs and that men found her attractive despite her physical disability. Meanwhile Don had started an electronics drafting business of his own, and he was working outrageously long hours with very little financial return.

The fissures in the relationship that Pam had largely ignored in the past grew suddenly deep and wide. Pam began to challenge Don's consumer habits and his more conservative political ideas. She found fault with his lack of involvement with their children and his refusal to do any housework even though Pam was going to school, raising their children, and working part time as well. Increasingly their times together were

49

fleeting and hostile, and their paths diverged "so totally that we just lived separate lives, especially from 1970 to 1973. He didn't know what was going on in my world, and I didn't know what was going on in his world."

Sensing that her marriage was slipping away, Pam urged Don to seek counseling with her. He refused until she gave him an ultimatum. Then he did go briefly, "but he was completely closed." Pam sought counseling for herself because she was "emotionally at the end of my rope," struggling to go to school full time, working part time, running the home, and trying to hang on to the new life she was trying to create for herself. After Pam unburdened herself to the intake counselor at a public mental health clinic, the woman asked her, "How heavy is your husband?" "One hundred seventy-five pounds," Pam answered. To which the therapist replied, "Aren't you tired of carrying him on your back?"

In the winter of 1973–74, ten years after they had moved to the Santa Clara Valley, Pam and Don divorced. Pam took the children, who were eleven, nine, and six years old at the time, and moved into an apartment. Because Don's business still was not turning a profit, at first he contributed no money to their support. Like Doreen, Pam was determined to complete her schooling, and so she relied on part-time work, public assistance, and her share of the proceeds from the sale of the house to support her new single-parent family.

Although Pam earned a teaching certificate, substitute teaching was the only job she could find. Dissatisfied, she became a management trainee at a chain store where she had worked several times before, but she found the hourly wages of $3.25 and the nighttime and weekend hours there untenable. The hours and pay were slightly better at her next job in a "one-girl-office" of a paper supply business, which her ex-husband had helped her find. Finally a friend helped Pam get a job teaching English as a second language to migrants enrolled in employment skills classes at a large county employment development agency. Pam worked there for eight years, moving into administrative positions that enabled her to qualify for the position she had assumed at SOS one year before we met.

Although the financial and emotional burdens of single parenthood were daunting, the satisfactions of Pam's new life soon began to outweigh them. As Pam's "back" began to mend, she, like Doreen, became high on independence: "I was on top of the world. There wasn't anything I wasn't capable of. I enjoyed having my own place, I was doing well at school, going out a lot, things were pretty good with the kids." Somewhat apologetically, Pam confessed that she also found pleasure playing with power reversals in relationships with men. She claims she began to treat them "as objects, you know, to give me pleasure like compliments, or take me out, or tell me a joke, or whatever. I treated them really without respect or caring." To maintain power and control, she refused to give her phone number to the men she dated, and she made a point of paying her own way. Retrospectively Pam judges this a defensive reaction to her history with Don. "I think I got to that place because I decided I'd made a terrible mistake in being married, and I'd been so totally ripped off that I was never going to let that happen to me again."

Of the numerous liaisons and affairs Pam enjoyed during that time, only one had lasting significance. Although Albert Gama lived in the same apartment complex as Pam and her children, they met at a singles' dance. Al was a carpenter, four years younger than Pam, recently divorced, and childless. After they had dated for a year, he moved in with Pamela and her children. Pam thought she would never marry again, and neither she nor Al even contemplated marriage at the time. Conflicts over Pam's children ultimately jettisoned their first period of cohabitation, which lasted for about one year. Pam found Al, who had never been a parent, intolerant and authoritarian with her children. After he moved out, Pam dated other men and even lived with one briefly, "but I would always wind up back with Al because it's obvious there was some kind of connection we both felt."

By 1980 Pam found herself in an introspective and discouraged frame of mind. She was increasingly unhappy with her job at the employment development agency, and the pleasures of the single life, particularly of single parenthood, had begun to wane. For the last several years she had been having difficulties with her children, all of whom were having troubles navigating the particularly jagged shoals of adolescent culture in the Silicon Valley. She worried that her son, who hated school, was experimenting with drugs. At fourteen Katie, her middle child, had become involved in a fundamentalist Christian youth group and tried to proselytize to her siblings and to Pam. Pam went along with her daughter to a few religious events, but she "just thought that the people were freaks. They were nice and warm, but they were sure weird." And Pam was disturbed "that they believed that the man should be the head of the home." Much more disturbing were Pam's travails with her oldest child,

Lanny, who had become an unhappy, rebellious adolescent. Without consultation, Lanny dropped out of high school and resisted all of Pamela's attempts to help her. Lanny fought her constantly, and Pam became so desperate that she considered placing her firstborn in foster care. Lanny moved out and lived with a series of friends before moving in with the truck driver who would become her first husband. Although today Pam's relationships with all of her children are exceptionally loving, intimate, and supportive, she still cannot forgive herself for what she regards as her past maternal failures.

Sobered by the tribulations of independence, Pam reconsidered many of the feminist goals and principles she had embraced in the early 1970s and found them rigid, artificial, and arbitrary. "They didn't make the kind of sense they'd made at one time." In particular, her opposition to marriage ceased to make sense to her. Al had begun talking about marriage, and Pam no longer found compelling grounds to refuse. Pam knew she wanted to relate to someone, "and I had determined that I'm a pretty monogamous person by nature," and "over the years I realized that Al and I had this strong bond that kept bringing us back together." Ample experiences with other men had convinced Pam "that there were problems with all of them." "Maybe it was better," she reasoned, "to just take Al." At least she knew what he was like, and he knew her children. Thus, Pam claims, with such minimal expectations she decided to give marriage a second try.

The honeymoon period was exceedingly brief, nonetheless, casting but a fleeting impression on the thick walls of Pamela's mounting depression. A back injury exacerbated the chronic physical problems caused by Pam's cerebral palsy. Job conditions at the employment training center deteriorated further. Her son, Jimmy, quit school, and because of his conflicts with both Pam and Al, he went to live with his father. Hoping a job change would lift her spirits, Pam applied successfully for an administrative position at SOS. And because she remembered how much she had enjoyed being in school, she enrolled in an external degree program to earn an MBA through correspondence courses. But nothing seemed to be working, and Pamela felt herself on the verge of an emotional breakdown. She tried therapy, antidepressant drugs, and "all this self-help stuff to try to turn it around" but could find only temporary relief. And her new marriage did not help either. Al could not understand her depression and blamed her for making herself miserable. Pam found herself with the same problem as in her first marriage: "No communication. We began to live really like just roommates, in a sense, and yet I still had to run interference between Al and the kids." Despite Pam's claims about her minimalist expectations, in marrying Al she had still been seeking intimacy. She had not found it, and she was lonelier than before.

Thus, about one year before I met her, Pam had "decided that everything was terrible, and that I really needed to be out of that marriage, bad." She moved into a condominium her parents helped her to purchase, and because by then Katie had gotten married, for the next six months Pam lived alone. "It was the first time in my life, the first time in my whole entire life that I was totally alone." At first it relieved some of the stress caused by conflicts in her second marriage. Although Pam maintained contact with Al, who campaigned for her to return, she resisted his entreaties. "Our relationship was just so superficial, just totally superficial. At that point, although I loved him on a certain level, I really didn't even like him, really didn't."

REDEEMING MARRIAGE

Unknown to me, Pam's narrative had reached its climactic threshold when my tape recorder signaled its need for a fresh cassette. Pam accommodatingly lighted another cigarette before recounting her dramatic tale of epiphany and conversion. Late one summer night several months earlier, and six months after Pam and Al had separated, Al severely injured a young woman in an automobile accident. Al had had a few drinks before the accident and was driving an inadequately insured vehicle registered in Pam's name. Several hours later, in the middle of the night, he arrived on Pam's doorstep, desperately shaken. All of their property, savings, retirement benefits, and future earnings were in jeopardy. "An awesome thing had happened to this young woman, and it looked like an awesome thing was going to happen to both of us. And Al had just never been in a place like that before. I mean, he just basically controlled his environment and shut off anything he didn't care to be involved in. Of course, this was one thing he couldn't shut out."

Terrified, remorseful, close to suicide, Al was driving to work several days later when "a voice came to him and said—which feels like it was God speaking to him—and said, 'Go see Katie,' which is our middle child."* A secular nonbeliever, Al ignored the voice at first, but as it repeated itself insistently, he surrendered. He delivered himself to born-again Katie, who received and guided him "through this big emotional thing where he accepted the Lord, and the whole bit, and asked for forgiveness for his sins. . . . And just suddenly this total depression he'd been in, this one where life just wasn't even worth living, suddenly he felt totally different . . . in fact still does to this moment, even though things are still real unsettled."

Quite suddenly, and without comment, Pam shifted from a third- to a first-person account in this revelation narrative. By so subtle a maneuver did Pam disrupt my preconceptions and redirect the future course of my research as she informed me that just as Al suddenly accepted Jesus into his life, she had accepted both Al and Jesus back into hers. "So we started going to just everything that Katie said, started looking for a church, began going to church. Global Ministries of Love [Katie's Christian community] has a lot of evening activities we went to. I hadn't had the experience Al had, but it felt totally okay to me because it was right in line with what I had been feeling all along."

Pam reminded me of her earlier church involvements, then continued the tale of their marital redemption. She and Al started reading the Bible together, praying together, rededicating their relationship to each other and "the Lord." "Because I really knew, clearly," Pam explained, "that there was something totally different about Al. And I knew on some very basic level that if we ever had a chance for our marriage to work out, it was right then."

Striking while the metal was pliant, Pam secured Al's agreement to attend marriage counseling with a secular therapist she had consulted before. "And Al was really pretty good there. He opened up as much as he could. He really tried to treat me different." But as they became more involved with Global Ministries, "a group that we just get drawn to, for whatever reasons," Pam and Al replaced secular therapy with "Christian counseling which is, you know, I think I've only told one person outside of that group that I'm going, because, you know, it seems, it's a big deal.

---

*Because Katie is actually not Al's daughter, Pam's sudden use of the plural pronoun symbolized the profound effects Al's conversion experience had on her subjective sense of family ties.

I even knew that before I went there, and I was kind of apprehensive about it."

Aware and respectful of my secular feminist sensibilities, Pam adopted a mildly defensive, confessional approach, one that disarmed and began to initiate me into the rhetoric, doctrines, and emotional attractions of fundamentalist discourse.[2] She understood the dissonance between her progressive and feminist political values and the moral and social doctrines of the evangelical community to which she found herself drawn, and she addressed the contradictions between feminism and Christian marriage principles head-on. "Christian counseling for a marriage is Bible-based. And if you know the Bible at all, you know it's submission, the husband is the head of the family, you know it's real clear. Of course, it also says that the husband should treat the wife as his own body, as Jesus treats the church. You know, if you can work out that kind of relationship, then who would care who's in charge, because it's such a total wonderful relationship? . . . I kept thinking, what am I doing there? You know, women's lib, and all that kind of stuff. This isn't going to fit with me at all. But somewhere along the line, just before we started going to counseling, I went through an experience similar to Al's, where I thought nothing's working for me, and I thought, I want to rededicate my life to God. I just seemed to feel at some basic place in me that that was where I needed to be and what I needed to be doing. So in a way this Christian counseling, was like, well, if it fits, it fits, do it; you know? And it's really worked out to be real good. Although it just seems so incredible to me. It really, really does, that I could go in there wanting to do it."

Whereas the talk of Al's conversion followed almost a textbook script of sin, crisis, repentance, and salvation, Pam's own rebirth struck me as unusually self-conscious, methodical, and strategic. She had not had a direct experience of Christian rebirth, but to secure for herself the personal and marital benefits it seemed to promise, Pam was willfully directing her experiences to achieve one. She reported that her efforts were being rewarded. "But now I'm in a much different place. I have some meaning to my life which has been lacking for a long time, some kind of purpose. And it's certainly not an easy life. It's a real demanding, disciplined life. But I feel good about doing it. In fact, Al and I are going to be baptized Sunday. That's going to be a trip. Baptism signifies you're putting away your old life, and kind of a rebirth. I'm feeding that part of myself right now. I'm really feeding that, and it's growing. . . . I just know it's good, it's where I want to be and what I want to do. My relationship with Al is far from perfect, but it's like a gigantic miracle took place, because here's this person that never related to anyone in his entire life, relating to people, including me, opening himself up, hanging in there when we have problems, just hanging in there for hours and hours and hours. And he wouldn't talk for five minutes before. And having that kind of support or commitment to working on a relationship is so incredible. It really is. It gives you a lot of good feeling, a lot of hope in the future."

Pam's account of the beneficial effects of Christian rebirth on her marriage unsettled me, and I pursued the question of how she reconciled patriarchal marital doctrine with her commitment to equality and justice for women. She did so with the same level of awareness and self-reflection she had applied to the conversion process itself. Her responses suggested a selective, instrumental, and highly creative approach to Christian marriage. Although a dozen years earlier Pam had rejected the traditional gender order and wifely subordination of her first marriage, now she was actively attempting to submit herself to Al's husbandly authority in order to renovate her second marriage. She did not do so lightly, fully, or unilaterally, however. "This is very considered. I consider everything about it. I even tell Al, I don't want you taking charge of my money. I really don't trust you. I haven't trusted him for years. I'm just beginning to learn to trust him. . . . But I am willing to submit to him."

When I pressed Pam to discuss the ways in which she was willing to submit to Al's authority, she described instead an instance in which he had helped her resolve her ambivalence about hosting a large family gathering. Yet she had done so by rejecting Al's advice to forgo the event. Noticing my puzzled look, Pam elaborated her understanding of the principles of Christian marital submission: "In the Christian marriage, they really encourage you, if you don't agree, you can still say, 'I don't agree.' They talk about people being like sanding stones for each other. The confrontation is good. So I thought about it for a while, and I was willing to go along with it, and then I thought in my heart, no, that's really important to me. So I went back to him, and I told him that, and he said, 'Well, okay, go ahead.' But I really was willing to just not have it even though I had real strong feelings that that's what I should do. I really was willing to just, okay, give it a shot."

Pam expounded on the efficacy of this rather "last-gasp patriarchy" marital philosophy by summarizing conversations she had held with other Christian wives. The views of wifely subordination Pam depicted struck me as remarkably strategic. "It's really interesting," Pam elaborated. "I found that more than one woman came from the place I came from. And the kind of things they described to me made sense. They said in the beginning, they thought, well, I'll do it, but all I'm doing is feeding his ego. That's all I'm doing. But they described what happened in their relationships, and I look at their relationships, and they have *good*, workable relationships. What happens is once they get past that, that frees the husband up a lot to behave in different ways. It's like he doesn't have to spend his energy fighting for his place. His place is well assured, and your support of him is well assured. So his energy doesn't have to go there anymore. His energy can go to a more positive place in the relationship."

As Pam's narrative progressed, I felt my preconceptions dissolving with the hours of the autumnal afternoon. Before that day I had harbored little respect for fundamentalist women. Like many feminists, I regarded the patriarchal ideology that governed their lives as a doctrine of male superiority and privilege largely imposed by men on the women they dominated. Women who accepted biblical male authority were mainly victims of a social system stacked against them, in my view, either mystified or resignedly adjusting their bids to our culture's androcentric deck of cards. Never before had I considered the independent appeals to women of fundamentalist communities, nor taken seriously the strategic possibilities of women's nominal subordination within these.[3]

Pam's narrative compelled me to reexamine my earlier views. She was no passive victim or dupe, no believer in the inferiority of women, and her turn to fundamentalist marriage was acutely self-conscious, willful, and articulate. Nor did this measured choice represent a simple repudiation of her earlier feminist and tolerant progressive politics. Indeed Pam was fully cognizant and wary of the potential threats that her new Christian course posed to these political convictions and to friendships based on such shared beliefs. She acknowledged the toll it had already begun to take, interfering most painfully in her close relationship with coworker Jan.

Pam hoped to sustain her old political convictions by isolating them from her new religious ones, but she recognized incompatibilities between the two and the possibility that she would relinquish the former as she became more deeply integrated into the Global Ministries community. "I know a lot of the people I'm involved with now are pro-Reagan," Pam worried aloud. "And I'm just totally not pro-Reagan. I'm frightened of the man. It's too early to tell if they'll affect me. I looked at some political literature they were handing out, and I saw that it was really slanted. They have convictions about homosexuality that I don't have. They have convictions about abortion I don't have. They have a lot of different convictions that I don't have. And I don't know if I'll be in-doctrinated and suddenly turn around, or not. I really hope that doesn't happen. . . . I really don't know. If there were a part of me that feels that it's not right, what I'm involved in, or what I'm not doing, it's maybe those things."

Although she worried about this prospect, Pam had developed a potent rationale for assuming the risk. "The only answer I have for that and for myself is that my life was a total mess. I wasn't doing anything on a humanitarian level, or a political level, for anyone or anything. I was totally preoccupied with what a mess my life was. I was a total zero in that area for quite a while there. If I have this belief in political systems, and I wasn't supporting them; if I have these beliefs in humanitarian values (although I think there's not very much conflict between the church and those kinds of things, except they hate the word humanitarian), and I wasn't doing anything to support the ideas I had, then what's the difference? I was a total zip. And I don't really get confronted with it 'cause the people I'm involved with don't spend a lot of energy on anti-abortion and homosexual problems. So, it's not that bad of a deal."

Thus, with thorough knowledge of her divided self, and not without misgivings, Pam had made a deliberate decision to proceed with her religious autoconversion. She had identified excessive rationality as a major source of her chronic bouts of depression and was choosing to submit herself to faith and patriarchal marriage to overcome these and to transform her relationship with Al. Pam's description of her method concluded with a riveting parable: "It's just that you have an experience where you say I'm going to follow this way of life. And you *work* on it. You study the Bible, you pray, you do a lot of things to try to grow and develop that side of you. And because of the fundamentalist personal relationship with God and with Jesus, you wind up having experiences that aren't all intellectual. I operate out of my head, most of the time. Most of the time, I never operate out of other senses. And you have experiences that reinforce your faith. Although there are also experiences that make you doubtful; but the best way I can explain it is this story that was told to me. A wise old man was talking to someone, and he was explaining that inside of him there were two dogs, and they were fighting: a gray dog and a spotted dog, and they were tearing at each other. And the person said, 'Well, tell me, in that fight, which dog won?' And the man said, 'Whichever one I fed the most.' So, it's like I'm doing a lot of feeding of that side of myself, and it's neat because I'm doing it for me, I'm doing it for my marriage; it's neat."

The jarring ring of Pam's telephone interrupted our dialogue, calling our attention to the lateness of the hour. The attraction between us and the desire to continue this discussion seemed to be mutual, and we agreed to get together again soon. Pam's story compelled, intrigued, and discomfited me. I was struck most of all by the contrasts in nominal and substantive authority between Pam's secular and Christian marriages. From her description of her current marriage, it was difficult to view her as a submissive wife, despite her formal accession to Al's patriarchal authority. Financially, occupationally, socially, and politically, Pam seemed to retain strong independence, or even control. Paradoxically she had described herself as far more submissive to her first husband, Don, and even to Al during the earlier, secular stage of their marriage than she was now that she had accepted Global Ministries' nominally patriarchal marital guidance. Moreover, Pam claimed to be making emotional demands on her Christian husband now that were far greater, and more effective, than those she had dared to make in any of her secular intimate relationships in the past. In short, I found Pam's commitment to male authority exquisitely subtle, a philosophy of "patriarchy in the last instance,"[4] the instance that never comes.

To no small extent, Pam's self-directed religious conversion seemed to be a strategy for achieving heterosexual intimacy, one facilitated by the surprisingly feminized view of a loving marriage implicit in her account of Christian marriage counseling. And in a relationship committed to struggling through conflicts to a mutually satisfactory resolution, no submission need ever occur. From Pam's description, Christian marriage was demanding more profound changes in Al's prior ways of relating than in hers. Perhaps that was why, despite her egalitarian convictions, the doctrine of submission did not strike her as a bad deal.

I was less persuaded than Pam of the triviality of formal subservience, however, and as I recorded field notes late that evening I registered some of my doubts:

> But I don't think patriarchy's last instance is insignificant. It may never come, but a whole institutional nexus comes with it. Christian counseling, however modernized in femalist terms, is likely to have subtle and eventually profound effects on Pam's other feminist and progressive values if she integrates into this community. She's aware and wary of this, the one thing about her new life that gives her pause. She hopes that this won't happen, because she thinks her progressive values are a more ingrained part of her than her views on marital relationships. I think the two are more intertwined and that the potential conflicts are serious.

I had stumbled upon a Silicon Valley woman in the midst of an unusual and notably self-reflexive process of personal and family transformation, a woman attempting to reconcile feminist with Christian fundamentalist views of marriage. My budding friendship with Pam offered me a unique opportunity to observe closely and discuss the evolution and effects of this project. Pam seemed flattered by my interest, and she offered to introduce me to as many of her relatives and friends as I cared to meet. Thus at an early moment in the process did I gain the privilege of studying Pamela and Albert Gama's efforts to develop a Christian marriage firsthand and to situate their progress over the next several years in the ever-shifting Silicon Valley framework of their kinship, employment, and community relationships.

4

Sprouting Some Odd Branches:
A Divorce-Extended Family

The extended family is in our lives again. This should make all the people happy who were complaining back in the sixties and seventies that the reason family life was so hard, especially on mothers, was that the nuclear family had replaced the extended family. . . . Your basic extended family today includes your ex-husband or -wife, your ex's new mate, your new mate, possibly your new mate's ex, and any new mate that your new mate's ex has acquired. It consists entirely of people who are not related by blood, many of whom can't stand each other. This return of the extended family reminds me of the favorite saying of my friend's extremely pessimistic mother: Be careful what you wish for, you might get it.

—Delia Ephron, *Funny Sauce*

One of Pamela's favorite Christian authors and radio personalities is Dr. James C. Dobson, who was an influential consultant on family and sexual policy to the Reagan administration. A member of Attorney General Edwin Meese's Commission on Pornography and of Reagan's National Advisory Commission to the Office of Juvenile Justice and Delinquency Prevention, Dobson also frequently counseled the U.S. Army Chief of Staff and members of Congress on family-related matters.[1] For more than a decade Dobson was a professor of pediatrics at the University of Southern California's School of Medicine and at Children's Hospital in Los Angeles. But the feminist agenda of the International Women's Conference held in Houston in 1977 convinced him that Christian family life was in mortal danger, and so he resigned these positions "in order to devote my full-time effort to the preservation of the home."[2] In 1977 Dobson founded Focus on the Family, a multimedia ministry designed to combat the dire threat to American family life that he perceived in feminism and in other symptoms of contemporary family instability.

During the next decade Focus on the Family grew and prospered along with the rest of the evangelical electronic church in the United States. From its two-room, one-secretary origins to the staff of 460 over which Dobson presided in 1987, Focus outgrew its six-building complex in Arcadia, California, and attracted an enormous popular following. By then Dobson's radio talk show, also titled *Focus on the Family,* was second in radio popularity only to Paul Harvey's news and commentaries, with 970 radio stations in seventeen countries broadcasting the program, often three times daily. Dobson alternates a folksy style of lectures and personal advice with interviews and panel discussions with invited familial experts, activists, and victims who address a wide range of contemporary family issues, from marital infidelity to disciplining children, from infertility to spousal and child abuse, from sexually transmitted diseases and drug addiction to conflicts with in-laws. He has also codified and marketed his philosophy on every imaginable facet of contemporary family life in popular advice books, which have sold more than 6 million copies, as well as in an ever-expanding series of videotapes, audio cassettes, films, pamphlets, newsletters, and magazines.[3]

Writing in his monthly newsletter in July 1987, when the aftermath of the Jim and Tammy Bakker scandal was taking its toll on the public esteem and coffers of the electronic evangelicals, Dobson sought to revive his audience's political and financial support for Focus on the Family by rekindling anxiety about the fate awaiting American families. To concretize his apocalyptic vision, Dobson compiled several pages of excerpts from a 1983 *U.S. News & World Report* article titled "When 'Families' Will Have a New Definition." The article, which summarized projections about the likely contours of U.S. family life in the year 2033, began with the description of the "odd branches" of relatives attending a futuristic family celebration that appears as an epigraph to chapter 1.

Dobson's newsletter continued with excerpts detailing the "confusing tangle" of kin relationships predicted to emerge as longevity increases and serial monogamy becomes normative: "Through the pattern of divorce and remarriage, a whole new network of kinship will arise. There will be double sets of grandparents, aunts, uncles, and brothers and sisters, as well as former in-laws and ex-spouses—all of them making up the new divorce-extended family." For Dobson, the family parameters "of the brave new world in which your grandchildren will be raised" threatened the very survival of society:

> If the authorities are correct, and I pray they are not, the Christian concept of the family will soon give way to even more widespread cohabitation, uncommitted marriages, casual divorces, joint custody of children, blurred sex roles, government intrusion in the family, and child-care centers to replace the mother-child relationship. What a depressing prospect for our future! Personally, I don't believe Western nations can survive such a radical departure from the value system on which they were founded. When the Scriptures declare "The wages of sin is death," they pose a warning not just to individuals, but to societies and nations, as well.

Thus, Dobson concluded with an appeal for funds to support Focus on the Family in its unswerving efforts to avert that calamity:

> Our purpose has not changed in the past 10 years. . . . we still believe in the permanence of marital relationships, in loyalty and fidelity between husbands and wives, in the value of bearing and raising children, and in the other tenets of the Christian faith. We hope you agree that we must not permit these concepts to fade from the memory of mankind. We *must* defend them with our very lives, if necessary. Why? Because the Creator of families knows how they work best. If we substitute the puny ideas of men for His marvelous design, we and our children will suffer the consequences of our folly.

A RING IS NOT A SHACKLE

Reading this newsletter in the summer of 1987, I thought back to a summer Sunday afternoon one year earlier when with my own small Jewish nuclear family, consisting of a working mother, my second husband with whom I had cohabited for ten years, and our only child—then a five-year-old veteran of commercial child care—I sat in a pew of a small Global Ministries Church. Pamela and Albert Gama, who had cohabited intermittently since 1975 and been legally married since 1980, were about to celebrate their reborn marriage with a Christian wedding ceremony. I recall being struck even then by the ironic incongruity between the occasion's script and its cast.

As Pam's son-in-law Eric, a Global Ministries deacon, ushered the fifty or so invited guests to their seats, Larry, an attractive young man with a guitar and one of Eric and Katie's communal housemates, asked us to "soften our hearts for this joyous day of celebration with Pamela and Al and Jesus" by joining him in song. Congregants clapped rhythmically or raised their hands in praise as Larry led us in folk-rock cadence:

> This is the day, This is the day,
> That the Lord hath made, That the Lord hath made . . .
> Let us lift up our hearts, lift up our hearts,
> And be glad of it, And be glad of it.

By the time Larry, accompanied occasionally by his pretty, guitar-strumming wife, Nadine, had finished playing numerous other hymns set to lively contemporary beats, the ambience in the sunny, modest church was warm, relaxed, good-spirited, and wholesome. Yet as I surveyed the assembled kith and kin, I gazed upon a family gathering remarkably similar to the anti-Christ vision Dobson perceived in the futuristic fantasy of the *U.S. News & World Report* article.

Serving as the official wedding photographer was Pam's ex-husband, Don Franklin, who was accompanied by Shirley Moskowitz, his live-in lover and would-be third wife. All of the wedding attendants were stepkin and step-in-laws to the groom. Pam's two daughters from her first marriage, Lanny and Katie, were her bride matrons, and Melissa, Lanny's young daughter from her own first marriage, was her grandma's proud flower girl. Joining Katie's husband Eric as Al's ushers were Lanny's second husband, Ken, and Pam and her ex-husband's son, Jimmy.

More than half of the pews were filled with members of four generations from the "confusing tangle" of former, step-, dual, and in-law relatives of Pamela and Al's divorce-extended family. And of the friends who joined Global Ministries shepherds and disciples in filling out the rest, most were fictive kin and former or current housemates to members of the wedding party. Sharing our pew, for example, was Pam's close friend Lorraine, sporting a stylish new punk haircut and flanked by her third husband, Carlos, and Corinne, the daughter from Lorraine's second marriage whom she had raised as fictive sister to Pam's son, Jimmy. Lorraine and Corinne had also shared Pam's single-parent household for two years after Lorraine had fled her second marriage. Meanwhile my young son focused his own rapt attention on the home-baked, three-tiered cake generously contributed by the divorced single mother of Lanny's second husband.

After a simple processional, an attractive young pastor, whom I correctly surmised to be the couple's marriage counselor, beckoned the nervous bride to join her husband and husband-to-be at the altar. Pastor Bill Jensen prefaced the proceedings with a brief speech highlighting the uncommon character of the ceremony we were about to witness. We had gathered, he informed us, to celebrate quite an unusual and special event. Pamela and Al "were choosing this day of joy and celebration to make their marriage covenant with Jesus, and to share their faith with their family and friends." Although they were legally married already, Pam and Al never had exchanged Christian vows, and thus this was a moment of great significance in their relationship. Pastor Jensen proceeded to draw a pithy contrast between a secular and a Christian marriage. A secular marriage, he told us, is based on a contract that, in turn, is based on a lack of trust. Secular marriages, as a result, do not last. Christian marriage, by contrast, "involves a covenant which is much deeper than a contract, a covenant based on trust in each other and in Jesus, and," he concluded, "that is why Christian marriage is permanent."

After outlining the major purposes of Christian marriage, Pastor Jensen addressed Pamela and Albert individually on the distinct roles and obligations of a wife and a husband in a Christian marriage. The husband has the larger responsibility, he reminded Al, because he is the head of the household, as Jesus is the head of the church. Accordingly "the wife must submit to her husband in all things as we all submit to Jesus," he told Pam. Submitting to her husband is submitting to Jesus, and thus, "she does so with love and trust, knowing that the husband must love his wife as his own body and as Jesus loves us."

Pastor Jensen interrupted this oration to lead us in singing "This Is Our Father's World," a hymn he described as one of Pamela's childhood favorites, which seemed to underscore his theme of benevolent patriarchy. He next quizzed first Al and then Pam on their readiness to exchange their Christian marital vows, asking each "Have you received the Lord

Jesus Christ as your personal savior? Does the Holy Spirit dwell within you?" Having ascertained that Pam and Al were indeed prepared to pledge their eternal love, obedience, and commitment to Jesus and to His divine plan for marriage, Pastor Jensen inaugurated the ring ceremony by explaining the doctrine of submission. The rings that Pamela and Al were about to exchange "symbolize union," he instructed them, "and they will always remind you of your love for one another and for Jesus." A rainbow looks like a ring from the vantage point of heaven, Pastor Jensen told Al, gently reminding him that "a ring is not a shackle, and marriage is not a relationship of domination, but of equality. You are the head of the household, Al, and therefore, you have the larger responsibility, but that has nothing to do with dominating a wife."

Turning to the congregation, the pastor informed us that Pam and Al wished "to do something different and special at this celebration": they were inviting other couples to join them in renewing their vows before Jesus. If there were married guests who had not exchanged Christian vows before or who wanted to renew theirs, they should step forward. The pastor paused for several moments, but no one advanced, and so he repeated the invitation. I expected that Pam's younger daughter, Katie, and her husband Eric, longtime Global activists and personal guides to Al's conversion, would relieve the mounting tension in the church by volunteering. I was startled when instead Lanny, Pam's older and unsaved daughter, suddenly nudged her second husband and joined her mother and stepfather at the altar. While Pam squeezed her daughter's hand and placed a grateful, loving arm around her waist, I wondered whether I was witness to a momentous decision. Had Lanny and Ken succumbed to the cumulative family pressure to join the ranks of the saved?

After mother and daughter each had pledged love, honor, and obedience to their respective second husbands and received their vows of love, honor, and protection in exchange, Larry and Nadine reappeared with their guitars to sing a ballad about loving Jesus and one another. Staring adoringly into each other's eyes every time they sang the chorus

I've seen many things in my life,
but nothing that moves me as much
as, when I see Jesus in your eyes,

66

they ended their duet with a kiss. A sermon about virtue, chastity, and righteousness followed; it centered on how only Jesus makes us pure because, despite our sinful nature, He "sees us as whiter than white, whiter than the driven snow, without a blemish," and made me uncomfortably curious about its reception by Lorraine's Black and Latino family sharing my pew. The communion ritual concluded the ceremonial portion of the wedding.

A long receiving line of divorce-extended family members slowed our descent to the small church basement for the reception, an informal party in which guests milled about or sat on metal folding chairs while sipping nonalcoholic punch and nibbling wedding cake or vegetables dipped in sour cream. After circulating among the many guests I had met before, I had a brief conversation with the groom. I asked Al if he had been nervous during the ceremony. "Of course," he replied, "it's a big responsibility I'm taking on." Agreeing to meet with me again soon to discuss this momentous event, Al advised me that we would spend some of our time together discussing ceremonies. "What was special about this one was that it was so personal; whereas most weddings the minister doesn't even know the people getting married. I know one church where the minister does three weddings in a day, like a factory—for the money, of course." Just then a friend of Pam's interrupted to say that Pam wanted to know whether Al preferred to open their wedding gifts publicly right then or later alone at home. Al seemed uncomfortable and asked which Pamela preferred. The friend did not know, and so the newly sanctified Christian patriarch responded as he had in the only episode of wifely submission Pam had been able to recall during that revelation interview two years earlier. He told her to do "whatever Pamela wants."

A MARRIAGE REBORN

Leaving the church after the festivities were over, and walking with my husband and son through the lively streets of the Asian neighborhood to our sun-baked car, I reflected on the significance of the day's events. I had come to know Pam fairly well in the two years since I had met her. I understood the wedding ceremony that afternoon to be a major public affirmation of Pam's commitment not just to Al but to the Christian course she had chosen to pursue. That is, I viewed this wedding as a symbolic banquet Pam had prepared to feed the "spotted dog" within. I knew too, however, that the "gray dog" still survived, despite its austere diet. Pam had not yet resolved the conflict between feminism and fundamentalism that raged within her;* nor, as the gift-opening vignette indicated, did the Christian wedding service signify her capitulation to a male-dominated marriage. I knew that her struggles with these issues continued then, as they still do today.

The wedding struck me also as an unintended affirmation of the remarkably harmonious set of postmodern extended kinship relations that Pam and her relatives had managed to construct. Indeed the major variation between that imaginary birthday gathering of a divorce-extended family in the year 2033 and the actual family gathering I had just departed was that few in this family appeared to share twenty-first-century Junior's wish for fewer relatives. During the two years I had, by then, spent in Pam's social world, I had witnessed the ways in which, despite the seemingly inhospitable context of chaotic, unstable work and household arrangements in which they lived, Pam and many of her female relatives actively strengthened these extended ties and were rewarded by the general appreciation of all concerned.

I found no small irony in the fact that evangelical Christianity, and even Dr. Dobson, far more than feminism, were facilitating their efforts. Particularly impressive were the uncommonly compatible accounts of the effects of Al's Christian rebirth on his character, his marriage to Pam, and their kin relationships that the diverse members of this postmodern family had conveyed to me during my time among them.

Perhaps no version of this narrative had surprised me more than the one Al himself had first relayed. The only person in this study who identified himself fully as a member of the working class and the only one who was native to the Santa Clara Valley, Albert Gama struck me

*Because Pam first described her new faith and church to me as "fundamentalist," I employ this term interchangeably with "evangelical." However, as I discuss in chapter 6, most contemporary fundamentalists in the United States distinguish their movement from the broader category of Christian evangelicalism. After Pam read a draft version of an article I coauthored about contemporary evangelicalism, she called to report Al's view that Global Ministries was best described as pentecostal or charismatic. These terms, which often indicate belief in the gifts of tongues and healing, also have a variety of meanings and usages. See Lawless, *God's Peculiar People,* for an informative discussion of pentecostalism and the Pentecostals.

as an unlikely mate to Pamela. A burly, swarthy, socially reticent construction worker four years her junior, Al is a fourth-generation descendant of Portuguese-American fruit farmers. Despite the fact that very few of Al's relatives have been employed directly by the electronics industry, the region's postindustrial transformations of the past three decades had visibly disrupted their traditional ethnic family and community. "I was brought up in a very small town atmosphere, family-oriented, hard-working," Al told me the first time we conversed, two years before the wedding ceremony, "and now it's turned into a high-tech center." When Al was growing up, "everyone had a family, there were hardly any divorced people; out of maybe twenty to thirty uncles and aunts, there were only two divorces. . . . But like among my cousins, divorce is a lot more common." Al estimates that 40 percent of family members in his own generation have divorced, Al and both of his siblings among them. His father's generation maintained their own thick endogamous communities, the barely changed remnants of which some of his aunts still inhabit, "but this whole other community has grown up around them, modern."

During the first ten years of Al's life the area was entirely agricultural, and everyone in his father's generation worked the small-to-medium-size farms they owned, assisted by hired seasonal laborers. But then "the subdivisions started appearing, pulling out the orchards." Although they lived in an area that was one of the last to be developed, "they noticed." By the time Al was a teenager in the late 1950s, property values in the area had escalated so irresistibly that his parents, who had been cannery workers during the Depression, sold the family farm and invested in small real estate ventures.

Al identifies himself as working class ("unfortunately; I'd rather be rich") because, since he had been nine or ten years old, "well, everyone just had to work." He blames his "antisocial temperament" and his "antisocial friends" for his antipathy to school, regretful now that he "never took advantage of it." Practical pressures, however, convinced Al to get his diploma before enlisting in the army in 1963, and volunteering saved him from serving in Vietnam. After three years in Europe, Al moved back into the small tract home for which his parents had exchanged their farm. A variety of short-term production jobs, including an extremely unpleasant and unhealthy one in a paint factory, preceded Al's offhanded entry into what became his life work in the construction trade. In 1969 it was easy to sign up for the union's four-year apprenticeship program, which offered on-the-job training and evening classes while paying 60 percent of a journeyman's wages—four to five dollars an hour in those days. But "now they start guys out much lower." Al had received "pretty good money, good benefits" since becoming a journeyman in 1973, because "if you work steady enough, you do very well." He estimated that when we spoke an average Silicon Valley carpenter was probably earning "twenty-five, twenty-six thousand dollars. It depends on how much you work. In a good year, you can earn forty thousand." Al's hourly wage at that point was about twenty dollars, and because he had worked "quite a bit" that year, he expected to earn more than thirty thousand dollars.

Equally diffident was Al's account of his entry into his first two marriages. In 1972 he married Candace, "a gal from back East" he had met at a military buddy's party, because "she seemed okay." "Just okay?" I quizzed him. "Well, she seemed good for a wife. —She worked, good housekeeper, pretty." Al claimed he was not actively looking for a wife, "but it just seemed like the right time to get married. I was getting to be about twenty-six, living by myself; it didn't seem too positive." Al liked being with Candace, and he "had a certain amount of feelings toward her," and so after several months of dating, they were wed.

The marriage lasted but a year, "not a very good year . . . a little bit like hell, I guess." Al found Candace very difficult to live with, demanding and critical; she found Al unemotional and antisocial. They liked different friends, had different interests, and because "we stopped liking each other," their marriage quickly disintegrated. Although Candace was the one who made the decision to divorce, Al claims he "didn't mind; I knew it wasn't going to work out." Thus, Al had been enjoying the single life once again when he met Pam at the single's dance in 1975.

I had been particularly eager to hear Al's account of his shared history with Pamela, expecting that he might interpret the patriarchal doctrines of Christian marriage far more rigidly than she. Although his narrative gave some support to my feminist suspicions, the compatibility between his and her oral records of their relationship was much more impressive than the dissonance.

Al described his second approach to premarital courtship with a bit more enthusiasm but portrayed himself as passive as in his first marriage. He "wasn't looking to get involved with anyone," but attended the singles' dance because "there was a lot of girls there." Al was attracted to Pamela physically and by her "aloof and independent air." And since they lived, coincidentally, in the same apartment complex, they began to see a lot of each other. Al describes that early stage of their relationship as "good—fresh and exciting." Gradually, because he was spending so much time in Pam's apartment, they decided that he should move in.

For the next several years Pam and Al played musical chairs with their relationship and residences, with Pam determining most of the changes. They lived together in an "up-and-down" relationship about eighteen months that first time, with conflicts over Pam's three children causing most of the downs. Al liked Lanny, Katie, and Jimmy but disapproved of Pam's permissive child-rearing practices, and Pam resented his more authoritarian responses to her children. Pam and Al had planned to buy a home together, but because Pam came to find the tension between Al and her children unbearable, she decided they should buy separate residences instead. Al claimed that he "didn't object strongly since we weren't getting along well," and thus they separated, without rancor, in 1976.

Al maintained occasional contact with Pam and with her children until her new live-in love affair caused a two-year breach between them. Although he felt slightly rejected by Pam, he also enjoyed regaining the freedom to date a lot of women. But then Pam "left the guy, and she didn't have a place to live, so she moved in with me for a few months." "How did you feel about that?" I asked. "Well, they needed a place to live." When Pam located a new residence and moved her family out again in 1979, Al "thought it was great because she could get on with her life." Al still wanted to be with Pam "a little bit," and, had it been up to him, they would have stayed together. He wished "at the time, that she could make up her mind more completely."

Suddenly Al interrupted his reluctant, awkward responses to my questions about his own emotional preferences with one that foreshadowed his impending redemption testimony. Acknowledging that he probably had wanted Pam to make a commitment to him, he volunteered that, had she done so, "I wouldn't have made a one hundred percent commitment to her" in return. Al would have lived with Pam again, "but it wouldn't have been mind, body, and spirit, all in one."

Absence once again restored the couple's mutual fondness, and Al was pleasantly surprised in 1980 when Pam agreed to marry him. Retrospectively he recognizes that Pam was in a depressed, reclusive phase, but because she did not discuss it with him, he "wasn't too aware of it at the time." The first three years of their marriage were not "too bad" from Al's point of view, except that Pam became more withdrawn and depressed. They did not socialize much, but this did not disturb Al, who had "always been pretty much of a loner." Al recognized the fact but not the depth of Pam's malaise because "she really doesn't talk to me about a lot of things." Al concedes he also did not encourage her because he is "not used to talking about such things."

As Pam's depression deepened and communication between the couple lessened, "she decided to make a change" by separating once again. Al reports "mixed feelings about the split." On the one hand, he "felt like a failure," and he did not want to live alone again. But he "was pleased with it too, if that was going to make her happy," and he experienced some relief from the tension. Al "felt good for her if maybe she could find something happy for her," a goal he did not share because "I never really considered myself an emotional person, and so I figured I could pretty well overcome most things."

Four months after Pam moved out, the tragedy Al could not overcome transformed his life. Numb, depressed, overwhelmed by fear of the consequences of the accident he had caused, Al turned to Pam for solace, because "she's a really caring, loving person." Pam succored Al through the ensuing miserable weeks until "I got converted." Quite suddenly, as if to demonstrate his personal transformation, this husky, unemotional, uncommunicative man collapsed in sobs as he gushed forth his conversion testimony. Repeating the narrative Pam had told me about the persistent voice that spoke to him on the freeway, Al described the morning "when I accepted the Lord into my life. Probably it's the most beautiful experience you can have. —It's a real experience; it's not an intellectual thing. Like I knew it had happened. You accept it, and it's like all the things you've ever done, are forgiven. There's a release of all the guilt, frustration, and a freedom." Al believes that the several hours he spent "crying, talking, and praying" with Katie and her Christian housemates are the most powerful experience he will ever have. "It's a rebirth. I don't know what other people feel when they're born again, but for me when I was going down that freeway, there was a voice talking to me; I mean something was talking to me. —The Lord talked to me. More than once; He talked to me three times. I ignored it at first, thinking it was my imagination, but the third time, I knew. As soon as Katie looked at me, she knew what had happened to me. And we were able to talk and to share things that in most situations most people can't. There's a complete freedom that I had never had before."

Although Pam seemed happy for Al when he relayed his conversion experience to her later that afternoon, he doubts that she really understood his rebirth at the time, because "if you haven't been born again you can't really understand it; it's not an intellectual thing, it's an emotional experience." Pam had been seriously depressed that morning too, and, warned that she was about to be fired from her job at SOS, she had come to Al's place for lunch and sympathy. Then, "miraculously," her boss had a change of heart and did not fire her when she returned.

Al had been willing to reconcile with Pamela throughout their separation, and now that she perceived the profound change in him she found reason to return. "Well, I think that she feels that God brought into her more love for me. God's power is the power of the Holy Spirit, and the Holy Spirit can fill you up." Pam's much less dramatic rebirth followed shortly thereafter, and Al agreed to her proposal that they seek Christian marriage counseling from Pastor Jensen.

Thus did Al explain the genesis of his resurrected marriage. If there were differences in each spouse's tale of the marital effects of their shared conversion, these were matters more of rhetoric and emphasis than of substance or degree. Al's rhetoric was more biblical than Pam's, his interpretation of Christian doctrine encumbered less by contrary political convictions. And while his commitment to the principles of patriarchal marriage was, as I expected, more enthusiastic than his wife's, his view of these was far less self-serving or autocratic than my preconceptions led me to presume.

Instead, Al's explication of Christian marriage lent support to Pam's perception that it had demanded greater changes from her husband than herself. More evangelical than Pam, Al was eager to convey the stark contrast between secular and Christian marriage counseling. "The main thing is that you make God the main focus of your marriage instead of yourself as an individual. That's the basis of Christian living. You try to live your life the way God wants you to, and the experience really brings you closer together. We went to secular counseling three times last summer. It was okay, but it's a little bit opposed to Christian. In Christian counseling you forget about yourself, and you're always trying to build up God. In secular, you're not involved with God, you're trying to improve your own self-image. In Christian, if I build up God, then He will

73

build me up. And that's what's important. Because I'm not really that important. You're kind of denying yourself in a sense, and you're trying to do away with pride, egotism, and all those other things." "How do you know how God wants you to live?" I asked. "Well," Al replied, "when all else fails, you read the Bible. The Bible's pretty explicit about it, that you shouldn't have jealousy, pettiness, to love one another, respect one another, not to judge others. I believe that the Bible is the Word of God. That's it; it's a matter of fact. The Bible is pretty clear-cut; it's not wishy-washy if you're a fundamentalist." The goal of Christian counseling, Al explained, "is to help you throw away your old self and begin yourself anew in Christ." The counseling focuses your attention on God and the Bible: "You try to picture your relationship as you want it, as it should be, and then try to live it out." Then by praying together frequently, you strive for honest effort and communication."

Readily conceding worldly barriers to the success of these techniques, Al also addressed the conflicts between patriarchal doctrine and contemporary gender ideology. "I don't always believe. It's not a magic wand. You live in this world. In the counseling you talk about actual things in your relationship—like sex, how to run a household. You talk about how to change your relationship. One of the problems in the New Testament, since the man is the head of the house, it comes into conflict with a lot of people's beliefs now. Especially since women are really running the household or running their own lives. So trying to correspond that to modern life—Some people take that to mean that the husband has a whip over the wife, which is not really true." Al proceeded to offer an interpretation of his Christian patriarchal responsibilities remarkably compatible with the one Pamela had conveyed. "Well, basically it means, I've got to get off my duff and get my wife to go to church, and I've got to lead our selves in prayer. I can't leave that responsibility to her. It's like being a leader. It doesn't mean I hold a whip over her, or try to get her to do my will. Being head of the household means being the spiritual leader."

Al did, however, entertain a somewhat broader view than Pam of the domain of patriarchal leadership. He thought the household head probably should also be responsible for managing a family's finances and apportioning household chores, but acknowledged that because of the litigation he had not yet assumed these burdens. Al was in danger of losing all his property in the legal case and worried that this would put him in a very dependent situation. Although he would find it pretty hard to be so dependent on Pamela, he did not consider the prospect a violation of Christian marriage.

The stress caused by the couple's legal worries and human frailty competed with the Christian counseling to maintain considerable turbulence in the Gama marriage, but Al blamed most of their difficulties on himself. "I'm not really an open person, and to be a truly loving person is not something you just get into being because somehow you get converted. I take most of the responsibility for our problems because it's up to me to make the difference, because I can't make her do anything, but I can make a change in myself. . . . I don't consider myself an honest person. I don't always say anything. I don't always have that need to be talking like she does. But you know one thing good about being a Christian is that, I tell you, sometimes you can just open up like you never did before. There's a certain amount of love that comes into your heart that was not there before."

Al completed his testimony with a description of his Christian marital goals—ones with which few contemporary feminists or other women would be likely to find fault: "I just hope that we can come closer together and be more honest with each other. Try to use God as a guideline. The goals are more openness, a closer relationship, be more loving both verbally and physically, have more concern for the other person's feelings."

A CHRISTIAN PATRIARCH

My first lengthy interview with Al challenged my preconceptions almost as profoundly as had the earlier one with his wife. I was not yet prepared for the self-effacing humility of Al's interpretation of his Christian patriarchal obligations. And despite the moving experience of his testimony, I still suspected and feared that Al's deepening involvement in Global Ministries would lead him to a more authoritarian stance. By the time I attended the wedding nearly two years later, however, I had learned to suspend most of my feminist prejudices. For in my experiences with the "re-newlyweds," I had encountered scant evidence that fundamentalism was cultivating in Al a greater appetite for dominating Pam or anyone else.

My visit with the groom one week after the wedding largely reinforced my new humble stance. Although I noted that Al's rhetoric had grown increasingly biblical and that certain of his political views about gender and sexuality had shifted in the predictably conservative direction, I detected little change in his conception of Christian patriarchy or in his description of his marital goals. If anything, Al's emphasis on his patriarchal obligation to be a loving, respectful, considerate, and committed mate to Pam had deepened over time.

Indeed Pam had scheduled my early-evening rendezvous with Al without consulting him first, so confident was she that he would not object. The apricot trees that framed the couple's two-bedroom cottage and screened its view of the adjacent shopping mall were in fruit when I arrived, an aromatic memento of Al's economic roots. I parked my car just as Pam drove up bearing a Kentucky Fried take-out dinner, which she invited me to share. We dumped the chicken onto paper plates while Al set out cans of soft drinks. Thirsty after an hour and a half of rush-hour driving, I was about to lift my glass when Al advised me gently that we would preface the meal by saying grace. Pam and Al joined hands while Al performed this task of spiritual leadership, expressing verbal gratitude to the Lord Jesus for the protection He had offered us that day and for the nourishment He was about to provide. Quietly Pam thanked Al for his thoughtful blessing, and we began the brief, informal meal.

Pam's ex-husband, Don, had already developed the wedding photos, and they shared the table surface with our food. Pam, Al, and I were commenting about the pictured guests when a snapshot of Shirley Moskowitz reminded Al of the Passover seder she had hosted that spring. He had enjoyed attending, he told me, but had been disappointed that the Jewish people present seemed not to take the occasion as seriously as he did. When the door had been opened for Elijah, for example, no one but Al and Pam seemed to know who the prophet was or why his presence should be anticipated. Embarrassed, I acknowledged my own scriptural ignorance, and Al launched into a lengthy theological discourse on the prophets of the Old Testament. Pam politely waited for a pause, then, claiming it would be more interesting and "fun" for Al and me to talk alone, she excused herself and began to leave the room. Seeming nervous, Al encouraged her to linger, but Pam insisted gently, kissed him lightly on the forehead, and departed for the bedroom.

Al and I moved into the living room onto cushioned easy chairs, which

Pam's daughter Lanny had recently reupholstered, to begin our appointed discussion of Christian marriage. During the next three hours Al expressed pleasure in his progress toward honoring the goals of love, commitment, respect, and consideration to which he believed a Christian husband was honor-bound. The wedding, he told me, had been his idea, a way to demonstrate his love to Pam. "I thought it would just probably show her that I did love her and was happy to be married to her. Just an outward sign. 'Cause you know there's a lot of work and preparation to go through, so you don't do it lightly." Their relationship had improved sufficiently that they were no longer receiving marriage counseling. They were getting along much better, Al reported. "We're just trying to help each other out more, I think. You know, not be self-centered, you know, and try to be more considerate of her needs, and feelings. I think that when you are able to work with your mate, you don't need someone preaching at you all the time." Al attributed this improvement largely to needed changes that faith had worked in him. "I think one of the things that happened to me, after I got converted— Before I was converted, though, if I had an argument with somebody, hell or high water would come, and I would never say I was sorry, or try to make amends necessarily. . . . And since, I think, since the conversion, at times I'm able to say, Hey, I may be right, I may be wrong, but right now it doesn't really matter. I just want to make up. And start over again."

Although Dr. James C. Dobson would have been delighted with Al's testimony to the marital benefits of salvation, he might have been less pleased to learn of another effect of Al's new Christian forbearance. For, unlike Dobson or imaginary Junior, Al expressed considerable affection for his divorce-extended family. When I commented on my surprise at seeing Pam's former husband serving as the wedding photographer, Al agreed that it was "a little bit unusual." But he was pleased about the increasingly warm relationships that had been developing between the two divorce-related couples and their respective kin. They frequently attended family dinners at each other's houses to celebrate birthdays, anniversaries, and an ecumenical array of Christian, Jewish, and secular holidays. "Whole families can get together, and nobody gets left out. I think it's great, really."[4] Al was looking forward to attending his first Jewish wedding when Shirley's daughter would marry her Catholic fiancé in a local synagogue that fall. Thus, I was no longer surprised when, after attending church with Al a few months later, I saw Pam and her daughters rush through Sunday dinner to wrap their gifts in time for Shirley's daughter's bridal shower that afternoon.

The positive familial effects of Al's conversion impressed me profoundly, because I knew how difficult his last two years had been. I had first met Al when he was poised, unknowingly, on the brink of serious occupational decline. Two years earlier when Al reported income from the good year he had just completed, neither of us realized that he was about to suffer the effects of the decline in the local electronics economy and of the Reagan-era assault on labor unions. Despite a geographic climate hospitable to construction work year-round, Al would be unable to find work more than eleven of the next twenty-six months, and he would be forced to accept piecework rates on nonunion jobs most of the times he was fortunate enough to work at all.

Approaching middle age as a unionized blue-collar worker, Al was a member of one of the vulnerable cohorts of the male victims of postindustrialization. As he began to perceive the decline in his trade and in his personal opportunities within it, he entertained fantasies of making a major occupational shift. Pam repeatedly urged Al to seek vocational retraining or to apply for white-collar forms of employment, and occasionally he would pursue some of the employment contacts she initiated. But Al was quite pessimistic about his ability to secure or succeed at a desk job, and thus his efforts were rather feeble and sporadic, and unrewarded.[5]

THE BOUNTIES AND LIMITS OF FAITH

Pamela was frustrated with Al's passive response to the deteriorating conditions in his occupation. Her pro-union upbringing and the sympathetic character of her early remarks about the effects of Silicon Valley developments on local workers led me to expect her to display political anger and union solidarity. Instead, Pam frequently complained to me about the union-instilled sense of entitlement to work and income that she believed prevented Al from taking steps to improve his own situation. He had been spoiled by his earlier experience, she seemed to think. "The trades were so good for so long. He just hasn't come to grips with the fact that the economy has changed and that he's going to have to put a lot more effort into finding work. He can't rely on it just coming his way, the way it used to. He can't count on just riding out the bad periods." Applying a gender analysis of the differences in male and female attitudes toward employment, Pam contrasted what she regarded as Al's passivity and inflated expectations with her own more realistic willingness to accept low, entry-level wages in whatever work was available and then to work hard to prove her worth and improve her position from within.

Pam thought Al was stuck. Not surprisingly, as the layoffs mounted and the periods of unemployment lengthened, he became depressed, lethargic, and withdrawn. Pam believed that her Christian wifely responsibility was to resist the impulse to withdraw from Al in turn. Interpreting this impulse as a spiritual weakness, Pam concluded that she should draw on her faith "to push Al and to confront him, to help get him off his duff." But she found that "the work issue is especially hard to communicate about, because of the male image problem and the history of each of us taking care of our own business." Moreover, because Al's imposed leisure time seemed to have the paradoxical effect of reducing his participation in housework, each time Al was out of work Pam vacillated between bouts of anger and attempts to employ a blend of Christian compassion and feminist psychology to comprehend and forgive his retreat.

Pam had herself weathered a prolonged work crisis and a decline in her personal employment status during the interval between conversion and the wedding. For reasons Pam could never quite determine, she had begun her position at SOS on the wrong foot with her boss, and she was never able to restore herself to his good graces. During the three years she spent as his subordinate, he repeatedly wrote Pam up, suspended her, and placed her on probation. Like Al, Pam regarded her boss's change of heart the day he had intended to fire her as evidence of the Lord's merciful work. Unknown to Pam, however, coworker Jan had also intervened on her behalf, performing a favor both friends would live to regret.

By the summer of 1985, Pam seemed to be on the verge of emotional collapse, despite the concerned support she was receiving from Al, her relatives, and her new Christian community. As I watched her never-robust health decline further and listened to her deepening anguish, I became seriously concerned. Faith and prayer did not seem to be providing sufficient solace, and Pamela decided that she needed to find a therapist. Because my husband is a psychiatrist, she sought my assistance in securing a referral for a consultation. However, Pam never contacted the woman my husband recommended because she feared that secular therapy might threaten her faith. Instead she located a Christian male therapist through a referral service whose telephone number appeared on the back cover of a Christian advice book she had been reading. Although Pam appeared to be oblivious to the symbolic significance of the gender order implied by this decision, she was fully aware that it was an attempt to buttress the religious course she had chosen to pursue.

The strategy was successful. The next time that Pam was suspended for insubordination at SOS, she began a serious job search. Her efforts were rewarded more rapidly than she had dared to hope, in contrast with her husband's experiences, in part because of her greater education and white-collar skills, in part because she was willing to accept a position with less status and autonomy than she had enjoyed at SOS. Pam entered her new position as a staff assistant in a county transportation department with modest expectations, but she was grateful for the fresh start and eager to succeed. She gleefully recalled the sardonic words of encouragement with which her predecessor at SOS had transferred the mantle to her three years earlier. "It might be the same old shit, but at least it will be new shit; enjoy the honeymoon period." Pam adjusted rapidly to her new job, and gradually her spirits lifted. She was disappointed and hurt, therefore, when her first job evaluation was less enthusiastic than she had expected and believed she deserved; but this time her use of Christian ideology effectively deflected the blow to her self-esteem. "I thought I deserved a much better review, but so what? You do work for the glory of God, not for the praise of men."

Several months after Pam's departure from SOS, she and Al received another sign of what they took to be the Lord's blessing—the unexpected out-of-court settlement of the legal case against them. Now their financial debts, although steep, were finite and manageable, and the relief from two years of anxiety did a great deal to reduce the strains in their marriage. Pam and Al began to enjoy a much-delayed honeymoon period, which encouraged Al's proposal to renew their vows later that spring.

Pam read all these improvements in her circumstances and marriage as the bounty of faith. She was continually amazed, she told me many times that year, by "the way Al is still hanging in there, the way he keeps trying to work things out when we have conflicts, keeps dealing with issues. I know there's no way he'd be doing this without being a Christian." Modeling her reform tactics after Pastor Jensen's wedding sermon to Al, Pam described how she initiated discussions about her marital grievances. "Sometimes I do it in very general ways. I talk about Jesus and the Bible, how Jesus was a servant, that He sacrificed himself for everyone, and He's the model of the ideal person." Sometimes Pam's approach was more direct. She was working to engage Al more actively in caring for his step-grandchildren, for example. When he failed to contribute what Pam regarded as his fair share of child care during an extended family birthday party for her ex-spouse, Pam waited until they were alone to tutor him with Christian rhetoric. He hadn't been the only tired family member present, she had told Al, "and if you really believe you are blessed to be a grandparent, you need to take more responsibility." "The remarkable thing," Pam reported to me, "is that these days Al really does seem to be hearing me." She had been especially delighted when during one of their evening prayer sessions together Al prayed for the Lord to make him more humble. Pam interpreted this as "a sign that he's really listening to me, and I felt really blessed."

Although most of the time Pam seemed to share Al's optimistic view of the progress of their Christian marriage, she remained more divided than he about the prospects for further change, or at least more open about her doubts. There were times when Pam volunteered quite negative assessments of Al's capacity for intimacy. "I'm having to accept the fact," she told me over lunch just a few months before the church wedding, "that Al just can't be very verbal about his feelings and isn't a particularly open person. And sometimes I think he just doesn't know how to empathize." Pam had been discussing this problem with her new Christian therapist, attempting to determine if Al "just doesn't have the capability, or if it's something that can be learned, and he just never learned it. He just isn't able to put himself in the other person's shoes." Al was still "hanging in there," trying to work out their difficulties, "but he often just doesn't get it." Pam diagnosed Al's incapacity as a response to deprivation: "He hasn't had the experience of being loved, and so he denies his own feelings. It may be just too huge a step to be able to go from that to imagining how someone else is feeling." With her Christian counselor's assistance, Pam had decided that she would "probably have to learn how to draw new boundaries, to find ways of protecting myself more," if it turned out that Al was simply incapable of change in this area.

Taken aback by Pam's matter-of-fact critical appraisal of Al's emotional abilities, I asked if she was worried that he was regressing to his preconversion character. Pam's response led me to revise my interpretation of the major attractions to her of Christian marriage. Al did seem to be slipping back a bit, she replied, but "he hasn't closed the door. Maybe he's not so open as he was immediately after the accident and the conversion experience, but he hasn't closed the door. And the important thing that's really changed, the big difference in Al now, compared to what he was like before the accident, is how much more committed he is to the relationship. That's the crucial thing. He's more committed, and he's more trusting. And he tries to be open. There are pathways."

What Pam was getting at, we both realized, was that she had come to value the security that "absolute commitment in marriage" offered more than the qualities of openness, communication, and emotional intimacy that first had permeated her rhetoric about the beneficial effects of Al's conversion. "I think that absolute commitment, that rock-bottom commitment, that's so important; otherwise everything is so contingent. You don't know what's going to happen if you're not as beautiful as you used to be, or you lose a job, or you get sick, or something like that."

Pam returned to this theme repeatedly over the next year and a half, particularly during moments of marital crisis. I came to believe that these discussions served Pam as a form of self-management, attempts to discipline her own occasional impulses to flee her marriage as precipitously as she had returned to it. She drew on her renewed faith to fortify her own wavering commitment to sustain her marriage, at least as much as she sought Al's commitment to her. I began to conjecture that Pam had felt as threatened as she was attracted by the level of honesty and open discussion of feelings that she and Jan had attempted in their friendship and that feminism seemed to demand. Perhaps this and Jan's self-reliant posture contributed to Pam's sudden retreat to a fundamentalist marriage where an absolutist commitment might provide Pam with shelter for self-protective boundaries.

A FAILING FRIENDSHIP

Jan's absence from the fundamentalist wedding, which may have been conspicuous to me alone, was a further indication of the nature of the priorities that drew Pam to her surprising Christian course. Jan was one of the very few significant friends whom Pam had failed to integrate into her extended kinship network. Each woman blamed the other for this failure, but its negative impact on their relationship was not in dispute.

I had been only partially correct in my original assessment of the warm friendship and supportive collegial relationship between Pamela and Jan. The bonds between them, which were deeper than I had imagined, had already begun to sever that first summer when we met. Jan experienced Pam's recent return to her marriage and her conversion to charismatic Christianity as a personal and political betrayal. As I got to know them better, both women gave me compatible accounts of the mutual attraction that prompted a unique friendship and professional alliance between the two soon after Pam arrived at SOS. Hired to administer the program in which Jan worked, Pam quickly recognized Jan's competence and promoted Jan to be her personal assistant. This took place during that reclusive period of Pam's deepening depression that her husband had noticed, but did not discuss.

Pam had turned instead to her new friend Jan, confiding at length her dissatisfactions with her marriage and her insecurities about the job. Jan had supported Pam's difficult decision to leave her husband, and during those months following the marital separation, which Pam had described to me as solitary, Jan had spent many evenings with Pam attempting—with success, she had thought—to help Pam rebuild her occupational confidence and to expand her vision of avenues to intimacy outside of marriage.

Proudly self-defined as a "woman-identified" feminist and a lesbian, Jan was shocked and deeply offended when Pam abruptly resumed the marriage she had described as so unsatisfying. Even more appalling to Jan was Pam's conversion to patriarchal Christianity. Not only were Pam's actions a cowardly violation of emotional and political integrity, in Jan's view, but they were threatening as well. Jan felt "ripped off" by Pam's turn to Christian marriage because "heterosexual relationships are inherently blessed through religion. It takes a lot more guts to say I'm not going to get this blessing, but I'm going to do it anyway." And Jan

83

interpreted Pam's conversion as a total rejection of her prior feminist convictions. "You didn't know Pamela before, but she used to have a very good rap, a lot about feminist consciousness. Then she gave it up totally. It's very upsetting that this could happen to Pam, that it could happen, and makes you worry—could it happen to me?"

Although Pam struggled to maintain her friendship with Jan, her conversion proved an insuperable barrier to their continued intimacy. Jan had "a spiritual side" herself but found fundamentalism unacceptable. She felt as if Pam had used her, and the mounting tension between the former friends made their shared work situation unbearable for both. From the moment I met them, each yearned for a new job to extricate herself from the painful daily reminder of their failed friendship. More than a year would slip away before either one took serious action to realize this goal. The relief that Jan and Pam both experienced when Pam departed SOS late in 1985 was palpable.

AN ECUMENICAL EXTENDED FAMILY

As our discussion about her marriage underscored, Pam was deeply committed to her extended family and unwilling to risk losing its supportive bonds. Like Al, and unlike Dr. Dobson, Pam was unperturbed by the role divorce and remarriage played in augmenting her kinship circle. During the period of this study she collaborated actively with her former husband's lover, Shirley Moskowitz, to create a remarkably harmonious, matrifocal, postmodern extended family. In the early days of this study, I had detected familiar remnants of divorcée hostility in Pamela's allusions to her former spouse. Reciprocal sentiments surfaced in the oral history I conducted with Don later that year. His prominent, supportive role at the Christian wedding signified the impressive restorative work Pam and Shirley had accomplished in the interval.

Whereas contemporary popular literature about postmodern family configurations echoes Dobson's emphasis on its negative, destabilizing features—the rampant opportunities it provides for hostility, jealousy, and competition between former spouses, their subsequent mates, and their assorted and recombined progeny[6]—Pam and Shirley optimistically exploited its more gratifying possibilities. They promoted an inclusive approach to familial exchanges and gatherings that worked to expand the social and material resources of all the members of their combined families.[7] Through their initiative, holidays and special occasions that might demand awkward or painful social decisions from members of many divorce-extended networks became instead affirmative rituals of expanded family solidarity.[8] One year the entire extended clan celebrated Thanksgiving at Pam and Al's house, the next year at Shirley and Don's. Pam invited Shirley and Don to the Christmas party she gave when Al's brother visited from Denver, and Shirley reciprocated by including all of her paramour's divorce-related kin in the Passover seder she conducted to demonstrate Jewish traditions to her daughter's Catholic fiancé. Pam even cooperated with Shirley to organize a fiftieth birthday dinner party for Don, and gradually the two couples began to socialize more casually. When Shirley and Don's next-door neighbors put their house up for sale, Shirley encouraged Pam and Al to purchase it and move in.

Pam had difficulty understanding my incredulity at each new symptom of harmony within her postmodern tribe. "Don't you think this is becoming more and more common today with all the divorces and everything?" Pam responded when I confessed my surprise at Don's role at the wedding. It seemed self-evident to her that everyone benefited from a gracious adaptation to the new conditions of family life, and she found the Christian doctrine of forgiveness a useful resource in its employ.

Shirley was equally enthusiastic about this "brave new world" family that was gradually replacing most of her natal and legal relations in her affections and plans. Like Pam, she offered a matter-of-fact explanation for the harmony that seemed to reign among them. "Well, this extended family is just a compatible group. It just works out. The kids aren't noodges. They do their own thing, believe what they want. Yet when you're together, you know there's love in the whole family." Shirley also agreed that Al and Pam's Christian conversion had abetted the warm feelings that permeated their postmodern familial milieu: "Great, I think it's great when people believe in something, and it makes them feel better. And, it's really improved their relationship; there's something that has bound them together much more. You can't define it, but you can sense it. There's more respect for each other, more warmth, love."

Shirley had even secured her official passport into this welcoming circle, her cohabiting relationship with Don, by way of strategic use she made of the ties she had formed with his daughters. Shirley had met Don in

1980 at Gateways, a Silicon Valley singles' club. But after the two dated intermittently for more than two years, Don got involved with another woman and stopped calling Shirley, who was disappointed and hurt. She did not allow this rupture to terminate the relationships she had forged with his daughters, however, and these proved to be the conduit back to a relationship with Don. "I'll tell you how we got together again," she recalled with pleasure. "I still remained friends with his daughter, Lanny. We bowled together. Actually I went to her wedding when she married her first husband, because I was seeing Don at the time. She lived nearby, and we had a real good relationship. We'd go to flea markets together and she'd call me, and I'd bitch to her about him all the time." Then when Katie planned her wedding, to be celebrated in her father's back-yard, Lanny encouraged her sister to invite Shirley. "I was kind of skep-tical whether I should go or not, but then I looked in the mirror and said 'Shirley, you look good. Go!' So I did. So when I left this house— the wedding was here—when I left, Don said 'I'll give you a call,' and I said 'Okay.' That's when it started all over again. I knew I'd *wow* him now."

Indeed, after that Shirley did succeed in forging a stable, long-term relationship with Don, and during the course of this study she appeared to be making slow but discernible progress in overcoming his strong resistance to making a third appearance at the altar. Don argued that marriage was irrelevant; they were already living like a married couple without the formalities. "I don't know that there is any difference," he tried to persuade Shirley. She disagreed with him, Don explained to me, because "she's stuck in the traditional stuff."

Shirley accepted this view of herself, as a traditional woman, despite a personal history and practice that belied it. Respect for conventional social norms was one of the motives beneath her desire for legal marriage, but she also sought to fortify Don's commitment to their relationship and the legitimacy of her membership in her new extended family. The lavish wedding that Shirley was proud to be making for her daughter was imminent the first night I spent several hours alone with her, and with a mixture of pride and anxiety she joked about how she would introduce her adoptive family to the East Coast relatives she hoped would come. "Oh, who's that? That's Don's ex-wife and her husband. Who are they? That's Don's ex-mother-in-law and father-in-law. Those are Don's grandchildren from his first wife, and so on. We share each other's families. It's really strange; weird."

As it turned out, however, Shirley had little need to rehearse these awkward introductions, because only her former husband made the trip from the East Coast to California to attend the wedding. Shirley was disappointed and insulted by this evidence of disregard by her formal kin and grateful for the enthusiastic support of her new extralegal relatives. Her definition of herself as old-fashioned—"I'm still back from the old days"—had not yet caught up with the dramatic changes in gender and family strategies she had pursued in the past decade, changes that the attendance patterns at her daughter's wedding signified.

A forty-eight-year-old executive secretary at a major Silicon Valley electronics firm when first we met, Shirley was the daughter of East European Jewish immigrants to the Bronx. This working-class girl came of age during the 1950s. While working in a factory office to contribute to sparse household funds during her high-school years, she had aspired only to marriage. In 1957, at the age of nineteen, Shirley succeeded in contributing to the nation's flourishing marriage and birth-rate statistics. Quitting work when the first of her two children was born the following year, Shirley became the homemaker accomplice to her young veteran husband's successful upwardly mobile career as an insurance salesman. She was also a willing participant in that period's mass migration to picket-fence suburban communities. With her children in school, Shirley wanted to supplement the family income to purchase long-denied middle-class amenities, so she took a part-time secretarial job in the engineering department of a nearby prestigious university.

Shirley remembers being happy with middle-class suburban life in a conventional modern nuclear family. "We didn't have a bad marriage. We had a good marriage. We got very active in the synagogue. We had a lot of friends, maybe too many." But sometime during the mid-1970s things seemed to unravel mysteriously. Shirley's husband began spending extravagant periods of time with an attractive woman friend who served with him on the synagogue board of directors. When Shirley confronted him with her jealous suspicions, she unwittingly "opened a barrel of worms." He denied improprieties but acknowledged his infatuation and failed to reassure her of his affections. "When I asked, 'Do you love me?' I was devastated when he said he didn't know. He couldn't tell me he

87

loved me; he couldn't even tell me he liked me." Shirley looks back on that period now and asks, "How did it start? Everything was hunky-dory. It seems to have just grown apart. It was like living with someone and being alone. I figured this man doesn't love me, why is he sharing a bed with me?"

A truly old-fashioned Jewish woman, like the one depicted as Golda, Tevya's wife in *Fiddler On the Roof,* might not have asked herself this question, nor drawn the conclusions that Shirley did when she answered it negatively—that they needed marriage counseling and, when that failed, a separation. But Golda never confronted the opportunity that Shirley did to participate, however unwittingly, in the broad-scale up-heaval in this nation's gender and family order that accompanied post-industrialization. By the time of her marital crisis, Shirley's employment schedule had increased to full time. Inspired by the unperceived influence of a militant feminist movement from which she held her distance, Shirley enjoyed options to an unsatisfactory marriage not available to earlier generations of women. She moved out, secured a job offer as her former boss's secretary in the Silicon Valley electronics firm to which he had moved, presented her husband with an ultimatum to relocate with her or lose her, and then when he refused, migrated cross-country in 1979 with her teenage daughter, while believing all along that "I didn't want from divorce. Everyone else gets a divorce."

Adjusting to sudden independence, reduced economic circumstances, and the Silicon Valley singles' scene was at first lonely and painful for Shirley and her daughter, but gradually they both replaced their former Jewish modern family and community with gratifying new lives in their respective interfaith postmodern families. Shirley's loyal support to her boss's meteoric Silicon Valley career earned her favorable reviews and frequent raises. In the space of eight years she doubled her salary to more than thirty thousand dollars plus bonuses, which placed her in the top 10 percent of female incomes in the country.[9] Sharing household expenses with Don, a successful packaging engineer, placed the income of the cohabiting couple well into the top quintile of "family income" in the United States and made them the most affluent economic beneficiaries of Silicon Valley development in my study.

As a consequence, Don and Shirley could contribute disproportionate material resources to an extended family that functioned as a mutual aid society, but in which the means and prospects of most of the other members were far more limited. They lived in the most affluent neighborhood and in the largest house, which Don owned and which provided ample space to house the unmarried children and prospective children-in-law who migrated in and out in response to changing employment and personal circumstances. Shirley subsidized housing costs for the struggling family of Don's daughter Lanny by renting them the condominium she owned at well below market rate. During one of Al Gama's periods of unemployment, Don hired him to remodel a bathroom, and when Lanny needed extra income, Shirley collaborated with Pam in helping her find middle-class houses to clean.

In short, Shirley was a wholehearted participant in Don's divorce-extended family, and she wanted the public recognition and legitimation of her position that legal marriage would provide. She worried about the day when her young grandchildren-by-proxy would learn that she wasn't "really their grandma," and she squirmed with discomfort each time her adoptive relatives stumbled with terms of address when introducing her to others. Pam and Al's Christian wedding had been a bittersweet experience for Shirley: "I felt good for them, bad for myself. They're having a second one, and I can't even get him to a first." Despite my feminist ambivalence about the institution, I found myself wishing that Don would relent. Nagging was not Shirley's style, however, and so as she and Don made plans to enjoy their retirement years together traveling in a mobile home, she waited patiently, hoping that "maybe there will be a time he'll decide he wants to do it." If Don takes the preferences of his extended family into account, I suspect and hope that time will come.

5

Pamela's Children: Spirited Youth in Stressful Times

During the 1960s and 1970s, most of the adult members of Pamela's kinship network reaped a share of the material benefits of Silicon Valley development. They managed to establish careers that paid incomes greater than their parents had enjoyed and that enabled them to own their own homes. The electronics industry provided some of these careers directly, such as those enjoyed by Shirley and Don, by the other former husbands of the East Valley circle of women, and by both of Al's siblings. Other occupational benefits were indirect, like the boom in local construction that secured Al's earlier success and the expansion of social services that rescued Pam and the other East Valley divorcées from poverty's vestibule. Moreover, like Pam, most of the women in her cohort, and a few of the men, had furthered their education by taking advantage of the expansion of the local educational infrastructure that accompanied the growth of the electronics industry.[1] I expected that Pam and Don would have transmitted their new middle-class status and opportunities to their children, just as my own upwardly mobile parents had done two decades earlier.

This did not appear to be so. Instead, coming of age during the Valley's boom period had had anomalous effects on the children's aspirations and prospects. Like Pam, all three of her children had been downwardly mobile after her divorce, which had subjected them at vulnerable ages to frequent shifts in households, neighborhoods, and schools. While grap-

pling with the effects of parental divorce, which psychologist Judy Wallerstein has found to be traumatic for youngsters even in the relatively
protected environment of affluent Marin County, California,[2] Pam's children were also obliged to contend with an adolescent drug culture that
reached devastating proportions in the Silicon Valley during the 1970s
and 1980s. In response, two had dropped out of high school and skated
the slippery border between "hard" and "settled living."[3]

Thus, while Pam's divorce encouraged her to pursue an education and
to achieve financial independence, it seemed to have had the opposite
effects on her children. None had sought higher education, nor had any
yet secured economic independence equivalent to what their parents had
attained at comparable ages. And the decline in the local economy, not
reflected in its inflated housing costs, made it unlikely that any of Pam's
uncredentialed children would soon replicate the material circumstances
his or her parents had enjoyed at an earlier stage in postindustrial
development.

STRESS JUNKIE

Lanny, Pam's oldest child, was twenty-four when I met her during the
last week of her second pregnancy in January 1985. She was already in
her own second marriage and a postmodern, blended family considerably
less harmonious than her mother's. Her rather skeptical, chip-on-the-
shoulder, older-than-her-years presentation contrasted with her pretty,
youthful appearance, but as I recorded the range and drama of Lanny's
personal history, I could understand why she claimed "I feel like I'm
sixty years old" and worried that she might be a "stress junkie."

Her parents' divorce when she was thirteen had hit Lanny hard. It
came as a shock. She did not know many people who divorced, and she
"didn't think it would happen to our family." Pam's move to a rougher
neighborhood just as Lanny entered junior high school surrounded the
girl "with kids into things I hadn't been around before—drugs, stealing,
smoking, family troubles—it was just a big pain." Personally frightened
by this milieu, Lanny still felt compelled to "put up with those jerks,
because there were no normal people there." Threatening "to beat up
on me" if she did not conform, her new friends taught Lanny to cut

school, smoke, do drugs, fight physically, and party every day. Lanny resisted the "heavy and weird drugs by making myself scarce at those times," but at fourteen she started dating a man she was soon to marry who did not share her antipathy to narcotics.

After attending five different schools in five years, Lanny dropped out of high school during her junior year without consulting her parents. When her exasperated mother threw her out, Lanny moved in with her boyfriend, a twenty-three-year-old army veteran who earned union wages as an auto worker. Lanny got "this funky job" as a minimum wage, on-call sales clerk at a department store but was economically dependent on her boyfriend. Shuffling from one friend's or relative's tumultuous household to the next, the young couple had moved ten times when they decided to use a Veteran's Administration loan to purchase their own home. Lanny was only nineteen. Soon Lanny "was crushed" to find herself pregnant, but her boyfriend's enthusiasm and her friends' graphic descriptions of the pain of abortion scared her into letting nature take its course. She married the expectant father and convinced him to move out of their "nice house in a terrible neighborhood, in the heart of the ghetto, very Hispanic, very high crime, a lot of drugs, robberies, low-rider capital of the Silicon Valley." Seeming to replicate her mother's earlier homemaker strategy, by the time Lanny was twenty-three she had parlayed her small family's real estate holdings into a third house, which cost over $100,000, financed by a $1,300 monthly mortgage payment.

At that time Lanny considered herself "pretty fortunate." She thought she had "an okay relationship. He treated me nice, except for the fact that he couldn't carry on a conversation." She thought, "Here we are on our third house, he's working, able to keep a job, unlike most of our friends." But her husband was away most of the time, working, or so he claimed, more than twelve hours a day, often seven days a week. Staying home with their baby, Lanny found herself isolated and unbearably lonely. Pam encouraged her daughter to enter a county agency drafting course, and soon, via various temporary agencies, Lanny found ready employment drafting electronics schematics.[4] But when mortgage interest rates fell and Lanny attempted to refinance their home, she discovered that her husband "had snarfed away" all their savings. Forced to sell "and take a bath" on their house, she convinced her husband to enter a residential substance abuse program. When he did, Lanny became a welfare mother. She hated drafting, but she job-shopped frequently to

raise her income sufficiently to support herself and her daughter. Taking
a new contract job every few months, Lanny was earning fourteen dollars
per hour (but without benefits) when I met her early in 1985. At one of
those jobs she had met Ken, an expediter in the purchasing department,
who earned only five dollars per hour. It "was love at first sight," and
having written off the husband who she felt had betrayed her, Lanny
invited Ken to move in with her clandestinely. Her two-year-old daughter's weekly visits to her daddy at the rehab center, however, made it
difficult for Lanny to keep her husband from learning about her affair.
When he discovered it, he became alternately threatening, suicidal, and
determined to win Lanny back.

Partly to convince her husband that her change of affection was irrev-
ocable, Lanny gave in to Ken's desire to have a child of their own. She
became pregnant again easily, then "wondered what the hell did I do."
Ken was eager to get married, and Lanny barely managed to overcome
her first husband's resistance to a divorce in time to marry Ken before
giving birth to their son. Nor had the divorce removed the primary source
of Lanny's anxiety. Instead, it immersed her in the sort of unhappy
postmodern family that popular stereotypes deride. Although she retained
custody of her daughter, her first husband received "reasonable visita-
tion" rights. He was still wasted and kept threatening to abscond with
their child. As a result, Lanny found that "every weekend is a nightmare.
I've gotten an ulcer since my divorce."

Despite this traumatic history, Lanny's second marriage was vastly
superior to her first. Lanny described Ken as "a great guy, very patient,
understanding, his life is real mellow. Problems don't really happen to
him, probably because he comes from a stable family." Even more important, in Lanny's view, Ken, unlike her first husband, was able to
communicate. "That's the biggest thing. You have to have somebody
who actually cares about what you're saying. And somebody who's intelligent enough to have their own ideas and to discuss them with you.
You don't have to agree always, but the fact that he's willing to sit there
and listen to me, and that when he talks it's interesting enough where I
want to listen back."

Although I soon came to share Lanny's positive evaluation of Ken's
personality, I found cause to dispute her description of his family history
and present circumstances. Over a hamburger at Big Boy's the following
week, Ken recounted how his mother, the creator of the traditional wed-

ding cake that had so delighted my son, had sacrificed her personal happiness to the struggle to support her four children after she divorced their alcoholic, lumberjack father when Ken was six years old. Depositing her young brood in Wyoming in the temporary care of her widowed mother, Ken's mother had come to the Silicon Valley in the early 1960s to attend a computer training program. She returned for her children one year later and supported them, without assistance from their father, on the salary her career as an information systems manager provided.

Additional serious problems had happened to Ken. He had suffered several major injuries, such as a severe thigh fracture that confined him to a wheelchair for most of his sophomore year of high school, which he credits with shielding him from the relentless peer pressure in the Valley to experiment with drugs. Several years later Ken's first fiancé was killed and Ken was moderately injured when a drunken driver crashed through the freeway divider into the car Ken was driving. Ken had graduated from high school and attended a local community college while working as a dishwasher. Lacking vocational direction, he had quit school after a year and begun a checkered career of employment in a host of service, sales, and unskilled labor jobs that he quit or was fired from at frequent intervals. In light of this history, it did not seem shocking that even easygoing, mild-mannered Ken, like his new bride, suffered from a bleeding ulcer.

When we first spoke, Ken was cautiously hopeful about his mobility prospects at Phonetek, where he had begun as a shipping clerk and progressed to the inventory control position that by then was enabling him to earn a salary two-thirds as high as what his wife then commanded. He did not yet earn enough, however, to release his wife from the electronics drafting work she despised. Thus, as soon as Lanny's six weeks of postpartum disability payments expired, she returned to the work she found grueling, boring, and insulting. Lanny dreamed of returning to school to become a clothing designer, but believed her family could not afford to relinquish its primary breadwinner: "I'm in a position where I can't afford not to work, so I think that's going to have to get put off for a while, I guess." Lanny had no interest in becoming a homemaker once again, nor any resentment about her disproportionate contributions to the family's finances. She even offered Ken the chance to quit his own lesser-paid, unsatisfying job and stay home with the children, an idea that appealed to him, "but he goes through this head trip because he knows that I hate my work, and he doesn't want me to do that just so he can stay home."

During the course of this study, however, the downturn and reorganization of the local electronics industry caused Lanny, like Al, to suffer a decline in her employment and earnings potential which began to effect an unsought reversal toward a more conventional division of labor and income in her household. The development of computer-aided-design (CAD) reduced the entire drafting work force and cut the wage rates for mechanical drafters like Lanny. As a temporary contract employee, Lanny could not get CAD training. She turned to moonlighting jobs in department store sales and as a domestic worker in order to ride out the lengthening layoff periods. As a result, sometimes Lanny worked more than sixty-five hours per week, leaving her husband feeling very lonely and shouldering the primary responsibility for the children. Several times Lanny enrolled in interior design courses, but a lack of confidence and recurrent financial pressures, such as the crisis caused by Ken's own startling layoff by Phonetek in 1986 ("The week before he left he got his five-year gold pen and pencil set; tacky!"), kept interfering with her commitment.

I visited a very discouraged Lanny during the winter of 1987 right after Ken had found a new job as an electronics firm "stockroom stupidvisor," as he put it. While Ken was thrilled that he had at last managed to equal Lanny's best wage as a drafter, her hourly wage had declined to twelve dollars, and she was determined never to take another drafting job at any wage. As a result, Lanny inadvertently recapitulated much of her mother's former employment pattern. She was spending most weekdays home alone with the baby and was supplementing her husband's income by joining her mother's friend Lorraine in cleaning a few houses and in selling secondhand merchandise at local flea markets. There had been a violent murder in the condominium complex the week before, and Lanny desperately wanted to move to a better neighborhood. But the couple could not afford to give up the rent subsidy Shirley provided, and Lanny feared realistically that she would never again be a homeowner.

Pam worried frequently about her daughter's unhappiness and did whatever she could to help out. But, as with her response to Al's economic reversals, Pam attributed much of the difficulty to Lanny's negative attitude. Her daughter had been harmed by the chaotic years after Pam's divorce and then spoiled by the heady taste of early affluence, Pam believed, and she blamed herself for having subordinated her children's needs to her own search for fulfillment. Lanny was aware that her mother felt she had abandoned her, but considered her mother's response to her adolescent behavior appropriate: "I was a witch; there wasn't anything she could do." And she resented her mother's lingering guilt over that period. "I didn't turn out so bad, did I?"

Lanny, in turn, worried about her mother's unhappiness and fragile health. She had had quite ambivalent feelings about the joint conversion of Al and Pam. During our first lengthy conversation six months after the event, Lanny claimed to hate the revivalist fervor that was spreading through her kinship circle. It had been bad enough years ago when Katie and her husband "went and got fanatical on us" and began pressuring everyone in the family to give over their lives to Jesus. Now that Al and Pam had converted, it was "no fun being the only person who isn't a Holy Roller in the family."

However, Lanny had also been pleased when she saw how much happier the conversion seemed to have made her mother and Al. "It's about time. She was so miserable for so long. And I'm glad Al's happy. He's been miserable forever too." Lanny fully confirmed the extraordinary transformation the religious rebirth had worked in her stepfather. She had loathed the unwelcome intruder when he first had moved into her mother's single-parent household; then gradually over the years, she had learned to tolerate him. But before the accident Al just "wasn't really someone you could get close to." Suddenly everything changed. "Now that he's gone through this big ordeal, you know, he's a different person. It's like night and day. He used to be a very grouchy, silent, hostile person. Now he's become a happy Christian, mellow, has feelings, loves everybody. It's like he sat down in a chair, fell asleep, woke up, and that was a different person. That's how fast he changed."

Lanny, like me, regarded her mother's conversion as more measured. She believed that at first "Mom was just going along for the ride," and Lanny felt better about it when she thought "that she was just doing it to humor Al." But gradually Lanny realized that while her mother "has a little bit more control over her fanaticism," she too "has gotten really into it."

As I spoke to Lanny intermittently over the next two years, it seemed that she alternately feared and flirted with the domino effect Christian salvation seemed to be inflicting on her family. A few months before her mother's Christian wedding, Lanny felt like the lone holdout and under a great deal of indirect pressure from her born-again relatives. She was also frantically worried about her mother's health. Pam had been losing weight and suffering from a mounting series of undiagnosed symptoms. Just as Lanny had had "one of my awful premonitions and fears" that her mother might have cancer, Pam had revealed that her doctors were ordering extensive cancer-detection tests.

The prospect of cancer struck Lanny as rankly unjust. For the first time in years her mother had had "a respite from all that stress, what with her liking her new job, with her and Al finally out from under the lawsuit and finally getting a chance to rebuild their relationship. If this is cancer, it's grossly unfair." Lanny was at once disdainful and envious of her sister Katie's response to the threatening news: "You know her characteristic, 'if it's the Lord's will. The Lord may have this purpose for Mom, and it's important to trust in the Lord.' "

Although the fatalistic interpretation offended Lanny, she appreciated the solace and support such faith could offer Pam were she to endure the trials that Lanny feared lay ahead. In fact, Lanny had become so distraught awaiting the test results that she had made a "private deal, a pledge to Jesus that if only my mother doesn't have cancer, I will come round and join this Christian business too." Lanny claimed that she still did not "believe in this stuff, and it wouldn't be from the heart if I did it, but it would be well worth it if it spares my mother." She reported that Ken had warned her "to count me out" after she confided her pledge to him. When I interviewed him the following week, Ken described himself as a tolerant, "laid-back worshipper" and confirmed his discomfort with the rectitude, fervor, and arrogance of evangelical conviction, but he also defined himself as more religious than Lanny, and he was troubled that she was opposed to baptizing their son.

Pam's medical tests proved to be inconclusive, and her symptoms persisted. She was so sick the week before her Christian wedding that it was nearly postponed. When she called to cancel our festive prenuptial lunch date, my own anxiety about her health nearly equaled Lanny's. These background events only intensified the emotional ambiance and symbolic significance when the wedding took place on schedule the next Sunday afternoon. Thus, when Lanny and Ken accepted Pastor Jensen's invitation to join Pam and Al in exchanging Christian vows, I imagined they had succumbed to their sense of familial fate. I was startled to discover that my own relief was not unequivocal when, as I passed through the receiving line, Lanny reassured me that she had simply acted to prevent the disappointment her mother would have felt if no one had responded to the special invitation. By then I had "gone sufficiently native" to believe that Lanny too might benefit from a religious conversion.

EQUALLY YOKED

Katie and Eric were the couple I had expected to step forward. Katie had been only twenty-one years old and expecting her first baby when I interviewed her for the first time one year before her mother's wedding. Pretty like her older sister, but softer, more innocent, and much less talkative or expressive, Katie seemed an unlikely source of the spiral of religious conversions twisting its way through her extended family. Yet the unwavering decision she had made when only thirteen years old "to let the Lord be in my life" appeared to have had this effect.

A girlfriend had recruited Katie to join an evangelical youth group sponsored by Global Ministries. Katie offered only a spiritual explanation for her attraction to the group, while her older sister's interpretation was instrumental. "At first she went there to meet guys," Lanny believed. If that was true, the strategy failed. Several years after converting, Katie fell in love with unsaved Eric while he was vacationing in the Silicon Valley. The infatuation was mutual, and soon Eric converted too, in response to Katie's loving ultimatum. " 'Cause at that point," Katie explained, "I realized, you know, to start a relationship with a nonbeliever is just stupid, you know. My friend talked to me about not being unequally yoked, with a nonbeliever. Which is—I guess they talk about oxen, you know, how the yoke is on oxen? And if you're unequally yoked, and one's going this way and one's going the other way, it just won't work. And so this really, it just really woke me up, and I said, you know, this is crazy. So when Eric moved back I, you know, I did share with him my feelings on that." Later, in their pickup truck honeymoon chariot, the young newlyweds converted Eric's formerly Catholic mother. Next Katie received and guided Al through his emotional rebirth, and just before she and Eric left for a crusade that was to plant them as missionaries for a year in Florida, Katie had jubilantly witnessed her mother's receipt of Jesus Christ as her personal savior.

At the respective ages of twenty-one and twenty-two, Katie and Eric already were seasoned evangelists who had dedicated their lives to serving the Lord as disciples and missionaries of Global Ministries. They subscribed uncritically to Christian patriarchal family ideology, as well as to all of their church's teachings, and they practiced certain "traditional" marriage and family principles with greater harmony and success than any of their relatives. The young couple did not live together before they wed, even though Eric had had grave difficulty affording housing after he moved to the Silicon Valley to be with Katie. To avoid premarital cohabitation, Eric had rotated stays among Katie's parents' separate households and an RV van. Theirs was the only intact marriage in the family comprised of two never-divorced spouses. They practiced the most conventional gender division of labor. Katie, the only one of Pam's children who graduated from high school, had enjoyed being the lone girl in her high-school welding class, and she had held numerous jobs in electronics assembly and the service sector during and after her high-school years. However, when she lost her fifth minimum-wage position shortly after marrying Eric, she retired happily to an unpaid career as a homemaker and part-time office worker for the ministry.

Affable, gregarious Eric, affectionately nicknamed "Mr. Charm" by his in-laws, was pleased to assume what he regarded as his proper and ordained responsibilities as the family breadwinner. "I mean, if it's my wife," Eric explained in the now quaint, chauvinist terms of the modern family ideology, "I'd rather have her home. Especially, you know, there's lots, there's plenty of work to do around the house. My wife could never handle working at a job. She can't even, she has a hard enough time, you know, there's a lot to do at the house. Especially when you got a baby, and especially when you want to have kids. Who wants to put kids in a preschool and all that? When they need their love at home, you know."

"But," I challenged Eric in my own predictably feminist cadences, "I suppose you could say that they need a father at home too. You could, you know. What do you think about that?" "Well, they, they should get that, that father," Eric agreed, momentarily unsettled by my secular, sociological logic. "The man, I believe that the man was, you know, the one who should go out and be the provider for the family. . . . No, I know, it's just a good question, it's too hard. It's too hard a question. But I know that this might not be a good enough answer, but there's a difference between a man and a woman, and a mother and a father. And there's no doubt that the way that a mother takes care of a kid, that motherly instinct, is needed, throughout the day, over the fatherly instinct. I mean I couldn't handle it as good, you know, taking care of the kid. You know, I can handle it, but not as good as my wife can do with the babies. No. There's something that was just, you know, they were designed for it to be able to be a mother. There is even in God, even God, I mean the Creator, has feminine and masculine parts to Him. And that's the way He made us, you know, so there's definite lines. There's a motherly part of God, and a fatherly part of God."

Despite their shared traditionalist, modern family values, Katie and Eric actually lived a highly unconventional family life that bore scant resemblance to that of the modern nuclear family. Ironically, the couple's deep involvement in evangelical Christianity was the source of their irregular family pattern. After being evicted from their first married residence in a trailer park beneath the freeway, Eric and Katie had decided "to move into community" as Global Ministry disciples. Since that decision, they had lived in a series of communal Christian households, including one that was interracial. The senior Global hierarchy primarily determined the shifting composition of these communes. Approximately twenty-two youthful adults and their seven or eight young children lived in the five or six suburban subdivision houses that the ministry purchased or leased for this purpose. During the course of this study, Eric, Katie, and a child born soon after I met them shared four of these houses with at least nine different adults and their children.

Recently called back from their missionary year in Florida when I first met them in the spring of 1985, Eric and pregnant Katie were sharing a house adjacent to one of Global's offices with Larry (the wedding musician), his pregnant wife Nadine, their two toddlers, and an unmarried man. They ate together, divided all housing, utility, and grocery bills among them proportionally, and shared the housework chores. The two women stayed at home and did most of the cleaning and cooking while the three men worked for pay. Katie and Nadine were not isolated homemakers, however. Caring for their children cooperatively freed the young mothers to work two or three days each week in the Global office. Moreover, their highly integrated home and work sites placed them at a hub of sociability. "I guess because they're Ministry homes," Katie explained, "these houses are constantly active. There's always people coming through here. Next door we have a clothes bank and a food bank, and there's people coming for food or, constantly, there's always something going on." The evenings were even busier, with frequent guests for dinners followed by Bible study, Global staff meetings, and missionary work among local youth groups, hospitals, detention centers, and refugee communities.

Whenever tension between the communards threatened household harmony, Global ministers intervened with Christian counseling. Although there were moments when Katie and Eric chafed under their subordination to slightly older Larry and Nadine and longed for greater privacy, Katie loved the flexibility, support, and "the growth" she experienced in their communal family. When the Global leadership decided to "yoke singles to married couples" and promoted Katie and Eric to lead a joint household shared with two young single men, Katie sorely missed the daily sociability and cooperative child-rearing arrangement she had enjoyed with Nadine. This experiment proved to be ephemeral, however, and by the time I withdrew from the formal fieldwork portion of this study in 1987, a young married couple newly recruited by Global Ministries had moved in with Eric, Katie, who was pregnant once again, and their two-year-old.

My experiences with the couple gave me no cause to doubt that deep religious conviction was their primary motive for living in Christian collectivity. However, I also could not help but observe the many ways in which life in this evangelical community served as an effective ballast against the limited occupational horizons and turbulent economic winds that buffeted their existence. Communally reinforced spiritual priorities relegated the rewards and tribulations of earthly labors to a sphere of relatively minor significance, while shared housing, food, and daily maintenance expenses and ready access to the ministry's food and clothing banks provided a measure of economic and social security available to very few working people in Reagan's America. Moreover, living in community as disciples to the adjacent Global ministerial hierarchy served as a form of potential employment apprenticeship with occupational mobility prospects greater than any Eric or Katie appeared likely to enjoy in the secular labor market.

Certainly the two were cognizant of many of these material and emotional side effects of their unusual spiritual life course. The ministry taught them to live spontaneously, from day to day, each of them told me: "The way that we try to learn to live is to live as though we're going to be here a hundred years from now, but also be ready for Jesus to come tomorrow." While Al was the only person I studied who identified himself as "working class," Katie was the only one to respond to a similar question about her class identity by claiming to be rich. "We're not poor. We don't have—I don't know, middle class, I guess. We don't have—I don't know, it's hard to say. I mean, he doesn't make big bucks, that's for sure, but we certainly don't ever do without. I would say rich, mostly, we never do without, we never go without. We have whatever we want. It's all taken care of."

Observing the asymmetry between the young couple's emotional equilibrium and their occupational status and income, I found reason to agree. Of all the people in my study, Eric and Katie appeared uniquely free of vocational or economic ambitions. Katie had no occupational goals whatsoever. She thought she might work for pay again some day, but she loved her unpaid work for the ministry, which was more meaningful, rewarding, and more compatible with child rearing than any paid job that she, or almost any other contemporary woman, could find. And I estimated that Katie received greater in-kind benefits for this labor, such as child care, counseling, and subsidized housing, than she would have been able to purchase with a full-time minimum-wage income.

Eric diligently pursued what he considered to be his ordained responsibilities as family breadwinner without aspiring to a worldly career. After moving to the Silicon Valley shortly after graduating from high school, Eric, like his brother-in-law Ken, had quit or been fired from a series of short-term sales and service jobs before Pam persuaded him to enroll in a clerical training program at SOS. Eric was unenthusiastic about the suggestion, but Pam convinced him of the wisdom of her strategy. "I was trying to figure out what kind of skill to take. She tried to talk me into taking office skills, and I just didn't particularly care for that. But she had an idea; she said that if you get into office skills, you would be a minority in that field, being a male, so that, and males move up faster in that type of a field, just because they're a minority. And, she said, like take for example a bank teller or whatever, something to that effect, so I decided to go with it. It didn't sound too fun. But it sounded like a true possibility. So I went to SOS, and they paid me too, to go there."

It appeared that Pam's strategy, rooted in an astute observation of the advantages enjoyed by men who enter characteristically female occupations, enjoyed initial success.[5] Soon after Eric had completed the six-month office skills training program, he was hired as a secretary by a small firm that leased and serviced computer terminals. There he received on-the-job training as a service technician and a 50 percent wage hike within two years. However, a sudden downturn in the industry in 1984 led Eric's boss to lay him off just before he and Katie had been scheduled to depart for a weeklong charismatic Christian crusade in Florida that Global Ministries had been invited to administer. The layoff influenced Global's leadership to encourage the couple to remain in the ministry's new missionary post in Florida at the end of the crusade. That spontaneously did the couple's year as "global" missionaries commence. And there too Eric and Katie lived "in community," sharing a comfortable suburban home with a senior missionary couple who led Global's first attempt to live up to its ambitious name.

It is difficult to imagine how the newlyweds would have survived the next year otherwise. Eric failed to find employment in anything but door-to-door commission sales of household appliances in which he netted less than eleven hundred dollars in the eleven months they spent in Florida. Yet it never occurred to the young couple to have Katie join the search for paid work, because Eric "just knew that God wasn't directing us that way at all." Instead Katie continued her unpaid service to Jesus in the ministry's office and as a volunteer in a Christian bookstore, while the couple trusted the Lord in His wisdom to provide. " 'Cause it's really hard to explain," Eric said as he struggled to do so, "but when you follow the Lord, you don't just do the logical, you do what He wants you to do. . . . You know logically you're not making money so you better get a job. See, we made it, we were, you know, we didn't go without the whole time, really. So we just didn't make it the way my mind would tell me I should make money."

After Katie became pregnant, Global leaders recalled the young couple home to its Santa Clara County headquarters, where they immediately resumed their communal life with Larry and Nadine. On their first day back in the spring of 1985, Eric said, "Another testimony of the Lord, right here. We got back, and I got the message that my boss that I used to have at Lease and Save Terminals [LST] wanted me, so I gave him a call and he wanted to give me temporary work. Another testimony of the Lord." For two months Eric replaced an LST serviceman who had recently suffered an accident. Despite a thorough job survey of every computer terminal firm within a three-county region, however, Eric could find no subsequent positions in this line of work.

Once again the ministry served as vehicle for the Lord's trusted provision. One of Global Ministries' pastors who worked for a dairy distribution company recommended Eric for a delivery route job. The hours were long, irregular, and unpredictable. Most days Eric began his route between 4:00 and 6:00 A.M. and worked until his deliveries were completed, eight to fifteen hours later. Under constant pressure to work faster so that the company was not obliged to pay him overtime, Eric often underreported his hours while worrying whether this dishonesty was a form of "cheating on the Lord." Nonetheless, he was pleased with his new work. The company allowed him to park the delivery truck at home, and so Katie and Nadine had daily use of Eric's pickup truck. Eric loved being on the move all day and getting to know the extended geographic area. Best of all, having survived the probation period, Eric had been admitted to the Teamsters' Union just in time to qualify for health and maternity benefits for Katie's delivery. And thanks to union-scale wages, which started Eric at close to eight dollars per hour, in one month he earned more than in the entire year he spent in Florida.

Job security and advancement opportunities were not matters of significant concern to Eric. At first he estimated that, if only he could learn to work faster, his prospects with the company were reasonably good. But speed remained a major problem, and by the time I left the field twenty months later, Katie was pregnant again and Eric was working longer and longer days under the constant threat of a layoff. While pushing himself to meet job demands that even uncomplaining Eric found to be unreasonable, the missionary framework protected him from deep anxiety about his future on this job. Eric explained to me that he was "ready for Jesus to come tomorrow. So that you know we do look ahead in that way, but on the other hand, we're ready for something to change, you know. So, yeah, I do look at the future, and I also know that I'm called to the mission field, so I don't foresee me staying with this company for twenty years, or something like that."

The social and psychological safety net Christian community life seemed to offer was so impressive that I came to believe Katie's youthful turn to evangelical religion had represented a search for stability rather than for guys, her own remarkably effective means of coping with parental divorce and the dangers of the Valley's adolescent culture that had inflicted damage on both of her siblings. Katie's younger brother, Jimmy, seemed to have glimpsed some of the comforting attractions of Christian conversion also, and, less cynically than Lanny, he had flirted with surrendering to them. But because this did not prove to be a viable option for him, Jimmy had suffered several years of social marginality and strife before devising a career strategy of his own that held some promise of success.

NOT YET "THIRTY-SOMETHING"

Jimmy was the last of Pamela's children and the one I met last, in part because he stood me up the first time we arranged to meet. It had taken me several months to try again, sufficient time for my fieldwork experiences to have diminished my capacity for surprise. Nonetheless, once again I found myself with preconceptions I had to shed. Uniformly Jimmy's relatives had portrayed him as an irresponsible, mixed-up, directionless kid who had problems with drugs and with discipline. I had heard that he, like Lanny, had dropped out of school and that one year later he had been forced out of the Job Corps after fighting with his mates. Jim seemed apprehensive when he agreed to talk to me, and after he forgot our first appointment, I found myself somewhat apprehensive as I set out for our second try. I feared that Jimmy might be a suspicious, withholding, and reluctant informant and that I would fail to establish with him a necessary modicum of rapport.

Instead I developed an instantaneous affection for Pam's youngest child, whom I experienced as one of the most gentle, sweet, and loving eighteen-year-old males it has yet been my privilege to meet. As physically attractive, indeed as pretty, as his sisters, Jimmy was shy rather than sullen, and guileless as well. I met him, it turned out, just as he was emerging from a prolonged and troubled adolescence and had begun to define and pursue a satisfying calling of his own. During my fieldwork period Jimmy was the only person in my study who made steady progress toward work and family goals.

Only six years old when his parents divorced, Jim's memories of the disruption were less vivid than his sisters', but its social effects seem to have been similar to those that Lanny had suffered. Like Lanny, Jimmy lacked confidence and was always unhappy in school. "Well," he remembered, "I was kind of shy in school, you know, and I didn't socialize a lot. I got a lot of bad feelings at school and I didn't like it. Ever since I been little I always hated school. I never really liked it. Now I wish I could go back. I feel like I'm missing something—the history— Like when people are talking about history I can't really get into that conversation 'cause I don't know too much about it." As soon as he was legally eligible, Jim emulated his big sister by dropping out of school and moving out of his mother's household.

Conflicts with Al prompted Jim to move into the far more spacious house owned by the father he barely knew. Pam and Al were not getting along, and it pained Jim to see his mother so unhappy. He knew that Al "was always a good guy down on the inside," but before the conversion "which really changed him a lot, it's just he had trouble showing it, showing his affection, love. I think when I was seven years old I was playing jacks on the floor. He thought that was weird for a boy to be playing jacks, so he stepped on my hand. I guess he was kind of mad that I was playing right there in the kitchen, but he had an idea of how a boy should act, and I always loved him, but he'd turn around and do something like that." Lanny's maturation strategy of romance, cohabitation, pregnancy, and marriage was not available to her brother, however, who was also less successful than she in resisting the allure of drugs. Without much reflection, Jimmy had started smoking dope at thirteen, the same age at which his middle sister, Katie, had accepted Jesus Christ as her personal savior.

Indeed, by Jimmy's account, the emotional effects of dope and Christian rebirth were rather similar. He spoke from direct experience. The year he dropped out of school, he had responded to the earnest proselytizing efforts of Katie and her betrothed and began attending church and Global Ministries events with them. Soon Jimmy too had become "a born-again Christian. Yeah. I felt God. That feeling that you get inside. You feel real happy. On top of the world and stuff. It's just like a high." "How does that happen?" I queried. "I think you got everybody there supporting you and everybody's real loving and nice. You see somebody, and you give them a hug. Guy or a girl—they all love each other, and they all love God."

Although Jimmy described himself as one who always had loved God and always would, his beliefs had proven too tolerant and his desire for earthly, sensual pleasures too compelling to allow him to accept the religious dogma and behavioral restrictions of his sister's faith. "My sister—it's like she was real interested in welding when she was in high school. She totally changed and just wanted to be a housewife and be with her husband. It took the spunk out of her. She's still a neat, great person. I love both my brother-in-law and my sister. It's just different. . . . I think it's like different strokes for different folks. There's so many different kinds of religions. How could one person say that this is the right one? I don't think there is no one way to love God. It's just loving Him. I do believe in it. I just don't think there's one way to love Him. . . . And it was just too, too binding or something. Seems like I couldn't have fun. I couldn't do the things my friends did."

What most of Jimmy's friends did was hang out, smoke dope, listen to music, and look for girls. After dropping out of school like his peers, Jimmy spent two years "goofing off" with them in this seemingly aimless, restless culture. He forgot about his childhood ambition to become a chef. Since the age of seven he had enthusiastically shared the household cooking responsibilities with his sisters and their recently divorced, working mother. Instead, like his friends and both of his brothers-in-law, Jim took a series of dead-end, minimum-wage, service-sector jobs like those at a car wash, a fast-food restaurant, and a parking garage, which he too quit or was fired from in rapid order.

Deeply concerned about her aimless son, Pam had intervened by recommending vocational training, just as she had to his sisters and to Eric. Through her contacts in social service agencies, Pam had helped Jimmy get a place in the local Job Corps, which offered courses toward a general education diploma (GED) concurrent with vocational education. Jimmy found the carpentry course there boring and the peer culture threatening. Remembering his boyhood interest, he switched to a course in culinary arts, but he thought that the cuisine they taught was pedestrian and the pedagogy weak. Then just after he received his GED, Jim participated in a brawl he claims to have entered in self-defense, and he was forced to resign from the Job Corps. He was drifting and goofing off again until Pam intervened once more. Through a friend who knew the owner of La Fresca, an expensive and popular Valley restaurant, Pam helped her son get the salad chef job he had begun five months before I met him.

After a shaky start, Jimmy seemed to have embarked upon the career of chef he had dreamed about for years. He had taken it to heart when his fictive sister Corinne, Lorraine's daughter, challenged his use of marijuana as excessive, for he had a growing sense of purpose. He was delighted to be learning to prepare haute cuisine under the tutelage of experienced chefs at a restaurant of quality that, even better, was also unionized. Proudly Jimmy displayed his Hotel and Restaurant Employees and Bartenders union card and a copy of La Fresca's ornate, extensive menu, while he detailed for me the complicated recipes he had already mastered. As salad chef, Jimmy prepared most of the restaurant's gourmet appetizers and artistically composed salads, and he had set himself the goal of progressing to sauté chef by the end of the year. Jim was surprised to find himself planning ahead, because, a child of the nuclear age, he had difficulty believing he would live to be twenty-one. "I can't see myself three or four years down the line," Jimmy claimed. "I think if something does happen, it's going to happen within the next three years. It's this weird feeling I got that I don't think I'm going to live to be twenty-one. It may just be me, but I can't see myself as twenty-one."

Later that year I had the pleasure of sampling gustatory evidence that Jimmy had succeeded in satisfying his six-month plan when Pam and I celebrated her exit from SOS over a leisurely lunch at La Fresca's. As we savored delicate capellini with basil and sautéed mushrooms that Jimmy personally prepared and served to us, Pam told me, with affectionate pride, that her son had begun to investigate the possibilities for receiving formal training and accreditation in culinary arts. Jimmy's enthusiasm for his fledgling career was so apparent and his prospects at success appeared sufficiently promising that Lanny, his once-disdainful sister, felt envious. The young brother whom she had thought to be a lost soul seemed to be developing the one thing for which she deeply yearned, but that continually eluded her—a life of creative and satisfying work.

By the time I concluded formal fieldwork among his kin in 1987, Jimmy had applied for admission to a culinary arts academy in New Orleans, which he hoped to enter the following spring. Fortunately, most of his real and fictive kin were enthusiastic about his plans, because, irrespective of his talent, without their support it is unlikely that he could have contemplated a serious culinary career. Even if Jimmy had secured the La Fresca job on his own, he barely could have supported himself independently, despite its union-scale wages. Started at $6.00 per hour and raised to $7.40 after a year and a half on the job, Jim worked a split shift with highly irregular and unpredictable hours determined daily in response to diner demand. An unexpectedly busy lunch shift, it turned out, had been the reason Jim forgot about our first appointment to meet. Rarely, however, did he work a full forty-hour week or take home more than $180. Only by living rent-free with Don and Shirley or, when their household was crowded or tense, with Pam and Al could the young man begin to save a small portion of his wages toward tuition costs. He would have had to live and save this way for many years if he did not have his generous and ever-supportive mother to turn to for an interest-free loan.

Like both of his sisters, Jimmy felt very close to his mother, "the best mom I could have," and it upset him, as it did Lanny, to know that Pam believed "she screwed up or something when she was raising me." Jimmy viewed his mother as "a real caring and loving person," who had taught him to be affectionate as well. He found himself much more comfortable and demonstrative with women than with men "because I've grown up around women. I have a mother, two sisters, Lorraine was living with us, Corinne was living with us, my cousin Vera was living with us. A household full of girls. I was the only guy. . . . Sometimes guys do think to be sensitive is sissy or something, not manly, but I don't feel that way."

Jim considered his mother's friend Lorraine "like my second mother," and her daughter Corinne, his best friend, "we're like brother and sister." Later Corinne described her relationship to Pam and Jimmy to me in identical terms. The harmony in Pam and Don's divorce-extended clan contrasted starkly with the bitter residue of Corinne's own parents' divorce, and she was glad to be included within its affectionate ranks. Corinne and Jimmy had been raised together since infancy until, when they were ten, Corinne's father had been transferred to Albuquerque. Jimmy had gone along to spend the first summer in New Mexico, and after her parents divorced, Corinne and her mother had moved back and shared Jimmy's female-dominated household for more than a year. Later, after Lorraine lost a child custody battle, Corinne moved away again to spend her high-school years with her father and his new Caucasian wife. The summer when I first interviewed him, Jim was pleased that Corinne had just moved back to the Valley. He was very proud of her, "a real smart kid" who, unlike any of his other friends, had graduated from high school and was planning to go to community college and to begin to train her operatic voice.

When Corinne returned to the area, I realized I had adopted the romantic fantasy enjoyed by several members of the family that some day she and Jimmy might wed. But this notion seemed incestuous to both, neither of whom, moreover, had any intention of marrying anyone within the next ten years, if ever. Both identified thirty as the age at which they would even be willing to consider such a prospect.

Corinne knew she wanted to have a child, but believed she would rather forgo a husband. "The only thing I think of," Corinne told me, "is when I get older that I'd like to have kids, but I really wouldn't want to have a husband. I'd like to have a baby but not a husband along with it. So I don't know. That might be weird . . . I could have artificial insemination and all that kind of stuff, whatever. Yeah, I don't really, in the future I don't see myself getting married. I'm not saying I'd never, but if I did, I know it would be ten years from now, at least ten years from now, at least when I got in my thirties or something."

Jimmy's family priorities were the inverse, but equally remote. "I can't see myself getting married in the near future," he echoed Corinne. "Right now I can't think of getting married. Well, I don't know . . . I think when I'm about thirty—about thirty I might get married if I find the right girl. I can't see myself having kids. I like kids but seeing what my sister has to go through with two kids; it's a lot of work."

Jim's concern about the parental burdens of child rearing reflected his strikingly egalitarian vision of marriage. Along with racial tolerance, emotional expressiveness, and sensitivity, he had absorbed his two co-mothers' views on the appropriate gender division of domestic responsibilities. In postfeminist fashion, Jimmy expected that any woman he would marry would want to work, not only "to help out on the bills" but also because "I kinda like the liberated woman, somebody who thinks for herself and takes care of herself, financially, physically. I don't know, it seems too phony just to be washing dishes and taking care of the house like that. Housewife. This is the eighties! You know, it's 1985. I don't think it's appropriate for a woman to be stuck in the house, used like a maid or something."

"Do you think you'll find one who'll want to do that?" I asked him. "Well, I guess there's still a few." "But," I probed, "they wouldn't interest you particularly?" His response seemed unequivocal. "No. I like a spirited person." And, although Jimmy hated housework, he expected to share these tedious tasks equally with a wife. "I was raised that way," he told me, expressing disapproval of the way his father treated Shirley "like a maid; I wouldn't do that to my wife." Corinne was confident that Jimmy's claims were more than ideology. She thought, "whoever marries him will be kind of lucky, because like I said, he had the influence of my mother and Pamela and all that, so he's not an average type of guy. . . . I think that he was influenced by the movement and everything else as well. So I think that he would be good for her; he would let her have her own freedom and things like that. He wouldn't tie her down."

On Valentine's Day of 1987, a mere eighteen months after the conversation with him just excerpted, nineteen-year-old Jimmy impulsively proposed a long-term engagement to Elena, his eighteen-year-old girl-friend of the past six months. Pam was tickled and already enthusiastically integrating the pretty young Chicana into her expansive kinship circle, but Lorraine, Corinne, and I were caught off guard by Jimmy's choice. Defying our predictions and his own, Jimmy seemed to have found and betrothed himself to one of the few, by his estimate, "unliberated" young women who still survived. A high-school dropout like himself, Elena had not looked for work since being laid off by a discount record store several months before. She seemed unmotivated and unambitious to Corinne, "not the type I thought would be for him"; "a born housewife," by Lorraine's assessment. Even Jimmy described her in terms quite different from those he had earlier applied to his imaginary mate. Elena was spirited, but she appeared to direct her assertive energies to making rather conventional demands. Jim found her "real possessive of my time" and resentful of his other friends. She was "sort of spoiled in a way" and unwilling to be rushed when getting ready to go out. Elena was not enthusiastic about Jimmy's plans to leave her for two years of culinary school in New Orleans. Not surprisingly, therefore, the couple were fight-ing quite a bit already, and, with Jimmy conceding that "it's still hard for me to comprehend marriage," I left the field lacking confidence the engagement would survive its six-year goal.

Instead I understood the rapid shift in Jimmy's willingness to consider marriage to be evidence of the steady improvement in his self-esteem and his relationships with his extended kin fostered by his occupational prog-ress. Although global armaments and military conflicts had continued their terrifying level of escalation since our first conversation, Jimmy's apocalyptic consciousness had declined markedly. He no longer worried as much as he used to about nuclear war. "I don't know. I was thinking about that the other day. I don't know, I guess I don't feel that strong about it, like I did before. Maybe it's 'cause just the things I was going through and stuff. But I hope I'm going to be here. No, I guess, because we just keep going on and nothing happens, so I guess I'll just live life, you know, until it happens and I'm not really worrying about it, I guess." Now that he could contemplate an attractive occupational future for himself, Jim was ready to seek adult status within the family network whose loving support he had come to appreciate. And postmodern though Jim and his relatives might be, like his mother and his would-be step-mother, he seemed to consider marriage the preferred route to legitimacy among them.

Coming of age under postmodern familial and postindustrial occupational and social conditions had had contradictory effects on Pamela's children. Parental divorce, Silicon Valley drug culture, and turbulent employment conditions contributed to a troubled adolescence for Lanny and Jimmy and to inauspicious class mobility prospects for them and Katie. On the other hand, the material and emotional resources of their divorce-extended family spared Pamela's children the most severe effects of the recent burst in the Silicon Valley bubble. All lived in housing provided or subsidized by their multiple parents or other housemates. All received periodic familial aid in securing job training, employment referrals, and multiple forms of practical assistance. Support from their extended kin helped Lanny and Jimmy to reenter "settled living" territory. Evading the threats of "hard living" from the start, Katie had brought increasing numbers of her relatives into the alternative world of kinship and community she found in Global Ministries.

6

Global Ministries of Love and New Wave Evangelicalism*

At that moment, Jesus called me to the greatest mission field in the world, the Silicon Valley; a land full of wealth, property, pleasure and recreation; a land full of people who think they have it all together. It is also full of people involved in theft, murder, drugs, homosexuality, and occult practices. These were the days of San Francisco's Haight-Ashbury district, and its influences had spread to the Santa Clara Valley. There were "hippies" everywhere. Young people left home to live in communes. Many spent every day blown out on drugs.

—Eleanor Morrison Garrett, *In Praise of Our Father*[1]

"Thank you, Lord, for giving her a goal, a vision, and the determination to write a book about your people in the Silicon Valley. We pray that you will help her to write her book and make it a good one and that you will help her to get it published. Help her, Lord, to write a book that will not only help her but the many other people who will learn from it as well. Thank you, Jesus, for bringing Ms. Stacey into our lives this afternoon. We feel blessed having a visit from one of God's chosen people, and we ask your blessing on her book and on the Jewish nation."

A flushed face and arhythmic heartbeat registered my acute embarrassment and anxiety as Eleanor and Paul Garrett concluded our four-

---

*Portions of this chapter appear in an article co-authored by Susan Elizabeth Gerard, "We Are Not Doormats: The Influence of Feminism on Contemporary Evangelicalism in the United States."

hour visit by praying for this book. Eleanor could empathize one author to another with the challenge that lay ahead of me. She herself was seeking a publisher for an autobiographical manuscript she had nearly completed. In fact, Eleanor was eager to have me, an already published author, read and advise her on the story of the ministry she had founded fifteen years ago, *Global Ministries of Love: In Praise of Our Father.* Agreeing to do so, I felt rather closer to Judas than to Jesus, but I was deeply uncertain whether disloyalty to my feminist convictions or to my fundamentalist research informants was my graver treachery. Although Eleanor and I hoped to publish books committed to incompatible social visions, she and Paul had extended toward me their infectious warmth, trust, and generosity. I felt gratitude, and shame.

Inexplicably, I had conducted more than two years of fieldwork on the case study of Pamela's family before I sought this interview with Eleanor Garrett, and almost as much time passed before I moved Global Ministries of Love in from the periphery of my research visual field. It took me that long to register the fact, or to perceive its potential significance, that the founder and spiritual leader of Global is a woman. I believed I had adopted a "deconstructionist" stance toward the meaning of the concept "family"—the family has no a priori, natural, essential, or universal meaning or form. Instead "family" is an idiom for signifying a fully socially constructed "institution." Yet residues of conventional definitions of the parameters of family and kinship still guided my research initiatives.

When, at last, I began to broaden my definition of the appropriate ethnographic field to include as Pamela's kin several members of the Global Ministries community to whom she was related not by blood, marriage, or long-term friendship, I sought out Pastor Jensen first. As the senior pastor of the ministry, the one Pam and Al both appeared to respect the most, and as their marriage counselor, Pastor Jensen seemed likely to have had pivotal influence on the couple's relationship and beliefs. For these very reasons, however, I worried that a research interview with him would strike even remarkably unguarded Pamela as an indecent intrusion on her marital privacy. I broached the subject gingerly and was surprised and relieved by her enthusiastic response. Willing, as usual, to deepen our mutual quest for cross-cultural understanding, perhaps Pam was confident as well of her spiritual advisor's personal appeal and hopeful it might assist her efforts to dislodge the feminist skepticism that filtered my comprehension of her emergent religious identity.

SUBMITTING IS A PRIVILEGE

Thus it was that in the fall of 1986 I came to spend the better part of my own husband's birthday engaged in a highly charged discourse on love, sex, and marriage with an articulate, genial, and attractive charismatic Christian minister named William Jensen. We met in the administrative headquarters of Global Ministries, a set of basement offices beneath a podiatry and fast-food establishment in one of the Silicon Valley's ubiquitous drive-in commercial malls. To establish rapport and gather contextual information before pursuing the more sensitive topics on my research agenda, I initiated a discussion of the ministry's history, activities, and purposes.

Pastor Bill was less reticent. Early in our conversation he signaled his preoccupation with contemporary gender issues, and he pursued these by conducting a personal and theological dialogue with and about feminism throughout the lengthy interview. With no prompting on my part, this boyish, thirty-six-year-old evangelical minister labeled many of his remarks potentially "chauvinist" or "offensive to women's libbers," responded to imagined feminist criticisms of his beliefs, validated numerous feminist criticisms of men, and espoused an ideal of heterosexual intimacy with few departures from that which Francesca Cancian, a feminist sociologist, has aptly termed "the feminization of love."[2]

Presenting his version of the origin tale of the fifteen-year-old ministry, Bill Jensen described the experience of "baptism of the Holy Spirit" that had released in a young widow named Eleanor Morrison "the gifts of speaking in tongues" and of "knowledge and prophecy" that led her to become part of the charismatic movement. "The Lord used Eleanor in this special way," Pastor Jensen told me, despite the fact that "at that point she didn't even believe in women ministers; she had been quite a submissive type, regular churchgoer, et cetera." But after the church with which she had been doing youth work dismissed her for the doctrinal deviation her new gifts implied, Eleanor sought God's counsel on "what

He wanted for her life." Soon "it became clear that God had given her a ministry in Santa Clara Valley." Fittingly enough, God's plan for Eleanor was to minister to the needs "of the rebellious ones" by founding "a ministry based upon Isaiah," that book of scriptures identified as a resource for "Peace in Time of TURMOIL," according to the spiritual reference guide on the first page of the Gideons' Holy Bible Pam gave me.

"Soon," Pastor Jensen continued, "the Lord called many people around Eleanor"—people like Bill who shared her mission "to reach people who weren't being reached." Interpreting Isaiah to suggest that "the wilderness was the world and that the desert was the church," Eleanor named her mission Global Ministries of Love, and she and the small group of missionaries she had attracted "made themselves freely available to churches, helping out with family problems, drug problems, teaching Sunday school." They brought the Word to "a lot of difficult kids, most of whom were atheist, often on dope, runaways, et cetera." They also volunteered their services to the youth ranches and shelters of the county's juvenile justice system.

Bill was not actually involved with Global Ministries at its inception in 1973. He was only twenty-three years old then and had arrived in the Silicon Valley with his young Christian bride just one year earlier. He was the son of Christian missionaries, and his marriage represented his return to a fold from which he had strayed briefly as a youth. During "a kind of Clint Eastwood adventurer phase," young Bill had smoked some pot, drunk some booze, and made plans to migrate to Australia as a machinist. But then in 1972 he met Loretta, a devout Christian teenager whose "love of the Lord" rekindled Bill's own. He "remembers throwing the pot seeds out the car window" and committing his life to Loretta and to the Lord.

Bill had married into a family that believed in the gifts of healing and tongues, and although he "had always been opposed to speaking in tongues, really turned off by Holy Roller types, pentecostals," he found himself actively seeking "the baptism of the Holy Spirit." He had just resigned himself to the failure of his repeated attempts, when the Lord quite suddenly rewarded him with an overwhelming religious experience. The Lord gave Bill "the gift of repentance" and washed the sobbing, weeping young man "like a fountain" so that he "felt scrubbed inside like S.O.S. pads." "It was indescribable," Bill proclaimed while describing the way that "laughter came from the depths of my being, incredible joy. I felt the presence of the Lord so close and realized that He was filling me with spirits."

Bill claimed that before this religious experience, he had never liked emotions or emotional people, but now he felt "the overwhelming presence of love," and God "began to release gifts within me that I didn't have." Bill had just begun to apply his new gifts for teaching and counseling youth when in 1974 Eleanor Morrison, a very emotional person, called and said, "we need you" to join Global Ministries. "It was funny," Bill volunteered, "and I can't explain how it happened that I accepted Eleanor, a woman, as a leader, because I had always been very chauvinistic and had been raised pretty traditionally and hadn't had a basis for accepting a woman in authority." Although "like a lot of things, it can't be explained sufficiently by the intellect," Bill did accept Eleanor's authority, because he knew "with a spiritual knowledge that this was right." Having a woman as a spiritual leader was not a theological problem, Bill hastened to reassure me. "It's obvious that often woman took the highest spiritual place; for example, Deborah and Juneas." And so, Bill claimed, he had not had difficulty accepting Eleanor Morrison's spiritual leadership.

My shorthand note-taking had scarcely recorded Bill's claims to these enlightened sentiments when he revised them. There had been times, he conceded, when he had experienced resistance to Eleanor, a woman, teaching him, a man. "I'm a rebellious person by nature," Bill explained, "and I have the natural emotions of a man. Men just want to be their own boss." Yet when I asked Bill why men were like that, he offered not a biblical but a cultural determinist, rather feminist, account of male "nature." Through books, television, and other cultural means, boys "are taught by society to repress emotions." Raised this way himself, Bill had found himself, at moments, resisting Eleanor's female authority and her highly emotional leadership style, even though he "knew this wasn't right."

Once again Bill needed no prompting from me to offer a metacommentary on his own gender ideology. With a sudden, self-reflective pronouncement, he signaled his desire to engage in just the sort of discourse about feminism, fundamentalism, and contemporary family life that I had been eager but hesitant to initiate: "I could say some things that would make me sound like a woman libber, and I could say other things that would make me sound like a chauvinist." With this disarming preface, Pastor Bill launched a dialogue about gender that he proceeded to conduct much less with me than with the hordes of imaginary feminists whose views he had selectively internalized, modified, and warded off. And because I had not yet done my homework on the belief systems of contemporary American evangelicals, I was again more surprised and fascinated than I should have been with the complex pastiche of biblical and feminist principles and of biological and cultural reasoning that composed Pastor Bill's views about love, sex, and marriage. Seldom did I need to interject a word of query or encouragement as Bill proceeded, in rather a Talmudic manner, to address my unasked questions on these matters. The fundamentalist Bill seemed to converse less with me than with his postfeminist alter-ego:

Bill #1: I believe a woman can be the leader in a marriage, an influence, in fact she needs to be an influence. In this society, that influence often turns into nagging, or people call it nagging. Well, sometimes it is nagging, but usually that's because she's so frustrated, because her husband doesn't listen. But she has wisdom, intuition, and all that he doesn't have.

Bill #2: On the other hand, according to the Bible, the man is provided as a covering to the woman, just as Christ is a covering to the church. Christ is our protection from Satan, from our enemies. And the husband is responsible directly to God for his wife and his family.

Bill #1: That doesn't mean that she doesn't have a direct relationship to God too. She does. And it's not because he's stronger or smarter. He's not.

Bill #2: It's just a matter of spiritual government. You've got to have some kind of authority and government. All institutions and societies need this. . . . It just so happens that the man is in that role. It's in the scriptures, which is the word of God.

Bill #1: But God isn't all male. God also has female parts to him.

Bill #2: I believe the Bible is the direct inspiration of God. I believe that the Bible is word-for-word correct.

Bill #1: But this doesn't make man any better or more privileged at all.

Perhaps I looked a bit skeptical or confused, or perhaps Bill perceived the tension between patriarchal and egalitarian principles implicit in his remarks, because he next attempted to resolve the apparent contradiction by reinterpreting the concept of submission to rid it of hierarchical or authoritarian implications. Indeed, authority is a burden and submission a privilege in the theological interpretation Pastor Jensen offered. Just as Bill's role as pastor is to serve his congregation, "the person in authority should actually be the servant." To be in a position of Christian authority is "not to dominate, but to serve," and thus, as Bill had reminded Al during the wedding ceremony, "the husband's job is to serve his wife." But to scrutinize Christian marriage through a judicial lens is to miss the point entirely. Using the same phrase that Pamela employed on the day she first told me about her conversion, Pastor Bill explained that Christian marriage is "a total giving relationship." Consequently, "you don't look at fairness and unfairness, at what you get for yourself. In fact it's ridiculous to apply standards of justice to marriage, because it's amazing how little we know about justice. Christian marriage is no fifty-fifty, give-and-take affair; in marriage it's one hundred percent."

In Pastor Jensen's view, feminist and other critics of evangelical marriage principles misunderstand the Christian concept of submission. "I believe all humans are made to submit. Men and women are both made to submit to God." Although "rebellious humanity" resists humility, "to be humbled is good," and "submitting, that's a privilege." Noting correctly, however, that "it's semantics what submission really is," Bill chose to define it as protection and to draw a "big difference between obedience and submission." Within this framework he reaffirmed Talcott Parsons's prescription for successful marriage—separate but equal marital spheres defined by expressive female and instrumental male roles. "The wife can be the heart of the marriage. A man can often go by the intellect."

Pastor Bill's evaluation of the expressive role, however, displayed far less affinity with the views of the late sociological theorist than they did with contemporary, female-centered popular psychology. Like many of the other contemporary evangelical theologians and popularizers I would discover, Pastor Jensen promoted the "feminization of love." And to add to the irony, feminist Cancian is critical of the woman-centered ideology of love that the Christian minister embraced. Compare her skeptical assessment of current love ideals with the more enthusiastic depiction of expressive love by Pastor Jensen that follows.

Cancian: A feminized and incomplete perspective on love predominates in the United States. We identify love with emotional expression and talking about feelings, aspects of love that women prefer and in which women tend to be more skilled than men. At the same time we often ignore the instrumental and physical aspects of love that men prefer, such as providing help, sharing activities, and sex. This feminized perspective leads us to believe that women are much more capable of love than men and that the way to make relationships more loving is for men to become more like women.[3]

Jensen: One of the greatest failures in marriage is communication. The husband is afraid to reveal his emotions. Women are generally much better at this. A man needs to learn to open up emotionally, to cry on his wife's shoulders. . . . And sex has so much more meaning than just the physical act. It's an ultimate expression of a spiritual and emotional relationship. Often men abuse this. Men often just want sex for its own sake. Women want more from sex emotionally. Sex is a sacred thing; it's not just physical. It's holy. But a lot of men expect their wives to make love to them without even communicating or regardless of what's going on between them emotionally. And they don't realize how abusive that is to a woman, because a woman integrates the sexual and emotional more.

Sounding often like a female respondent to Shere Hite's surveys on 1980s heterosexual malaise, Pastor Jensen legitimated many feminist criticisms of men. He also affirmed tolerance for such liberal feminist political goals as equal pay and access to political office, including the presidency. Indeed the pastor interpreted feminism as a reaction to men's unjust, abusive treatment of women: "Women have been so abused, made a sex object, and all. So they're trying to regain it, their self-image." For just that reason, however, Bill judged feminism to be inherently flawed. "Women's lib is the result of women not being allowed to take their proper place. Men have abused women. But women aren't getting their rights in women's lib; they're being abused more. . . . Women's lib tries to be in one sense the same as men. And so they give up what's special about women. Women's lib is a reaction to men, to chauvinism, but it's not a calling."

The reactive character of feminism and its defensive denial of gender difference, in Pastor Jensen's view, condemned it to failure. "The problem is the attitude, the desire to prove something. Women libbers want to prove that they can do it." But women should not have to prove anything, because women and men "are equal in Christ." Even worse, Bill maintained, feminism misleads women, who are naturally expressive and submissive, into forfeiting these spiritual and emotional advantages by competing with men for earthly success. Far from meeting women's needs, this hardens women, thereby exacerbating marital difficulties and deepening women's pain.

Christianity, by contrast, offers women a superior alternative, Bill believed, indeed the only reliable resource for securing the fulfillment, love, and satisfying marriages women crave and deserve. As Global Ministries' principal marriage counselor, Pastor Jensen actively tried to assist women's efforts to reform their marriages to these ends. Fusing ancient scriptural doctrines and his version of feminized love ideology with contemporary human potential movement tactics, Bill prepared betrothed couples for the challenge of Christian marriage and counseled couples like Pam and Al through their tribulations and crises.

The first, most important lesson in Bill's counseling curriculum was teaching the couple "to focus on Jesus as the center of their marriage." For Bill that meant that each spouse must serve the other: "You have to come into marriage with a servant's attitude." Bill's next goal was to teach couples to communicate successfully, a process, it appeared, of developing skills for intergender translations of cognitive and emotional data. Like feminist psychologist Carol Gilligan, Bill had concluded "that men and women think differently. It's not that one way is better than the other. It's just that different things make them feel secure. And so they have to learn how each other thinks."

Finally, Bill devoted much of his instructional time to remedial work on the subject of love. Here he preached his version of the doctrine that true love is will, "agape is the purest, highest form of love," which the authors of *Habits of the Heart* found to be a characteristic evangelical conviction.[4] Bill recognized that "to most people, and even to me before I really understood it, the idea that love is will doesn't sound too appealing." But, he assured me, the advantages of this view are many. Realizing that they can choose to love empowers people to have the marriages that might otherwise elude them and to save those that would otherwise fail. Even when a couple believes that they made a mistake in marrying or that they are no longer in love, they "can choose to reverse the lack of love in a marriage." Bill has seen and helped this happen: "If you commit yourself to love, then you can make enormous changes. . . . You begin refusing negative thoughts about the other person. You begin selflessly loving that person." This optimism of the will works, because it vanquishes the major source of marital difficulties—selfishness. "Selfishness is the opposite of love. Most people think hate is the opposite of love, but that's wrong, because where there's hate there's still strong emotion. But to the degree you're selfish, you can't love, and vice versa."

Pastor Jensen had never seen a troubled marriage that could not be saved if the couple were willing to commit themselves to love. Matters were much more difficult, he conceded, when only one party made this commitment, unless that party was the husband. A committed, loving husband generally could win back an estranged wife, because women usually respond to love, but "it's harder for a woman, in the submissive role, to win him back, because he's often hardened. In a Christian marriage, there are usually problems when the man has turned away from the Lord."

Bill had even counseled unfortunate wives to remove themselves from bad, abusive marriages with unbelieving husbands. "I'm not liberal about divorce, but I'm not legalistic," he explained. This reminded me that I had begun to notice a number of divorced converts like Pam and Al within the Global fold. Bill confirmed and dismissed my observation. A divorce before baptism was irrelevant to evangelical morality. "I don't care what a person's done outside of Christ—rape, murder, the most awful things don't change it, if people completely repent."

A CHRISTMAS BANQUET

I attached greater significance to Bill Jensen's tolerance of divorce than he did and found myself deeply curious about the source of his many feminized and postfeminist attitudes toward heterosexual love. Presuming these were aberrant among evangelicals, I suspected that Global's female founder might be responsible for this doctrinal revisionism. Lunching with Pam shortly after my interview with Pastor Jensen, I expressed my growing interest in Global's founder. Pam immediately volunteered to ask Eleanor Morrison Garrett to consent to an interview, and then she rather defensively invited me to attend a Christmas season recruitment banquet the ministry had planned. Eleanor and her new husband, Paul, would preside over this event; technically the dinner and entertainment were to be free, but Pam warned me to expect "some heavy-duty" fund-raising appeals.

The balcony-striped towers of the pastel concrete and glass motel were visible from the congested freeway I exited a few evenings later, but I still lost my way beneath the labyrinth of road ramps. Fearing that I had missed the opening ceremony, I ran awkwardly across the parking lot in my uncustomary high heels. Pam and Al, who were greeting newcomers, laughingly handed me a name tag and led me to the seat they had saved for me at their table.

The dining staff had just begun to serve a lavish meal to the three hundred or so diners who occupied perhaps two-thirds of the places that had been set. I estimated that one-fifth of the diners were members of Global's small congregation. The remainder included a mixture of relatives, members of other Silicon Valley evangelical churches, a handful of potential recruits, and a smattering of freeloaders. Two Black couples (one, the new housemates of Katie and Eric) and a few Latinos peppered the otherwise racially homogeneous assembly.

While live musicians played a round of "Deck the Halls," a beaming, robust woman mounted the stage. Eleanor Garrett bid us all a hearty welcome and an appetite to match. Saying grace on our behalf, Eleanor thanked the dear Lord for blessing the banquet and all the devoted Global disciples who worked so selflessly and enthusiastically to bring it to fruition. She thanked Him too for sending so many wonderful new friends to share this evening of joy and celebration with so many beloved, familiar ones. After Eleanor thanked Jesus for the meal we were about to receive, she urged us to dig in and enjoy it, promising teasingly that we would be hearing more from her than we might wish after our bellies were sated.

Her husband, Paul, was with her when Eleanor returned, as our dessert dishes were being cleared, to make good on her promise. The program that the couple were about to host was, in fact, a long one. Seeking to reinforce the commitment of the converted, to convert the unsaved, and to elicit generous financial donations for the ministry from all, it combined entertainment with revivalist preaching and fund-raising. First, with pride and good humor, Eleanor introduced the premiere public showing of a short, self-produced promotional film documenting Global's diverse spiritual and community services. Next the couple performed a sample

123

"Word for the Day" dialogue, a five-minute radio spot of spiritual advice they were broadcasting daily on local Christian radio stations. The Word for that evening cited scriptural support for the need for loving communications in marriage. Testimonials from the saved, an inevitable evangelical event, followed. Eleanor effusively introduced one brand-new and several veteran believers who were willing to share with us their individual tales of how each "had come to meet the Lord and be saved." Carlos, one of the few Latinos in attendance who, Eleanor informed us, had been newly rescued from the ranks of derelicts inhabiting the nearby urban streets, offered a brief, embarrassed thank you to his earthly and higher-ranking benefactors. More loquacious witnesses followed.

Having become familiar by then with the rhetorical formula for witnessing among evangelicals. I was prepared for the ensuing tales of sin, repentance, salvation, and earthly reward. Several Global leaders offered seemingly well-rehearsed narratives in this genre. Still, one of these intrigued me. With barely restrained maternal pride, Eleanor handed a microphone to Stephanie, a former drug addict, bar dancer, and unwed mother who had been sheltered and brought to Jesus by Global Ministries. Now Stephanie was engaged to marry a man she had saved and about to lead a ministry to shelter, aid, and rehabilitate young women in crisis. According to Eleanor, Jesus had directed her to establish a temporary shelter for abused and wayward girls, to appoint Stephanie to be its full-time director, and "to pray and seek out those who would regularly support her."

Before the audience was asked to finance Stephanie and her ministry, Eleanor yielded the stage to another exuberant woman, quite a talented soprano/ventriloquist, who entertained us with her naughty, wooden sidekick Joby and led us in Christmas carols. When the time arrived at last for the banquet's climactic event, the audience was well fed, good humored, and responsive. I was quite unprepared, however, for the power of that event, or for the nature of the responses I was about to witness and experience.

Women had dominated the decidedly "expressive" proceedings until that moment, but now that it was time to execute the "instrumental" fund-raising function, the banquet's featured event, Eleanor turned the honors over to a man. We all had been blessed, she told us, because Pastor Anthony Leonetti had accepted her invitation to serve as guest preacher. My quick visual inventory of the tall, dark, handsome man ascending the stage suggested at least some cause for assent. Learning that Pastor Leonetti was a pentecostal minister with nearly three decades of revivalist preaching experience aroused my interest further. So minimalist is my personal religious background that to experience directly a professional revivalist sermon qualifies as a first encounter of the exotic kind.

I was not to be disappointed. For the next hour and a half, Pastor Leonetti, a commanding figure whose personality gave me new appreciation for the term "charismatic movement," harangued, delighted, and mesmerized the crowd. He worked us over verbally, lacing his rapid-fire delivery of a montage of Hell, fire and brimstone threats, and inspirational scriptural promises with Henny Youngman's borscht-belt style of "now, take my wife" humor. The theme of his sermon, "The Sun Is Setting," prophesied that a corrupt, Godless, materialist era was coming to an end and the Lord had selected the Silicon Valley to be the nucleus of an imminent, global, spiritual revival. Leonetti punctuated his rousing sermon with artful demonstrations of his ability to employ the gift of tongues.

The pastor's oratorical skills were so persuasive that I was comforted he chose not to apply them to overtly political directives. Only a single dismissive allusion to Pat Robertson's then-budding presidential candidacy—"and they tell us if we just get rid of Reagan and get Pat Robertson, everything will be all right"—peppered the preacher's scornful litany about the woeful corruption of contemporary churches "with their six-inch deep pile carpeting and attaché case–carrying ministers and *no Jesus*."

Leonetti directed his remarkable rhetorical talents instead to the entwined tasks of securing souls and funds. And at this latter chore, he was stunningly successful. Praising Eleanor, Paul, and Global Ministries for the magnanimous and pivotal services they had already rendered to Jesus' divine plan for the Silicon Valley, the preacher assured us that Global was destined to play a vanguard role in the region's coming Christian renewal. Hence, Jesus now was calling upon us, through Leonetti's auspices, to support and extend Global's good works. Having been fattened and disarmed by the banquet and show, he quipped, we would now be eager to reciprocate our hosts' generosity by pledging lavish amounts to Global Ministries' deserving treasury. I forgot to breathe when Leonetti announced the precise amount the Lord had established as the evening's fiscal goal—$100,000.

This was preposterous, I reassured myself, as Pastor Leonetti reassured the rest that collectively, and to our everlasting glory, our individual contributions would attain this celestial numeral. Instructing us to listen closely to the Lord who would tell each how much to pledge, Leonetti revealed a few highlights of his personal conversation with the deity. Twenty banquet diners, the Lord had informed him, would give five hundred dollars each; twenty more would give one thousand dollars; and the Lord would direct ten others to give greater amounts that had biblical significance.

After asking the Lord to answer our prayers for individual guidance in this matter, the pastor initiated an auctionlike public bidding proceeding by donating a used twelve-seat van to the ministry. He then waited in expectant silence for his prophesy to be fulfilled. Soon the first donor rose to pledge one hundred dollars to Global Ministries; several others followed suit. Pastor Leonetti's response was appreciative but not effusive. The next bidder, he promised, would donate one of the designated numbers; and the next two donors each pledged five hundred dollars. I sat spellbound as one by one donors I knew to be of quite modest means pledged immodest sums. Perhaps half of the evening's target had been pledged when the preacher decided to up the spiritual and fiscal ante. The next bid, he instructed, would be one of biblical significance. We waited in anxious anticipation. Suddenly Al rose and with a trembling voice pledged $3,300 to the ministry. Responding as if Al had cracked the Axis code, Leonetti gushed his approval. This was indeed the correct figure, a sacred, biblical numeral, he explained, because Al had pledged $100 for each of the thirty-three years Jesus had spent on earth before He was crucified. I observed no signs that Al had consulted Pam before he made this startling declaration, but she appeared proud and fully supportive. The evening's events had stretched my own capacity for empathy, however, to the limits of my decidedly secular, sociological imagination. As soon as Leonetti concluded his triumphant public fund-raising, I sealed my anxious contribution of thirty dollars (calculated as fair tariff for the dinner) in a pledge envelope, offered my thanks and excuses to Pam and Al, and departed hastily.*

Long past my ordinary bedtime that night, I recorded field notes

*The next issue of the Global Ministries monthly newsletter announced that Pastor Leonetti had raised $90,495 in pledges to the ministry at the Christmas banquet.

struggling to understand and allay the anxiety provoked in me by the evening's events. Much that I had observed at the banquet reinforced my prior insights concerning the postmodern character of Global Ministries and the nature of its appeal to some of my Valley friends. Nonetheless, I warned myself, it would be a mistake to explain contemporary evangelical beliefs entirely in such terms. "On some ultimate level," my field notes confess,

> there's a belief system here that has a power of its own, that's not reducible to these needs and interests; and it's certainly one that's inaccessible to me. I can understand the appeal of such beliefs, but I really can't comprehend how people actually believe this stuff. And on some deep level it depresses and disturbs me that they do.

Most intimately, it upset me to recognize how deeply involved Pam had become in a world I found so alien. I had neither absorbed nor accepted Pam's conversion so fully as I had imagined.

My impulse was to grant myself a brief respite from my field study, but when Pam called early the next day to say that Eleanor had agreed to an interview, I could not refuse. Three days later I spent the afternoon with Eleanor and Paul that concluded with their (at least partially effective) prayer for this book.

QUEEN OF HEAVEN, WOMAN OF EARTH

A large passenger van in the driveway helped me to distinguish the Garrett residence from its neighbors on the cul-de-sac in the comfortable suburban tract house development. A friendly young man I recognized as one of Global's pastors let me in and offered me a seat on an embossed sectional sofa flanked by poinsettia plants. He summoned Eleanor through an intercom, and minutes later a woman much larger than I had expected limped her way with a cane into the living room. Dressed in a Hawaiian-patterned sun dress, Eleanor greeted me enthusiastically, offered me a Diet Coke, and started to tell me about the autobiography she was hoping to publish. Readily permitting me to tape record an oral version, Eleanor plunged into her effusive delivery of a more processed oral history than I had gathered from other participants in this study. She told a personal story with sufficient trauma and awareness of abuse of women to have climaxed in a feminist transformation.

In her early fifties and but three happy years into her second marriage when we met, marital success was a recent novelty for Eleanor and her forebears. It was a point of pride as well as pain to her that she came from a lineage of unlucky, but strong, midwestern single mothers. "So we're tough womenfolks." When Eleanor was five, her prominent father ran away with his young secretary, leaving Eleanor and her siblings to be raised alone by an embittered mother who tried to teach her daughter that "you just can't trust men; they'll just leave you. You can make it on your own."

The cultural gender messages that celebrated domesticity in the post–World War II years of Eleanor's adolescence must have been more persuasive than her mother's, because in 1952, at the age of seventeen, Eleanor dropped out of high school to marry Simon, a marine she met while visiting a married sister in southern California. For a few blissful years, the teenage groom worked as a truck driver and construction worker to support his adoring bride, but before Eleanor could settle into her 1950s dream marriage, tragedy intervened. Soon after the birth of the first of the couple's two children, Simon developed a mysterious mental illness that, compounded by his heavy drinking, made him alternately violently self-destructive and fearfully dependent.

Eleanor's matrilineal resources stood her in good stead as she assumed financial and emotional responsibility for her young family. So, she believes, did the nascent electronics industry. She took a job as an assembler. "I don't know *why* they let me go to work there. The newspaper said you gotta have a high-school diploma. And so I've just believed all these years that God got me in that electronic industry because He knew I was going to have to have it to support these kids and raise this family. And I just thank the Lord for the electronic industry, Silicon Valley. It's certainly helped me a lot." The headquarters of the firm were in the new high-tech mecca, and because several of Eleanor's and Simon's relatives had already migrated to the Silicon Valley, a few years later they followed suit.

For a decade, breadwinner Eleanor practiced a major gender-role reversal strategy, struggling to heal the afflicted, housebound husband she still loved, to save her troubled marriage, and to support her family; yet her husband kept deteriorating. Afraid for the safety of her home and children, in 1962 Eleanor initiated divorce proceedings. Had it been a decade later, Eleanor might have found affirmation and support from the women's movement. Instead the woman friend at work who reached out to Eleanor in her time of misery offered a more traditional form of sustenance: She introduced her to her conservative church, where Eleanor gave her "heart back to Jesus."

Although this conversion brought Eleanor exquisite relief and a new sense of purpose, it also presented the distraught wife with a dilemma. Eleanor knew that "the Bible says divorce is no good," but she knew also that her marriage was untenable. She prayed and proceeded with the divorce. "And yet in my heart somehow I felt that it [the divorce] would help him, and the Lord had given me strength now to move out, to let him rehabilitate so he wouldn't be dependent on me." A few years later, and before the divorce was finalized, Simon died of a sudden heart attack. This made Eleanor a respectable widow who, she notes with irony, through social security and veterans' benefits, was better supported by a dead husband than she had been by a live one.

Conditions for women working in the electronics industry prompted some to file sex discrimination complaints, but Eleanor refused to join them. She knew that she and other women were paid less than the men, but she did not compare herself to the men, and because she received frequent raises, she never felt underpaid. She felt it would be "unscriptural" to join the feminist protest. Eleanor presented a thoroughly positive reading of her experiences as an electronics employee. Working from the late fifties until the early seventies, during the headiest years of the industry's development, she advanced steadily from assembler to lead lady to an engineering assistant assigned to work on defense contract space projects that she found thrilling. Eleanor loved her employers, she told me, and they loved her. Her total loyalty to her firm did not spare her periodic layoffs during recessionary cycles, but Eleanor claimed to have welcomed these forced vacations as opportunities to pursue her expanding missionary work with youth at the church. Similarly, she portrayed the irregular and extraordinarily lengthy work shifts positively, as evidence of the challenge of the work and of the mutual flexibility in her relationship with her employers. Because she was flexible with them, they were flexible with her, she maintained, allowing her to adjust her hours when family demands were urgent.

No single parent could have met such demands for "flexibility" without an extensive social support network. Eleanor created such a system with her local relatives and her ever-widening church community. Although fifteen years separated her two marriages, Eleanor never lived alone with her children. She shared households and domestic responsibilities with women friends, with her mother, and with fifteen of the adolescents whom she recruited to the church and then chose to foster. Gradually as Eleanor's kinship circle grew along with her missionary zeal, her passion for these overtook her love for the electronics industry.

By the early 1970s, Eleanor had become too "radical" for her church. She had had the experience of baptism of the Holy Spirit and received the Lord's direction and His gifts for missionary outreach work among rebellious and outcast street youth whose scruffy appearances and involvement with drugs, alcohol, and crime did not endear them to church members. She had formed coalitions with other local religious activists involved with youth work, and they convened a meeting "to decide what God wanted us to do next." That morning at breakfast, Eleanor opened her Bible, "and the Lord gave me a Scripture, Isaiah 43. And it says 'Do not ponder the things of the past. Do not look to your old established ways. Behold, I want to do a new thing, and it will spring forth now.' . . . Or something like that. I paraphrase. Anyway, I felt like that was really directed to me . . . that God was directing me to take the church out to where people are."

Thus it was that in the very years when the radical, new thing many American women did was form women-only consciousness-raising groups to recruit women to feminism, Eleanor was meeting with men to form Global Ministries of Love to recruit converts for Christ. She was the only woman at these meetings and at the many others over the years, Eleanor volunteered, as she went on to describe the abuse she has suffered in consequence. She attributes the phone threats, slashed tires, and the hate mail mocking the audacious "queen of heaven" that she has received since founding Global Ministries to the "warped minds" of people who "don't see that people are equal with God. They have their old-fashioned ideas and ways—men's ways."

None of this deterred Eleanor, who succeeded in persuading less bigoted men like Bill Jensen to join her expanding ministry projects in the county's juvenile halls, prisons, mental health facilities, religious hospitals, and on its meaner streets. When Eleanor injured her leg in 1975, she decided to leave the electronics industry to devote her full-time energies to Global. Drawing disability in addition to the social security benefits that her mother and her still-minor daughter each received brought Eleanor's household more income than she had earned as an engineer's assistant. "I guess the government started this ministry," Eleanor quipped, explaining how she had interpreted the benefits as "God's provision for me to just phase out of the secular job and come into the ministry."

For the rest of the decade Eleanor led a full and satisfying life as the anomalous unmarried matriarch of a charismatic Christian ministry. "I started this ministry, just poured myself into this work, and that became my life. And I knew then that I would probably never remarry. I would just spend the rest of my life serving the Lord, and trusting Him, and letting Him take care of me." Eleanor credits her devotion to Jesus with helping her to change what she judges to have been a negative attitude toward men. To my feminist ears, however, her reformed view of the other gender sounds matronizing and somewhat forced. "I began to see men differently. I realized Jesus Christ was a man. If I was going to serve and love Him all my life, I certainly needed to love men. And I saw I had overexpected of them all these years. I expected them to be perfect, something that I couldn't be. And yet I could be almost anything. So they always fell below my standards. Then, when I realized they're really just sort of little boys grown up, they need a lot of help, I began to respect them much more."

Paul Garrett, a lapsed Christian thirteen years younger than Eleanor, was one of those grown-up little boys in need of help, "a divorced man, very broken, very hurt," when his mother's pastor sent him to Global Ministries in the late 1970s. Paul had been busted on drug charges after his first wife ran away with their children and another man. He found the help he needed by helping younger drug victims to receive the Lord and the forgiveness and acceptance to which this initiation rite into the Global community entitled them. Eleanor did not have much to do with Paul during his first years in the ministry. "I was the leader, and he was one of the sheepies." But when she began actively to educate her flock in the skills of deep friendship, "learning to be open and transparent and trust in one another," Paul notified his leader that he would like to spend his homework sessions with her.

It did not take many months of talking openly, working, praying, and playing with Paul before Eleanor was distressed to realize that she had fallen "head over heels in love with him. It was just like you hear about in the storybooks." She sought professional counseling to extinguish the unwelcome feeling that "man, this man is the only thing I want in this whole world," a feeling that threatened to "destroy my whole life." Instead, her counselor and friends in the ministry encouraged Eleanor to delight in her new feelings and to risk expressing them directly to Paul. It was Paul's turn to feel fear when she did so, and once again Eleanor's disciples intervened to offer cupid an assist. Bill Jensen spent a day walking and talking with Paul in the nearby tawny hills, helping him to pray for release from his fears and for guidance in determining his relationship with Eleanor. The Lord and Bill both told Paul that the time had come to make a decision.

Eleanor was about to narrate the climactic resolution of her romantic tale when its protagonist entered the living room. "Is he here to edit this?" I teased. "I'm here to see if you guys need anything," Paul parried. "Anybody want a glass of water, or a cup of anything . . . ?" Eleanor affectionately beckoned Paul to sit beside her because she was about to tell "how sweet you are." "On that day," she continued, "the Lord told him he had the privilege to choose. And so therefore he made a choice to love me. And it took." Paul nodded in confirmation as Eleanor gushed the fairy tale's happily-ever-after conclusion: "When he made that choice, then he just changed instantly. I mean, every guard, everything was down. I mean, he just was filled with love. This man is the most affectionate, romantic person you could ever, ever—I can't even imagine me desiring such a person. And I just eat it up. I love it."

They married in 1983. For their honeymoon, Eleanor took her groom to Florida, where she opened the Global Ministries station to which she would dispatch Pam's daughter Katie and her husband Eric the following year. When the newlyweds returned, Eleanor continued her maverick record of providing her husbands with housing and employment. Paul moved into his new bride's lodgings above the ministry's Silicon Valley headquarters. Delighted that she had secured the male "covering" deemed necessary by most of her Christian colleagues, Eleanor appointed her self-selected head-of-household to codirect the ministry.

PATRIARCHY IN THE LAST INSTANCE

Discussing Christian gender principles of love and marriage with Eleanor and Paul that afternoon reinforced my suspicion that Eleanor had been the primary source of the surprisingly feminized, even protofeminist, doctrines I had discovered among her disciples. Like Pam and Al, and even more thoroughly than Pastor Bill, Eleanor promoted an ideology of female subordination best described as "patriarchy in the last instance." She readily accepted my characterization of her ministry's gender beliefs as egalitarian. "Well, the Bible says that whether Greek or Jew," Eleanor began. "Slave or free," Paul contributed, allowing his wife to finish paraphrasing and interpreting St. Paul's Epistle to the Galatians: "—slave or free, male or female, they are all equal to God. It doesn't mean one's better than the other. And that's kind of the attitude I have. I don't feel like 'Well, I'm going to show those men a thing or two.' That's just something that would be totally wrong for me to have, that kind of an attitude. But I do feel free to be me. I feel free to do, be me, whatever I want to do. And they can like it or lump it."

"What about the idea that the man is the head of the family?" I inquired, pointing out that this concept did not seem to describe Eleanor's experience. "Well, it hasn't been, although I've promoted that because that's what the Bible says, and I believe that today." Perhaps I looked as perplexed as when Bill Jensen had tried to explain the biblical concept of submission to me, because Paul found cause to assist his wife's analysis of Christian organizational hierarchy. "To be the head doesn't mean that you rule over something, or that you usurp something. It means just the opposite actually, that you serve them with love and with respect."

Still skeptical, as I had been when Pam first described Christian patriarchy to me, I pursued the question of a husband's practical authority over his wife. Like Pam, Eleanor tried to explain that if it came "down to the bottom line," a disagreement irreconcilable through discussion, the Bible would oblige her to yield to Paul's authority. But just as with Pam, Eleanor was hard-pressed to supply an empirical illustration of an occasion when she actually had done so. In fact, the couple claimed, they resolved all their conflicts through discussion, and soft-spoken Paul conceded that he was more likely to yield to loquacious Eleanor than the other way around: "I have the responsibility to listen to her too, because she may just be the one with the answer." "That's really true," Eleanor affirmed.

The exegesis on submission and authority that followed suggested strongly that Eleanor had supplied much of the lexical inspiration for Bill Jensen's views. Submission is not subjection, Eleanor repeated, but an attitude of teachability; authority is a responsibility; and they complement each other in a successful marriage like the Garretts'. The couple believe that their "loving teamwork" union serves as a great model of Christian marriage in the work they do. In their counseling work and marriage seminars, Eleanor tries, by demonstration, to teach women not to "cower back" in order to build up their men. "It's a terrible bondage for a woman to be in that" sort of marriage, she explains. Eleanor prods the women to challenge their husbands instead. "Just let me be me, and you get ahead of me. You know what I mean? And it does, it motivates him. He needs to be up in front, and so he's got to go some to be there."

Likewise, Eleanor had begun actively to hold up her successful second marriage as a leadership model for the youthful pastors and their wives in Global Ministries. She was encouraging all the pastors and their wives to become teams who practiced her feminized doctrine of love: "Play together, talk together, do like he and I do; just learn to communicate and become one person together." Why then, I asked, were there no other women ministers in Global? There was another woman minister, they corrected, reminding me of Eleanor's foster daughter, Stephanie, who had testified at the Christmas banquet. And there was another one who, unwisely Eleanor believed, made the choice to leave when she became a wife. It was true, however, Eleanor conceded, that even in revisionist Global Ministries, women ministers have been exceptional. Not too many women feel the call as Eleanor did, perhaps because "there's a lot of persecution." But things are getting better for women in the church. "It's a lot more acceptable for a woman to become a minister" now than it was when Eleanor founded Global fifteen years ago, Paul pointed out, without noting the temporal coincidence of this progress with organized feminism. It delighted Eleanor to see more women preaching on Christian radio and television programs, and she was proud that four of the five young interns that Global was training, with the assistance of theological correspondence courses, to become ministers for foreign missionary stations were women.

Political successes that the profamily backlash and its phalanx of new right televangelists enjoyed during the Reagan era caused many once-borns like myself to presume all born agains suffer acute nostalgia for the vanishing [1950s] nuclear family. Perhaps Eleanor's traumatic experience with family life in that decade bred her more creative profamily strategies. She had put her long-practiced matriarchal skills to great effect, I believe, shaping Global Ministries into her own matrifocal, postmodern, extended family.

Having spent fifteen years as a single, working mother, Eleanor had learned to appreciate the benefits of extended households. She treated her domestic sites as accordion constructions whose membership expanded and contracted frequently. Blood and marital ties determined some of the participants in Eleanor's matrilocal domicile. Her divorced mother lived with her for several years, and later when her daughter married a young Chicano who joined the ministry, not only did Eleanor welcome her new son-in-law into her household, but she ordained him as well. Not all who shared Eleanor's living quarters were formal relatives, however. She had been foster mother to fifteen adolescents, a few of whom made her a foster grandmother also. Eleanor forged enduring bonds with some of her foundlings, like Stephanie, whom she integrated into the Global ministerial staff.

Indeed, Eleanor had achieved much more sociospatial integration than most feminists or other progressives who decry the modern schisms between public and private worlds, between work and family life. Wherever she lived was also Global's organizational and social hub, the site of its staff meetings, its recording studio, and its public relations office. The Garretts had only recently moved to the commodious split-level house where I interviewed them in 1986 while a rivulet of Global staff and callers with personal or business needs politely interrupted us. Before then they had shared a smaller house with Global's central offices, the offices in which Katie and her housemates worked and from which they managed the food and clothing banks that overflowed Eleanor's garage.

Global's matriarchal leader encouraged her "sheepies" to form joint households also. The ministry purchased and leased several adjacent houses that it subleased to Global staff and recruits so that they too would derive the benefits of "living in community." These Christian communes served as a laboratory for Eleanor's attempts at social engineering, the experimental terrain for her activist approach to family reform. Eleanor pointed out the economic advantages of communal households that I had observed directly during my visits with Katie and Eric. The ministry provided full support to four pastors and their families, all of whom lived "in community" with others who subsidized their rent and food expenses at the same time they reduced their own.

Eleanor was even more enthusiastic about the social benefits of co-operative living. The communes provided a means to integrate single people into Global family and community life. The long years she spent as a divorcée-widow made her unusually reflective about the social needs of single women and probably fostered her activist responses to the single-woman "crisis." I had already noticed that Eleanor herself and other Global women like Stephanie had reaped matrimonial benefits from the ministry's not-always-casual matchmaking services. But Eleanor did not rely on romantic attachments alone to extend kin ties and familial arrangements to the unmarried. She self-consciously sought to maintain a balance of married and single members in the community and regarded the communes as an opportunity to bridge the social gulf that might divide them. "In fact," Eleanor explained, "there's a Scripture that I love, that the single belongs in the family. And we feel, Paul and I both agree on this, that singles in the family of God are there to serve the family. And the families are also to serve the singles by providing that that they need. I think single people need to see married people, they need to be around them, because they need to see something good and positive in that kind of a relationship. So that's why we have singles living with all of our marrieds." Since marrying Paul, Eleanor had made it Global policy to "yoke" singles to married couple–headed households. This prevented social isolation for the singles and antisocial withdrawal by the marrieds.

Single women "yoked" to married couples who were to model the benefits of conjugal relationships might legitimately resent the implied denigration of their own single status. The delight Eleanor took in her second-chance romance with Paul probably had inclined her to privilege conjugal over single life. However, not all the forms of support or the messages that Global directed toward women celebrated coupledom. As Pastor Bill had claimed, the ministry did not offer legalistic opposition to divorce or support to marriage. It celebrated a particular vision of Christian marriage against which many earthly representations might well be found lacking. When the deficiencies were severe, Global officials encouraged women to trade in their abusive husbands and lovers for a more rewarding marriage to Jesus. "You will find Jesus the most interested and responsive Lover ever," Eleanor and Paul promise readers of a column they titled "Romancing Jesus" in one of Global's monthly newsletters. Emulate brave "Ms. Loveless," suggests a cartoon in another, depicting a working mother who receives the Lord and ousts the man who exploited and beat her: "Jim, I'm afraid you will have to leave. I have decided to live *for* Jesus so I can't live *with* you anymore. Now I have someone that I don't have to take care of Him, *He* takes care of me and the kids!"[5]

Marrying Paul also led Eleanor to reevaluate her former antagonism to all forms of status segregation. To protect anyone from feeling excluded, she had always opposed all separatist social events. Living with Paul had taught her "that you can be together and separate," and, in consequence, she had begun to organize some separate groups for men, for women, and for singles. The day before she married Paul, for example, a vision inspired by the Song of Solomon led her to establish monthly breakfast meetings for Global men. Eleanor realized that Paul "has such a soft heart" that he "had a lot to teach other men." The purpose of the breakfasts is to teach men to be "open, honest, and meek." Once each year, Eleanor attends a men's breakfast where she personally delivers one of her feminized theological discourses.

Almost everything Eleanor and Paul told me or that I observed during the long afternoon we spent together seemed to confirm my belated realization that the gender of Global Ministries' founder had profoundly influenced the entire character of this evangelical community. Eleanor appeared indeed to be the source of the unexpected blend of fundamentalism and feminism, of formal patriarchal principles and informal egalitarian practices, and of the strikingly feminized doctrine of heterosexual love that I had encountered among her constituents. Eleanor rejected feminism, but she propagated a gender ideology that had been deeply informed by it. Although she accepted the nominal patriarchal authority principles of the Bible, she read the scriptures as selectively as do other religious faithfuls, and her reading preferences seemed to have been shaped by personal and political events that challenged traditional patriarchal values.

Eleanor is an impressive "mover and shaker." I could easily imagine this strong, spunky woman as a grass-roots feminist activist. I regretted the vagaries of biography and history that prompted her instead to employ her protofeminist impulses in a direction that so effectively absorbed, depoliticized, and deflected feminist challenges to male institutional authority. Certainly Eleanor's first marriage had been sufficiently traumatic to permanently undermine the 1950s domestic ideology she had tried but failed to realize. Had feminism been as visible and vigorous when Eleanor abandoned her marriage in the early 1960s as it was to become less than a decade later, she might now be organizing feminist rather than Christian shelters for battered women.[6] Recently divorced women have proven particularly responsive to the criticisms of conventional family life that second-wave feminism generated.[7] But by the time Eleanor would have learned of such criticisms, she had already integrated her own single-mother family into a supportive Christian community.

I must admit that a portion of wishful fantasy governs my if-only reconstruction of Eleanor's chosen path. It is equally plausible that no delay in the timing of her divorce would have attracted Eleanor to a feminist rather than a Christian conversion. Whereas most second-wave feminist criticisms of marriage denounced as oppressors the men who benefited from its institutionalized powers and privileges, Eleanor viewed her own disturbed first husband as an unfortunate victim. Never having experienced wifely dependency—"the problem without a name"—she might have found little incentive to join forces with middle-class women who were angrily challenging their domestic confinement. Eleanor had already proven herself capable of greater independence than she wished to experience. More exhausted than outraged, she was seeking a community of interdependence and affirmation rather than one of opposition and resistance.

Drawing on resources she found in the contemporary Christian evangelical revival, Eleanor crafted such a community in Global Ministries of Love, which became her own postmodern, matrifocal extended family. Global disseminated a gender ideology and supported family practices sufficiently flexible to be palatable to a feminist like Pamela, who was also seeking release from anger and fatigue as well as support for efforts to renew and reform her second marriage. Even before my interviews with her new religious teachers, I had begun to understand the appeal to Pam of the love and support she was finding in this seemingly maverick charismatic Christian community. But the prayer session that concluded my interview with Eleanor and Paul afforded me a more direct experience of its seductive power. The prayer embarrassed me, but its simple words of encouragement and praise warmed me as well, and made me wistful. How rare it is in the deeply secular academic and political worlds that I most frequently inhabit to give or receive such unsolicited expressions of support. My flushed face may have betrayed more than discomfort.

NO DOORMATS

Several months after the interview with Eleanor and Paul I terminated my active fieldwork among Pamel's kin. By then I had come to perceive Global Ministries as a deviant evangelical community whose gender ideology and family relationships were anomalous, the product of the sort of fringe social landscape that people like to regard with amusement as an only-in-California excrescence. Remembering the early challenge I had received from the neighbor of the other Silicon Valley family featured in this book, that they were too unusual to merit detailed study, I worried that Pamela's Christian community was even more aberrant than the Lewisons'. Had I wasted nearly three years of my field study of changing American family life on people whose kinship views and strategies were so far outside the mainstream that they could justifiably be dismissed as social oddities?

This worry led me to an examination, by then long overdue, of the literature on and by participants in contemporary American evangelical Christianity. There I found much to reassure me about the social relevance of my ethnographic "sample" and a great deal likely to astonish most feminists and other "secular humanists." Sampling the literature of contemporary evangelicals taught me quickly that I had given Eleanor Morrison Garrett too much credit for the originality of her unorthodox gender views and family practices. She and Pam are not unique in finding the born-again movement to be a flexible resource for reconstituting gender and kinship relationships in postmodern and postfeminist directions. Indeed, feminist ideas and practices have diffused broadly throughout evangelical Christian discourse in the United States today.[8]

During recent postindustrial decades, evangelical religions have flourished while mainstream churches declined and women have swelled the burgeoning ranks of the former in proportions even greater than they outnumber men in the latter. Estimates of evangelicals range from 18 percent to 40 percent of the adult population, and more than 60 percent of the participants in this fastest growing variety of religious orientation in the United States today are women.[9] This growth in numbers, visibility, and respectability has alarmed feminists and other progressives, who have assumed that evangelicals are a politically cohesive, conservative, and antifeminist constituency. Certainly this is true of the best-organized factions of white evangelicals, but, as few besides those who study American religion recognize, evangelicals are remarkable diverse.

Evangelicals believe in the full truth and authority of the Bible and in its usefulness as a practical guide to the conduct of everyday life. They have differing views, however, on the nature of biblical truth. While strict constructionists attempt to interpret the Scriptures literally, many evangelicals incorporate metaphorical and contextual readings of the book that they all consider to be the inspired Word of God. The most definitive characteristic of contemporary evangelicals is their conviction that a deeply personal relationship with Jesus Christ is the only path to a meaningful life and to salvation after death. Most have had a "born again" or conversion experience that led to an emotionally intimate relationship with Jesus, whom they view as a friend who intervenes personally in their lives. As his evangelicals, they commit themselves, in turn, to spread the "Good News" by bearing public witness to their faith.[10]

Born-again Christians do not share a unified political perspective. With the crucial exception of their more conservative views on abortion and homosexuality, they hold views on most political issues almost as diverse as those affirmed by once-born Americans.[11] Most analysts characterize fundamentalism as the right wing of evangelicalism. Fundamentalism is a separatist movement that formed at the turn of the century in reaction to mainstream Protestantism's adoption of the social gospel. In this separatist spirit many fundamentalists think of themselves as the only true evangelicals. Partly in response to fundamentalist insularity, a less separatist movement called neo-evangelicalism arose in the 1940s. It shares the conservative theology of fundamentalism but is more ecumenical in spirit and more "in the world." Billy Graham, the most prominent neo-evangelist, brought the evangelical message to the ears of presidents and to the living rooms of middle Americans. The respectability Graham brought to this movement paved the way for its explosive growth during the late 1960s and 1970s. A number of right-wing televangelists built large ministries in this period, but evangelicalism also achieved an appeal to members of the urban middle classes with middle-of-the-road and even liberal politics. In 1976 the United States elected its first evangelical president, Jimmy Carter.[12]

The secular new left that emerged in the same period inspired parallel political developments, not only within mainstream Christianity but among evangelical Christians as well. A small but vocal minority of left-wing evangelical Christians have formed communal living and working groups. They publish an evangelical brand of liberation theology in such periodicals as *Radix, The Other Side,* and *Sojourners,* the most prominent of these journals. The March 1988 issue of *Sojourners* featured articles on the religious beliefs and pretensions of presidential candidates, peace protests at the Reagan-Gorbachev summit, a Lutheran bishop's work in El Salvador, and a sermon on healing in the community and nation as well as in personal lives. There also was a short item on the women's budget of the Women's International League for Peace and Freedom, a column analyzing the puerile, male-fantasy content of newspaper comics. and an announcement of two job openings at the magazine for which "women and minorities are encouraged to apply."[13]

The rise of evangelical feminism paralleled that of secular feminism. It had early ties with the evangelical left, but soon developed as an autonomous movement. Evangelical women published critical feminist articles in Christian magazines as early as 1966.[14] When in 1973 a meeting of the left-wing Evangelicals for Social Action was convened to discuss social issues, women struggled successfully to include in the meeting's final declaration: "We acknowledge that we have encouraged men to prideful domination and women to irresponsible passivity. So we call both men and women to mutual submission and active discipleship."[15] The organizational base that feminists established at this meeting enabled them to found a feminist evangelical monthly, *Daughters of Sarah,* in 1974. One year later an evangelical feminist conference in Washington, D.C., attended by 360, endorsed the Equal Rights Amendment (ERA) and formed a lasting organization, the Evangelical Women's Caucus.[16]

Evangelical feminists are serious about both their evangelicalism and their feminism, and each belief system modifies the other. They bring feminist criticism to their Christian communities and theology, and their deeply felt Christian commitment shapes their feminist ideology. "Biblical feminists" or simply "Christian feminists," as many identify themselves, contend that the inspiration for the notion that women are the equals of men is not the affairs of the world but the teachings of the New Testament. They confront patriarchal church leaders and attempt to win evangelical women and men to feminism; consequently they scrupulously seek, and find, scriptural justification for their feminist beliefs. Evangelical feminists have focused most of their energies on three issues: claiming women's right to leadership roles in the church, including ordination; demonstrating the need for the Bible and its interpreters to employ "inclusive language" that presents God not as male but androgynous[17]; and challenging the scriptural basis for the subordinate role of women in marriage.

Biblical feminists have made their greatest impact on evangelical theology and gender ideology in this last area. To counter evangelicals' standard patriarchalist biblical reading of the scriptural foundation for women's subordination to their husbands, Christian feminists have elaborated the ingenious and, to my mind, somewhat forced doctrine of mutual submission that Pastor Jensen and Eleanor Morrison disseminate in Global Ministries. Biblical feminists argue that the essence of Christ's message and practice was a radically egalitarian challenge to prevailing society, a society so profoundly patriarchal that Jesus was compelled to couch his subversive and implicitly feminist teachings in terms comprehensible and tolerable to his compatriots. When read in this context, those troubling passages in the Bible that direct wives to submit to their husbands, such as Paul's notorious message to the Ephesians, can be understood to mean instead mutual submission:

> It is in the context of mutual submission that we must read the famous passages about the submission of Christian wives to their husbands, in particular Ephesians 5:22 and following. . . . Therefore, when Paul speaks of wives' submitting themselves to their husbands, he is building upon the concept that every Christian is intended to submit to every other Christian, to serve every other Christian, to defer lovingly to every other Christian. . . . The Christlike husband takes upon himself the form of a servant, humbles himself, and dies to himself by living for the best interests of his family. He loves his wife as he loves his own body, because he and his wife are one flesh.[18]

A doctrine of mutual submission leaves little room for feminist anger. Biblical feminists challenge unequal marriages as un-Christian. They also take feminist positions on many issues unpopular with most fundamentalists, such as their support for the ERA, for singlehood as a worthy option for women, and their (far less enthusiastic) acceptance of homosexuality and abortion as matters of personal conscience.[19] However, their writings lack the righteous anger that characterizes much of secular feminist literature. Instead, like Eleanor Garrett, evangelical feminists believe that the key to women's liberation is not anger but love. Women must learn to love themselves, and women and men must learn to love each other in a Christlike way:

> According to the New Testament, the Christlike person exhibits the best in human qualities: love, joy, peace, patience, kindness, goodness, faithfulness, gentleness, self-control, humility, integrity, meekness, sensitivity, empathy, purity, submissiveness, confidence, courage, strength, zeal, determination, compassion, common sense, generosity, and self-sacrifice.[20]

Although only a minority of evangelicals are feminists,[21] the impact of feminism on evangelical discourse has been profound and diffuse. Some prominent male theologians have absorbed and now teach feminist ideas,[22] and feminist influence on evangelicalism goes well beyond this self-conscious engagement by evangelical leaders. According to a 1980 Gallup Poll, although the political views of evangelicals on "social issues" were predictably more conservative than those of nonevangelicals, the majority of the former (53 percent, compared with 66 percent of the latter) still favored the Equal Rights Amendment.[23] Moreover, there is considerable evidence that a pervasive postfeminist ideology has infused evangelical culture. James Hunter, a sociologist who studies American religion, surveyed students in evangelical colleges and seminaries. He found them affirming a curious amalgam of conservative and feminist attitudes toward gender and family relationships.[24] Although a majority claimed that the husband should have the final say in a family's decision making, most also found sensitive, gentle men and assertive, self-reliant women as appealing as more stereotypical men and women. Most students agreed that a woman should put her husband and children ahead of her career (although some commented that a man should also put his family ahead of his career). However, they did not agree with the statement "a married woman should not work if she has a husband capable of supporting her." In these respects, their views are only slightly more conservative than those of the U.S. population as a whole.[25] The strong emphasis evangelicals place on family life, however, leads them to value male participation in early child care, albeit not equal participation, even more than do their less religious counterparts. The overwhelming majority (about 98 percent) of Hunter's respondents believe that both father and mother have the responsibility to care for small children.[26]

Popular Christian evangelical literature displays this same pervasive postfeminist ideology. *Today's Christian Woman* (*TCW*) and *Virtue,* for example, portray women working outside the home as a taken-for-granted arrangement; in fact, the subscription pitch for *TCW* says it offers "practical ideas for coping with the challenges of marriage, family and career." Concrete advice to women for building satisfactory Christian marriages dominates the pages of Christian women's magazines, and much of this advice suggests feminist influence. A fairly typical statement by one advice columnist echoes the biblical feminists' view of Christian marriage: "A healthy marriage allows both partners to be themselves. Balancing personal needs with the needs of the relationship requires compromise and negotiation. But if one mate continually subordinates her or his needs in order to please the other, the relationship suffers."[27]

Christian journalists offer readers strategies for improving the emotional quality of their marriages, and few of these advocate the mixture of submission and Saran Wrap Marabel Morgan once peddled.[28] A fairly typical article in *Virtue* contends that women's frustrations about lack of intimacy in their marriages spring from the fact that women and men see relationships differently. The authors blame men and their difficulties with self-disclosure for this lack and conclude: "It's not up to the woman to be the one responsible for the level of intimacy in the marriage relationship."[29]

Even James C. Dobson, the right-wing evangelical founder of antifeminist Focus on the Family whom we met in chapter 4, shows postfeminist influences. He tells women in troubled marriages that the Bible does not demand that they tolerate disrespect or abuse from their husbands: "Please understand that I believe firmly in the biblical concept of submission, as described in the book of Ephesians and elsewhere in scripture. But there is a vast difference between being a confident, spiritually submissive woman and being a doormat. People wipe their feet on doormats, as we know."[30]

While popular evangelical literature decidedly exalts heterosexual marriage, it also offers a surprising amount of support for singlehood. Women's shelves in Christian bookstores display such titles as *Finding Your Place after Divorce* and *Helping Women in Crisis*.[31] Even Dobson views being "single by design" as "a legitimate choice which should be respected by friends and family alike." "Believe me," he remarks, "a bad marriage is far worse than the most lonely instance of singleness."[32] A record review in *Virtue* also gives the stamp of approval to singleness: "This new release also presents a song called 'The Gift,' encouraging Christians to give special honor and support to those who are called to a life of celibacy, serving God as single adults rather than as married couples."[33] And, within evangelical churches and communities, singles' ministries and groups designed both to support and, perhaps, to reduce the ranks of the uncoupled, flourish.

As Barbara Ehrenreich, Elizabeth Hess, and Gloria Jacobs have pointed out in *Re-making Love*, elements of the sexual revolution also have "penetrated" the Bible Belt,[34] but sexuality remains, I believe, the most conservative aspect of evangelical gender ideology. Even most biblical feminists find it difficult to overcome scriptural and personal antipathy to homosexuality and abortion, and the popular evangelical literature is almost uniformly reactionary on these issues. The new Christian right appears to have scored its most disturbing and significant ideological victory in this political arena.[35] Nonetheless, the Metropolitan Community Church, one of the largest gay churches in the country, is evangelical, and Christian women's magazines show modest signs of recognizing moral complexities to antiabortion politics.[36]

Secular feminists can find numerous other surprises in Christian women's magazines, including information on rape self-defense, criticism of social pressures for thinness and youth, and reviews for books celebrating friendships between women. Such literature lends support to Hunter's provocative claim that despite the small numbers of evangelical feminists, "feminist sensibilities are, nevertheless, ingrained within substantial sectors of Evangelicalism."[37]

"Postfeminism," in my view, better characterizes the dominant gender ideology of contemporary evangelicals. Generated partly in reaction to feminism, it also selectively incorporates and adapts many feminist family reforms. Under postindustrial conditions even wifely submission has lost its traditional meaning. Told that an evangelical feminist interprets submissive Christian women as fearful of divorce, Julie Cabrera, coordinator of women's Bible study at Crossroads Bible Church in the Silicon Valley, responded: "Nonsense. I am in submission to my husband by choice. I do this in order to please God. He has put our husbands in the head of us. We choose to be in this position. We are not doormats."[38]

JESUS PEOPLE INFORMATION CENTER, INC.
4338 Third Avenue, Sacramento, CA 95817
NEWSLETTER   Editor: Tom Adcock
I Am Woman

JERUSHA ADCOCK, 9 YEAR OLD 1st DEGREE BLACK BELT, AMERICAN TAEKWONDO ASSOCIATION.

7

The Gray and Spotted Dogs

There is an old Yiddish saying, "To a worm in horseradish, the whole world is horseradish." . . . Psychotherapy can help us face up to the fact that the world we live in is horseradish. . . . It can teach us to adjust to this world and be less frustrated by it. But it cannot whisper to us of a world we have never seen or tasted. Psychology can teach us to be normal, but we must look elsewhere for the help we need to become human. The question of whether life has meaning, of whether our individual lives make any real difference, is a religious question . . .
— Rabbi Harold Kushner, *When All You've Ever Wanted Isn't Enough*

If this ethnography has succeeded in reproducing the fitful progress I made in understanding the character of Pam's evolving family reform strategies, it should also have created the false impression that participation in Global Ministries enabled Pam to resolve her internal conflicts about feminism, fundamentalism, and postmodern family life. Had I lost contact with Pam after I arbitrarily concluded my active fieldwork period, I might have concluded that this was true. I might have forgotten the portentous significance of the parable about the fighting gray and spotted dogs that Pam had relayed to me the day we decided I should study her.

Remember that just before I met Pam she had decided to nurture the appetite of her "gray dog" for spirituality, marital security, and emotional support. She fed that hungry hound quite generously during the period of our active work together, and I attentively observed and interpreted the consequences. But throughout this period Pam also served a richer menu than I then recognized to her "spotted dog"—the cravings for rationality and critical self-reflection and for the democratic and feminist elements of her political identity that she had subordinated but not extinguished. Indeed, Pam's decision to become a central figure in this study, I should have realized, represented the depth of her attachment to this spotted canine. She was agreeing, after all, to subject her life, words, and sentiments to critical scrutiny by a secular feminist. The process was to serve Pam, I came to believe much later, as a means to mediate some of her internal conflicts on issues of our shared concern. And, I suspect, to some extent this research may have served a similar purpose for me.

It required several months of cautious study for me to learn that I had entered Pam's life at a particularly volatile moment. Her decision to follow Al into evangelical Christianity was both recent and raw. While in part a response to the inner turmoil and depression that she had been suffering, Pam's abrupt identity shift generated new sources of conflict. I believe that her relationship with me assisted this difficult transition. Regarding me simultaneously as a nonjudgmental researcher and as a feminist, Pam used our collaborative work to ease her way into charismatic Christian womanhood without abandoning her feminist identity.

REFRACTED VIEWS

The Former Friend

Reconciling her new and former selves, particularly her fundamentalist and feminist convictions, posed greater challenges to Pam than I have yet conveyed. The most immediate of these stemmed from the irreparable damage that Pam's conversion had inflicted on her relationship to her friend and coworker Jan. Jan felt injured, baffled, and abandoned by Pam's sudden conversion, and Pam, in turn, felt threatened, rebuffed, and highly vulnerable to Jan's profound disapproval of her actions. The unwitting support provided by my feminist research forum helped Pam to cope with these painful emotions without renouncing feminism.

Jan's brand of feminism was not reconcilable with born-again Chris-

tianity, not even with its most revisionist versions. Jan was deeply offended when Pam attempted to include both her gray and spotted pups
in SOS's annual conference for welfare mothers. At that conference I
attended a workshop on "family wellness," listed on the program as
"Survival Techniques for Families in the 80s." The workshop defined a
"healthy family" in terms sufficiently pluralist and postmodern to satisfy
the most anti-"traditional" feminist or secular humanist. "Composed of
two or more individuals who promote the health and well-being of those
living together," such a family, the workshop leaders reassured us, could
include marrieds or unmarrieds, homosexuals or heterosexuals, one parent or more, and related or unrelated people. However, Pam also invited
a local minister to deliver an ecumenical religious invocation and Global
Ministries to staff an informational table. The event proved to be the last
that the two former friends would administer together—Jan was furious
at Pam for "cramming her new religious views down everyone's throats."

Jan remained an unambivalent second-wave feminist, the most striking
exception to the trend toward postfeminist consciousness that I encountered during my Silicon Valley fieldwork. "I'm still very much a feminist.
Never say die, that's me," she proclaimed over lunch soon after Pam had
left SOS in 1985. Jan had inherited Pam's program director job, and she
was brimming with ambitious plans to make the program "*The* county
center for services to women." She hoped greatly to expand its services
in order to address a panoply of women's needs that feminists had identified, such as child care, shelters for battered women, housing, education,
legal services, and counseling. Yet Jan defined feminism more in psychological than in political terms: "I really see feminism as not being
male-identified, demanding cultural awareness as a woman."

Jan found men of little interest. "I don't see men in the world," she
asserted with a hint of pride. "I'm not oriented to them at all. I don't
take them as seriously as I probably should. I'm just not male-identified
in any way." Jan was gratified that she had developed her impressive
physical and mechanical aptitudes sufficiently to avert reliance on male
assistance. She looked to herself and other women rather than to men as
the "source of power and strength." But, she hastened to add, "I'm not
a separatist. I'm inclusive, but on an equal basis." Both on the job and
after hours, Jan worked amicably and effectively with men. She participated actively in electoral politics, supporting progressive male as well
as female candidates, and she enjoyed unusually positive relationships

with the same male superiors at SOS who found so much fault with Pam. "I don't know what's going on, but they just love me around here," she marveled after her boss (and Pam's former nemesis) had just awarded Jan her third major promotion and hefty pay raise in one year. "I get to eat lunch with the boys now. Pretty good for a kid from Richmond, don't you think?"

Jan's lesbian identity did not seem to be an issue for the "boys," nor did she find cause to make it so. "They don't know; they don't want to know." During the 1986 campaign against a LaRouche-sponsored antigay state initiative,* Jan wore her "No on 64" button to work and encouraged her colleagues to participate in the campaign. She also brought her new lover to the office Christmas party, but no one said or asked Jan anything about her personal life. "So maybe they suspect or know, but it's not an issue. None of that garbage like 'bring your boyfriend to the party.' "

Crediting feminism with effecting enormous improvements in her life, Jan was not inclined to retreat from identifying herself with this out-of-fashion label. Nor did she believe that many "original believers" like her (or me) were jumping ship. The problem lay in "the next generation of women; they don't have to do any struggle to get it, but it's available to them on demand." Feminism, as a result, was "not moving forward, partly due to exhaustion, but it isn't retreating either." And, as it grew older along with stalwarts like Jan, the women's movement had matured. Jan, like Pam, had lost some of her appetite for indignant anger and was relieved to find the ambience of the 1980s women's movement to be more tolerant and humorous. "Earlier feminism had more anger for anger's sake," Jan mused, recalling a former lover "who was much the feminist, always harping on me for every little thing, like every word I used, every small detail. It used to drive me crazy, even though I could see the point." It was a relief to "lighten up." Jan was equally pleased to relinquish "the idea of women as victims who are owed something because of it. I don't think I'm owed something anymore. I just want a fair opportunity, but no one owes me anything."

Thrilled to be in a position to help create fairer opportunites for other women, and wondrous that she was earning unanticipated sums to do so, Jan overflowed with strategies for empowering less fortunate sisters.

---

*The right-wing political sect led by Lyndon LaRouche sponsored an initiative to bar homosexuals from public school teaching positions. Extensive media attention to a range of conspiracy theories and beliefs propagated by LaRouche helped to defeat the initiative.

"I realize I have to start small," she conceded, "but I have so many plans for this job, I might have enough to keep me here for almost two years." Unimpressed with the magnitude of Jan's anticipated job tenure, I asked why she limited her commitment to two years. "No moss grows on this girl," she explained. "If it starts to feel damp, I run to the desert." "I'm not like Pam," she elaborated, unable to resist an impulse to fling a barb at her former friend. "I prefer challenge to security."

Although Jan's SOS tenure forecast proved to be prescient and her self-characterization largely apt, she had allowed an uncomfortable set of entanglements to constrain her family and work decisions. Throughout the three-year period of the rise and denouement of her intense coworker friendship with Pam, Jan had been mired unhappily in a postmodern family of her own. She had shared her mobile home with her long-term lover Paula and on a biweekly basis with Dylan, Paula's young son.

Young Dylan's custody and kinship arrangements were decidedly avant garde. He had begun life with three coparents—his biological mother, Paula; her then live-in lover, Adele; and Tom, a close friend of the couple who had committed his sperm and his long-term cooperation to their parental aspirations. Adele and Tom began early to assume major responsibility for the infant's care, and when Paula and Adele separated three years after Dylan's birth, Adele became the toddler's de facto primary parent and her home his primary residence. Jan and Paula became lovers shortly thereafter, and Jan voluntarily entered Dylan's custodial network by inviting Paula to move into her "mobe." "Dylan's family history is pretty complicated and screwed up," Jan acknowledged, "but he's a remarkably together and wonderful kid. He's bright, friendly, sociable, has friends, seems fine. We must be doing something right."

Custody conflicts gradually disrupted these harmonious arrangements. Adele received an enticing job offer in San Diego, and Tom supported her wish to accept the job and to take Dylan along. Paula vented some of her anger at this on Jan, whom she blamed for earlier encouraging her to leave Dylan in Adele's care. Jan denied any responsibility for Paula's maternal plight; she thought the accusation "sums up what's wrong with Paula; her movie is being the victim."

Jan was quite attached to Dylan and committed to remaining in his extended adoptive kinship network, but she found herself ever more estranged from Paula. Despite the thickening "moss" of her disaffection, however, before Pam entered her life, Jan had taken no steps to exit this unhappy relationship. Pam's entry at SOS presented Jan new trailways to the "desert." As the friendship between the women blossomed, each confided her dissatisfactions with her own mate. Pam was the first to translate words into action. Jan applauded Pam's separation from Al, from which she also gleaned a measure of inspiration and more tangible benefits. Living alone, Pam had more time to spend with Jan and a couch she offered on those nights Jan chose to avoid her own unhappy domicile. Drawing sympathy and support from Pam, Jan began to extricate herself from her unsatisfying relationship with Paula.

These circumstances help account for the depth of the shock and the intensity of the emotions Jan experienced when Pam returned to Al and converted to charismatic Christianity. Matters worsened when Pam, newly enamored of long-term commitment, tried to encourage Jan to rededicate herself to Paula. This was just the fate Jan had been struggling to escape. Engulfed with rage, Jan retorted, "Hey, you're trying to paint my picture. That may be your movie, but it's not mine." It was not that Jan was uncompromisingly opposed to committed intimacy, she explained to me, but that she drew a keen distinction between authentic and false security needs. And Pam's bond with Al, as well as her own attachment to Paula, Jan located unequivocally in the latter column. Such judgments intensified Jan's already heated political disapproval of her friend's startling turnabout.

"Pam's religious trip is a cop-out, a flight from reality, a way to hide," she fumed. "I can see how some people need the idea that their marriage is blessed by God," she continued, "but that's just a grab for false security, a rubber crutch, and I thought Pam was too intelligent for that." Learning to accept loss as "a major fact of life" and to grow from the experience of bearing it was one of Jan's existential principles. Nonetheless, she was hostile only to the form of Pam's desire for spirituality, for Jan had developed spiritual longings of her own. One day I visited her while she tended sunflowers and zucchini on her small plot in an incongruous community garden nestled defiantly adjacent to the blare and fumes of an interstate freeway. Surveying the profusion of color and cornucopia that surrounded us, Jan lamented, "I look at this and I wish that relationships were like this; that is, if I put this much effort in, I'd get this much bounty back. I've learned through the years that I need to believe in something, some meaning to life. Believing in people, in relationships isn't enough. I tried that. You need something more."

Pam's exit from SOS seemed to release Jan to seek ways to satisfy both her emotional and spiritual desires. In a matter of days Jan fell deeply in love with a new woman. Together they began attending the weekly meetings of an Al-Anon group for gay and lesbian "codependents." Jan, her new lover, and other members of the group viewed themselves as drawn to and complicitous with people who had drinking and substance abuse problems. The leaderless, loosely structured group followed a version of AA's twelve-step program, and Jan rated "the spirituality component" of the group high among its multiple appeals: "I ignore the corny stuff and the excessive male God trip in it. It's a spiritual program, but it's explicitly nonsectarian and nondenominational, so you can relate to any spirit you want. They have this saying—most of the sayings are cornier than shit—but they say 'take what you want and leave the rest,' and that's what I do. If something there bugs me, I just don't put it in the computer." The AA teachings that Jan found most helpful bore striking resonance to lessons Pam seemed to draw from her born-again faith—extend greater tolerance to oneself and others, assume responsibility for one's decisions and deeds, relinquish anger, and practice forgiveness. "They teach you to take responsibility for changing yourself and for your responses to things, but also to accept yourself and when you're wrong to make amends. One thing I really like is learning to leave it behind. If there's something you can't change, accept that. Learn to walk away from things, especially anger."

True to her prediction, just before two years were up, Jan walked away from her heady job at SOS. "The shit just got too high, and the snakes were slithering through," she explained. Still in love, she had moved in with her new mate and was "enjoying a lovely life." Perhaps Jan's new emotional security encouraged her to trade the economic security of her SOS salary and benefits for the challenge of starting her own business. The desktop publishing company she established was nearly prototypical of Silicon Valley private ventures, and to subsidize the venture Jan also took an evening job teaching desktop publishing in a local school. Yet her identity was so firmly planted in feminist, lesbian, and countercultural communities that she and I both had difficulty regarding her as a fully legitimate member of my research "sample."

Despite eight years of employment in Santa Clara County agencies and of active engagement in county politics, Jan maintained a view of herself as "not really part of Silicon Valley at all." Claiming to hate the region, she scrupulously parked her mobile home outside the county borders. To Jan, as to most observers, Silicon Valley signified electronics, and she believed that unlike most county migrants, she was in the Valley not because of but in spite of that industry. To me, Jan seemed too familiarly connected to my own politico-cultural milieu to qualify as sufficiently working class or "other." We both harbored these respective conceits against significant empirical challenges.

The daughter of a Polish auto worker, Jan had a more conventional working-class family background than Pam, a background she drew upon quite effectively to establish rapport with low-income ethnic students and clients at SOS. Nor was her employment in the region as arbitrary or as unrelated to the electronics industry as she preferred to believe. SOS was an important component in the region's response to the demographic, occupational, and social upheavals spurred by its emergence as a high-technology frontier. The jobs Jan performed there—drafting instructor, skills training classes supervisor, Southeast Asian refugee project administrator, and women's services director—existed largely because of the electronics industry, whose infrastructural needs they served and whose social dislocations they attempted to mitigate. Moreover, the influx of a significant number of countercultural and progressive political veterans of the 1960s, like Jan, challenged the dominant political and cultural landscape of the county. She and I both were mistaken to imagine her presence in Pamela's milieu an irrelevant fluke. Pam's receptivity and attraction to cultural diversity was an unusual, but far from unique, response to the postmodern character of Silicon Valley culture, a hybrid rather than an organic culture in which received and innovative forms intermingle without homogenizing.

Pam's turn to evangelicalism, however, had strained the cultural ties binding her to Jan too far, releasing Jan to judge harshly a gender strategy she viewed as irreconcilable with feminism. Even so, Jan did not consider Pam's conversion conclusive. "I know I have this tendency to stereotype Pamela now because of this fundamentalist thing," Jan conceded, "but I know that's too simple. Just when I'm seeing her as a fanfold, computer printout, she'll do something that surprises me, proving that she can't be boxed into a simple category like that." Convinced that Pam had fled the burdens of freedom, Jan predicted—wishfully I thought—that eventually her former friend would return. "Maybe it won't be until she's in her sixties or seventies, when she stops worrying about what her relatives and other people think; but one of these days she'll stop looking to men and marriage for security, and she'll give up on false formulas for salvation."

A Mother's View

No one else among Pamela's kin disapproved of her Christian conversion as keenly as Jan did, but others found it disconcerting and doubted the permanence of her commitment to Global Ministries. Several expressed their reservations long before I perceived the instability of that commitment. Just two days after Pam and Al's Christian wedding ceremony, for example, I interviewed Martha Porter, Pam's then seventy-nine-year-old mother. Martha had approached me during the reception, openly disappointed that I had not yet seen fit to include her in my study. Apologetically I agreed to rectify this negligence at her earliest convenience.

Two days later Martha and I claimed the lone shaded bench in the same noisy community garden where Jan revived her spirits by cultivating produce. Unwrapping a new tape cassette, I asked Martha how she had enjoyed the wedding. Martha liked the music and the convivial Global spirit, and anything that pleased Pamela pleased her too, she readily assured me. Then, pausing briefly, she volunteered a response to the service more feminist than I had allowed myself to suffer. "That's why Sunday, it was a little confusing to me that Pamela would renew her vows the way she did—with the minister saying that the man is the master and all that. I couldn't listen to the beauty of the marriage because of that. I know Pamela doesn't believe that. I know that she doesn't do everything the way Al wants it. The pastor came on pretty strong, didn't he?"

Martha's sensitivity to this issue, I soon realized, had been honed by recent developments in her own half-century-long marriage. After suppressing resentment of her subordination to her own husband for nearly fifty years, Martha had won a late-life struggle for marital equality. Although her husband, Fred, now was seriously incapacitated by declining health, his still-vigorous wife judged their marriage to be "better now than we've ever had."

Martha was proud to report, and I was gratified to learn, that thanks

155

in part to the women's liberation movement, the most important progress in her marriage had preceded her husband's physical decline. When a grass roots feminist movement revived during the fourth decade of the Porter marriage, Martha held her distance. "I never took part in the marches or in the meetings, or I never even sent money." But she had observed the movement's growth and listened to its rhetoric with spontaneous sympathy and keen personal interest. She had always been aware of men's injustice to women, she told me, and "I've always read books." Martha read some of the new angry books, like Kate Millett's *Sexual Politics*, that feminists began to publish, and these inspired her victorious personal rebellion—a battle for greater financial autonomy.

"Yes, I think that was one of the things that made me insist on the check deal," Martha mused before recounting the tale of her struggle for a checking account of her own. Although she had earned a steadier income than her husband, Fred had always controlled the couple's finances. Accustomed early in life to turn over any money she earned to her widowed mother, Martha easily acceded to Fred's demand that she transfer her paychecks to him. "It seemed to be the better part of wisdom to let him handle the money," she recalled. "And there were many times when he spent money on himself and I did without. But I didn't mind it. I never minded it. Uh, and if I had it all to do over again, he wouldn't have had a servant; he would have had a partner instead."

What Martha seemed to mean was that she had not allowed herself to acknowledge how much she had minded Fred's domestic fiscal control until media coverage of second-wave feminist challenges to male authority encouraged her to confrontational tactics of her own. The year before Martha retired, realizing that "it was now or never," she informed her husband that she would be happy to write any checks he needed on her new, independent account. Fred resisted vehemently, but resolving not to relent, Martha successfully deployed the ultimate spousal threat. "Well, I stuck to my point. I said, you can either get a divorce, and I'm willing, or you can do things my way, and we'll both write checks. Well, he wouldn't write a check again for two years."

Martha's victorious bid to turn servitude into partnership garnered the Porters several years of egalitarian marriage. The couple spent these healthy and pleasurable retirement years traveling throughout the continental United States in their mobile home. When Fred's health began to fail, the Porters parked their trailer in a Silicon Valley motor home park, and Martha's unmarried sister rented a trailer nearby. There the two septuagenarian sisters aided one another and received the benefits of integration into Pamela's postmodern extended family.

Martha bypassed the "modern" family en route to Pam's postmodern one. She never had been a full-time homemaker supported by a bread-winning husband. After her father died when she was nine, Martha grew up poor in Okie territory in a migratory, female-headed household. Shunning several marriage proposals, she worked her way through high school and several years of college before learning of the Works Progress Administration and Federal Emergency Relief Administration programs of Franklin Delano Roosevelt's New Deal. Inspired by the new president's progressive ideology, in 1933 Martha moved to Texas where she met Fred who, like her, taught current events and workers' rights courses to farm workers in a FERA program.

Martha told me that she was thrilled to go to Houston with Fred and other FERA friends to see FDR nominated for his second term.* Sharing political commitments and working together to organize beet workers in Colorado and pecan workers in Texas, Martha and Fred found their friendship deepening. In 1936, when Martha was twenty-nine and Fred was thirty-five, they "just drifted into marrying." Each of the three times that unplanned births followed at two- to three-year intervals, the couple contemplated an abortion.

Neither marriage nor motherhood, not even the difficult births that inflicted spastic cerebral palsy on the Porters' last child and a milder athetotic condition on Pamela, interrupted Martha's long history of paid employment. Far from objecting to a "working wife," Fred relied on her contributions to the household budget he controlled. Martha tried to find jobs, like door-to-door selling, that could fit around her mothering responsibilities. Then in 1947 she secured a teaching credential. For the next twenty-three years she taught in public schools—kindergarten at first, then, motivated by her youngest child's burdens, special classes for the physically handicapped. Her pay was modest, but it yielded the family more reliable income than the proceeds from Fred's far more erratic occupational history.

Most of Martha's family history also bypassed the "modern" nuclear

*The Democratic presidential nominating convention was actually held in Philadelphia in 1936 and in Chicago in 1932. It is possible that Martha attended a state primary convention for FDR.

household form en route to the Silicon Valley trailer park. Her widowed mother moved in with the Porters after they settled in California, pooling modest resources while easing her working daughter's considerable child care burdens. A "premodern" family history like this left Martha unprepared for, and disappointed by, Pamela's decision to choose early marriage over a college education. She liked her daughter's fiancé, but she worried that without an independent career, Pam would easily be dominated by her husband. Martha was not shocked, therefore, when twelve years later Pam arrived at a similar conclusion and wanted to divorce. "And Don didn't want a divorce," Martha remembered sympathetically, "and Don is, he's a fine guy, but he has a way of putting women down. And, it, so when that happened, why, we supported her in every way possible."

Martha found it easy to sympathize with her daughter's newfound feminist principles. After all, she had been reading feminist literature herself. There Martha found striking parallels with the literature about the handicapped with which she was already deeply familiar. "I think maybe that women's rights also come in line with handicapped rights, and all three of my children were partially or wholly handicapped,"* Martha pointed out. "And reading about handicapped problems is similar," she explained, "because women are handicapped. And the two readings went side by side."

Thirteen years later it was much more difficult for Martha to understand her daughter's conversion to fundamentalism. "Now do you want to know what I think about religion?" she asked me quite abruptly after concluding her analogy between the handicapped and women. Indeed I did. "Sometimes I think it is the biggest farce," she proclaimed, before conveying more modulated religious views. "I believe in God, and I believe in kindness, empathy, children having a chance in life, and always letting a person have face, letting them not feel guilty. I believe in—I'm not sure whether I believe in Jesus as the son of God, or not. I don't think it's important. And that's where I keep my mouth shut around Pamela and around the rest of them."

As her opening comment about Pam's wedding had signified, Martha objected strongly to the patriarchal gender ideology that defenders of her daughter's new faith disseminated. "I do believe that some of the men

*Two of Martha's children were born with cerebral palsy. The third had learning disabilities.

there are —they are not racist; what do you call them?—chauvinistic?"
She found laughable the defense of husbandly authority I had received
from Eric, her granddaughter's husband—that someone had to be in
charge to resolve irreconcilable differences of opinion. "I think he's not
mature," Martha retorted. Yet despite objections to the sexism and other
reservations about evangelical theology, Martha fully supported her
daughter's involvement in Global Ministries. "Oh, more power to her,"
she affirmed. "It's not the Methodist, it's not the Baptist, it's not the
Lutheran, but it has intrinsic values. And—that I believe in. The, you
see, there are grandchildren, and there are great-grandchildren now coming along. And Melissa is beginning to grow in the church,* and I believe
in that. You have to belong to something. This is part of the thing I used
to tell in parent conferences. You cannot raise your child alone. Society
has to enter into it and be a part of it. So if there is any way that I can
help, I'll do it."

Martha's support for Pamela's new faith was not simply rhetorical.
Nickel-and-dime religious books for Pam and Al became regular bargain
bounty of the flea markets Martha loved to frequent. Daydreaming their
way through objectionable portions of the service, Martha and her sister
enjoyed their sporadic Sunday visits to the Global Ministries church.
And, while Martha claimed never to have contributed money to support
feminist efforts she had favored, she frequently donated funds to Global
Ministries "because it means a great deal to Pamela." Indeed, Martha
had just influenced her sister to make Global's ministry for pregnant
teenagers the beneficiary of a major five-hundred-dollar gift she had
decided to donate to a worthy cause.

Martha and I had talked for nearly three hours when she began to
worry that she had left Fred alone for too long. Hastily concluding our
visit, Martha blurted a prediction about her daughter that mimicked
Jan's. "I think that Pamela will grow away from this church," she announced. As I drove Martha to her bus stop, she denied my request for
elaboration and parted with these prophetic words: "Well, let's save that
for another time. Because of that, because I think it will eventually begin
to eat on her. The difference, given her background and her feelings.

*Actually Melissa is the daughter of Lanny, Martha's more secular granddaughter, and thus
she is not growing up in church. Melissa had been the flower girl at Pam's wedding, however,
and Martha's minor factual error here helps to underscore her point that social participation
is more important to her than doctrinal details.

Pamela can't help—you either grow or shrivel, and Pamela spent too many years the other way. Pamela believes in religion. I know she does. But she believes more in man's kindness to man than in Christ the son of God."

A Loyal Friend

When Jan had predicted Pam's eventual return from fundamentalism, I interpreted this as self-justificatory and wishful. Yet during the fortnight immediately following the Christian wedding—the very period when Pam had most publicly affirmed her commitment to Jesus as her personal savior—kin who were far less hostile to Pam's conversion echoed this prediction. Pam's mother was the first to do so, Pam's friend Lorraine, the second.

The wedding had inspired me to extend my oral history forays among Pamela's kin, and I placed Lorraine second on my postnuptial priority list. Sharing the church pew that afternoon with her, her new husband, and her daughter, Corinne, I had noted that, besides myself, she seemed to be the only friend of Pamela's in attendance who was not a member of Global Ministries. Reminded thus of Lorraine's kinlike ties to Pam, I made an early date to interview her more formally. Several days after my garden visit with Martha, I made my way to Take-off, a prison halfway house for women that SOS operated. Pam had helped Lorraine to secure her job as an evening-shift counselor here. Lorraine enjoyed the job, but its meager wages did not cover her expenses. Thus, in order to support her daughter, Lorraine still filled some of her available daytime hours with housecleaning jobs.

It required little conversation before I recognized that Lorraine is one of the more unusual Black women in the United States. Her views on domestic work first alerted me to her exceptional racial history. Depicting housecleaning employment more positively than do other minority group domestic workers portrayed in sociological literature,[1] Lorraine reminisced, "Pam and I, when we were going to school and also when we had hard times, we'd always do housework, because that's the best thing that you can do. It's quick money, and you feel good doing it, because it's a good job, and if you've got other worries, it's just kind of a therapy thing." She never had encountered racist employers, Lorraine claimed.

Indeed, Lorraine claimed that she never had experienced racism at all. "And people say, 'You lived in America and you haven't had any racism?' And I say 'No, I can really say I haven't.' " This extraordinary experience was partly a function of Lorraine's remarkably easygoing ability to ignore small offenses, but her eccentric personal history probably explains more of the enigma.

Lorraine, it turned out, had come by her own social tolerance quite "naturally." She had not grown up in the United States; nor had she been reared by a Black family or community. Adopted at her birth in 1933 by a white interfaith couple in England—her adoptive mother a Jew and Laborite, her father a Protestant "royalist"—Lorraine came of age in war-ravaged Europe exclusively in white company. She was four-teen before she actually saw another Black person. Two years later, two years after World War II, Lorraine eloped to Paris with a French air force man she had met at a London dance. The marriage lasted but three years before Lorraine, stunned by her husband's infidelity, returned home pregnant with her first child.

The Korean war brought a new wave of American servicemen to Eu-ropean bases, and attending base dances once again, Lorraine was sur-prised to find herself attracted to a "Yank." That he was Black strikes Lorraine as incidental: "No, I don't think race had anything to do with it. It was just something about Arthur's manner and how he conducts himself and stuff like that." Lorraine quickly agreed to marry Arthur and to return with him to his parents' home in Baltimore. In the United States too Lorraine, then twenty-one, encountered conditions unusual for members of her race. Arthur's parents had achieved greater affluence than the vast majority of African-Americans. His parents' lucrative beauty products business financed a higher education for Arthur, cul-minating in an engineering degree, that launched him on his successful, and highly mobile, career as an engineer. Crisscrossing the country with each of Arthur's new promotions, Lorraine considered herself happy in her work as full-time mother to the couple's two young children and as a homemaker in their frequently shifting homes. In 1966 Arthur moved his family to the Silicon Valley. They became the first Blacks to buy a house in the neighborhood where Lorraine's future family and work life would mingle inextricably with Pamela's. Lorraine and Pam each soon gave birth to Corinne and Jimmy, their youngest children, whom they raised as near siblings. From the last few years that the women spent as happy housewives of upwardly mobile Valley engineers, through their liberated, struggling single-parent days, and onto their respective re-marriages to less occupationally successful men, the two fast friends have shared more than two decades of personal and social transformation.

Lorraine's racial and gender consciousness was awakened by the sec-ond Black woman who appeared in the neighborhood. In turn, Lorraine prompted Pamela and the eight other members of their happy housewife circle to enroll in the new reentry program at East Valley Community College. The neighborhood's previously tranquil households never re-covered. "When Edna dropped in our life, that was when things started to happen to all of us," Lorraine recalled with humor. "She was like the catalyst. She just started to say, 'Why don't you go here?' and 'Why don't you go there. . . . come on, there's this women's group talking at San Jose State, now you come down and listen.' " So Lorraine and Pam and their friends went here and there, and they listened to the quietly subversive rhetoric of second-wave feminist consciousness raising. "It was women's rights, and why should women be in the kitchen, and it was all really strange to all of us," Lorraine continued. "Well, they would ask us all 'Don't you have any complaints?' 'No, we don't have any complaints,' " she parodied. " 'except sometimes it gets boring, but then everything gets boring.' "

Echoing Pamela's tales of the irreversible effect the East Valley pro-gram wreaked on these previously tranquil marriages, Lorraine described their husbands' mounting resistance to the developing assertiveness of their wives. Arthur protested when Lorraine accompanied Edna to Black Panther meetings in distant Oakland. But Arthur and Don did not protest when their wives proposed entering the East Valley program. They were too amused at first. "We asked our husbands," Lorraine recounted, "and they said—well, I think Don, he laughed. I remember the night that we told them too that we were going to take some courses at East Valley. Donald laughed and fell on the floor. My husband said, 'Oh, what next?' Or something good. And none of the husbands were in agreement, but it was like 'Oh, yes, dears, go on,' you know, the little pat, 'go on, this is something else these little dears are getting into; just let them go, they'll be happy and be off our backs, and we won't be saying we won't let them go,' So that is exactly what they did. They thought it was just a cute little thing, what the suburban housewife is doing now."

The joke paled quickly, however, as the women began to devote more of their attention to their courses than to their husbands' careers. When the East Valley English teacher invited the bewildered husbands to join their wives in discussing the implications of wives returning to school, they met in Lorraine and Arthur's house. "And I always remember my husband saying that he didn't know what was the matter with women, because the men were all making excellent money; they gave their wives and children everything they needed; what was wrong with them? He really couldn't see."

Seemingly successful marriages began to dissolve. Pam and Don separated first. The demise of Lorraine and Arthur's marriage was more prolonged and brutal. Lorraine refused to move with Arthur when he was offered another out-of-state promotion. " 'Well, I can't because I can't take that much time away from school,' I explained to him, and that's when I remember him getting really angry again; he said, 'That's gone too far.' " Arthur went ahead alone and bitter, while Lorraine completed the reentry program and joined Pam's experiments with the quasi-single life. A blend of nostalgia and embarrassment surrounds Lorraine's memories of this period. The reentry women used to meet for coffee in a motel adjacent to the campus. "So there was a group of us used to meet and go to dance and stuff . . . You know, when I look back on that, it was really short-lived, because it was all new to all of us, with this thing of 'I am woman, I'm going to do what I want.' . . . It was a good period and we did have some good times, but then there was a lot of sad times in with it too."

Her East Valley degree in hand, Lorraine did join Arthur in Albuquerque for what proved to be the rapid demise of their marriage. She found that her husband too had been making extensive use of local bars. Although Arthur had rarely drunk before, now "he was drinking really heavy, and when he was drinking the most, he became a totally different person." Arthur became abusive, and after he beat Lorraine badly a second time, she filed for her second divorce.

The only paid work experience Lorraine had accumulated during the twenty-five years of her marriage to Arthur was in the clandestine housecleaning career she and Pam had shared. Lorraine chose work at a battered women's shelter—the first full-time employment in her life—to support her financially and emotionally while she successfully fought Arthur's suit for custody of their daughter, Corinne. Lorraine cannot imagine how she could have endured "the really horrible experience" of the custody struggle without the support of Pam and her family. "So it was hard," Lorraine recalled, "but Pamela's family are just like a mum and dad to me; so if I hadn't had them, it would have been really tough." When the bitter battle was won, Lorraine returned to the Silicon Valley with Corinne to share a household with this second adoptive family.*

Even with mutual support, sharing the truly single life with Pam was far more difficult than Lorraine had expected. As soon as Lorraine left New Mexico, Arthur reneged on the alimony and child support payments that he had agreed to in the divorce settlement. Lorraine took a series of odd, and ill-paid, jobs including, predictably enough, one as an electronics assembler. She found the latter so odious, however, that she returned, with Pam's assistance, to social services and to housecleaning.

It was during the two and one-half years that Lorraine, Pam, and their children shared a household that Pam first began to date Al. Neither Lorraine nor their other friends could understand this attraction. "When she first got involved with Al," Lorraine explained, "Al was so different from the Al he is now. He was so chauvinistic. . . . And all of her friends would say 'Why is she going with him?' " Lorraine remembers Al as an angry, antisocial boor, a "miserable person" whom Pam's children hated. Lanny moved out, and Jimmy begged Lorraine to "go and live somewhere else so I can come and live with you, because I don't want to live with Al." Pam shocked her entire household, therefore, when she announced her intention to marry Al. "And I started laughing," Lorraine confesses. "I said, 'I don't believe you two guys are going to get married!' And she said, 'Why?' I said, 'Your relationship is so bad!' But they got married anyway."

Lorraine was neither surprised nor sorrowful when Pam and Al separated. Pam's recent religious conversion and marital reunion surprised her somewhat more, but she responded with characterisitc equanimity. The benefits to Pam were apparent. Lorraine missed the more spirited, fun-loving Pam of those East Valley days, which she judged to have been her friend's happiest period, but she was relieved to see that her chronic depression of recent years seemed to have lifted. And Lorraine felt she must give credit where it was due. Al had truly changed, she acknowledged, adding her voice to the chorus of witnesses to this not-so-minor

*Corinne, Lorraine's fourth and youngest child, was the only minor at the time of the divorce. She moved back and forth between her parents.

miracle. "I can see that the marriage is a lot better because he's supporting what she needs."

Lorraine was attuned, these days, to the benefits of successful conjugal life, having remarried recently herself. Her third husband, Carlos, a Central American immigrant, had been a cook at a nursing home where Lorraine worked before Pam helped her get the job at Take-off. Lorraine characterized her third marriage as egalitarian, relaxed, and independent. She and Carlos shared the household chores without conflict. "He'll cook, he'll clean and do the washing, and you don't have to ask him," she declared with pleasure. She also valued her husband's respect for her autonomy. "He's got very good attitudes," she explained, "and it's the type of marriage that I like. Because I couldn't go back to where I have to make sure he's comfortable before I can do what I wanted to do."

Lorraine had been a bit nonplussed during Pam's wedding ceremony, therefore, when she heard her friend vowing to be an obedient wife. " 'Did you sit down with the preacher beforehand?' " Lorraine claimed she had queried her friend after the ceremony. " 'Did you know what he was going to say?' And she said, 'No, we just told him that we wanted to confirm our vows.' And I said, 'You know I did get a little worried there when I heard 'obey this' and 'obey that,' and I thought, oh no, Lord, you can't have it all like that.' . . . Even Corinne said, 'Oh, Mom, what is going on here?' " But, because Lorraine thought she did understand what was going on, Pam's vows had bothered her less than they had Corinne, Pam's mother, or me. Taking the long view of Pamela's conversion, Lorraine had adopted a wait-and-see approach to its future course. "It's just an area that she's going through," Lorraine assured me as she too reminded me that Pam might easily change again. "And I know Pamela; she gets into things, and like I say, they become her whole life. And then she'll just look at it, and she might just toss it out; you never know. I think she might change again. Because I've seen her go through changes, so it wouldn't surprise me if she did, if she went just totally the opposite."

Pam on Pam

As I write this chapter in December 1988, more than two years have gone by since Lorraine, Martha, and Jan forecasted Pam's return from evangelicalism, and Pam has not yet "tossed out" Global Ministries or "gone just the opposite." Pam and I have maintained occasional contact since then. During our phone conversations and visits she has reflected repeatedly on the changing character of her religious and familial commitments. Pam's personal speculations, which suggest that her dog fight continues, underscore the indeterminacy of her future course. Believing that she should be granted some last words in this revisionary chapter, I conclude it with a chronological selection of summaries and excerpts from my "post-fieldwork" field notes.

The ensuing dialogues took place during a major setback period for charismatic Christian televangelists. News that broke in March 1987 that Praise the Lord media minister Jim Bakker and his associates had paid off church secretary Jessica Hahn to cover up Bakker's illicit liaison with her proved to be but the first and splashiest of the sex-and-money scandals that have tarnished the reputation of the moralistic and entrepreneurial Christian revivalist movement. An exposé of fiscal malfeasance in Jim and Tammy Bakker's evangelist empire ensued, followed by the highly publicized power struggles for control of PTL resources by Jerry Falwell and others. Marvin Gorman, a lesser-known Assemblies of God televangelist in Louisiana, was the next sexual sinner to be defrocked. Then one year later Gorman took his revenge on the more powerful rival who had accused both Jim Bakker and him when he exposed Jimmy Swaggart's own sexual transgressions. These scandals shook the confidence of even many of the faithful in the integrity of the contemporary Christian evangelical movement. They formed a backdrop and catalyst for many of Pam's reevaluations of Global Ministries' leaders and practices that I have recorded in the field notes from which the following summaries and selections are drawn.

March 31, 1987

My own father's recent death had interrupted my contact with Pam, who, I learned when I reached her at work this day, had just suffered a loss of her own. She and Al had recently returned from a visit to her brother in Nevada right before he died of lung cancer. Pam was preparing to speak that night at a small family service at which she planned to reveal that her brother had died peacefully because he and his daughter had secretly "accepted the Lord." Yet during this same phone conversation Pam told me that she and Al were thinking of leaving Global Ministries. The Bakker scandal was the precipitating factor.

"So it's a very big deal," Pam explained, "that Falwell who's a Baptist is taking over a pentecostal ministry." Pam had no use for Falwell, she claimed, "in fact I can get pretty violent on the subject," but she did admire his Bible teachings. However, she and Al had found themselves in grave conflict with Global leaders' responses to the Bakker revelations. Both Eleanor and Pastor Bill had defended the Bakkers from the pulpit, appealing to congregants to pray for them, love them, and forgive them, and to defend them against those media piranhas who were ever poised to persecute those doing the work of the Lord. While Pam proclaimed herself more than willing to forgive and pray for the Bakkers, she was not prepared to view them as victims of secular humanists. Rather the Bakkers had committed "the grave error of looking to themselves as important, rather than to God." "In a hundred years, who will remember any of us, or even any of the supposedly important people?" Pam continued. "The problem with Jim and Tammy Bakker is they got lost; they began to think that they were important; they lost sight of God, which is the whole point anyway." This is a recurrent problem with religious leaders, she had concluded, startling me by drawing an analogy to Jonestown. "Any time we hand over our responsibility for our faith to a leader, any time we say to them 'you lead me, you tell me what to do,' we're in trouble. Faith is a personal thing between you and God, and you have to be responsible for your faith. That's the kind of problem that led to Jim Jones and in other cults—people abdicating their responsibility for their own faith."

A troubling family argument had occurred recently, Pam reported, when Al had expressed similar sentiments to Katie and Eric. Pam acknowledged that she wished her daughter and son-in-law "weren't so indoctrinated. They are so isolated; they don't read the newspaper or anything, so they believe whatever Global leaders tell them." The defensive response of the Global hierarchy to the Bakker debacle had transformed Pam's latent doubts about the local ministry into manifest grievances. "We think we're getting sermonized rather than Bible teaching," Pam complained. Nor was she confident that "Global is using its time or money properly either."

Mounting disaffection was leading Pam and Al actively to consider leaving the Global fold, but Pam did not know how they would find a

167

more satisfying religious community in which to practice their still-secure, born-again faith. And concern for Katie and Eric was a more serious barrier to defection. "It would be hard on them if we left, and so it would be hard on us too," Pam worried aloud.

May 20, 1987

Pam and I spoke for the first time since I had returned to teaching. She declared herself delighted to hear my voice, claiming that I had been on her mind because she was reading a "terrific" book by a rabbi named Harold Kushner, titled *When All You've Ever Wanted Isn't Enough*. Years ago Pam had read and appreciated an earlier best-seller of his, *When Bad Things Happen to Good People*, and she was excited to discover that his new book was based on Ecclesiastes, "one of my *favorite* books of the Bible." Praising a rabbi's books prompted Pam to confess her ecumenism and to confirm thereby her mother's assessment that she believed more deeply in tolerance and humanity than in evangelical salvation doctrines. "I don't know that I have the Christian attitude one hundred percent. I'm not sure I accept the view that you have to have Christ as your personal savior or otherwise you're lost. I believe it for myself, but part of me is not sure that everyone has to accept Christ in this way."

After a lengthy exchange of family news, Pam and I resumed our conversation about the implications of the Bakker scandal. The topic unleashed a new torrent of Pam's disaffection with Global Ministries. "Al and I have been having our problems with the ministry lately," Pam lamented. They were "getting fed up" with continuing exhortations from the pulpit urging them to support and love the Bakkers "and to present a united front." It was fine "to practice forgiveness, but you also have to take this seriously and look at its lessons"—a task she found the ministry staff disturbingly reluctant to undertake. "Our days with Global are probably numbered," Pam predicted.

Yet in a talmudic spirit congruent with her then-current reading tastes, Pam shifted immediately to a discourse "on the other hand." She found herself increasingly committed to the evangelical work she and Al were doing with hospitalized psychiatric patients. They were visiting the mental hospital three times a week and finding the personal rewards manifold. "You know, there but for the grace of God," Pam explained. "I can see women in there for whatever reasons, they just haven't been able to handle things; life just battered them." Ministering to these unfortunate women, Pam reported, seemed to have a salutary effect on her own marriage. She and Al might enter the ward in the midst of a serious marital conflict, but shared work among the much more severely afflicted generally led them to find their own difficulties trivial. It would be hard to break their ties to these patients.

On the other hand, Pam was deeply troubled by the mounting tele-vangelist scandals, which she found "symptomatic of a widespread problem. It's of a piece with a kind of world where people expect to turn things over to the experts. People don't want to think for themselves, take responsiblity. They want people to tell them how to do everything. I used to make a joke that was half serious about how I'd start a business managing people's votes for them for a fee, and they wouldn't have to bother learning anything for themselves. I was sure I could make a fortune this way." Then without a word of transition, Pam announced, "I'm getting pretty sick of evangelicals lately."

July 7, 1987

After several years of teasing about our desires for personal transformation, Pam and I had arranged to splurge on a beauty "makeover" at a stylish San Francisco salon. When I called to convey final details about our appointments, Pam gave me an unexpected earful. She was in the mood for a "total makeover," she asserted. That past weekend she and Al had had their worst fight since his conversion. Worried that they "were slipping into bad habits," Pam was feeling "a need for things to be different in our relationship." Her anger had been so intense that she had heaved her wedding ring at Al and spent Sunday night alone in a motel. Now she was feeling more elation than remorse. Although she had reclaimed her ring and domicile the next day, she was not "rushing back in to resolve things with Al." Pam was determined, she informed me, to secure "some real changes on all sides," and she had already taken dramatic steps to effect significant self-reform.

In the meanest moment of last weekend's battle, Al had accused Pam of being alcoholic and self-involved. Ruminating postbellum alone in her motel room, Pam had decided not to let pride prevent her form confronting the possibility that more than malice motivated Al's charge. She had worried privately about her reliance on wine and tranquilizers; the next day she took public steps to examine this dependence. Pam called a friend "who's also someone who uses alcohol to relax with," and together they had attended an Alcoholics Anonymous meeting. "It was uplifting; I had a great experience," Pam enthused, describing virtues in the AA program similar to those that had once attracted her to Global Ministries. She had found support, sincerity, humility, and commitment in the AA group, and she planned to continue with the program.

July 9, 1987

Our makeover day was deeply pleasurable. No fashion scout asked us to model for a beauty magazine, but we enjoyed being pampered, indulged, and adorned. Pam reported with enthusiasm that she had spent the past three evenings attending AA meetings. I began to wonder whether she was in the midst of realizing Lorraine's prediction that she might throw herself into another life change as wholeheartedly as she had converted first to feminism and later to evangelicalism.

December 23, 1987

The passage of time and the press of teaching demands diminished my contact with Pam. By the time we met again just before Christmas, I was eager to learn whether or not she had left her marriage, her church, or both. I did not need to ask. Pam announced almost immediately that right after the New Year, she and Al planned to set themselves a deadline for departing Global Ministries together. "Give me a mainline denominational church any time," Pam proclaimed, as she initiated the most scathing appraisal of Global she had ever offered to me. "Our church is such a joke," she lamented. "If it were ever a joke before, now it's really a joke. We're going to look for another church."

So far as I could gather, no major events or significant changes in Global doctrine or practices had taken place since last we spoke. Rather, continuing media attention to the questionable moral and fiscal principles of prominent televangelists seemed to have provided Pam with a plausible narrative structure into which she could recast her prior doubts and grievances. Eleanor, Pam had decided, was becoming more dictatorial and sectarian, "and Bill Jensen is right in there with her in this. Eleanor is pushing quite a little nest for herself and her husband. She's back to being head again. No more of this pushing her husband forward like she was doing for a while. I wonder how she squares this with principles. It doesn't conflict with mine, but I wonder what she does with this." Disaffection with the ministry's uncritical response to the Bakker scandals was widespread, Pam maintained, and "people are dropping [out] like flies." She had discussed the situation with a friend from a Bible study group at her workplace who had warned her, "Hey, Pam, stay away from the Kool-Aid." "We're there because we love Eric and Katie and their baby, and we don't want to leave them there," she continued, answering a question I did not pose. "We don't want to leave them behind." However, it was just a matter of time, Pam repeated, before she and Al would find another church. "Stay tuned," Pam seemed to be saying. And I did.

April 14, 1988

Another teaching term and another major televangelist scandal intervened before next I checked the channel. Less had happened than Pam or I had anticipated. The fall of Jimmy Swaggart had deepened Pam's cynicism about moral hypocrisy and corruption among evangelical leaders, and she seemed ever more inclined to perceive these sins in the Global hierarchy. Pam scoffed when I again asked about the ministry's denominational affiliations. Eleanor, she reminded me, had selected and ordained all her ministers herself. Now they were trying "to set up a Project Foster which is some sort of a Bible school to ordain ministers, which I think is completely flaky, a joke." Nonetheless, Pam and Al had taken no steps to leave the ministry. "We are probably crazy, but we're still going," she mused. Once more she identified Katie and Eric as the primary cause of their inertia, and in my field notes I recorded my belief "that the community reinforcement and social structure for these family ties is something P would miss."

April 21, 1988

A leisurely Japanese lunch with Pam disabused me of such a simplistic reading of her attachment to the Global community. Worse, it threatened the basic structure of my analysis of the ministry's ironic contributions to postmodern family bonds. Embedded within a litany of the now-familiar criticisms of the ministry that Pam recited over our teriyaki was a new, provocative charge that Global was one of those greedy insitutions[2] that aggressively compete with the family for an individual's devotion and time. "They give you no support to helping or being with your relatives unless they're in the ministry," Pam complained.

Having completed, by this point, drafts of all but this chapter on Pamela's kin, I was not eager to summarily abandon its central interpretive lens. My resistance bred what I like to believe was the creative tension that generated subtle refinements in my understanding of Pam's gender and kinship strategies. It still was correct, I reassured myself, that the hybrid ideologies of Global Ministries could support many postmodern family renovations. However, it was crucial to emphasize how actively Pam selected from these, and from all other cultural resources, that which she found useful, meaningful, and attractive, while she ignored, rejected, or modified less appealing features. Pam found feminism, evangelical Christianity, and now AA, I decided, adaptable to her always-evolving, personal family reform goals.

Ever the cooperative research collaborator, Pam quickly offered fresh support to my revised view of her cultural strategies. She had continued, she informed me, but with declining frequency, her attendance at AA meetings and was finding progress through the twelve steps beneficial to her marriage as well as to her substance use problems. Relations with Al were secure and satisfying again. "We still fight," Pam observed, "but even the fights are good because we really let it out, because we have that confidence in the relationship which is so important." Pam's confidence in her marriage had deepened; she could now risk a greater integration of her faith and her feminism than she had previously been willing to attempt.

At Pam's request I had brought some literature I had recently discovered by evangelical Christian feminists, and she enthusiastically quizzed me on its contents. She recalled that soon after her conversion she had learned of this literature, but had chosen not to seek it. "I was trying to make a full commitment to Al and to my new faith, to focus on my new relationship," Pam explained, "and I didn't want to drag in parts of my past that might be disruptive." Consequently she had also consciously suppressed her feminist responses to mainstream evangelical literature. "When I came across some of the reactionary Christian literature on women's role, where all that women should do is stay home and bake cookies, I just dropped it," she recalled. Because Pam "didn't want to take it on as a confrontation," she had reassured herself with biblical passages more compatible with her views. Now, however, with her marriage and faith more secure and her illusions about Global Ministries gone, Pam believed she might be ready to engage with Christian feminism, to negotiate, perhaps, a reconciliation between her gray and spotted dogs.

May 12, 1988

Pam appeared well launched on this project. She sent me a copy of a special issue of *Christian History*, an evangelical periodical, devoted to women in the early church. The entire contents consisted of contributions by and in response to biblical feminists.

September 9, 1988

Inertia continued to reign supreme the last time I visited Pam before writing this chapter. She was still participating, skeptically, in Global Ministries, still attending AA, still a supporter of feminism. She had not reconciled her discordant selves but had reconciled herself to discordant realities. Global leaders, she decided, were not intentionally dishonest, but their deep desire to believe led them to proclaim dubious miraculous healings and to inflate the significance of their work. Most of the Global congregants, meanwhile, were "very good, loving people" whose company and affection Pam had come to value. Pam and Al continued to challenge managerial practices in the ministry, but they no longer spoke of "breaking fellowship." And, while Pam had thoroughly enjoyed an AA conference for women that she had attended recently at a nearby campus, AA had not replaced Christian counseling as the dominant force in her personal life.

My mild disappointment with the inconclusive character of this last installment of field notes alerted me to the vicarious, as well as literary, investment I had staked in Pam's personal narrative. Perhaps I had hoped to conclude this portion of the book with news that, as her past and present kin had predicted, Pam would be "tossing out" her evangelical identity, or that, as I had begun to anticipate, she was joining the Christian feminist movement. Either development could have enhanced the dramatic structure of this ethnography. But as Pam offered no evidence that either course was likely soon, my readers and I must learn to live without narrative closure. A postmodern woman, Pam finds good reasons to feed a heterogeneous kennel.

II

THE LEWISONS: HIGH-TECH VISIONS AND BATTERED DREAMS

8

The Last "Modern" Family in Town

To say that they clashed in many ways and in many ways disappointed each other is to say no more than that they were married, and for a long time. They acted out the possibilities of the form.

—Phyllis Rose, *Parallel Lives*

On a mid-November afternoon in 1984, I drove my made-in-Japan automobile to Foothill Vista, a Silicon Valley town whose corridors of semiconductor firms and shopping malls partition residential neighborhoods composed primarily of post–World War II, single-family, "crabgrass frontier" dwellings.[1] It was one week after my fateful revelation interview with Pam and one week after Reagan's landslide reelection. I came to Foothill Vista in search of a white working-class family with an electronics industry occupational history, the sort of family that the media had depicted as the most socially significant base of Reagan's support. I was seeking families for my study with more conventional white working-class patterns and histories than Pam's or than the unmarried welfare mothers I had interviewed at SOS. I hoped to find nuclear families based on long-term, intact marriages with male primary breadwinners whose employment records had been reasonably steady—families whose gender norms and attitudes, therefore, I presumed, would be more conventionally working class as well.

A weathered limestone signpost marked the entrance to Orchard Park, the 1950s tract house subdivision where the Lewisons resided, and where I found cultural markings reassuring to my social stereotypes. The pastel rows of modest, aging "contemporary" ranch houses, their driveways filled with American-made vehicles (with pickup trucks and RVs in generous supply), the plethora of plastic low-riders, trikes, and fantasy artillery strewn across unevenly tended lawns, gave Orchard Park a personally resonant appearance. It had the familiar, if somewhat shabbier, look of the subdivision where in 1955 my own parents had established an isolated modern nuclear household after spending the first thirteen years of their marriage in an extended family with my maternal grandparents.

Outward social indicators at the Lewison household seemed particularly promising. Smoke rising from a chimney and the soundtrack of a daytime TV movie gave visual and auditory signs of life to a dwelling otherwise blocked from view by the five vehicles in varying states of repair that overflowed its two-car driveway and surrounds. The draperies were drawn, but the rain-warped screen door revealed a dark, smoke-filled living room crowded with well-worn furniture, family photographs, and bric-a-brac. My appointment was with Dotty Lewison, but her heavily tattooed husband, Lou, answered the door instead. Dotty was finishing her bath, Lou informed me, as he invited me in and offered to reheat a cup of coffee on the micro-go-round. Accepting Lou's hospitality, I attempted to introduce myself to a youthful, and uninterested, couple whom I found snuggling, smoking, and sipping cola on the sofa.

As Lou placed a coffee cup and a jar of powdered dairy substitute for me on the large, cluttered dining-room table, another caller rattled the screen. A neighbor's teenage son was delivering Dotty's order from a Gifts and Gadgets party that his mother had hosted.[2] The mounting social chatter seemed to hasten Dotty's sudden, theatrical entrance. Out of the bedroom hallway emerged a large, lively woman clad in a floor-length black negligee ensemble who lighted a cigarette as she greeted kin and callers with gusto. Thanking and hugging the courier while she relieved him of his burden, Dotty piled the cargo in front of me on the table's densely littered surface. "My kids call me a pack rat, Judith," Dotty announced, addressing me, as she was always to do, by my formal, given name rather than by the informal "Judy" preferred by most of my acquaintances. "And they're right." She giggled proudly, thereby triggering a coughing fit that failed to interrupt her chain-smoking.

After Dotty had supplied herself with water, coffee, cola, and an ashtray, she sat down beside me to unpack and savor her new wares. With the zeal of a game-show hostess, Dotty exhibited each of her three purchases. The first, a set of plastic clamps designed to keep opened bags of potato chips from wilting, she promptly put to use. "I think that's so clever, don't you?" Dotty bubbled. "And it's good for my diet, because I won't feel like I have to finish the bag to keep from wasting it." Dotty was equally excited about her second acquisition, two families of porcelain mice fashioned into hooks for hanging Christmas stockings above the fireplace. "I think they are just adorable, and I bought enough for all the grandchildren to hang a stocking at Grandma and Grandpa's house." Finally Dotty unveiled the *pièce de résistance,* a massive, elaborately gilded, white Bible. "Isn't it just gorgeous, Judith?" she enthused. "Our old one was getting really shabby, and I just couldn't resist."

The aftershocks of my recent interview with Pam and of Reagan's conservative electoral triumph were still reverberating in my secular feminist soul. I struggled to assume sufficient sociological detachment to cushion the impact of the unwelcome political sentiments I expected the Lewisons to express. Seldom have I been as pleased to have my prejudices exposed. During the ensuing three hours, while Lou, as backseat archivist, monitored the accuracy of his wife's account from his TV armchair, Dotty filled my tape cassette with precisely the sort of Silicon Valley working-class family narrative I had hoped to "discover." So direct was her manner and so warm her personality that no detachment on my part was possible; nor, fortunately, was it needed.

Transcribing the tapes from this interview the next day, I decided euphorically that I had stumbled onto personal and sociological paydirt. The Lewisons satisfied all the criteria, and then some, that my former colleague and I had established to identify bona fide members of the electronics industry working class. Dotty and Lou's then thirty-year-long marriage had survived all three tumultuous decades of Silicon Valley development. And Dotty, Lou, and four of their five adult children, including the romantically engrossed youth occupying the living-room sofa, had worked in the electronics industry in a broad array of companies, at a wide range of lower- to middle-level occupational categories, and with startlingly diverse mobility patterns.

Minutes after we met, fifty-year-old Lou had told me how a severe heart attack several years earlier had forced him to retire from a successful career as a line maintenance mechanic and supervisor. Former home-maker Dotty, then a part-time office receptionist, once had been an assembly worker in semiconductors. The Lewisons' oldest child, Kristina, a single mother, was succeeding, Dotty boasted, as a designer-drafter at one of the biggest semiconductor firms in the world. Two married daughters and the temporarily resident youngest son, however, had less auspicious histories as occasional assemblers and operatives. Lou, Jr., a married son serving in the military abroad, was the sole family member to avoid employment in the electronics industry. Receiving mechanical training from the military as his father once had done, "Loujoo," as the Lewisons called him, was his father's pride and pleasure, and the U.S. base in Europe where he lived with his wife and baby served as the prime incentive for Dotty's paid employment. She was working, Dotty informed me, to save enough money so that she and her husband could visit the junior Lewison household the following summer.

Not only did the Lewisons satisfy formal criteria for inclusion in my study, but also I could scarcely have been more satisfied with the narrative depicting their family and work histories that Dotty and Lou constructed jointly during my first visit. It closely matched my preliminary notions about the relationships between the rise of the electronics industry, feminism, and white working-class family transformations. The Lewisons portrayed their conjugal history as that of a struggling, but warm and loving, 1950s-style family. I deduced they had achieved that ephemeral "modern" family structure partly because of the mobility opportunites that the electronics industry had at first extended to white men.

Dotty had been a teenager in 1954 when she met and married Lou, a sailor mechanic who had dropped out of school in the ninth grade. She bore their five children at nearly regular two-year intervals during the first decade of their marriage while also making occasional forays into the world of paid work, including one two-year stint in the late 1950s assembling semiconductors. But Dotty neither perceived nor desired significant opportunities for personal advancement in electronics or any occupation at that time. Instead, several years later she pushed Lou to enter the industry. This proved at first to be a successful strategy for *family* economic mobility, but one that was to have contradictory effects on the Lewisons' marital relationship as well as on Dotty's achievement goals. With his mechanical aptitude and naval background, and with on-the-job training, Lou steadily advanced to the position of line maintenance engineer. Then, as he explained, "the companies didn't have many choices. No one even knew what a circuit looked like. . . . But you can't find many engineers starting out now who don't enter with degrees, because the companies have a lot more choices now."

The industrial bough that had nestled the Lewison cradle, however, also later hurled it from the tree. With residual anger and some bitterness, Dotty and Lou detailed the catastrophic toll that the industry's work schedules and demands had exacted from Lou. They spoke of the twelve-to-fourteen-hour days and the frequent three-day shifts that led work-aholic Lou to neglect his family completely, precipitating a marital crisis and two-year separation in the mid-1970s. Dotty had become a grass-roots community activist by then, as 1960s' social currents stirred her imagination and nudged the traditional female volunteer labors she per-formed for the public schools and her Methodist church in less traditional directions. She organized local food co-ops and joined grass-roots efforts for multicultural education and fair housing reforms. These activities seemed to lead organically to her involvement in local feminist activities, including the shelter movement for battered women.

Dotty implied that engagement in feminist groups, in turn, led her to reappraise her deteriorating marriage and gave her the confidence to risk living as a single mother. Thus in 1974 Dotty asked Lou to move out. Like Pam and Lorraine, Dotty found the challenges of single-parent life both daunting and exhilarating. Enduring the humiliations of poverty and the welfare system, Dotty enrolled, as Pam and her friends had done, in women's reentry courses at a local community college. There she too gathered strength and self-esteem. "Emotionally it felt a lot better. I felt a lot stronger. Going to school, earning a 4.0, working part time, I felt really great about myself." Dating other men also "was okay, but it wasn't okay," Dotty hedged. "I think I was terribly spoiled being married to him."

Dotty seemed proud of this history of community activism and inde-pendence, but in remarks like the preceding, she also led me to believe that, to a large extent, these had been creative responses to neglect by her workaholic husband. She affixed unequivocal blame for their near divorce on Lou's overly dutiful response to outrageous industry demands, and Lou offered corroborating testimony. "You can believe," Dotty as-serted in response to my question about the reasons for that separation, "that it's because he worked forty million hours. He was married to his job. I *hated* it!" "He was so in love with work," she continued, "I just couldn't handle it anymore. I told him if he was just going to be at work he might just as well live there because he wasn't doing any good here. He never saw me or any of the kids." Lou supported his wife's account, explaining in his more diffident manner that while he had enjoyed his work, he had had to work like that "just to do the job."

More pointedly, Dotty blamed the electronics industry for the devastating heart attack Lou suffered in 1976, which permanently disabled him and forced him several years later into his reluctant state of early retirement. "I attribute his health directly to the fact that he worked so damn many hours; and so did the doctors." But, an irrepressible believer in the silver-lined cloud maxim, Dotty also credited Lou's heart attack with prompting their reconciliation and ensuing marital reforms. "I think that brought everything to a head for me. I decided this is really ridiculous. I think what I really want is him, and I don't want him to die." Thus Dotty had invited Lou back home, and his disability contributed to a gradual restructuring of the household division of labor. Forced to retire after a second heart attack followed his return to work, Lou came to do most of the housework, and as her taste for community activism waned, Dotty turned to part-time paid work to supplement Lou's disability payments. Lou's brush with death also bequeathed him a renewed appreciation for life and a more tolerant attitude toward his wife, children, and others. So, "thank God for the heart attack," Dotty sermonized.

What excited me most about the Lewisons was how they promised to allow me to have my cake and eat it too. They fit all the formal criteria for inclusion in my working-class sample and my hunches about links between occupational and family structural changes, but not my social prejudices. Dotty, for example, lent immediate, unabashed support to my observation that they seemed to have lived a paradigmatic Silicon Valley drama. "I know, I know," she assented. "I have other friends whose husbands worked in electronics, and they're now separated and divorced." Yet the Lewisons' gender practices and political views appeared to be far more progressive and feminist than I had imagined I would find among white working-class people in the Silicon Valley. Although no longer politically active, Dotty still expressed support for feminism, "depending," she quickly inserted, "on what you mean by feminism." And Lou, despite a Southern rural upbringing and military background, seemed sympathetic to Dotty's political views and proud of her feistiness. Finding these challenges to my preconceptions much more gratifying than those Pam had dealt me when she "came out" as a born-again the week before, I eagerly accepted Dotty's invitation to return soon for another lengthy interview. That second visit led to a third, and without planning it, I found I had embarked on an in-depth study of a second set of Silicon Valley kin.

REVISIONS/RASHOMAN

Increasing contact with the Lewisons, as ethnographic work is wont to do, quickly introduced numerous revisions and confusions into the plot. Most of the time the varied voices in Pamela's family could be harmonized. But, the more I spoke with the Lewisons, and the more Lewisons I spoke with, the more I recognized that, with all due respect to Tolstoy, under postmodern conditions "happy" families are not all alike. Any unitary family history imposes arbitrary order upon the multiple, and often contradictory, subjectivities of the individuals whose diverse narratives it attempts to distill. It masks, thereby, those telling discrepancies between the His and Her marriages,[3] as well as the Yours and Mine parent, child, sibling, and extended kin relationships that all families contain. The unitary portrait of the Lewisons just presented approximates the manner in which Dotty and Lou jointly chose to represent their family history to me during our first encounter.

Faint signals that more traumas than those inflicted by Lou's work history had disrupted the Lewison household flashed fleetingly across the screen during my second visit to Orchard Park. Dotty depicted numerous occasions when she had assisted victims of rape, sexual molestation, and wife and child abuse in their deceptively tranquil-looking neighborhood. Discussing her work in the local shelter movement on behalf of battered women and children, Dotty recalled how shocked she had been. "I just couldn't believe," she claimed at first, "that people could lose control like that!" "And yet, you know," she added with several pregnant pauses, "even though you're shocked, having had five children, I can certainly sympathize. And I understand how you can get to the point where you are just so snowed under—and you feel like your cup is empty—and there's just so much coming down on you—that you just want to kill everybody—and yourself included."

Not all the abuse victims Dotty had assisted, I soon realized, were extrafamilial. Dotty mentioned the time when at fourteen her youngest son had been enticed into the playroom of a neighborhood man who molested young boys. Dotty believed, but was not certain, that Danny had been spared molestation. Her first grandchild, Tommy, however, had suffered a serious sexual assault by a babysitter when barely a toddler. And battering so severe that it damaged her kidney underlay the divorce of Tommy's mother, Kristina. Nor did it seem that the Lewisons were always innocent victims of external abuse. Describing her childhood in rural California, Dotty reminisced about the humanitarian treatment that her grandfather, a police officer, habitually extended to adolescent offenders in the youth detention center he had administered. Then, by contrast, she slipped in without elaborating how poorly her son Danny had been treated in a Silicon Valley juvenile hall. Just in passing also, while discussing her growing involvement in a "metaphysical" church, did Dotty mention her concern about Loujoo's "violent karma." He had narrowly escaped death a few years back when he participated in a racial altercation in boot camp.

Pursuing the subject of Dotty's feminist history also produced muted revisionary notes to the prior week's narrative of marital accord. Lou repeated his appreciation for Dotty's assertiveness and his claim that he had always supported her political work, but she cautiously reminded him of times when he "had had some trouble accepting some of the things that I got really radical about" and how he had resented coming home to meetings in their house. Just as gently Dotty challenged Lou's claim that they had always divided housework "according to what each likes." She saw the current equitable division of labor as a postreunion achievement.

As I made ready to conclude our second visit and Dotty agreed to help me try to interview their children, she alluded to additional closeted family skeletons. Although eager to facilitate my study, Dotty did not want to send me to the home of her third daughter, Carole "because it reminds me of Tobacco Road, to be quite blunt." With a blend of embarrassment and contempt, Dotty depicted a chaotic, unkempt, joint household that Carole, her husband, and their three young children shared with some of Carole's in-laws and assorted, transient others. It was supported by the underpaid employment of women dominated and exploited by men who were "creeps." "The women do everything, and the men order them around," Dotty elaborated, her normally resonant voice constricting with ire, "and let me tell you, I get *very angry,* I get angry—God, that pisses me off—I can hardly be nice to that prick, oooh, God it pisses me off. And it makes me so angry at my daughter! How dare she?! She has been raised better than that!"

How *had* the Lewison children been raised, I began to wonder, as I pondered these first glimpses of tarnish on the sheen of the happy family image I had been savoring since leaving Orchard Park the week before. How harmonious a marriage had Dotty and Lou enjoyed prior to his all-consuming electronics career, and had other fault lines presaged their mid-seventies' cleavage? As if she perceived and wished to allay my budding doubts, Dotty spontaneously reaffirmed her attachment to her husband. She believed, she said, that we are all put on earth for a purpose, and hers might be to help Lou, "because he is terribly important." In fact, a "past life reading" of Dotty had revealed that this was the third life in which she and Lou had been together. "And I can believe that"— Dotty chuckled—"We just kind of fit so well."

It seemed time to enhance my own past life reading of the Lewisons by interviewing the central parties separately. I decided to avoid, or at least defer, establishing a dyadic female bond with Dotty that might threaten her husband and exclude him from the study. Joking with taciturn Lou about how his loquacious wife had been dominating my air waves to shield me from his views, I asked if I could visit him alone next while Dotty was at work. "It don't bother me none," Lou agreed.

LOUIS LEWISON: "IT DON'T BOTHER ME NONE"

"Hello, young lady," Lou greeted me, with chivalrous disregard for facial data, when I interrupted his television viewing two days later. "Come on in; I just made a fresh pot of coffee." Danny, who was stretched out on the sofa in his long johns, seemed to take my entrance as his cue to exit. Left alone together for the first time, both Lou and I were ill at ease. I was nervous about asking, and Lou about responding to, questions he might consider too personal or embarrassing. I had more cause for concern than he. I both worried and hoped that my private inquiries would elicit major revelations and deviations from the sanitized version of their marital history that Dotty had transmitted with his assistance. I had failed to reckon, however, with Lou's socialization as a rural Southern male that had rendered him "articulate in the rhetoric of silence."[4] Lou confessed that he would hate my "kind of work—talking to people— I would find it boring as hell, just not my cup of tea." And while he courteously answered all of my questions, he accurately depicted himself, echoing Al, as "not a very open person."

Accordingly, Lou was circumspect at best whenever our conversational focus was on his marriage or emotions. In understated terms he relayed the painful circumstances of his childhood. The eighth of eleven children, Lou was born in 1933 on a prospering farm in Georgia. But Lou's father was "a drunkard" and brutal to his wife and children. Shortly after Lou's birth his father's heavy drinking problem cost the family its farm. Lou claimed to remember a time from his early childhood when his father had beaten his mother so badly that Lou's older brothers had tied their father to a bed on the front porch and kept him there for two weeks. But the battering continued, and when Lou was eight his adult siblings forced their father to move out of the house for several years.

Growing up in this large, downwardly mobile, single-mother household, Lou and his siblings all had worked as early as they could. Predictably Lou spoke about his work history with greater ease and fluency than of his affective life. With an alloy of pride and resentment, Lou explained that he had quit school in the ninth grade because "I always had to work." He joined the navy in 1952, which he described as "the best thing that ever happened to me." The navy "got me away from the house," it trained him in hydraulics as a metalsmith, and it brought him to Santa Clara County, where he met Dotty on a blind date.

If I had thought our lengthy wind-up would encourage Lou to pitch a few curves into the seamless narrative of his marital history, I was to be quickly disappointed. Instead Lou reaffirmed, and scarcely amplified, that text of a good marriage temporarily thrown off track by his preoccupation with his once-promising and demanding electronics career. Although the pace and pressures of his job had been grueling, Lou conceded that he had "loved the work. I enjoyed my work tremendously. I was learning something all the time. I hate to do something when I'm not learning something. I was learning something every hour." Lou claimed not to have noticed Dotty's disaffection or that his work was causing "that much of a problem." So far as he was concerned, his marital troubles began abruptly in 1974 with a separation he neither anticipated nor desired. "She's the one who wanted all this stuff; you'll have to ask her why," he declared, portraying himself as Dotty's passive victim. He had been shocked and devastated by the rupture, but felt that "there was nothing I could do about it." It pained Lou deeply when he realized that Dotty was seeing others, but he had never returned the insult himself, he claimed, partly because he "didn't want to bother" and in part because "it never entered my mind that we wouldn't get back together."

Dotty was at her sons' high-school football game with their coach, her live-in lover, and Lou was there working the down chains when he suffered the nearly fatal heart attack that was to make his reunion prophecy come true. Dotty rode in the ambulance that took Lou to the hospital and, although he told her that "she didn't have to bother," she visited him every day. A few months later, shortly after Christmas, Dotty invited her disabled husband to move back home. Lou claimed not to know how or why Dotty's relationship with her lover ended. He had never asked. "Why bother? It just makes it worse." He was simply gratified that Dotty had taken him back and seen him through his period of gravest need.

Since then the Lewisons' marriage had improved "one hundred percent," Lou estimated. His "stubborn, male ego" lost several years of battle to continue working, but once he made peace with his disability, his marriage and family relationships reaped the benefits. He was more affectionate than he used to be, and he had a better understanding of how to sustain a good marriage: "better communication, more communication; don't be so stubborn; let the other person know what you're thinking." Lou professed attitudes toward the household division of labor that seemed a model of nonsexist rationality. He did the housework now that Dotty was working part time, claiming that they "had never had any big conflict over who does this or who does that; this is a man's job, or this is a woman's job. I always thought that was stupid. What difference does it make whose job it is?"

Lou expressed the hope, and then a note of doubt, that his sons would exhibit equally sensible gender values. He was confident, he claimed, that Loujoo was a similarly enlightened husband and father, "but the youngest one here, I think, is gonna be, try to be, domineering as hell." Danny, the object of Lou's criticism, occasioned his father's first display of intolerance. Lou viewed Danny as a spoiled, lazy, foolish moocher, and he seemed to blame these ne'er-do-well traits on Dotty's coddling. Two years ago Lou had "finally convinced Dotty to quit catering to Danny, quit doling out money to him, that he has to get out and learn on his own." The couple had kicked Danny out of the house, but recently the boy had appealed to Dotty for temporary shelter. Despite Lou's objections, she had allowed her youngest to return. "Been me, he wouldn't a never," Lou volunteered with sudden gratuitous hostility. "I could've cared if he had slept out on the sidewalk in the rain."

Quickly regaining his equanimity, Lou provided more temperate, often empathic, characterizations of his other children. He also began to represent himself as more racially tolerant than he had been raised to be. We had just begun to discuss some of the racial attitudes that Lou had developed growing up in a declining white Southern family when a knock on the door interrupted us. His family was "very against the colored," Lou whispered to me over his shoulder as he greeted the Filippina wife of Loujoo's Black recruiting officer. Wishing to retrieve my own son from his extended day-care program, I took the woman's entrance as an opportunity to exit. Once more I left the Lewison household as I had come, bearing an intact narrative of its intact marriage.

DOTTY LEWISON: "I'M NO ANGEL"

Time alone with Dotty after we had established a relationship of substantial rapport and trust radically shattered the homey tale of a rescued, wayward Silicon Valley marriage that the couple had presented for scholarly scrutiny. I had spent two months of continuing visits with Lou alone and with Dotty and Lou together, during which time I attained modest glimpses of conflicts over child rearing, money, and church attendance that long predated the couple's mid-seventies marital crisis. At last Dotty and I decided to begin meeting unchaperoned together outside the Lewison home. Straight away quite a different, indeed nearly an inverse, narrative emerged.

In place of the fable of a cohesive, happy family disrupted by the inhuman demands of the electronics industry, Dotty plied me with stories about a trauma-riddled, fractious household, one afflicted by a virtual litany of disorders featured in textbooks on dysfunctional families. Dotty's tales of wife-battering and child abuse, of alcohol, drug, and legal trouble, of sexual infidelities and emotional breakdown provided humbling testimony to the clichéd aphorism that things are rarely what they seem.

A fifth-generation Californian, Dotty, like Lou, grew up on a farm in conditions of greater material and emotional comfort than her husband, but with even less household stability. Soon after her birth, her father deserted the family. Dotty's mother remarried, only to become widowed by or divorced from four additional spouses. Dotty was a young teenager when brought to the Bay Area by her second stepfather. A new school friend arranged Dotty's auspicious blind date with Lou. Despite the model of marital instability her own mother had provided—or rather, partly because of it—Dotty rushed into marriage without "an inkling" of what lay ahead. "I had this goddamned Pollyanna idea that my generation seemed to have been taught and bred, or whatever, that marriage is peaches and cream and it is *the* way to live, and it's, nothing ever goes wrong, it's just this rosy little healthy glow around it—all the bullshit. And I bought it—hook, line, and sinker. . . . My God, my mother was married six times! You'd think I would have picked up on some of that shit. No, I was gonna be different."

Marriage to Lou did prove to be more permanent and different from Dotty's mother's numerous unions, but it was also radically different from what Dotty had anticipated. The struggling young couple's material circumstances surpassed those in which Lou was reared, but they represented notable downward mobility for Dotty whose fifties domestic fantasies soon received more serious bruises. From the earliest days of their marriage, Dotty revealed, violent conflicts between the young couple, particularly over child-rearing differences, had resulted in a cycle of battering, separation, and reunion. Lou replicated his father's brutal disciplinary methods, and Dotty's efforts to protect her children often resulted in spousal physical combat. She generally was able to stop Lou from beating their children, Dotty claimed, but "I could not stop him from beating me." Lou would beat her when "he felt trapped" and when he felt "provoked" by her angry outbursts. Then, as Dotty became trapped with young children in her violent marriage, she too "would lose it with the kids once in a while."

Numerous brief marital separations preceded the rupture in 1974 that Lou defined as the beginning of their troubles. According to Dotty, early in their marriage the couple developed a repetitive pattern in which after a period of battering, she would kick Lou out of the house for a week or more. When tempers cooled, she would agree to reconcile only if Lou agreed to marriage counseling. With a counselor's aid their relations would improve for a while. As soon as the counseling safety valve was capped, however, the vicious cycle of entrapment and violence would resume.

By the early seventies Dotty felt that she "just couldn't take any more shit" and that if she and Lou did not separate soon, "one of us was going to get killed." Viewed in this frame, the links between Lou's workaholism and the couple's near divorce appeared considerably more dynamic than first reported. Lou's escape into work seemed as much a response to as it was a cause of their marital crisis and a source of familial relief as well as neglect.

Unlike Lou, Dotty experienced the big separation as a liberation: "It was terrific, it was terrific, it was great. Oh, my God, it was like night and day." "The kids were happier," home life was peaceful, and before long Dotty became romantically involved with Ed, her sons' football coach. Nor had Lou behaved quite so chastely or patiently as he had claimed while awaiting the reunion that he regarded as inevitable. "Didn't he tell you about Ellen?" Dotty quizzed, then chuckled as she perceived my ignorance of the woman from Lou's assembly line that he had dated. "Oh, that fucker, he didn't tell you; too bad." Dotty owned that her romantic liaison had been more serious than Lou's, and "it became a little hairy" when Lou discovered that Dotty's new beau had moved into his former bedroom. In a spirit I found remarkably good-humored, Dotty recounted how Lou had "kept coming over and peeping in windows, and shit. Yeah, it got really sick." On several occasions Lou brought a shotgun onto the community college campus where Dotty was enrolled in courses. Scared that he would hurt her or someone else, Dotty finally decided "screw it, so I'll quit school."

Lou's devastating heart attack probably was the underlying cause of Dotty's change of heart, but much less directly so than he had imagined. Dotty and the Lewison children assumed caretaking responsibilities for Lou, and the family crisis subjected Dotty's romance to substantial strain. But it was not until her live-in lover abruptly and hurtfully deserted her that she invited her permanently disabled husband (and his disability pension) to move back home. Wielding the undeniable emotional balance of power in the relationship, Dotty could do so on her own rather harsh terms. She would have total autonomy over her time and her relationships, she claimed to have warned Lou, and she would never again tolerate even a threat of violence.

Although her sympathy for Lou, her own convenience, and other pragmatic interests weighed more heavily than renewed affection in her decision to rebuild her marriage, Dotty did confirm her husband's view that their relationship had improved substantially since then. Marital counseling had played no role in this successful reconciliation, because this time, ironically, Dotty was the one who "flat-ass refused to go." Instead the Lewisons had taught themselves how to live together non-violently. The main source of their hard-won marital harmony, Dotty believed, was that "the issues are gone." With the children mostly grown and (mostly) out of the house and with their economic circumstances improved, Lou and Dotty found much less to brawl over.[5]

The role reversal in the Lewisons' division of labor had also contributed to the couple's successful marital reconstruction, but it had been far more difficult to achieve than Lou maintained. "An awful lot of yelling went into that adjustment," Dotty reported, remembering how coming to terms with the medical urgency of his retirement and learning to stay at home had almost destroyed Lou. Dotty viewed his previous attitudes toward family and work roles as far less enlightened than he acknowledged. He had bitterly resented her stints in the paid work force when the children were young, Dotty insisted, tolerating brief episodes only when family economic needs were acute. Thus, Lou had found particularly galling the two years that Dotty earned a higher wage as an electronics worker than he was receiving as a gas station attendant. Later Dotty had found it difficult to cede most of the house and garden work to Lou. She did so in order "to give Lou a sense of accomplishment and to help him feel needed," but this was a sacrifice at first: "I felt like he was trying to take over my whole realm of living."

Those spontaneous expressions of affection that Dotty showered on Lou in my presence, such as "he'd better not die; he doesn't dare leave me," were, she confided, another instance of self-conscious service to Lou's injured ego. "I think he needs to hear that, and it doesn't hurt to tell a little white lie sometimes if it makes him feel better. It's terribly important to him to feel—well, hell, who isn't it important to feel needed to?" Lou's death would upset Dotty seriously, she believed, but she believed also that "my life wouldn't end."

Time alone with Dotty afforded altered angles on most intrafamilial relationships, such as Lou's antagonism toward his youngest child and his partiality toward Loujoo. Danny's birth coincided with one of Dotty's earlier love affairs ("Hell, I'm no angel," Dotty conceded), and the ambiguity of Danny's paternity differentially affected Lou's and Dotty's affection for him. Loujoo reaped surplus paternal rewards from this, Dotty believed, including a portion of paternal myopia. Loujoo modeled himself after his father, but far less laudably, in Dotty's view, than Lou perceived. He too had a violent streak, which Dotty had seen him visit upon his wife as, in earlier days, he had abused his siblings.

Having commenced my case study of the Lewisons partly to mitigate the personal threat that Pamela's born-again revelation represented, my respite proved to be short-lived. After typecasting the Lewisons as a harmonious, progressive working-class family, I found Dotty's revelations of abuse at least as disturbing as Pam's religious conversion had been. In addition to underscoring the wisdom of Jessie Bernard's characterization of His and Her marriages, the irreconcilable discrepancies between much of the couple's independent testimony on their shared history suggested the need to augment my roster of family witnesses. Supplementary perspectives, such as those summarized next from the oldest and the youngest of the Lewison offspring, confirm the existence of Yours and Mine parent-child and sibling relationships, while doing little to resolve textual dissonance.[6]

KRISTINA: THE VIEW FROM A PARK BENCH

One mild California January afternoon in 1985, Dotty and I were visiting in a public park when she pointed out a small duplex apartment building as her eldest child's residence. Kristina was home on one of the weeklong "vacations" that Advanced Semi-Conductor (ASC) imposed on its employees during the industry recession that occurred in 1984–85. Pride in her firstborn and a desire to assist my study overcame the surprisingly deferential anxiety Dotty displayed as she decided to appear with me unannounced on her daughter's doorstep. Kristina greeted me with skeptical reserve, but not hostility, and agreed to meet with me soon "to set the record straight."

Although twenty-eight-year-old Kristina was a high-school dropout and a single mother, she was nonetheless the most ambitious and occupationally successful of the Lewison children. Like Pamela's firstborn, Kristina was an electronics industry drafter, but her career as a "permanent" employee was more successful, demanding, and gratifying than were Lanny's temporary job shop gigs. Kristina's high-pressured position as a designer-drafter with supervisory responsibilities demanded levels of commitment and work schedules that occasionally rivaled those of her father.

Indeed Kristina identified Lou as the central source of her driving career ambition, but claimed that he served as a negative inspiration. Her career, Kris insisted, "was a vendetta—out-and-out vendetta" against a father whom she resented bitterly, yet so clearly also admired and for whose affection and approval she seemed to hunger. Once Lou had warned Kris that she was going to wind up "sleeping on park benches with any hobo that was around," and while the parents both dismissed his remark as passing sarcasm, Kris "vowed that some day my father would eat his words." In vengeance, she had determined to best her father's highest earnings and to purchase a park bench when she did.

It took Kristina no time at all to best her mother's narrative of the Lewisons' violent family history. With her tough, no-one-messes-with-me demeanor, Kris presented the harshest view of her family I was to encounter. She had grown up in a "war zone," Kris asserted, where "it was always like gloom and doom. Everything was such a trauma, everything." Severely critical of her parents, Kristina viewed herself as the functional mother who had contested deficient parents for authority in a violent, chaotic household parented by a father who "worked eighteen hours a day or however many stupid hours he worked, and a mother who would take off and be gone." "My father is a battering parent, severe battering," Kris announced just minutes into our first interview, insisting on the present tense as she cited brutal incidents that occurred even after Lou's disabling heart attack. While Kris claimed her father's brutality as her earliest family memories, her portrait of her mother was less consistent. Dotty had protected her children at times, Kris conceded, but she also would "check out" intermittently, or lapse into violence herself and become "totally out of control" at others. According to Kris, her mother was often unable to cope, and consequently her father had always done most of the housework.

Kristina's views of her siblings were equally unflattering. She admitted to a jealous rivalry with Polly, her father's favored daughter, and was contemptuous of, rather than sympathetic to, Carole's plight as an exploited, abused wife and mother of three. Kris minced few words about her brother Loujoo: "He's a very evil person. He thinks nothing of mutilating someone physically." And Danny, in Kris's view, was an incorrigible "airhead." Coming of age in a combat zone had tutored Kristina too in martial arts that she admitted practicing against her siblings and even her parents. Combat skills were a necessary defense, she believed, in a "cuckoo" household where even water fights with garden hoses might occur indoors. Under circumstances like these, Kris claimed, she used to beg her parents to divorce.

Although Kristina's dominant stance toward her father was one of bitter hostility, eddies of grudging sympathy and identification were easy to tap. She believed that Lou's own violent upbringing was difficult to transcend and, "that's one of the most terrifying things, I think, in my life, knowing that statistically battered children become battering parents."* Kristina claimed to have been so fearful of this fate that she had once considered terminating her pregnancy, "because I have a lot of my father in me, although it chokes me to say that, and my mother." Becoming a mother proved instead to be the impetus to Kristina's determination to succeed, as well as a bridge to an improved relationship with her father.

Kristina had discovered that she was pregnant soon after she was jilted by her first love with whom she had been cohabiting in an adjacent county. Forced onto welfare by a difficult pregnancy that Kristina believed might be her last chance to bear a child, she resisted the impulse to abort and decided to take control of her life. At that point, her oc-

---

*This belief in a "cycle of family violence"—that battered children are particularly likely to become battering parents—is widely believed by mental health professionals and laypeople alike. Linda Gordon (*Heroes of Their Own Lives*, pp. 177ff.) suggests, however, that it is not readily supported by statistical data. Poverty correlates with a history of abuse and with battering, but there is no good evidence for a direct relationship between an abused childhood and abusive parenthood. Similarly, the relationship between alcohol consumption and abuse is indirect, mediated by cultural support for violence. See Kantor and Straus, "The 'Drunken Bum' Theory of Wife Beating."

cupational history indicated little progress toward the purchase of her park bench. Like an astonishing one out of every fifteen Americans, Kristina's first job had been at a McDonald's.[7] Since then she had worked in a variety of subminimum wage service-sector jobs followed by assorted temporary electronics production jobs.

Scarcely had Kristina recovered from a traumatic childbirth and from the repeated hospitalizations that plagued sickly Tommy's first year of life, when she plunged into her bootstrap ordeal. Days Kris studied drafting in a county training school, "where all the welfare workers, carryovers, and South-of-the-border people go"; nights she worked as an electronics industry security guard. One night Tommy was molested and assaulted by his baby-sitter. On the verge of an emotional breakdown, Kristina moved back with her son into her parents' house. Consumed with guilt, Kris found it unbearable to be near her child, and so she left him in her parents' care while working two electronics jobs eighteen to twenty hours each day. After a year of this frantic existence, motivated in part by her desire to secure a father for her victimized son, Kristina accepted a marriage proposal from a construction worker whom she barely knew, only to become a serious battering victim again herself. Perhaps violence was so familiar to her, Kris speculated, that she failed to recognize the danger signals. Tommy's attachment to the only father he had known also weakened her defenses until the kidney injury after six nightmarish months of this marriage jolted Kris into divorcing her husband in 1981.

By then Kristina had secured a foothold on the occupational ladder that she had been climbing at ASC, while living alone with Tommy. When I first interviewed her in 1985, she had just received a new promotion and a raise that brought her annual earnings to $30,000, almost enough to secure her vendetta triumph. (One year later I arrived to find a shiny Sears park bench dwarfing the small apartment's cluttered furnishings.) Kris dreamed of owning her own home, but recognized that prohibitive local housing costs might compel her to leave the state to do so. She pinned her hopes on a corporate transfer to a branch in a southwestern state where the real estate (and labor) markets were considerably cheaper. Her sister Polly's corporation had transferred her to the Southwest several years ago, and Kristina thought that "by moving like that I probably could afford to ship my parents out there" also. Kris still dreamed of finding "the right man," but here she perceived meager grounds for optimism. "Every working-class man I know," Kris told me,

195

was just like her abusive husband, "intimidated by me because I am a strong-willed person, and I am very forceful. They're intimidated by my stature; they're intimidated by my salary; they're intimidated completely." Yet, because Kris found the middle-class, professional men that she dated "ridiculous"—arrogant, selfish, and weak—she did not sustain much hope that she would be sharing her park bench with a suitable mate.

The devastating portrait of life in the Lewison household that Kristina rendered revived my fear that the family was not suitable as a case study of Silicon Valley families. To my amazement, Kris did not believe that her family was so unusual. "I'm trying to think of all the people I've met and all the families that I know," Kris reflected aloud when I raised the topic. "I think we're kind of middle of the road, actually. I think there's definitely some, you know, real bizarre things that go on in my family, but . . . when you have that many kids and that many relatives that are in the same area, come on, you're going to have something. . . . But, you know, when I think about it, I cannot think of one person that I've met that doesn't have some pretty weird things go on." Kristina predicted that the main distinguishing characteristic I would find in her family was its openness about its hostilities and traumas. She, for one, Kris assured me, had learned early on not "to believe in fairy tales."

DANNY: "I'M NOT LOST YET"

In June 1985 a distraught Dotty told me that Danny was being held in a maximum security unit at the county jail. From her rather murky account of the precipitating events, I gathered that one month earlier, police had arrested Dan for driving under the influence and found a stolen gun in his van. Danny had skipped bail and hidden out in another state before returning and being captured. A few weeks after this conversation, I paid a visit to Kristina and found the convict, out on probation, mopping his sister's kitchen floor. Danny readily accepted my offer to buy him a meal in exchange for an interview a few days hence, but he and Kristina both warned me that I would have to call to remind him of our date before I left my house. I did.

Kristina's long-haired, youngest brother fulfilled his sister's prediction that I would find most members of her family more willing than others to talk openly and easily about their warts and wrinkles. Twenty-one-year-old Danny agreed with his sister that the Lewisons were unremarkable. "It's probably an average family," only unusual in that, unlike most of his friends' families, his parents did not split up. Dan did not, however, replicate his sister's narrative of family violence. In his view, his father had been "just a crab," but not brutal, and his mother, generous and permissive. "I remember a couple of times that I deserved to get my butt spanked and I got it. There was a lot of slack when my dad didn't live there. Things were easier around the house. And then Kris, the boss, wasn't living there either. I like my mom a lot better than my dad. My mom has a sense of humor. I have a good sense of humor and I like to joke a lot. Yeah, all my friends like my mom." Dan was glad that his parents had stayed together, "because I've seen other people from broken families, and they're just lost. I'm not lost yet."

If he was not yet lost, Danny was still the first to admit that he was also a long way from saved. "Drugs. I still can't get out of them." "Do you want to?" I asked. "No," Dan conceded. "I don't really want to. I guess I've grown used to the life-style, I don't know. It's fast-paced, exciting . . . not really being in touch with reality, you know, yeah, not caring about too much."

Danny had started dealing small-time dope when he was thirteen with his brother Loujoo's crowd of friends. He could make twenty dollars in a day then if he put his will to it. By fifteen he was averaging one hundred dollars daily. He attended school until he was eighteen without earning sufficient credits for graduation. "I was never at school, but I always had money, so it wasn't really important to me, school; I had other things to do." Besides drugs and partying, there was romance. During his last year of high school, Dan fell in love with Amanda, the young woman who had been sharing the couch with him during my first visit to the Lewisons. For the next two years Danny and Amanda cohabited as transients, sharing residences with his parents, with his sister Carole's household, and then with a drug-dealing friend, or living, when they could afford it, in an apartment of their own or in Danny's illegally parked van when they could not.

Danny and Amanda each would take a job from time to time, but each would also quit if the other was unemployed. Dan interspersed bouts of short-term, low-wage employment in electronics or assorted odd jobs, like hauling, with his far more lucrative trade in drugs. Nor was it difficult, he informed me, to integrate these lines of work. On the last electronics production job that Dan held, for example, his boss and coworkers openly used crank (speed) to endure the double shifts they were frequently pushed to work. Another boss "was so loose that he didn't hire anybody who didn't do drugs. I'm serious. He'd call break time, everybody in the whole building would stand around and smoke their joints, and he'd smoke them too. I mean, this guy was eating mushrooms and working."

The young couple progressed to heavy drug use when they shared a cramped household with Carole, her husband and three children, and another couple. "That was the lowest time I ever had in my whole life. I got really down. I got really into doing drugs and not working, and not even—I don't know what it was; I guess it was the whole atmosphere down in that house. It was just down and out." During the five months that they lived there, no one but Carole had a steady job; everyone else stayed home doing drugs and watching TV. Dan and Amanda moved out after discovering that the other couple had stolen their things, but they fell into an even bigger-time drug scene living with a dealer friend of Dan's. Soon they were hooked on a coke habit that cost six hundred dollars a day, and twice Dan had to rescue Amanda from a life-threatening overdose.

The fast life came to a crashing halt when Dan's dealer friend, and patron, was jailed. Homeless, hooked, out of work, and in debt, Dan decided to get off hard drugs and try "to get it together." He took a $4-per-hour job through a temporary agency as a materials handler for an electronics company. "Like I was working my butt off and they didn't give me a raise. I was like a slave around there, shop slave. . . . I got fed up with them 'cause they tried to rip me off on all my paychecks, it seemed like, like short-changing me."

That past fall, shortly before I had first encountered the couple, Amanda became pregnant, and everything unraveled. She moved to her parents' home in a nearby state to carry out her reluctant decision to have an abortion. Danny quit his job to follow her, only to be "bummed out when she shined me on." It was in that demoralized and destitute state last winter that Dan had appealed to Dotty to rescind his father's eviction notice.

Dan had been out of work ever since. "It's day to day for me, one day to the next." Kristina was pushing him to try to find a job, but unlike his sister, Dan had few motivating dreams. "I guess I got a really shitty attitude. I'm a radical. I consider myself a radical. Oh, I don't care about much at all. I'm a troublemaker. I like to live dangerously." Dan's radicalism was an existential rather than a political identification. "Yeah, I don't even like politics, that's nothin'. I don't like the government. I like Reagan. Yeah, I like Reagan, 'cause he's a good, strong president. . . . Like he doesn't take any crap from anybody, and I guess that's the way I am too, you know. I think we should spend more money on the defense of our country. Last year I almost voted, but I never got around to it."

Although he seemed to admire Reagan's macho defense policies and his personal authority, Dan expressed views on gender and marriage less patriarchal than those Lou predicted he would hold. "I'm for equal rights myself. You know, women are capable of taking care of themselves. No doubt. Yeah, and they don't get a fair shot at everything, you know. They gotta work a lot harder." Indeed, unlike his father, Dan had no intention of assuming the burdens of a patriarchal marriage. He had resented the periods when Amanda "was just pretty much living off of me, and here she's talking about how her parents are so rich and all that shit, and why the hell am I supporting her then, you know?" Dan did expect to marry and have children, however, and he took for granted that his wife would work. "Sure it takes two people these days, it does, definitely. Yeah, of course women should support themselves, you know, because shit, I have a hard time supporting myself, so how am I gonna, you know, let alone support someone else?"

Talking about kids and about Amanda evoked Dan's ambivalence about his radical life. Now that he looked back on it, he almost regretted going along with Amanda's abortion. "I wouldn't have minded having a little kid right now. Maybe we coulda made it. We were doing pretty good there for a while. It was just good to share my life with her, and I want to do that with somebody else. I'm not looking into the future right now. I've got a bad attitude. I'm not ready for it right now. I know what I've got to do. I just don't really want to do it. But I know I have to someday." When that day came, Dan hoped his marriage would be as successful as his parents'. "I'm happy for them that they got it together. Yeah, they're sitting on top now just looking down saying 'Wow, we did it.' That's what I want. Once I get married, I don't want to get divorced. I want to make sure that it's right."

199

Dan blamed his shitty attitude on his neighborhood rather than his parents. "I think growing up in the area that I did, not necessarily in the Silicon Valley, Bay Area, we're talking Orchard Park. Yeah, just the type of people that are there, the people are bad there. Bad people, drugs. I don't know, when I was growing up there was a lot of Mexicans there and you know, I always had racial problems with the Mexicans, because I'm white, you know, and I'm proud, and I guess I'm just as proud as they are, you know, so we don't get along, and I was always fightin' with the Mexicans, and then, as far as the whites, there was always a lot of bikers around, so I knew all these biker people, and you know, they're doin' drugs, so, I guess me and them too. It was a rowdy neighborhood." Danny could imagine only one hope for his future. He would have to leave the area. "I wanna get out of this Bay Area, Silicon Valley. I don't like it anymore. I don't know, there's just something inside me that's saying 'Get out, while you got a chance.' "

Dotty had come home for lunch by the time I brought Danny back to Orchard Park. She gave me her customary bearhug, then chortled as she handed me a copy of a flyer bearing these words:

**YOUNG ADULTS
&
TEENAGERS**

IF YOU ARE TIRED OF
BEING HASSLED BY
UNREASONABLE PARENTS
NOW IS THE TIME
FOR **ACTION!!!**—

LEAVE HOME AND
PAY YOUR OWN WAY WHILE YOU
STILL KNOW EVERYTHING!

POSTPARADIGM FAMILY PORTRAIT

I came to the Lewisons in quixotic search of a "modern" family, but found only its postmodern and narrative remains. My mid-eighties field-work amid the Lewisons garnered multiple accounts of the family's ten- to fifteen-year-long modern nuclear period, which had terminated more than a decade earlier. These often incongruent narratives did not readily synthesize into a paradigmatic Silicon Valley family story. It still seems correct to observe that the unusual window of occupational opportunity that the early electronics industry had offered the region's white working-class men combined with the federal government's generous VA mortage program to finance the Lewisons' ephemeral modern family period. Little else from this chapter's opening narrative, however, survives unchallenged.

If Dotty had embraced Lou's electronics career and the male breadwinner-female homemaker family form that its structure both demanded and threatened, she had done so via a compound of coercion and consent. During the late fifties and early sixties, the male family wage strategy was still the best one available to support the large family that Dotty, much more than Lou, wanted to raise. Family crisis conditions preceded Lou's entry into the electronics industry. And grueling career demands provided him and Dotty some relief from their violent, tumultuous marriage at the same time that it added to the causes of the family's deepening disarray. Indeed, instead of the stable family of my fantasies and of Dotty's fable, the Lewisons, far more than Pamela's kin, inhabited the dangerous border country between hard and settled living. And, as ensuing chapters will reveal, a series of tragedies befell the family during my field study that caused most of the survivors to migrate indefinitely below the settled living line.

Family life cycles, of course, render all household structures impermanent, but the Lewisons had failed to sustain Talcott Parsons's ideal pattern long before their young left home. Nor did Dotty and Lou transmit that pattern's prerequisites and ideals to most of their progeny. None of the Lewison children had reasonable prospects of becoming homeowners in the region. At least three of the couple's five children seemed to be on a descending economic course, while the child with the greatest occupational ambitions and prospects was a daughter and a single mother. One Lewison son and two sons-in-law attempted the military route to occupational mobility that Lou had traveled three decades earlier. Unlike Lou, however, two did so only after early marriages and parenthood underscored the gravity of their limited local occupational options. One had already failed, and the long-term prospects for the others seemed much less promising than Lou's had been. Dotty's housewife strategy, on the other hand, was less available or acceptable to her daughters when they came of age in the late seventies and eighties than it had been when she practiced it in her own prefeminist past.

My search for a modern nuclear family had landed me instead, I concluded, in another postmodern one, a fluid family system where gender and kinship strategies were less predictable than in the "modern" past. Dotty and Lou now practiced a partial gender reversal, although she remained economically dependent on her husband, as his disability pension far exceeded her service sector earnings. All five of their children had cohabited with lovers, and one had willingly become a single mother before marrying and then divorcing an abusive man. Married or single, all of the Lewison daughters and their daughter-in-law were generally employed even when their husbands and lovers were not.

Despite its many late-twentieth-century features, the Lewisons' postmodern family bore as much similarity to the premodern working-class families with unstable marriages and working mothers in which Dotty and Lou each had been reared as it did to the modern one they made and unmade in between. The Lewison household between 1984 and 1987, my period of active fieldwork, might best be described as a matrifocal, accordian structure. Expelled like his father for battering his wife, Lou too had been readmitted to the matrilineal fold in his declining years on conditions of good behavior. Intermittently thereafter, with Lou's acquiescence and without it, the couple shared the family domicile with various of their adult children along with their legal and extralegal mates and offspring, as well as with assorted needy friends and neighbors. Kristina and Tommy had recuperated from their molestation and battering crises there. During my field study period, Danny, with Amanda or alone, moved in and out of his parents' home before another serious encounter with the criminal justice system prompted him to heed the internal voice urging him to flee the area. Likewise, an eviction notice caused Carole, her husband Bobby, and their too rapidly increasing brood to spend six months of stressful coresidence with Dot and Lou. Periodically, visiting or displaced friends of Dotty's and of her children also occupied makeshift quarters in the Lewison garage on a short-term basis. The women who inhabited the Lewison residence worked for pay more frequently than the men, but never at jobs that paid a family wage.

Danny was correct to give his parents credit for evading the shoals of marital defeat. Dotty and Lou had temporarily rescued the family ship, however, only by shifting course from modern to postmodern channels. Feminist beacon lights, as we shall see, guided a portion of this journey.

9

To Feminism and Partway Back

I don't know anymore how families should be. In the early days of the movement we thought we could do without them. Then we created a model of equality that left the children waiting at the window for someone to come home. Then we floundered and demanded day care and deprived women who wanted to watch their two-year-olds pound pegs into holes of their earnest desire. We woke up to discover that our goal of equality had created a generation of gray flannel suits who played tennis to win and could tell you all about IRAs and CDs and nothing about Winken, Blinken and Nod. Now I am exhausted, a secret I am not yet willing to tell my friends and colleagues.

—Anne Roiphe, *LovingKindness*

Entering a high-school cafeteria in midsummer 1985 to attend the annual SOS conference for poor single mothers, I scanned the cinderblock shell for familiar faces. Neither Pamela Gama nor her estranged friend Jan, the conference organizers, was the first to greet me. Instead, encasing me from behind in her inimicable embrace, Dotty startled me, her very presence a taunting exposé of the artificiality of the discrete boundaries that I attempted to sustain between this study's two postmodern kin sets. Dotty's arms swaddled me noticeably longer that morning than was even her affectionate custom. Like many of the several hundred women flocking through the cafeteria doorways at that moment, Dotty Lewison was in pain.

"I was so bummed out that I cried almost all day yesterday, Judith,"

Dotty confided as she explained the cause of her distress and her presence at the conference. Just the day before she had been fired summarily from her insurance office job, granted two weeks' notice and no severance pay. Although she had been devastated, even more hurt than angry, Dotty claimed that fountains of tears and her metaphysical philosophy had already healed the emotional wound. "There's a reason for everything," she proclaimed. "I don't know what the reason for this is yet, but there is one." Perhaps, she speculated, she had to be available for a better job or, less optimistically, to contend with the difficult trials that lay ahead that year. Last week's reading in Dotty's psychic class had predicted the deaths of both of her aging parents.* She had been annoyed with the overdrawn sympathy with which her classmates had responded to this reading. It was hardly a tragedy for people in their late seventies to die, particularly as "psychics know that people continue to come back, to cross over," after they do. "Why get so upset?" Dotty fumed, exasperated by people she found to be "so irrational!"

Dotty's friend Marilyn was to be recognized at the SOS conference that day for her voluntary service to county women, and she had coaxed Dot to come along. To get her mind off her troubles, and perhaps to rekindle some of her dormant feminist spirit, Dotty had agreed. "Maybe it's time for me to get involved in this kind of work again," she theorized, indulging momentarily in nostalgia for the activist feminist past she and Marilyn had shared. "I loved the work when we were doing it," Dotty reminisced, "but it sure does burn you out."

FEMINISM AND THE UNMAKING OF THE MODERN FAMILY

Both Dotty and Marilyn felt nostalgia for their feminist history. Chapter 8 alludes to but understates the contribution feminism made to disrupting the "modern" marriage and family system that had once ensnared the two friends. In the mid-1970s, a few years later than was true for Pam and Lorraine, feminism had supplied Dotty and Marilyn with similar energizing anger and confidence and an interpretive lens through which

---

*Dotty had reconciled with her biological father.

to reconstruct their lives. Their modern marriages joined that decade's mounting casualty lists as feminist passions sparked their journeys along differing postmodern family courses.

A fortnight after the SOS conference I encouraged Dotty's romantic reveries about her wilder, more militant years. By sporting her to a dinner at her favorite Mexican restaurant, I hoped to lift her spirits. Dotty had just received another in the daunting series of trials that were to befall her throughout the remainder of this field study. A drug bust in her daughter Carole's "tobacco road" residence had prompted its landlord to evict the young family. Dotty felt compelled to house the insolvent brood despite the threat their shared residence posed to Lou's health and to the Lewisons' hard-won marital harmony. Adding to Dotty's alarm, a recent psychic reading that would prove disturbingly prophetic warned that she and Lou were going to wind up with Carole and her soon-to-number four unruly offspring. With future prospects appearing so dismal, Dotty was glad to relive brighter days.

Declaring that she had no regrets, she recounted bawdy and illicit escapades from her rebellious homemaker period, savoring memories of bar parties with her set of "typically dissatisfied suburban housewives" while their overemployed husbands worked and of the adulterous love affairs that followed. To fill her days with distractions from her domestic despair, Dotty involved herself in voluntary community activities. In the activist ambience of the period, these had turned progressively political. Organizing food coops in 1971, she met Marilyn, who recalls her shock at Dotty's unladylike speech and manner. "She scared the hell out of me," Marilyn remembered. "She was so extreme. On my first encounters with Dotty, she used words that I had never heard a woman use before at that point. And I was taught women were supposed to be polite and quiet, and here along comes Dotty—she doesn't like something? she says, 'What the fuck are you doing?' in the middle of the meeting. And there's a deafening silence." Together the new friends poured their frustrated energies into community school reform and then into housing reform that led them to the battered shelter movement, and to feminism.

Feminism turned their lives downside up. Brazen on the outside while trapped inside an abusive marriage, Dotty remembers how badly she "needed to have my stamp validated." Feminism supplied the inkpad— a rhetoric and forum for reappraising self and suffering. Dotty was not worthless, but devalued and oppressed, and she had the right and the capacity to reconstitute her life. Feminism reassured her that "it was okay not to feel subservient" and that she need not remain with a husband who beat her to make her so. The movement's oppositional ideology deepened the chasm in her marriage and gave her the courage to risk its dissolution. Recalling those heady days, Dotty harbored no regrets. "I look back on it, and it was so much fun. I'm not sorry I did a damn thing. I'm really not. I'd do it all over again. Some things I'd do twice."

Some things, like entering and exiting conjugal union, Dotty's best friend Marilyn had already done twice. When I interviewed forty-two-year-old Marilyn several months after the conference, she narrated the details of yet another textbook Silicon Valley family story. I began to believe that postindustrial forces were inverting Tolstoy's dictum. But for the details, all unhappy families had come to seem alike. Although Marilyn, like Dotty, had been reared by a divorced mother outside the hallowed modern family, she too had "bought the whole fifties fairy tale." Marilyn believed she was about to realize her fantasies when in 1965 at twenty-one she married Richard, a stable and committed air force–trained aerospace engineer whose promising career prospects brought the young couple to California's postindustrial frontier.

Frontierland, however, had alternative plots in store. Soon Richard, like Lou, was engrossed in sixty- to eighty-hour work weeks and an ascent up the corporate ladder. Marilyn, "vegetating, and very bored," at home with the couple's two young children, tried hobbies before venturing onto the volunteer trail that lured her incrementally and irresistibly into feminism's mind-jolting lair. Volunteer work led Marilyn to her first paid employment since becoming a mother, a staff position coordinating the very community schools project to which she and Dotty had been donating their labors.

Immersed in an intense, activist political environment, Marilyn met people with different and challenging ideas that her conservative husband and marriage could not withstand. "I started questioning things that I hadn't questioned before." Marilyn met feminists who encouraged her to introduce women's studies courses into the community schools curriculum. She joined a group of women organizing shelters for battered women and worked with an SOS group organizing its first conference for female family heads. One political project led to the next, and before long Marilyn was working an eighty-hour weekly schedule that outpaced her bewildered and outraged husband's. Richard, for his part, was posing questions of his own. Why was his formerly devoted wife now centering her life around work, friendships, and politics that offended him? "I was so very busy I didn't notice that anything was going on or not with my marriage, virtually." Soon Richard was going on with another woman, and the demise of one more modern marriage helped make 1977 another record year for divorce statistics.

WOMEN'S SPIRITS IN THE EIGHTIES

I feel this strong force of white light coming down, but you haven't quite managed to connect with it. I sense a hesitation, a holding back from new experience. You need to reach for it, make contact. Once you open yourself, you will have a wealth of new energy and spiritual experiences.

Dotty gripped my elbow supportively as I rose to retrieve my Navajo necklace from the Reverend Hannah's workworn hands. It was a balmy evening in the spring of 1986, and I had joined Lou and Dotty for Sunday services at the Universal Temple of the Spirit. Following a few Protestant hymns and prayers and a rather vacuous sermon on the power of love and determination, the minister called for healers to take their places behind three vacant metal folding chairs. Dotty, the octogenarian Reverend Hannah, and a casually dressed, burly gentleman complied. As the minister's wife played muted chords on her portable electric organ, congregants in need of healing presented themselves for the laying on of hands.

Her rehabilitative efforts completed, Dotty returned to our row, linked her loving hands to mine and Lou's, and anticipated the climax of the service—psychic readings of our personal effects. Each of the score of people who entered the rented fraternal hall that evening had been invited to deposit an item in a small basket to be read during the service by one of the psychics in attendance. Vibrations from Dotty's key chain and from Lou's wristwatch moved their interpreter to complementary readings, revelations a bit more specific and less hopeful but as accurate as the one my necklace had inspired. In a prophecy I had learned to judge distressingly safe for the Lewison household, the Reverend Hannah "sensed" that Dotty and Lou each were suffering "from the troubles of a loved one, someone close to you." Less presciently, alas, the well-intentioned spiritualist predicted that in three to five weeks time these troubles would subside. Also on the unduly optimistic side, the Lewisons' psychic reader foresaw a long-awaited trip "coming in the future, probably July or August," and she urged the owners of the key chain and the wristwatch "to make those plans, save those pennies, and save a little leftover because there will be something happening when you get home that you will need some of those pennies for."

Indeed more than one of the Lewisons' loved ones was in serious trouble at that moment, and while there was to be good cause for Dotty and Lou to save their pennies, none would be spent on the long-awaited trip to Europe. Loujoo's volatile marriage was on the brink of cleavage, and he had asked his parents to postpone their visit indefinitely. Daughter Carole's life and marriage were in even more catastrophic straits, threatening to realize the ominous psychic reading Dotty had received the previous summer. The prior week, just one month after Carole and Bobby had finally managed to move their family out of the Lewison household into an apartment of their own, Carole found a love letter to her husband from a woman claiming to be pregnant with his child. In response Carole attempted suicide. After thwarting his wife's desperate action, Bobby announced his plans to leave her and their four children for his new lover. Danny was in jail again after being picked up on a burglary charge while high on PCP. And mercifully unknown to the most visionary among us, a far more tragic year lay ahead.

"Maybe that's why this religion is so good for me," Dotty reflected as she drove us back to Orchard Park after the service. "It helps me understand that no matter what you do, things are going to be the way they're going to be, that really it's all karma. At least that's what I take from it. With one kid in jail and one trying suicide, I mean I figure they have to live their lives, I have to live mine. It seems to me that you're really responsible. Well, you have to be responsible for yourself, but it makes it easier to accept all of this. Otherwise I don't know how I would deal with this. I'm responsible for myself, but I have to take this to mean that maybe there's something that I need to learn in going through this, all of this experience, there has to be something good in it for me. Or

209

maybe it's something I have to pay back for some sins or whatever that I committed in the past life. There has to be something like that, because goddamn, it's heavy. Goddamn, it's heavy."

What Lou liked best about this church was the undogmatic way it allowed you to "do your own faith." In direct contrast with Global Ministry's commitment to doctrinal uniformity, the Lewisons' spiritualist denomination permitted "you to believe what you want to believe." Nonetheless, Lou somewhat defensively pointed out, I should not construe the spiritualist service as "so different from a regular Christian service." Almost all denominations believe in prophecy and healing. "It's just a matter of how open it is, whether they do it publicly or more privately."

It was easy to concede Lou's point. Despite the enormous doctrinal contrasts between church services at Global Ministries and the Universal Temple. I had observed a number of unexpected similarities. Both encouraged a personal relationship with a loving God; set time aside for direct, oral prayers for those in need; allowed significant spiritual roles for women; and preached an ideology that fused fatalism with a "keep on truckin' " self-help credo. Living their fifth decades during the 1980s, both Dotty and Pam seemed to find greater solace in their respective small, maverick, grass-roots, spiritual communities than in the activist feminist world each had so valued a decade earlier.

SECOND THOUGHTS ON THE SECOND WAVE

Dorothea

Dotty confirmed this interpretation a few months later as we sought respite from the summer afternoon's smoggy heat sunk in the naugahyde swivel chairs of a refrigerated cocktail lounge. She had lengthened her name to Dorothea, she informed me, but I still could call her Dotty. Dorothea sounded more mature and professional, she thought, and better suited her current position as a receptionist at a cable TV office. Dorothea was just as self-aware that she selectively appropriated reassuring teachings from her spiritualist religion. "I can't say that's what the religion really says, but that's what I take from it, because that's what I believe.

And I've had to believe this; it comes from necessity." Loujoo was supplying Dotty's most recent need for solace. By battering his wife he had also smashed his parents' dreams. His wife was leaving him, waiting for the military to cut orders to transport her and her toddler home, and all the excitement had gone out of the Lewisons' travel fantasies.

Yet even with her stated incentive for paid employment eliminated, Dotty displayed no interest in retiring. Nor had I detected a hint of renewed political activism during the year that had nearly passed since she had surprised me at the SOS conference. Instead Dot had immediately found another part-time service-sector job, and when her next employer laid her off, she accepted a cable television service job that entailed a significant wage cut. The year had not proven to be one that rekindled her interest in feminism.

While Dorothea was on the subject of her current beliefs, I directed our conversation toward these earlier ones. She did not think her beliefs had changed very much. "What's changed is my involvement. Mainly I got burned out." Dot reminded me that she had "never been totally in agreement with the angry, militant feminist, all-men-are-evil kind of thinking. The militants had turned people off. Hell, they used to turn me off. No wonder there's such a backlash against feminism and women's rights." She seemed to identify the militants with lesbianism, and she vacillated between blaming the media for homophobic distortions and believing these herself.

"Still, it's a damned shame," Dotty continued, "that there are a lot of idiots out there, like those damned religious right-to-lifers" who were so effectively undoing crucial feminist gains. Dotty still bristled to recall the pre–*Roe* v. *Wade* abortion she obtained in 1967. She had had to threaten to leave Lou in order to secure his signature on her application for a medically approved procedure. What a pity it was now that "those religious fanatics have more money and are more dedicated to their cause, and people like me have dropped out."

More than homophobia and ideological misgivings, Dorothea believed, it was burnout and shifting midlife priorities that explained her withdrawal from feminist activism. "I'm just too tired, there's too much other shit to deal with," she exclaimed. "But," I challenged gently, "with five young children, an abusive husband, and much less money, you must have been more exhausted and beleaguered when you did participate in the women's movement." Dorothea lighted a new cigarette with her old one, munched her chili nachos, and ordered a second bourbon before responding.

"I guess that's true," she conceded thoughtfully. "I guess I really don't need feminism as much as I used to." Partly due to the feminist-assisted success of her marital reform struggles, Dotty had less need for feminist support. And she was no longer in the mood to rock the conjugal boat. "We're kind of coasting, it's not a great working marriage. I get sick of it sometimes. But it's financially easier, and he's not so bad. It's someone to care about, and I don't want to be alone. I don't want the single scene anymore, even though it was a lot of fun and I wouldn't have missed it for anything." Dotty's concluding words challenged me in turn: "You can't always be a feminist, Judith."

Marilyn

Marilyn agreed. We drank coffee in the living room of the comfortable suburban rented house she shared with her teenage daughter and with her divorced mother, an electronics production supervisor who had been laid off scant months before her retirement eligibility. Marilyn and her brother were filing a class action suit against the company on their mother's behalf. Marilyn was also contributing occasional volunteer hours to the electoral campaign of a progressive woman candidate for city council. Yet she defined feminism as "kind of peripheral" to her present priorities. "You know, I get these pangs of consciousness occasionally, but this is sort of a laid-back time. I'm not as laid back as Dotty, but I'm not as active as I used to be." "Laid back" did not strike me as an optimal adjective to characterize the current circumstances or sensibilities of either Marilyn or Dotty. Posttraumatic stress more than tranquility seemed to underlie the two friends' differing degrees of disengagement from feminist activism.

Marilyn had been stunned by her first divorce. Although she had scrutinized her marriage through feminist lenses and found it wanting, she had not prepared herself for its demise. When it came, the support of her feminist friends and ideology did not spare her deep feelings of guilt and despair. "Immediately after we split, I was massively depressed. Massively. I suppose I felt like I had failed at whatever it was. I didn't go one hundred percent, you know . . . I felt that I had screwed up and screwed up the kids.''

The trauma of her unanticipated divorce froze Marilyn's already flagging political energies and brought her to one of those times Dotty had identified when one could not be a feminist. "I was burning out on all of it, and I did. I mean I just wanted to get away from it. I didn't reapply for the Women's Commission, and I didn't reapply for this, I stepped down from that board and started just stepping back from a lot of stuff." Perhaps reactively, certainly audaciously, Marilyn threw herself instead into a new romance, falling for a lover guaranteed to incur the disapproval of her feminist friends.

Mitchell was another engineer, and even more politically conservative than Richard. Although Marilyn, like her friends, found her new lover's political convictions offensive and "intractable," these did not chill her ardor. "Well, obviously nothing was enough of an issue at that point. I was totally infatuated. And I made a conscious choice, at that point. Friends would always be there; if you needed them, they'd still be there. But I didn't know that he would. I wasn't sure how long it was going to last; so I just enjoyed it while it was." Mitchell proved to be a costly passion, but one Marilyn still refuses to regret. She and Mitchell and the children from their earlier marriages lived together for two years, and then, succumbing to pressure from her relatives, they both paid their second visit to the altar.

The sanctified union survived but one year. Their sharp differences and the incompatible emotional needs of their unhappily blended new family jettisoned the marriage. Mitchell exited Marilyn's life in early 1981 even more abruptly than he had entered it, leaving her in far worse straits than when they had met four years before. This time Marilyn's devastation was material as well as emotional. Having forfeited child support payments from Richard when she married Mitchell, she was a single mother once again with insecure, underpaid employment and without a house. Drawing on skills she had developed writing grants for political projects, Marilyn took accounting jobs in computer companies and grant-writing contract jobs on the side. She was laid off by three different computer companies within the year.

Only marginal improvements characterize the years that followed. Because Marilyn's employment opportunities in contract consulting and grant-writing jobs are always feast or famine, she relies on steadier but "boring" employment in accounting to meet her expenses. Marilyn's mother and grandmother had migrated to the Valley a decade earlier. When the latter died in 1985, Marilyn and her mother pooled their resources by forming their current three-generation matrilineal household.

Marilyn viewed all of these arrangements as temporary. She anticipated that in several years her daughter would leave home, her mother would move back East, and she would enter a new independent phase of life that she intended to enjoy. As for men, Marilyn "wouldn't mind the income, but I want to skip the relationship." Perhaps she would get more involved in politics again some day, but right now she "had to work too many hours," and she, like Dotty, did not find conditions conducive to feminist activism. The two friends had not repudiated feminism but placed it in remission. Their modern marriages dissolved or reformed, their family and work lives demanding and insecure, both lacked the time and the incentive to do public battle with patriarchy.

POSTFEMINIST DAUGHTERS

Reckoning by the calendar, Dotty's three daughters, like Pamela's two, are members of the quintessential postfeminist generation. To varying degrees all have distanced themselves from feminist identity and politics, at times in conscious reaction against what they regard as the excesses of their mothers' earlier feminist views. At the same time, however, each has selectively incorporated feminist principles into her expectations and strategies for family and work.[1] The complex effects of birth order, personality, and intrafamilial dynamics have influenced the notably diverse gender and kinship strategies that Dotty's daughters display.

Kristina: "I'm an Equal Opportunist"

Two of Carole's children were competing for my lap as I sat with their mother and Lou watching a midmorning game show, when Danny, looking wasted, appeared in his pajama bottoms and beckoned me to the

FEIFFER®

phone. It was Kristina calling from work to cancel our plans for lunch and the private tour she had promised me that day of the prototype production line in her division. Advanced Semi-Conductor Corporation, in a major economic crisis, had just announced plans to lay off more than five hundred of its local workforce. Kristina's own job did not appear to be in immediate jeopardy, "although you never know." As a member of lower management, she was required to lend her grip to the axe handle that would cut half the employees in her small design department. Kristina had spent the night awake dreading her awful responsibility. "After all, they all have families too," her anguished voice whispered.

Kris was in surprisingly ebullient spirits, however, when I called her one week later. She had just received a promotion that allowed her a stock option at a fixed rate for ten years. "This is great timing," Kris explained, "because shares are so low now that this could mean a lot of money; this can probably put me in a house." "No wonder you sound so high," I commented. "Yeah, well, are you ready for this? The main reason is, I'm in love!" Kristina was in love with Frank Hopkins, who, she was embarrassed to tell me, was three years younger than she. She was less troubled by Frank's lesser occupational and income achievements. He earned half her salary working as a materials handler for an aerospace corporation. Frank was not new in Kristina's life. They had met and dated briefly four years earlier when he was the dispatcher on the security job Kristina had moonlighted, but then she had found Frank, with his middle-class background and cultural interests, "too nice and too easy. I could take advantage of him, and I always thought that I don't like too easy." They had become friends instead of lovers, and since then Kristina had taken periodic advantage of Frank's willingness to contribute occasional baby-sitting and other support services to her precariously maintained, single-parent household.

Now, however, for reasons she could not fathom, Kristina had abandoned her reservations about Frank and defined herself in love. For the duration of the active fieldwork portion of this study, she somewhat ambivalently, and unsuccessfully, pursued a marital or at least a cohabitational commitment from her seemingly devoted, dependent, and deferential yet highly resistant new flame. The first nine months of the couple's approach-avoidance romance coincided with a prolonged work crisis at ASC for Kristina that brought her to the razor's edge of an emotional breakdown. This may have heightened her desire to locate an alternate source of personal security and esteem, but it did little to improve the likelihood that her needy endeavor would succeed.

Throughout Kristina's work crisis, Frank willingly supplied his new lover with vital household support services. The predictable hours of his own less demanding job enabled him to care for Tommy on those numerous occasions when Kris felt compelled to work through dinner and even through the night. Several of those evenings, I visited with Frank while eight-year-old Tommy consumed his habitual heaping portions of violent TV fare. Remarkably flexible in his attitudes toward gender norms and seemingly unthreatened by Kristina's greater career drive, income, and age, Frank, like Lanny's husband, Ken, impressed me as a strikingly postfeminist man. He takes for granted the gender revolution in work and family organization that divides his parents' generation from his own. Although Frank was raised in a thoroughly conventional modern middle-class household by a full-time mother whose husband's corporate career opportunities dictated periodic geographic migrations for the family, he "can't imagine having a wife with a nose ring following her husband around from place to place."

Frank does not know how he came to hold such ideas, they just seem "obvious" to him. "Maybe if I had been in high school and college during the early seventies," Frank speculated when I asked if he thought the women's movement had affected his thinking, "I would have been more conscious of feminism, feminist issues. But I guess I just grew up taking a lot of it for granted." By the time that he went though high school in the late seventies, Frank believed, "these weren't issues anymore."

If Frank cannot imagine dominating a wife, it is also difficult for him to imagine having one at all. During the very month when Kris informed me that she and Frank were planning to live together and that I might yet be able to include another wedding in my book, Frank told me that he "could not be in a marriage-type commitment right now" because he needed to be flexible and open to career opportunities. "Marriage is not pressing. It kind of falls where it will. I like being single and don't see myself as the marrying kind." Nor did Frank perceive himself as the parenting kind. Tommy's attachment to him contributed to Kristina's romantic interest in him, and Frank seemed to return a portion of Tommy's affection. Nonetheless, Frank claimed antipathy to children and expressed "no desire to have my own kid." He had even considered having a vasectomy, but discovered "there was some hesitation there."

217

Hesitation, Kristina believed, was Frank's major characterological deficiency, one that she, with her own characterological assertiveness, was then determined to correct. Several years earlier he had accepted her advice to seek counseling to overcome the insecurity that Kristina diagnosed as the root of his perennial ambivalence. He had made considerable progress since then, she believed, and she was hopeful that continued progress would enable him to commit himself fully to their relationship. For Kristina, in contrast with Frank, had set lifelong commitment, "the bottom line in a relationship," as her unambiguous goal. When Frank asked her why they could not just continue as they were indefinitely, she warned him that she "had no interest in standing in place." "He'll have his walking papers yesterday," Kris assured me, "if he thinks I'll put so much effort into improving a relationship that's so easy to throw away."

Also unlike Frank, Kristina was committed to parenting. The relationship she treasured most was her maternal one, and she openly regretted the "fact" that her career did not allow her to have a second child. And perhaps because she had come of age at the height of militant feminism in the earlier seventies, and in a household where gender struggles were overt and consequential, Kristina was somewhat more self-conscious than Frank about her rather ambivalent relationship to feminism. Like him, Kristina took numerous feminist gains for granted. That she could choose without shame to cohabit and to become a single parent, that she could enter a male-dominated occupation and compete successfully for corporate rewards—these feminist achievements Kristina exercised as her inalienable birthrights.

This is not to say that she was unaware of gender discrimination. Indeed, she frequently regaled me with infuriating incidents of sexism at her workplace. But Kristina was equally antagonized by feminism, from whose unsavory connotations she was eager to distance herself. "The word 'feminist' is dirty—I don't know how to explain that," she tried to explain, as her associations drifted rapidly toward her mother. "I do not feel like a feminist, because to me my mother is a perfect feminist. If someone asks her to make coffee, she first has to determine if it is because she is a woman. I guess it is the word 'feminist' I don't like, because of the way I was brought up with it. It meant slapping people in the face with it, and it becomes a reverse discrimination; and I don't like to think of myself in that particular way, and I think most feminists do that."

It troubled Kristina to see feminists picking on men. She understood that there was a long history to female subordination, but "you know, I can't blame the people today for what was initiated centuries ago. So no, I don't. That's the main reason I don't call myself a feminist. An equal opportunist, maybe!" After observing Kristina's thoroughly individualistic relationship to feminist issues, "equal opportunist," with its classical liberal capitalist connotations, came to strike me as apt. Although she competed aggressively in a man's world whose sexist excesses she resented and resisted, Kristina could not imagine participating in political action on any issue, not even one like battering, which she suffered as a daughter and a wife. Kristina had channeled the righteous anger she felt toward her battering father into an individualistic achievement drive whose temporal and ideological demands were incompatible with political activism. Perhaps her unresolved anger toward her mother for failing to protect her and resentment of the time Dotty devoted to political causes helped to fuel Kristina's distaste for political issues. "I leave them for people like my mother who can make issues out of that, because I don't see it that way. I'll help the neighbor next door whose husband is beating her to death, but I do it my way. My way is not in a public forum. I am *very* different from my mother."

Polly: "They Were Going Too Far"

None of Dotty's daughters was as different from she as her second child, Polly. Twenty-six-year-old Polly was the least feminist Lewison daughter and the only one with a satisfying marriage. She also enjoyed the best living conditions of the sisters, largely because she had left the Silicon Valley in 1983 when Conductex, the electronics company she worked for, opened a branch in a southwestern state. I interviewed Polly when she returned with her new husband to visit her parents during the Christmas holidays in 1985. Dodging a Nerf ball, I entered the Lewisons' living room where Carole's unruly brood were ravishing each other's Christmas presents and clambering atop the couch, which held two pregnant sisters in their flannel nightgowns chain-smoking in front of the TV.

Although Polly had agreed to an interview, it took some effort for me to coax her out to a coffee shop for a private conversation. She seemed surprised by this idea and not enthusiastic. Before she dressed, she extracted my promise that I would not separate her from her husband for very long. As soon as I told Polly that I was studying contemporary family life, she boasted about her happy marriage. "Paul and I have a great marriage. We hardly ever argue. I don't have to"—Polly laughed—"I always get my way. I always have."

Polly was accustomed to having her way, she told me, because she had always been her father's favorite child. She attributed her privileged marriage to her cautious spouse-selection methods. She had made it a point to become friends with Paul before they had become intimate. "Just get to know him as a person before you get to know him as anything else" was the premarital advice she extrapolated from her experience. In fact, however, Paul had literally rescued Polly from the grip of a more typical Lewison relationship. He intervened when she was being beaten by the boyfriend with whom she had been livng for nearly one year. By delaying marriage and childbearing longer than her sisters and their mother, Polly seemed to have narrowly evaded the violent Lewison marital fate.

Although Polly had suffered developmental difficulties that placed her in special education classes, she was one of only two Lewison offspring to graduate from high school. She lost her first paid job as a nursery school aide when her parents' marital reunion disqualified her from the CETA rolls. Because she was unhappy in her second position as a live-in baby-sitter–housekeeper, Lou helped his favorite daughter get a temporary job at Conductex packing integrated circuit chips. After Polly was laid off without notice six months later, Lou intervened again, and for the next five years Polly fabricated wafers at Conductex, frequently working twelve-hour swing or graveyard shifts.

Polly's residences also alternated frequently during her years as a single woman. She moved in and out of her natal home between the first time she cohabited with a lover and later when she shared an apartment and even a bed, Chinese factory dorm "hot sheets" style, with friends who worked opposing shifts. Then in 1983 when Conductex sought workers to seed its new southwestern branch, Polly bid successfully on a job as a production technician and moved.

Working conditions and relationships in the new plant were not what Polly had expected. Her new supervisors resented Californians, and "they discriminated against women. They weren't used to having a girl as a technician, and you got treated different. They expected more out of you, and if you did something wrong they made a point of it to tell you and to embarrass you in front of everybody else, but if it was a man that did it wrong, they wouldn't say anything." Instead of the greater career opportunities Polly had anticipated, she suffered a demotion and a pay cut soon after the move. Then, adding injury to insult, Polly fell off her work stool and damaged her back and ankles.

At first Polly's romantic life was equally inauspicious. Arrested for drunk driving, she met a trucker in "DWI school" (Driving While Intoxicated) whom she soon foolishly invited to move into her apartment. During the year that they lived together, Polly learned the painful way that her boyfriend abused alcohol, drugs, and women. Fortunately Paul, a friend from work, visited in time one night to rescue Polly from a final violent struggle. Although she suffered a broken nose, black eyes, and further damage to her back, Polly was proud that she "threw the first punch." Paul bounced Polly's batterer from her apartment and moved in to protect her. The new roommates had already been friends for a year, and they waited another year before deciding to marry.

Marriage enabled Paul, an air force veteran, to qualify for a VA mortgage loan, and the newlyweds bought their first home right away. Alone among the Lewison children, Polly felt, with reason, that she was living the American dream. She was pregnant by a husband with a budding career who pampered and adored her and who did not insist that she contribute income to the household budget. During the course of this field study Polly moved toward a "modern" family pattern. Just one month after her marriage she suffered a second work injury from a sulfuric acid spill. In response, she overcame her husband's initial objections and answered a Conductex call for volunteers for lay offs. Polly then enrolled in a vocational school to avoid the job-seeking requirements of unemployment benefits eligibility, but when she became pregnant a few months later, Paul decided that she should quit school to stay home with their baby. Polly was quite happy to comply. "After eight years with a shit company, I really don't like to work. You know, I've had too many hassles in work, especially down there, because I figure, you know, during the whole time I was at work, I didn't really learn much, just what we had to do. It became routine, there was nothing to it. You were like, you got there, and they turned you on, and you did what they did, and they turned you off, and you went home, and I forgot everything."

Kristina, whose grueling work was far more challenging and rewarding

221

than Polly's, and whose marital experience was much less encouraging, thought her sister a fool to forfeit a career for conjugal dependency. "Lady Astor will pay for it later. I'd rather be self-sufficient. What's going to happen to her if Paul dies, and she doesn't know how to do anything? Call my attitude feminist if you want. I call it survival." While Kristina had chosen to emulate the father she resented, Polly found a husband who replicated her adored father's career, interests, and virtues but seemed to be free of his vices. Paul, like Lou before him, was a responsible, diligent worker who had pursued a military training route to his upwardly mobile, and hazardous, career as a line maintenance mechanic at Conductex. There he too suffered from extensive overtime demands and high-voltage injuries. Paul also shared Lou's avid interest in hot-rod racing as well as his willingness to participate in housework. Unlike Lou, however, Paul was an affectionate, accommodating, nonviolent spouse. Polly considered him an ideal husband. "What makes for a good husband?" I asked her. Polly laughed as she answered, somewhat smugly, "Somebody patient that likes to cook. Paul does all the cooking."

Dotty's least favorite daughter, Polly was also the least sympathetic to her mother's feminist politics. Polly had "never really cared for" feminism. "They were fighting about being equal, and I thought we were equal. My mom was always into signing Ms. instead of Mrs. or anything, and I thought it was kind of stupid. She gets out of hand. Like Carl's Jr. doesn't support the ERA, and we weren't allowed to eat there. Stupid stuff like that. I thought it was ridiculous. If I like the food I'd go eat there anyway and just not tell my mother. I thought they were going a little too far."

Instead of fostering feminist anger in Polly, gender discrimination at her workplace hastened her exit from the labor force. "That's one reason why I'm not there anymore. I found out one of the guys who was doing the same job as me, he had less than three years in the company, and he was making fifty cents more an hour than I was. I had eight years in, and that doesn't seem fair. But I couldn't do anything about it." And now that Polly had retreated from the world of paid work, she concluded that feminism "doesn't really have anything to do with me anymore."

Although Polly had been an adolescent at the time when her mother's feminist activism was at its height, she believed that she "really didn't pay much attention to it." Nonetheless, Polly, like Kristina, had complacently appropriated some of the benefits of hard-fought feminist campaigns. As a married woman, she expected and elicited her husband's active participation in housework and child care. As a single woman, Polly had nonchalantly exercised women's now-threatened right to an autonomous sexuality. She had felt free to take lovers and to live with them without marrying, and she had delayed childbearing by aborting an unwanted premarital pregnancy. Ironically, thanks in part to such feminist social gains, Polly appeared to be succeeeding at her mother's prefeminist modern family strategy, and in a period when this had become quite an aberrant achievement.

Carole: "I Feel Like I'm Missing Something"

Both Dotty and Kris disapproved of Polly's decision to pursue the homemaker course, a gender strategy that also held little appeal for Carole when I first interviewed this youngest of the Lewison daughters in September of 1985. However, one month later changes in family and work conditions pushed luckless Carole into an undesired homemaker role that bore far more resemblance to the oppressive one from which her mother had escaped than to the more privileged one her sister Polly enthusiastically embraced.

For reasons that the next chapter will reveal, I find it very difficult to write about Carole Lewison Kellner. I consider her to be far and away the most misfortunate and oppressed woman in my study. By all accounts Carole, the Lewisons' third child and third daughter, whose birth in 1961 deepened her parents' economic and marital crisis, grew up the most neglected, least favored of the five Lewison offspring. It is a sad irony, I believe, that the Lewison daughter who most admired her mother, had the greatest sympathy for Dotty's progressive and feminist politics, and whom I judged to be in greatest need of the family and work reforms that feminism seeks was also the least able to attain any of these benefits or to negotiate a tolerable alternative gender stategy.

Although I made several efforts, I never did get to visit Carole's "tobacco road" home. Instead I first met Carole, her husband, and their children when they moved back into her parents' home after being evicted. Carole was then twenty-four years old and pregnant with her fourth child. Her husband was none too pleased that she was leaving him in charge of their first three to spend the evening being interviewed by me. Believing that I could mollify Bobby somewhat by expressing interest in him too, Dotty nudged me to request a future interview with her son-in-law. Bobby, who was even more heavily tattooed than Lou, looked surly and suspicious, but, perhaps because I caught the young father off his guard as he wrestled a toddler into pajamas, he initially agreed to my request. Two days later, however, he "changed his mind back again" and canceled our appointment. As Bobby never changed his mind back the other way, I cannot include his perspective on the troubling tales about his character and behaviors that his wife conveyed with circumspection and his in-laws, with outrage.

Just one week after Carole became the second of the two Lewison children who graduated from high school, she met Bobby Kellner, a new Orchard Park neighbor. The mutual attraction between the young couple was instantaneous, as well as fateful and ill-starred. The night they met, Bobby staked his permanent claim to Carole: "He told me I'm his girl. Anybody that looks at me wrong, he was going to beat up, and if I look at anybody he would get me." The next day Bobby proposed marriage to Carole, and while she claimed that she "thought he was off his rocker," she began living with him three months later. She married and intentionally conceived a child with him three months after that. That precipitously did Carole link her fate to this eighteen-year-old youth from a family far more troubled than her own.

Bobby had entered Orchard Park temporarily to join the household of his divorced, remarried father, a man Carole consistently described as "a lazy, male macho son of a bitch." Bobby and his four brothers all did drugs, burglary, and time. In fact, Bobby had been jailed for three months after a drug bust that provoked another eviction early in their marriage and left Carole alone with their first young child. "It was the worst time of my life. I became an alcoholic at that time. It was the first time I had ever been on my own. I went bonkers."

This was quite a different relationship to life and liquor than Carole grew up intending to enjoy. She had hoped to become a bartender, because "I have one basic qualification that is really needed—a good listener—that, and I like mixing drinks." Carole had not hoped to get married or have children. "No, I swore up and down that I would never get married, never have kids, because I didn't want to be tied down. Me and my friend, we were going to get a place together and live the wild and fast life." While Carole's life did prove rather wild and fast, it was also overburdened by marital and maternal responsibilities. While she and Bobby intentionally conceived their first child, the next three "just kind of happened." Before she met Bobby, Carole had had a legal abortion at age sixteen. Ironically, the consequences proved to be opposite to the autonomous childbearing decisions that Polly reaped from her early abortion. Carole had found the experience so traumatic that she vowed never again to choose to terminate a pregnancy. Hence, the three contraceptive failures that rapidly followed her first child's birth ensnared Carole in a family life that was a continual series of traumas and abuse.

When Carole met Bobby, a "jack of all trades" but steady worker at none, she was working at a minimum wage, fast-food job. As the young couple began to plan a family, Dotty's friend Marilyn helped Carole get a job with better wages ($4.50 per hour) and insurance benefits on the electronics assembly line that her mother supervised. Although the company's management "hassled you a lot," penalized the whole line for minor errors, and "wasn't really too neat to work for," Carole liked the Mexican and Vietnamese women that she worked with: "It was like one big family, everybody pulling for each other." She also enjoyed the challenge of assembling PC boards and demonstration kits from schematics. "It was interesting working with your mind as well as your hands. It was a challenge." After working until the day her first child was born, Carole took two months of unpaid maternity leave before returning. She was shocked and depressed when, after she became pregnant again the next year, the company laid her off without notice to avoid paying her insurance.

From these not-so-glorious heights, Carole's occupational history skidded steadily downhill. Having been forced out after three years on her "permanent" job, Carole was compelled to accept two years of "temporary" employment at another Valley electronics company. Then in March 1985, just before the birth of her third child, Carole received her second layoff. Bobby, for his part, had just failed in his attempt to pursue a military route to income and occupational training. Kicked out of boot camp for fraud and insubordination, he spent a month in jail once again. Financial desperation and the electronics slump compelled Carole to take a further cut in pay to $4.10 per hour at a graveyard-shift job stuffing photographs into envelopes. Daily fluctuations in the company's workload determined daily fluctuations in Carole's schedule and income. And three months after the birth of her third child, Carole was pregnant once again.

These were the circumstances that lay behind their second eviction, which sent the desperate young Kellner family into its tense coresidential household with Dotty, Lou, and Danny. Bobby at last secured entry into a promising unionized job as a roofing apprentice, and he hoped to earn enough to keep his wife at home with their expanding family. "He tends to fall back on his father's ideas, which is the woman should be subservient and stay home with the kids, keep the house clean, have the meals cooked," Carole told me. Despite her growing brood and experiences in the labor force far more discouraging than Polly's, Carole still did not find her husband's goal for her appealing. "I don't know if I could handle that. I can't stand to sit around. I'd rather do something constructive. Sitting at home and taking care of the kids and keeping the house clean is not my idea of real constructive." Carole dreamed instead of owning a home with animals in the country and of opening a stained glass workshop that she and Bobby could operate together.

Scarcely one month after my first interview with Carole, she was forced to shift from a nondomestic to the homemaker strategy she previously abjured.[2] On the bright side, Bobby was progressing toward full union status, benefits, and income, and Lou had taken charge of his earnings to insure that these would secure independent housing instead of drugs. Within six months Bobby might be able to support the modern family he claimed to want. The negative factors, however, were more decisive. Quite simply, Carole could no longer afford to work for pay. She lost the photo-stuffing job she hated in a seasonal layoff, and now that she was expecting a fourth child, there were no jobs available to her that paid enough for the cheapest child care available. "In fact, I can't afford to work. Before I couldn't afford not to work; now I can't afford to work. It's weird, a head trip." Necessity fostered accommodation, and one year after Carole had claimed that she would hate to stay at home, she had concluded that "only if I absolutely have to" would she return to the work force. Instead she hoped to supplement family income by doing part-time electronics work at home.

Carole's moment as an optimistic homemaker was brutally brief. Discovering Bobby's infidelity the month they moved out of her parents' home drove her to attempt suicide. She kicked her errant husband out, but took him back as soon as he claimed to repent. By then her options were limited and grim. Alone among the Lewison daughters, Carole seemed fated to replicate her mother's prefeminist pattern, the underside of Polly's more privileged course. Bobby, like Polly's husband Paul, re-sembled Lou in many ways, but unfortunately for Carole, he shared far more of her father's vices than his virtues. Like Lou, Bobby had been an abused, neglected child who developed a tough don't-bother-me-none stance and a violent response to stress—unsavory male defenses untem-pered by the chivalrous norms of Southern civility to which Lou had been bred. Bobby was also like Lou in his native mechanical and physical abilities, but he came of age after the postindustrial window of opportunity for uneducated white working-class men had been shut. And perhaps because of the seductions of the local drug culture, Bobby, like Danny, never developed Lou's work discipline and responsibility.

With her self-esteem so low and her options so limited, Carole embraced the quixotic goal of reforming her husband. "Bobby is basically like his father. I am trying to get him a little bit more towards my idea of a good husband." She hoped to wean Bobby from his hard drug and alcohol habits and to curtail his tendency to "come home drunk and stoned at four or five A.M., which is not my idea of a decent hour." In this, Carole found her mother to be a source of inspiration. "She's always been the head of the house to me. She was very dominant. When my mom and dad separated, my mom dealt with it all. She didn't show anything was getting to her. I really look up to that lady. She gives me the inspiration to try and do better." Carole's admiration for her mother seemed to have fostered an intuitive sympathy for feminism. "I felt proud, very proud of her. I don't really know what a feminist is, but I like to take charge of my life, try to be the best I can be in whatever I'm doing. I don't know if that's a feminist or what."

I saw few signs that Carole would find the resources to emulate her mother's family reform strategies. Dotty felt as exasperated as I did when Carole agreed to take "that s.o.b. creep of a husband" back, but she held on to hope longer than I did that this was but a temporary relapse along the painful road to female self-determination. Dotty, who had the personal history to allow greater empathy with Carole's plight, also claimed the psychic capacity to "see" a happier resolution than I could envision. "My God, Judith, I just *saw* that Carole will have to repeat this, go through this a number of times before she'll be able to change things." I, on the other hand, limited by my secular, terrestrial-bound imagination, worried that Carole was correct when she told me "I feel like I'm missing some-thing." Not only was Carole missing the self-esteem to enable her to refuse her husband's degrading and abusive treatment, but she had also missed the period of feminism's most infectious empowering energy. She had missed an opportunity to participate in a sisterhood that might have compensated her for this fateful legacy of her disadvantaged family position.

Having come of age after feminism's most militant period, Carole seemed to have imbibed much of its awareness and its goals, without benefiting, as her mother and Marilyn had, from the movement's spurs to self-affirmation or social opposition. Like her sisters, Carole directly experienced and resented gender discrimination at work: "You do more work and you get paid less money." Carole's resignation to this injustice was more poignant than Polly's. "That's the way things are for the moment." For unlike Polly, Carole dreamed of a better world. Although Bobby was outraged at the thought of "a woman running the country, you got to be kidding," Carole had hoped that Geraldine Ferraro would succeed in her bid for the vice-presidency. "I said that's bullshit. You guys have done this so far and look what you've done. I mean, if a woman can run a household, why can't she try to run a country? She might do a better job. They could talk things out instead of going to war all the time."

Perhaps because Carole suffered the most exploitative family and work conditions among her sisters, she had developed the most progressive political instincts. Although she, like most of her siblings, never got around to voting, sheer exhaustion rather than indifference kept her from registering her political discontent. Unambivalently in favor of welfare, peace, and labor unions, Carole had spent her working days wanting to be organized. "Everybody that talked about a union, they immediately got silenced. I was always hoping that someone would come in and say, 'How about a union?'" I too wished that somebody had mobilized Carole, and I mourned her sadly unconsummated attraction to feminism. The vagaries of her familial and historical birth order struck me as consequential, and lamentable. Least resistant to, and most in need of, the transformative vision of feminism, Carole's postfeminist adolescence as the third Lewison daughter seemed to have denied her its rewards.

None of Dotty's daughters had fully embraced or repudiated feminism. Instead, in their efforts to negotiate family and work relationships under postindustrial conditions, all three took for granted many feminist convictions from which each, according to her resources, derived differing measures of gain or pain. Unacknowledged feminist campaigns paved the ground for Kristina to wage her successful vendetta as an unwed mother and career woman. Polly's retreat from exploitative and discriminatory postindustrial employment to her promising modern family strategy also rested in part on her exercise of reproductive rights that feminists now are struggling to preserve. I find more painful, however, the irony that feminist consciousness, because it underscored the chasm between her democratic aspirations and her oppressive circumstances, may have increased the suffering of Carole, the postfeminist daughter who appreciated and needed gender justice most of all.

10

If Wishes Were Fishes: Surviving Loss in a Matrifocal Family

If wishes were horses,
Beggars might ride.

—English proverb

It was the second day of Rosh Hashanah, the Jewish New Year, in October 1986, when I attended Sunday religious services not in a synagogue with my own family but in a neighborhood Methodist church in Orchard Park with three generations of women from Dotty's. Lou, who was not feeling well that morning, had stayed home to watch a football game, and I was seated between Dotty and Kristina when Dotty's mother, Lorna, joined our pew. Lorna was a recently recovered alcoholic who, citing AA's pledge of anonymity as the cause of her refusal, earlier had declined to participate in my study. Doubting that Dotty had prepared her mother for my presence that morning, I sat worrying about situational ethics and etiquette. Soon the minister, the Reverend Landman, would deliver a sermon about overcoming stress advising me not to worry.

Sunday services at Orchard Methodist Community Church crossbred theology and forms of worship observed at Global Ministries of Love with those at the Universal Temple of the Spirit. The ethnic and racial composition of the fifty or so worshippers in attendance was more diverse, including an African-American couple and several Asian and Latino families, but congregants appeared to inhabit the same working-class and modest middle-class milieu as did the members of those other two small Silicon Valley congregations. Most, like Dotty and Lorna, seemed to appreciate the blend of evangelical and human potential movement ideology and practices that filled the morning program.

Pastor Landman and his parishioners employed linguistic forms resonant of those in use at Global Ministries. Prayers and testimonies expressed the same direct, personal, and conversational relationship with Jesus. The service began with hymns and prayers of praise and thanks to Jesus, with the minister's wife playing the piano as her handsome husband invited the Holy Spirit "to enter and be among us." The pastor next invited parishioners to offer public "praise reports" to Jesus for the good He had brought into their lives that week. Dotty was the first to comply. She thanked the Lord for leading her back to this church. Another woman gave thanks that Jesus had enabled her to help a coworker to pray about his serious illness and had then rewarded him with the news that he did not have cancer. A Filipino man, thankful that his brother had joined the family in church that morning, introduced him to the congregation.

Orchard Methodist employed an equally personal format for intercessory prayer, and the pastor's call for these unleashed a litany of local travail. Once again irrepressible Dotty responded first. A former neighbor of hers had died at forty-two that week of ailments induced by alcohol. For several months, years ago, while the woman fled her brutal husband, Dotty had sheltered her friend's sons. Now Dotty asked parishioners to pray for the orphans for whom she was no longer able to provide more material forms of assistance. A second parishioner called for prayers for the survivors of a shocking murder that had been committed in Orchard Park that week. An adolescent boy was the primary suspect in the violent death of his mother. Next a man requested prayers for a homeless friend of his, and the pastor asked the congregation to pray for the resolution of a severe financial crisis that threatened the survival of a large church in the area.

Before the time came for the reverend to deliver his weekly sermon, the second in a series on overcoming stress, parishioners had displayed abundant evidence of their interest in such a goal. The sermon, a sampler of Christian faith embroidered with stress reduction maxims from the human potential movement, recalled the boosterist, optimistic discourse of the spiritualist church Dotty and Lou had recently abandoned. Its twin themes were trust in God and don't worry, be happy. A printed insert in the morning's worship service program listed ten steps for over-coming stress, each paired with a biblical textual citation. While several advised prayer, intimacy with Christ, and trust in God, more recom-mended attention to one's physical and practical welfare. "Pace yourself," "Get rid of all hindrances," "Make the most of every opportunity," "Rest and be refreshed," and finally, "Care for your body," the pastor's guide-lines advised. His own well-tended, athletic body exuding health and confidence, Pastor Landman drew from Corinthians a biblical injunction for physical fitness. "Do you not know that your body is a temple of the Holy Spirit within you, whom you have from God, and that you do not belong to yourselves? For you were bought and paid for; then give God the glory with your body."

In a folksy, good-humored manner, interjecting personal anecdotes about his own family and neighbors, the Reverend Landman advised his listeners not to worry about the future but to live in the present. I was confident that, at least in my pew, the doctrine he preached found a welcome, sympathetic audience. "There is enough trouble today," Land-man acknowledged, "you don't need to add to it by worrying about tomorrow's troubles. Worrying never helped anything anyway. Anxiety never added inches to anyone's height." "Or years to anyone's life," I imagined Dotty to be thinking, with Lou transmitting his extrasensory assent. Take time to play, Pastor Landman instructed, in a spirit also certain to win Dotty's approval. "Remember that a joyous God created you to have fun with you."

Albert Gama and most Global Ministries worshippers, in contrast, would surely cringe, I remember thinking, if they were to hear the Rev-erend Landman's views on proper Christian living. "I don't believe God established a hierarchy of needs and goals," the pastor announced, while acknowledging contending theological positions on this matter. "On the radio, you often hear pastors say that the most important thing is your relationship to Jesus, or living by the Word, or addressing your spiritual needs, but I don't believe that we can separate or prioritize our spiritual, social, physical, and emotional needs; they all work together, as we must do."

Unlike Universal Temple, the Orchard Methodist church displayed substantial concern for the social problems that afflicted the region and times. The Reverend Landman prefaced his sermon by labeling the Silicon Valley a high-stress capital whose inhabitants shoulder "unbeliev-able stress on their jobs." He reinforced the parishioner's intercessory prayer for a homeless friend by lamenting the large and growing number of homeless in a region of unparalleled affluence,[1] and he urged contri-butions to a missionary project for these unfortunates.

Orchard Methodist differed from Global Ministries in the character of its response to social inequities and need. It joined a social gospel to its spiritual ministry efforts. Eleanor Garrett Morrison could have penned the pastoral note on "the Good News that we have received in Jesus our Lord and Savior," which prefaced the October monthly newsletter from Orchard Methodist, as she would have endorsed the "spiritual warfare seminar" announced within its pages. But Global Ministries newsletters were unlikely to include an insert soliciting support for a national ethnic minority scholarship program for church leadership training, such as the one we received at the Orchard Methodist church that morning. The Methodist newsletter also advertised a women's prayer group in which the Lord's Prayer would be offered in Spanish and French, with "other languages welcome," and it encouraged church members to join Care for the Poor, a local antipoverty coalition to which their church had sent a representative. "You know, most of us think of the poor as desperate, grubby bums or something—but these days many people are actually middle-class people—like us, who have lost their job, their home, or their family," tutored the newsletter report from this representative. While Global Ministries also ministered to the homeless poor, it gave more attention to saving their souls than to ameliorating the social sources of their misfortune. Still, the impact of the human potential movement on all three of the small churches I had visited was unmistakable.

When the service ended, Kristina left us at the coffee reception while she gathered Tommy from his Sunday School group. Earlier that morn-ing, she had led his Bible study class. Kris's active involvement in this church was quite recent, as was my awareness of her active belief in God. I had misread her instrumental, worldly drive, her supreme impatience with human "irrationality," and the disparaging comments about fun-damentalists that she volunteered from time to time as decisive evidence of thoroughgoing secularism. Yet Kris considered her life to be firmly rooted in religious faith, an abiding belief in God that was not constrained by denominational distinctions. Despite the paucity of sleep that her grueling work schedule allowed, Kristina set her alarm for 6:00 A.M. each

233

Sunday to listen to "God Talk," a religious radio talk show hosted by a liberal Catholic named Bernie Ward, whom Al Gama had disdainfully described to me as an errant "social gospel humanist." During the segment of "God Talk" that I had listened to en route to the Lewisons' that morning, Ward actively opposed censorious Christian attitudes. He provoked the ire of many listeners by defending a single mother who worked as a topless dancer to support her two children, and he supported the Catholic dissenter, Father Curran, in his struggles with the church hierarchy. Kristina was not persuaded by Ward's defense of the dancer, she told me, but she appreciated his attempt "to bring the Bible up to date" and enjoyed being challenged by his views.

As we assembled tuna sandwiches and diet soft drinks back at the Lewisons' after services, Kristina expressed similarly positive but not uncritical sentiments about Orchard Methodist Community Church. Like her mother and grandmother, Kristina appreciated the informal ambience at the church and the minister's friendly, warmly personal manner, but she did not share Dotty's enthusiasm for the "touchy-feely" parts of the service. The hand-holding and sentimental praise reports that comforted her mother embarrassed Kristina. She shared her parents' belief in prophecy, however, and believed, with them, that the Methodist church did so as well. "I don't know why they call it a gift, though," Kris remarked, explaining that she had been born with this far-from-desirable ability. "It's really a burden, the burden of the message," which, Kris said, she had "prayed to be relieved of" several years ago after "seeing" her brother Loujoo's death in a racial altercation in boot camp. Intervention by alerted authorities had spared Loujoo that time, his family believed, and this in turn had reinforced their faith in mystical religion. But not for long.

IF THERE IS A HELL

Two months before attending the Orchard Methodist service, I had returned to California after a month's absence to find a wrenching letter from Dotty. "I decided to write you a note, because I didn't think I could stand telling you over the phone," it began ominously, "that our son Louis was killed in a wreck in France." Loujoo had died at twenty-three in a car crash. I was not the only one who had missed his funeral. Determined efforts to locate Danny, who had "skipped town" prior to being sentenced after his most recent drug and burglary conviction, succeeded only after Loujoo had been laid to rest in a military cemetery. Danny sneaked back for a brief visit two days late, then left again. "It's like losing two sons," Dotty mourned.

Loujoo's tragic death had precipitated his parents' decision to abandon Universal Temple and return to their neighborhood Methodist congregation. Dotty and Lou had been profoundly wounded, then enraged by inept, indifferent responses to their grief by the metaphyscial minister and church members. The minister had failed to minister to the Lewisons in their time of deepest pain, and few church members attended Loujoo's funeral or offered personal condolences. "I'm glad I never converted you to that spiritualist church," Dotty retorted one day when I informed her that she had finally converted me to microwave. "I can't believe they can be so cold." Dotty recognized that the metaphyscial church subscribed to a different emotional reading of death, but found the lack of empathy unforgivable. "Death isn't supposed to be such a sad thing, because it's not really an ending. But *still*, that was our *child*, for God's sake." The Reverend Landman, in contrast, had paid daily visits to these former parishioners, even though he had never met them before, and the grateful Lewisons rewarded his compassion by returning to the Methodist fold.

"It should have been me," Lou stated flatly when he greeted me on my first visit after my trip. It was the hardest death he had ever had to bear. "In fact, the stress almost killed me. But I guess I wasn't meant to die, because I'm still here," he continued, as he launched into an uncharacteristically lengthy explication of his fatalistic creed. "When your number's up, it's up. Everyone's put here for some purpose, or to learn something. You can't change your fate. Why do you think two people can have the same accident, or the same disease, but one of them dies and the other doesn't? It's fate. You die when you're meant to die. I can't figure why I'm still alive, but apparently I wasn't meant to die yet." His speech concluded, Lou left the room to tend his garden while Dotty whispered in my ear, "I thought we *were* going to lose him too. We came pretty close."

Too close. Loujoo's death proved to be but the first of a tragic series of events that devastated the Lewison family that year. One month after the church service we did lose Lou. Scarcely a week after he and Dotty had returned from visiting their newest granddaughter in Arizona and their oldest friends in Colorado, the heavenly banker called the loan on what Lou had considered borrowed time. Lou's stricken heart succumbed at fifty-three to a final assault. One month after that, twenty-six-year-old Carole received a diagnosis of a fatal cancer tumor, while Danny, who had returned home for his father's funeral, was in jail again after being arrested with PCP and hundreds of hypodermic needles. Four months later, released under strict court probation terms, Danny fled the state just before Carole's death left her husband contesting Dotty and Kristina for custody of his four young children. And these are merely the most significant of the ceaseless calamities that have battered the Lewisons since Loujoo died. Judging my research relationship to their mounting tragedies ghoulish, I curtailed fieldnote recording sessions and deferred writing about the Lewisons, this chapter of their lives especially, as long as possible.

As part of their valiant attempt to recover from their grief over Loujoo's death, and with money saved for the European trip that was not to be, Dotty and Lou took an anniversary trip to visit first their daughter Polly's newborn and then the friends who had arranged their original blind date more than thirty years before. The trip provided the last moments of shared pleasure Dotty and Lou were to enjoy.

When they returned home Carole was in a hospital hemorrhaging internally after a tubal ligation. She had been forced to defer this surgery and to undergo an abortion one month earlier when a preoperative examination revealed that she was pregnant once again. Persuaded by her doctors that the unexpected pregnancy represented a grave threat to her health as well as to her capacity to care for her four children, Carole reluctantly violated her vow never to have another abortion. She blamed the hospital's bureaucratic ineptitude, however, for confronting her with this moral quandary and trauma. The hospital had failed to complete the paperwork to implement Carole's request for the tubal ligation immediately after delivering her last child. "Can you believe it?" Dotty exclaimed, reporting this latest of the Lewison tribulations. "God, is there any end? And if so, is it good or bad?"

My pen was in hand, poised to record fieldnotes, when I telephoned Kristina's home on a Friday evening one week later. Frank answered the phone and informed me awkwardly that Mr. Lewison had died several hours before. A blur of sorrow and hubbub suffuses the days of mourning and regrouping that ensued. Dotty's friend Marilyn took charge of organizing the cadre of women volunteers who shouldered the considerable domestic burdens of enacting the social rituals of parting with the dead. Veteran attendants to the grieved, Dotty's women friends repeated the invisible labors they had performed two months earlier of notifying, transporting, housing, and feeding the Lewisons' extensive network of kith and kin.

Dotty and her children and friends set about gathering the mourners who would assemble to bid farewell to Lou. While none of Lou's surviving siblings was sufficiently healthy, affluent, or motivated to make the transcontinental air trip, all of Dotty's biological, step-, and half relatives set out to attend. Polly and Paul bundled their infant for her first marathon road race, Loujoo's widow and daughter were quickly airborne, and Dotty's biological father, his wife and brother, and both of Dotty's half siblings stocked their van for the long drive from the inland to the coastal valley. Feverish efforts to locate Danny succeeded more rapidly than they had when Loujoo died. He arrived two days before his father's funeral on a flight paid for by Kristina and Frank.

Following Marilyn's directive, I drove Dotty and Danny to the funeral home for a private family viewing of Lou's body, while Dotty balanced on her lap a pottery soup tureen made by Loujoo, the vessel she had selected to receive his father's ashes. Kristina had opposed her mother's plan to cremate Lou. It was "unnatural," she argued. "The Bible says you'll go back to the Lord the way you came." But Dotty was unswervable. She found it comforting to anticipate sleeping next to Lou's remains, and cremation spared the costly expenses of a casket and monument. If Loujoo hadn't died, perhaps she might have afforded the expense, but Lou would have disapproved, and "ashes are good for the earth; it puts something back in," she reasoned.

Well immunized from cares or affect by his ready supply of chemical mood synthesizers, mellow Danny nodded to a private beat. Knowing that his mother depended on more social coping mechanisms, I promised to bring her taped recordings of my early interviews with Lou. "I love you, Judith. You're a good friend," she thanked me. But moments later, perhaps unwittingly, Dotty evoked the unconventional and asymmetrical character of our friendship. She thought that I would find it as funny as she did, she told me, that I had annoyed her mother the day before by asking questions about Lou's death. "I think it's funny that she's so uptight about you." I, however, felt more defensive than amused. Declining Dotty's invitation to visit Lou before the public viewing, I tended Polly's newborn until she returned, weeping in Paul's arms, from the family viewing. Then murmuring excuses, I departed earlier and more hastily than I had planned.

I leave it to post-Freudians to conjecture why I, a skillful map-reader and habitually punctual individual, barely found my way back to the funeral chapel the next day in time to attend Lou's final service. The Reverend Landman intoned the first prayer as I rushed into one of the few remaining seats. "Provide your personal help and comfort to this inordinately aggrieved family," the pastor beseeched the Lord. God knows the pain you feel, he tried to assure Lou's intimate survivors, because He sacrificed His only son. A chandelier, swaying in a slight breeze, seemed to nod in agreement when the reverend reassured Dotty that her husband, now with God, was still with her in spirit. Lou might have disapproved of the money his family spent committing him to the ages, but I felt confident that he would have approved of his eulogy, a narrative not unlike the one he had first relayed to me, about a hardworking man who, despite the deprivation and hardships in his background, struggled successfully to overcome his often troubled history with a wife and children to whom he was devoted. "Good-bye, young lady," I imagined Lou murmuring as we mourners filed past his casket while the chapel's sound system played the country and western song his family had chosen to conclude this ceremony of farewell.

Back in Orchard Park, the seasoned volunteer catering committee served a potluck, postmortem banquet. Grateful to be usefully employed, I arranged platters of deviled eggs, macaroni, chicken wings, and luncheon meats, as I tried self-consciously to avoid exploiting this opportunity to expand my fieldwork acquaintance with Dotty's reunited extended kin. This proved an impossible, perhaps a disingenuous goal. Between bouts of sobbing admixed with nostalgic humor, Dotty introduced me to relatives and friends. Nor was it possible for me to ignore or condone Bobby's abusive treatment of Carole or to be indifferent to the deferential appeasement strategy with which this underappreciated young woman attempted to deflect his verbal blows. Where Bobby, by my cultural code, should be comforting his genuinely grief-stricken wife, instead Carole struggled to placate her irascible mate, leaping to his demand that she remove "the brats" while he drank his beer and shot a B.B. gun at a crow foraging in Lou's fallow tomato patch.

Danny's former sweetheart Amanda, however, made the trip to comfort Lou's least-favored offspring and to encourage him to surrender to authorities. Stoned throughout the mourning rituals, Danny appeared willing to consent. He had agreed, Dotty claimed, to turn himself in right after Christmas. Before his resolve could be tested, however, and scarcely a week after Lou's tragic death, a police officer picked up Danny and his dealer buddy in an unregistered car loaded with illegal drugs and paraphernalia. Compelled to seize her small comforts wherever she could find them, Dotty conceded a portion of relief at this latest traumatic event. At least now she would no longer be in a constant state of anxiety, worrying about whether Danny would overdose again, or fearing another police raid on her house. The Reverend Landman's ten-step plan for overcoming stress could not have anticipated the levels of anguish Dotty was required to endure. The death of her husband spelled economic as well as emotional deprivation, because Dotty lost the monthly disability checks that had supplied the mainstay of the household budget. As Dotty steeled herself to return to work after the three days of her allotted bereavement leave had expired, she summarized the season's events: "I honestly believe that if there is a hell, this is it."

But Satan had further abominations in store. The cruelest of these was Carole's cancer. The unexplained hemorrhaging Carole had experienced after her tubal ligation, her difficult pregnancies, an unhealed swollen muscle, and a myriad of random symptoms that she had suffered in silence assumed ominous coherence when the laboratory diagnosed her death sentence. Before six months elapsed Carole was dead of rhabdomyosarcoma, a rare and virulent cancer. I would like to be able to report that her tragic and tortuous demise reformed her husband who eased her painful decline by reciprocating her devotion and affection. Empirical constraints, however, forbid this sentimental flight of fancy. Carole suffered and forgave her young, unreconstructed macho husband who, until the end, failed to sweeten. Rallying greater reserves of anger and resistance than in healthier days, Carole turned her outrage instead on the medical personnel whose diagnostic negligence she blamed for her impending death. In a valiant, futile effort to bequeath her children a modicum of financial protection, Carole expended her final energies preparing a medical negligence lawsuit against the hospital that misdiagnosed her early symptoms. She also fought courageously to preserve the life she had tried to forfeit one year earlier, before surrendering with dignity to the unvanquishable foe.

WITHOUT A SHOEHORN

With Carole dying and Lou and Loujoo dead, Kristina vied for C.E.O. control of the remnant matrilineal family of which Dotty remained the emotional headquarters. Most of the women and children in the Lewison kin set had lost or forsworn their ties to that seemingly endangered species—the domesticated working-class male able to earn, and willing to share, a family wage. Polly alone still enjoyed such privileged circumstances, but as Dotty and Kristina both noted, her security, tethered to the stability of her marriage, was fragile, perhaps illusory.

One month after Lou's funeral, his widow discussed how shocked she was to discover the depths of her dependency on him. Dotty recalled with wistful wonder how confident and assertive she had felt when she set the stringent terms for their reunion a decade earlier. "Hell, I was so adamant about my independence; yet I gave up so much. I used to know how to do everything. Now I've forgotten everything. I don't know, Judith. He always took care of me. Lou was my shoehorn. I don't remember how to do things. I always said that any woman who allowed that to happen to her was a goddamn fool, but there I go." Fear honed Dotty's grief over Lou's passing into levels of distress she had not anticipated. Now that his income was gone, were she to lose her job again, she might lose her house as well. "What the hell is going to happen to me, Judith?"

Kristina, the only Lewison woman who had never attempted the "modern" strategy, was ready with an answer. Dependent on her own earnings instead of a man, she believed herself in greater control of her life, and she was willing, even determined, to assume primary financial and managerial responsibility for her mother's fate. Kris's seeming autonomy, however, did not exempt her from the debilitating high-stress culture that stalked her family and the region. Beset by work-induced anxiety and by a myriad of health problems aggravated by stress, fatigue, tobacco, and irregular nutrition, Kris survived on adrenaline and Xanax, which she supplemented from time to time with visits to a psychiatrist. During the season of death that decimated her natal family, Kristina lived under constant threat of a potential layoff, spending twenty-one days on an unpaid "vacation" when ASC shut its plant to reduce costs during a cyclical decline in orders. Kristina actually worked without pay a good many of those days, struggling to meet her company's unrealistic project deadlines.

Kris's boyfriend Frank, in the meantime, actually did suffer an unexpected layoff, and this shortly after he had wrecked his car. While this sequence of misfortunes increased his dependency on Kris, it did not, at first, diminish hers on him. On the contrary, the sudden loss of her brother and father seemed to strengthen Kristina's interest in marrying Frank. She sought emotional companionship and parenting support rather than a breadwinner in her man. "This has really brought us closer together," Kristina reported a fortnight before Christmas in 1986. "I don't want to be without him, and he's hardly left my side." The two were discussing mariage again, Kristina claimed, seriously this time. "Well actually, it started with Tommy asking Frank to marry me, and Frank made a joke out of it, but we've been talking about it seriously since then."

Kris perceived no contradiction between her simultaneous efforts to marry still-resistant Frank and to return to and reorganize her natal home. Indeed, the same evening that Kris reported the progress of her marital goals, she also detailed her efforts to assume her father's familial roles. She told me that she was shielding Dotty from both loneliness and undesired wellwishers by spending every lunch break with her mother and eating dinner with her almost as often. Determined to take care of her mother, Kristina lobbied strenuously to overcome Dotty's misgivings and resistance to a family reconstitution strategy she had devised. She wanted Dotty to refinance and remodel the house to transform it into a quasi-duplex. Then Kris could move in with Tommy and, if she had her way, with Frank as well, and she would assume primary responsibility for mortgage payments and household expenses.

Wouldn't such a plan further diminish Frank's lack of enthusiasm for her wedding plans? I asked. Kristina instantly reassured us both. "No, I already asked Frank how he'd feel about having my mom sort of living with us if we were married, and that was no problem." Unconvinced, but eager to share Kris's bid for relief from the season of anguish, I endorsed her conjugal inclinations. "It would feel good to attend a happy family event with the Lewisons for a change," I conceded. "I would love to end my fieldwork with a wedding." "You'll have to go to one more funeral first," Kris responded somewhat matter-of-factly. She and Dotty both had "seen" her grandmother Lorna's death.

The shocking news that the next family funeral would mourn Carole instead provoked a dramatic turnabout in Kristina's plans, serving indirectly to terminate her wedding dreams and to foster the formation of a matrilineal household. Two months before her sister died, Kristina found sudden cause to abandon her interest in Frank. He had finally found another job, as a security guard once again, and he was "still hanging around; like right this moment, he's watching TV with Tommy in the living room," Kris whispered into the phone. "But," she added with cold conviction, "Frank is definitely on the way out. I'm planning to get rid of him for betraying me." Frank's betrayal was not carnal but spiritual. In the midst of this time of extreme emotional vulnerability, Frank had undermined Tommy's religious faith and, thereby, Kristina's child rearing. In Kris's view Frank had betrayed her by telling her son that he did not believe in God. "And he did that after I explicitly told him *not* to tell Tommy that. I won't be betrayed, and I won't have anybody undermining my childrearing. That's it, he's through."

Although Kristina defined Frank's transgression of her parental authority as the central cause of her disaffection, she also displayed deep personal disappointment over his lack of faith. "I always knew that we were unevenly yoked," Kris lamented. Nonetheless, she acknowledged that she had hoped Frank would come to recognize and share the faith that she viewed as the source of the very strength in her he so admired. She had "hoped to bring him around indirectly," but she read his "betrayal" as brutal evidence that her plan had failed, and of their fundamental incompatibility.

Reading the Bible "kind of frantically " over the past few months, Kristina had been groping her way toward a different reading of God's will. Following a guide for daily Bible study from Orchard Methodist Community Church, Kris read the Book of Job as she coped with family tragedy. "You shouldn't blame God for your troubles," she concluded. "God doesn't take people; He accepts them, and that's a big difference. God has a plan." Accepting Carole, Kris had begun to speculate, might be the divinity's attempt to offer her sister's deprived and undisciplined children a chance to escape their troubled home environment. Kristina believed that her nieces and nephews were in dire need of therapeutic attention. If she could take custody of them, she reasoned, her medical insurance benefits would provide them with the health care and counseling services she seemed to think they needed more than their mother's survival.

The sad truth was that financially Carole was worth more to her children in death than in life. Survivors' benefits checks, which their custodial caretaker was entitled to receive, equaled $720 per month. This was the principal reason, Dotty deduced bitterly, that her son-in-law contested her appeal for custody of his children. Initially, Bobby's presumptive parental rights prevailed, and Dotty and Kristina were awarded only alternate weekend visitation rights. It did not take Bobby very long, however, to jeopardize his custodial rights by demonstrating many of the negligent and illicit behaviors that had driven his wife to her suicide attempt one year before her death.

Within six months of Carole's death, and without benefit of architectural reforms, Kristina and Tommy did move into Dotty's household. By then Bobby had been arrested for speeding in an unregistered car and had lost his job. He informally placed his children in Dotty's care so frequently that she soon won temporary legal custody of them. It did not take very long, therefore, for Dotty to find herself reliving the same double bind that had entrapped her daughter, as it had ensnared her decades before. One week before Dotty was scheduled to spend a week visiting Polly and several of Lou's relatives in the South, she contracted hepatitis. When Dotty's sick leave lengthened during a busy season at work, she lost her job, and by the time she had recovered, she was far too distraught and disorganized to seek or hold another one. Nor was she likely to have found another that she could have afforded to accept. The jobs available to her did not pay wages equivalent to the child care expenses they would oblige her to incur. Thus, Dotty came to be trapped as a full-time homemaker again, not in a modern family this time, but in an increasingly fractious, matrifocal joint household. So battered and debilitated were Dotty's spirits, she could no longer even manage to get herself to church. Indeed, she rarely mustered sufficient energy or incentive to dress herself or the children. Only home visits from her mother, stalwart friends, church volunteers, and social service workers parted the ponderous curtains of once-gregarious Dotty's social isolation and disarray.

243

CALAMITY CULTURE

I do not count myself, I am ashamed to report, among those stalwart friends. Troubled by the moral ambiguity of my relationship to the mounting list of tragedies that were decimating the Lewisons during the season when I had planned to withdraw from fieldwork, I attempted to define an arbitrary endpoint to our research collaboration. I sought a boundary line that would exclude Carole's impending death from my study's "proper" terrain of concern. This futile enterprise was driven by my emotional responses to the extremity of the Lewisons' misfortune. Overwhelmed and threatened, I recoiled from what I had come to perceive as the calamity culture that most of the Lewisons inhabited. I worried too that readers might also seek to distance themselves from the ill-fated Lewisons by defining the family, like its skeptical neighbor once had done, as beyond the province of sociological inquiry.

As Dotty lost her hold on the barest semblance of "settled living," it became clear just how precarious and ephemeral had been her family's tenure in that respectable status. The conditions of the Lewisons' lives made it impossible to distinguish clearly between effects of sheer ill fortune and of socially patterned malaise. Vulnerable to the volatility of the local postindustrial job market and to its many social and environmental evils, the Lewisons suffered a substantial level of social risk. Cumulative exposure to these hazards fostered a fatalistic credo and the rebellious, devil-may-care bravado of their "hard living" existential stance that compounded their travails. Life in their working-class fast lane mated the considerable physical and financial dangers of their work environment to equally hazardous off-the-job behaviors.

Most of the Lewisons lived hard, drove fast, spent impulsively, and partook liberally of high-risk diets, tobacco, alcohol, and often, drugs. Their leisure-time preferences—gambling, flirting, racing, shooting—reflected and reinforced the provocative and ambivalent character of their relationship to social stability. Deficiencies in medical insurance coverage and self-denying cultural norms conspired to prevent most from receiving preventive health care. Personal and social pride diminished their access to the inadequate and declining forms of public assistance available in the eighties. The Lewisons were victimized by an inordinate share of tragic events, but their circumstances and the lives they lived made them accidents waiting to happen. Ill fate or a merciless deity assured that the waiting periods were unconscionably brief.

Ironically, Danny, who took the baldest walk on the wild side, repeatedly escaped its fatal snares. He had fled the state again when he was released from jail on probation, and, the last time I inquired, Dotty described her youngest as living under an alias, married, employed, and "clean." Few of Danny's relatives shared his Teflon karma. His brother Lou, Jr., had died driving his newly purchased BMW at its maximum 120-mph speed in a fogbank at night after an explosive conflict with his wife. Lou, Sr., had blamed fate and excessive job demands for the lethal heart disease that did not deter him from chain-smoking until his early end. "They're trying to worry the American people to death," Lou used to fume whenever he encountered antismoking or dietary "propaganda" in the media. Dotty too thumbed her ceaseless cigarettes and a high-cholesterol diet at her asthma and high blood pressure. Carole played roulette with reproduction, then carried two of her pregnancies without benefit of prenatal care until alarming symptoms forced her to seek medical assistance for the indigent. She rightfully blamed hospital negligence for the late diagnosis of her cancer, but her own reluctance to acknowledge or seek treatment for her symptoms also contributed to at least a portion of the delay.

ON LOSS, LEARNING, AND LAUGHTER

As the tragic year unfolded, Dotty, Kristina, and I scavenged our disparate temperamental, spiritual, and cultural resources for interpretive schema and coping strategies. Dotty vacillated among diverse responses to her pain. With despondent faith she pondered the source of God's cruel greed. "Why did God need to take both of them?" she asked me plaintively immediately after her husband's death. "I could understand Him needing one of them, but why did He need to take them both?" Convinced there had to be a cosmic rationale for her suffering, Dotty sought comfort in her metaphysical convictions. Her belief in an afterlife and spiritual reincarnation provided a modicum of consolation. "Life doesn't stop when you die," Dotty asserted, as we discussed Lou's funeral a fortnight later. "The person's spirit survives, maybe not always in the form you would like, but they're still there." Loujoo's spirit, Dotty explained, was the force behind the swaying chandelier that had caught my attention during his father's funeral service. Dotty, Kristina, and Loujoo's young widow all had noticed the movement and recognized it as a sign that Loujoo's spirit had come to soften their grief. It was a bit more difficult to feel the spirit of Lou, Sr., because his was not as powerful as his son's, but Dotty managed to feel her husband with her in Orchard Park, watching out for their neighbors, lending them his metaphysical hand.

Less frequently, Dotty indulged the frightening fury suppressed beneath her grief, the impotent rage she felt toward more corporeal and tangible agents of her misery. At these moments Dotty railed against the fast-track life in Silicon Valley, condemning corporate negligence and greed for the unbearable losses she was suffering. Despite the recklessness of Loujoo's final ride, Dotty blamed his death on the failure of his seat belt, a failure she attributed to cost-cutting deficiencies in the manufacturing process. She continued to hold the inhumane, exploitative work demands that her husband's employer had exacted responsible for Lou's fatal coronary disease. Similarly Dotty identified the corporate bottom line as the unforgivable source of the medical malpractice that delayed the diagnosis of her daughter's malignancy. Gradually she also began to suspect that toxic substances Carole had breathed and handled in her work environments might be the carcinogenic culprits of her daughter's deadly affliction.

Through even the grimmest period, however, Dotty struggled to maintain her saucy sense of humor, her most practiced and potent coping resource. The week that Dotty returned to work after bereavement leave for Lou, I arrrived to take her out for lunch. As I sat waiting for Dotty's supervisor to give permission for her to leave, it cheered me to observe Dotty flirting with clients and coworkers. A Latino man arrived to shut off his cable TV service. "Hi, how are you?" he returned Dotty's welcoming greeting. "I'm gorgeous, but you know that," she parried without a blink, before consoling him on the recent layoff that had placed cable service beyond his reach. "You sure can see some gorgeous guys from here," Dotty announced, gesturing toward an attractive man crossing the parking lot in front of the office. Then winking at her African-American coworker, Dotty added. "And I also get to hear her husband's great bedroom voice." "There seems to be a hint of that in yours as well," I teased her back. "There ought to be; I've had enough practice."

Less practiced in the mirthful arts than her mother, Kristina employed more instrumental coping skills. The pragmatic reading of divine will that she gave to her sister's death typified, and served to justify, her best defense, an impetus to deploy her ample repertory of managerial capacities. "Didn't my father tell you he wanted me to take care of my mother after he died?" Kris interrogated me at the funeral, appealing for confirmation of her conviction that she was her father's designated legatee to be the family chief executive officer. Kristina did not await an electoral mandate to appoint herself the family's frontline contact person for the voluminous bureaucratic rites that attend American mores of death and dying. She rummaged through her father's unsorted papers to decode the access routes to his survivors' benefits; she located lawyers to advise Carole on her medical malpractice complaint; she battled the health maintenance organization to transfer her sister to a specialized oncology center; she fought the county welfare department to provide child care and hospice services; she arranged grief counseling for her mother and a Big Brother for her son.

Kristina's anger, when it surfaced, preferred individual to corporate targets. At moments she held her sister-in-law responsible for the final domestic rupture that preceded Loujoo's reckless ride. Kris fumed over Carole's irresponsible childbearing and over Bobby's perfidy and opportunism. She bemoaned her mother's disorganization and locked horns with her over their incompatible child disciplinary practices. And Kris never did forgive Frank for undermining the religious buttress of her parental authority. Action and anger seemed to resuscitate Kristina when her spiritual resources ebbed.

I turned to sociology for solace, but found it lacking and my project morally suspect. To treat the Lewisons' losses and grief as data, grist for milling sociological generalizations about the lives of working people, seemed another form of betrayal. Yet to excise this chapter from the text would be disrespectful both of their lives and of social reality. My unsolicited, yet warmly welcomed, ethnographic presence fixed this irrevocably ambivalent character of my relationship to the Lewisons' suffering. I genuinely grieved over Lou while unable to suppress awareness that my research must unavoidably profit from his departure. His funeral exposed me to a broader array of kin and community than I might

247

otherwise have met, while his death freed me to write much I might have censored had he lived. More deeply yet I mourned the tragedy of Carole's life almost as much as I mourned her death. I felt implicated somehow in the failure of feminism to touch her life in time to avert what I regarded as the unnecessary abuse and oppression she had borne. I wished I had found something more effective to offer Carole than the gift of a lucky gold charm, which she accepted so appreciatively before my cowardly retreat from the field.

Protected by educational and social-class privileges from the worst ravages of our calamity-prone culture, I could indulge a morose response to the Lewisons' miseries. As Elenore Smith Bowen observed in her fictionalized ethnographic account of the Tiv in Nigeria, "only in a very sheltered life of the sort made possible by civilization can one maintain a fine and serious sense of the tragedy of misfortune. In an environment in which tragedy is genuine and frequent, laughter is essential to sanity."[2] One need hardly live in tribal Africa, however, to lack such a sheltered life. Preserving her capacity for sardonic realism to the last, Carole concluded a poignant letter of gratitude and farewell with a favorite family aphorism. She wished, Carole wrote, that she were not being forced to leave all those she loved and to forfeit the chance to mother her children to maturity. But then again, Carole reminded her survivors,

> if wishes were fishes,
> we all would be fried.

CONCLUSIONS

11

The Postmodern Family, For Better and Worse

It is the belief that kinship, love and having nice things to eat are naturally and inevitably bound up together that makes it hard to imagine a world in which "family" plays little part. This mythologized unity must be picked apart, strand by strand, so that we can understand its power and meet the needs of each of its separate elements more fully. In part, this can be done by analysis and discussion, as we have tried to do here. But it must also be done by experiments in new ways of living and by political campaigns to transform not the family—but the society that needs it.
—Michele Barrett and Mary McIntosh, *The Antisocial Family*

BACKWARD TOWARD THE POSTMODERN FAMILY

Two centuries ago leading white, middle-class families in the newly united American states spearheaded a family revolution that replaced the premodern gender order with a modern family system. But "modern family" was an oxymoronic label for this peculiar institution, which dispensed modernity to white, middle-class men only by withholding it from women. The former could enter the public sphere as breadwinners and citizens, because their wives were confined to the newly privatized family realm. Ruled by an increasingly absent patriarchal landlord, the modern,

251

middle-class family, a woman's domain, soon was sentimentalized as "traditional."

It took most of the subsequent two centuries for substantial numbers of white working-class men to achieve the rudimentary economic pass-book to "modern" family life—a male family wage.[1] By the time they had done so, however, a second family revolution was well underway. Once again middle-class, white families appeared to be in the vanguard. This time women were claiming the benefits and burdens of modernity, a status we could achieve only at the expense of the "modern" family itself. Reviving a long-dormant feminist movement, frustrated middle-class homemakers and their more militant daughters subjected modern domesticity to a sustained critique. At times this critique displayed scant sensitivity to the effects our antimodern family ideology might have on women for whom full-time domesticity had rarely been feasible. Thus, feminist family reform came to be regarded widely as a white, middle-class agenda, and white, working-class families its most resistant adversaries.

I shared these presumptions before my fieldwork among Silicon Valley families radically altered my understanding of the class basis of the postmodern family revolution. White, middle-class families, I have come to believe, are less the innovators than the propagandists and principal beneficiaries of contemporary family change. African-American women and white, working-class women have been the genuine postmodern family pioneers, even though they also suffer most from its most negative effects. Long denied the mixed benefits that the modern family order offered middle-class women, less privileged women quietly forged alternative models of femininity to that of full-time domesticity and mother-intensive child rearing. Struggling creatively, often heroically, to sustain oppressed families and to escape the most oppressive ones, they drew on "traditional" premodern kinship resources and crafted untraditional ones, lurching backward and forward into the postmodern family.

Rising divorce and cohabitation rates, working mothers, two-earner households, single and unwed parenthood, and matrilineal, extended, and fictive kin support networks appeared earlier and more extensively among poor and working-class people.[2] Economic pressures more than political principles governed these departures from domesticity, but working women like Martha Porter and Dotty Lewison soon found additional reasons to appreciate paid employment.[3] Eventually white, middle-class

"We used to be old-fashioned. Now we're postmodern."

women, sated and even sickened by our modern family privileges, began to emulate, elaborate, and celebrate many of these alternative family practices. How ironic and unfortunate it seems, therefore, that feminism's antimodern family ideology should offend many women from the social groups whose gender and kinship strategies helped to foster it.

If this ethnography serves no other purpose, I hope it will shatter the image of the white working class as the last repository of old-fashioned, "modern" American family life. Stories of gender and kinship portrayed in this book document postmodern family arrangements among working-class people that are at least as diverse and innovative as those found within the middle class. The sarcastic quote from Delia Ephron with which I introduced chapter 4 mocks familial bonds within the contemporary divorce-extended family, warning those nostalgic for the "traditional," extended family to "be careful what you wish for." But working women like Pamela, Shirley, Jan, and Dotty have found ways to transform divorce from a rupture into a kinship resource, and they are not unique. A recent study of middle-class divorced couples and their parents in the suburbs of San Francisco found one-third sustaining kinship ties with former spouses and their relatives.[4] It seems likely that cooperative, ex-familial relationships are even more prevalent among lower-income groups, where divorce rates are higher and where women have far greater experience with, and need for, sustaining cooperative kin ties.[5]

Certainly, the dismantling of welfare state protections and the reprivatizing policies of the Reagan-Bush era have given such women renewed incentives to continue their traditions of active, expansionary kin work. The accordion households and kin ties crafted by the Lewisons, by Global Ministries, and by Pam, Shirley, Jan, and Lorraine draw more on the "domestic network" traditions of poor, urban African-Americans described by anthropologist Carol Stack and on the matrifocal strategies of poor and working-class whites[6] than they do on family reform innovations by the white middle class. Ironically, sociologists are now identifying as a new middle-class "'social problem" those "crowded," rather than empty, nests filled with "incompletely-launched young adults," long familiar to the less privileged like the Lewisons.[7] Postindustrial conditions have reversed the supply-side, "trickle-down" trajectory of family change predicted by modernization theorists. The diversity and complexity of postmodern family patterns rivals that characteristic of premodern kinship forms.

FAREWELL TO ARCHIE BUNKER

If, as this book suggests, postindustrial transformations encouraged modern, working-class families to reorganize and diversify themselves even more than middle-class families, it seems time to inter the very concept of "*the* working-class family." This deeply androcentric and class-biased construct distorts the history and current reality of wage-working people's intimate relationships. Popular images of working-class family life, like the Archie Bunker family, rest on the iconography of unionized, blue-collar, male, industrial breadwinners and the history of their lengthy struggle for the family wage. But the male family wage was a late and ephemeral achievement of only the most fortunate sections of the modern industrial working class. Most working-class men never secured its patriarchal domestic privileges.

Postmodern conditions expose the gendered character of this social-class category, and they render it atavistic. As feminists have argued, only by disregarding women's labor and learning was it ever plausible to designate a family unit as working class.[8] In an era when most married mothers are employed, when women perform most "working-class" jobs, when most productive labor is unorganized and fails to pay a family wage, when marriage links are tenuous and transitory, and when more single women than married homemakers are rearing children, conventional notions of a normative working-class family fracture into incoherence. The life circumstances and mobility patterns of the members of Pamela's kin set and of the Lewisons, for example, are so diverse and fluid that no single social-class category can adequately describe any of the family units among them.

If the white, working-class family stereotype is inaccurate, it is also consequential. Stereotypes are moral (alas, more often, immoral) stories people tell to organize the complexity of social experience. Narrating the working class as profamily reactionaries suppresses the diversity and the innovative character of many working-class kin relationships. The Archie Bunker stereotype may have helped to contain feminism by estranging middle-class from working-class women. Barbara Ehrenreich argues that caricatures which portray the working class as racist and reactionary are recent, self-serving inventions of professional, middle-class people eager "to seek legitimation for their own more conservative impulses."[9] In the early 1970s, ignoring rising labor militancy as well as racial, ethnic, and gender diversity among working-class people, the media effectively imaged them as the new conservative bedrock of "middle America." Thus, *All in the Family*, the 1970s television sitcom series that immortalized racist, chauvinist, working-class hero-buffoon Archie Bunker, can best be read, Ehrenreich suggests, as "the longest-running Polish joke," a projection of middle-class bad faith.[10] Yet, if this bad faith served professional middle-class interests, it did so at the expense of feminism. The inverse logic

255

of class prejudice construed the constituency of that enormously popular social movement as exclusively middle class. By convincing middle-class feminists of our isolation, perhaps the last laugh of that "Polish joke" was on us. Even Ehrenreich, who sensitively debunks the Bunker myth, labels "startling" the findings of a 1986 Gallup poll that "56 percent of American women considered themselves to be 'feminists,' and the degree of feminist identification was, if anything, slightly higher as one descended the socioeconomic scale."[11] Feminists must be attuned to the polyphony of family stories authored by working-class as well as middle-class people if we are ever to transform data like these into effective political alliances.

While the ethnographic narratives in this book demonstrate the demise of "*the* working-class family," in no way do they document the emergence of the classless society postindustrial theorists once anticipated.[12] On the contrary, recent studies indicate that the middle classes are shrinking and the economic circumstances of Americans polarizing.[13] African-Americans have borne the most devastating impact of economic restructuring and the subsequent decline of industrial and unionized occupations.[14] But formerly privileged white, working-class men, those like Al, Lou, and Don who achieved access to the American Dream in the 1960s and 1970s, now find their gains threatened and not easy to pass on to their children.

While high-wage, blue-collar jobs decline, the window of postindustrial opportunity that admitted undereducated men and women, like Lou and Kristina Lewison and Don Franklin, to middle-class status is slamming shut. Young white families earned 20 percent less in 1986 than did comparable families in 1979, and their homeownership prospects plummeted.[15] Real earnings for young men between the ages of twenty and twenty-four dropped by 26 percent between 1973 and 1986, while the military route to upward mobility that many of their fathers traveled constricted.[16] In the 1950s men like Lou Lewison, equipped with VA loans, could buy homes with token downpayments and budget just 14 percent of their monthly wages for housing costs. By 1984, however, carrying a median-priced home would cost 44 percent of an average male's monthly earnings.[17] Few could manage this, and in 1986 the U.S. government reported "the first sustained drop in home ownership since the modern collection of data began in 1940."[18]

Postindustrial shifts have reduced blue-collar job opportunities for undereducated sons of working-class fathers, like Danny Lewison, Carole's husband, Bobby, and Katie's husband, Eric. And technological developments like computer-aided design have escalated the entry criteria and reduced the ranks of those middle-level occupations that recently employed uncredentialed young people like Kristina and Lanny.[19] Thus, the proportion of American families in the middle-income range fell from 46 percent in 1970 to 39 percent in 1985.[20] Two earners in a household now are necessary just to keep from losing ground. Data like these led social analysts to anxiously track "the disappearing middle class," a phrase that Barbara Ehrenreich now believes, "in some ways missed the point. It was the blue-collar working class that was 'disappearing,' at least from the middle range of comfort."[21]

Postindustrial restructuring has had contradictory effects on the employment opportunities of former working-class women. Driven by declines in real family income, by desires for social achievement and independence, and by an awareness that committed male breadwinners are in scare supply, such women have flocked to expanding jobs in service, clerical, and new industrial occupations. For many of the women portrayed in this book, these provide the means of family subsidy or self-support and self-respect. Apart from the tenuous success of Kristina's vendetta, however, few women enjoy earnings or prospects equivalent to those of their former husbands or fathers. Recent economic restructuring has replaced white male workers with women and minority men, but at lesser-paid, more vulnerable jobs.[22]

A particularly ominous feature of postindustrial employment and social patterns is the rampant narcotics economy and culture. Currently devastating those minority populations who dwell in urban neighborhoods that most industrial employers have abandoned,[23] this epidemic also threatens many offspring from former blue-collar, white families. Pamela's and Dotty's children all confronted this threat, their sons more directly and vulnerably than their daughters. Greater family resources and intervention rescued Pam's son Jimmy, but the calamity culture inhabited by the less stable or affluent Lewisons made their sons and their son-in-law particularly vulnerable to drug and alcohol abuse. With a thriving narcotics economy as the seductive and destructive underside of postindustrial employment shifts, the permeable boundary between "hard" and "settled" blue-collar family life threatens to become more of a one-way street.

FAMILY QUARRELS

Recent books with such titles as *Falling from Grace* and *Fear of Falling* convey widespread suffering and anxiety among once-settled, middle-class Americans.[24] And Americans, as historian Linda Gordon noted, recurrently frame social anxieties in familial terms. Sociologists may attempt to reassure an anxious populace that family life is "here to stay," but, as political analyst Andrew Hacker once observed, "it is hardly news that families are not what they used to be."[25] The modern family system has lost the cultural and statistical dominance it long enjoyed, and no new family order has arisen to supplant it. The postmodern family is a site of disorder instead, a contested domain.

The passionate public response to the Moynihan report of the 1960s signaled a prolonged era of national conflict and confusion over which gender and kinship relationships are to count as "families" in postindustrial America. And in this family quarrel, gender and sexual politics occupy pride of place. Which relationships between and among women and men will receive legal recognition, social legitimacy, institutional and cultural support? In the postmodern period, a truly democratic gender and kinship order, one that does not favor male authority, heterosexuality, a particular division of labor, or a singular household or parenting arrangement became thinkable for the first time in history. And during the past several decades, family visionaries and reformers have been organizing struggles to bring it to fruition. They have met, however, with fierce resistance, and, as feminists have learned with great pain, it is not men alone who resist.

Why do many people of both genders recoil from the prospect of a fully democratic family regime? While there are multiple motives, including theological ones, this book suggests compelling sociological sources of popular ambivalence about family reform. Not only would a democratic kinship system threaten vested gender and class interests, but even under the most benevolent of social orders, it promises also to bring its own kind of costs. A fully voluntary marriage system, as this century's experience with divorce rates indicates, and as Pastor Jensen underscored during the Christian wedding ceremony he performed for Pamela and Al, institutionalizes conjugal and thus parental instability. A normless gender order, one in which parenting arrangements, sexuality, and the distribution of work, responsibility, and resources all are negotiable and constantly renegotiable, can also invite considerable conflict and insecurity. These inescapable "burdens of freedom" have been magnified monstrously, however, under the far-from-benevolent social conditions of this turbulent, conservative period.

Many men, African-American men most of all, have suffered from postindustrialization and the eroding modern family order, while, thanks to feminism, numerous women, particularly white, middle-class ones have achieved substantial gains.[26] The resilient gender inequality of the transitional period, however, places the vast majority of women at disproportionate risk. In exchange for subordination and domestic service, the modern family promised women a number of customary protections and privileges, principal among these, lifelong support from a male breadwinner. Scarcely had working-class women like Dotty, Shirley, Lorraine and Marilyn achieved access to this "patriarchal bargain,"[27] however, before it collapsed in a postindustrial deluge. With few social protections provided to replace the precarious "private" ones that the modern family once offered, many women have found good cause to mistrust the terms postmodern conditions appear to offer in its place. Women have been adding the burdens and benefits of paid labor to their historic domestic responsibilities, but men seem less eager to share the responsibilities and rewards of child rearing and housework.[28] Moreover, as feminists have demonstrated in depressing detail, women have suffered numerous unexpected, and disturbing, consequences of egalitarian family reforms, such as no-fault divorce, joint custody provisions, shared parenting, and sexual liberation.[29] Consequently, as Deirdre English, former editor of *Mother Jones* once observed, many women have come to "fear that feminism will free men first."

The insecure and undemocratic character of postmodern family life fuels nostalgia for the fading modern family, now recast as the "traditional" family. Capitalizing on this nostalgia, a vigorous, antifeminist "profamily" movement was able to score impressive political victories in the 1980s. It successfully, if incorrectly, identified feminism as the primary cause of the demise of the modern family, rather than the mopping-up operation for postindustrial transformations that were long underway. Defining the ERA and abortion rights as threats to the family, it placed feminists in the same defensive posture that housewives had come to assume. And partly because the profamily movement could draw on the volunteer labors of the disproportionate numbers of housewives it attracted to its political ranks,[30] the backlash movement was able to achieve political visibility and victories far in excess of its numerical strength. Former President Reagan assured this movement a profound and lasting political legacy by rewarding its contribution to his "revolution" with antifeminist appointments to the Supreme Court and the federal judiciary who promise to inhibit the progress of democratic family reform well into the twenty-first century.

Many feminists, like myself, were caught off guard by the retreat from feminist activism and the resurgence of profamilialism that characterized the 1980s. During the 1970s family instability seemed to swell the ranks of the women's liberation movement. Feminist ideology, disseminated not only by the media but in flourishing grass-roots community activities and women's reentry programs, served women like Dotty, Marilyn, Pam, Shirley, Lorraine, and others of their generation well to ease the exit from, or the reform of, unhappy modern marriages. Even older women in successful long-term marriages, like Pamela's mother, Martha, employed feminist principles to improve their relationships. Second-wave feminism also supported women's efforts to develp independent work lives and career goals. With high divorce rates and women's paid work continuing throughout the eighties, feminist activism and family reforms might have been expected to progress apace.[31]

Yet optimistic projections like these did not reckon with the ravages of postindustrialism. Neither feminism nor other progressive family reform movements have been as useful in addressing the structural inequalities of postindustrial occupational structure or the individualist, fast-track culture that makes all too difficult the formation of stable intimate relations on a democratic, or any other basis. In these circumstances, many have sought support for troubled family relationships from organized religion, particularly from fundamentalist varieties.

The unsettling conditions of postindustrial society and the global economy seem to have intensified cravings for security and spirituality. The ensuing retreat from rationalism and secularism has fueled an unanticipated resurgence of fundamentalist religious revivalism worldwide. It has been challenging and painful for feminists to understand why women even more than men are drawn to such movements. Why do women who have been exposed to feminist ideas voluntarily embrace an ideology of male headship and female submission, often attempting, like Pam's daughter Katie, to convert their more secular husbands? For, at least in postindustrial America, although male supremacy is alive and well, participation in a formally partriarchal marriage is a woman's choice. The social and material conditions that underwrote the modern family—the family many fundamentalists erroneously portray as the biblical family—are long gone. As a recent ethnography of a fundamentalist community notes, no fundamentalist husband today can dominate a wife who does not choose to submit.[32] That is why Julie Cabrera, the coordinator of women's Bible study at Crossroads Bible Church in the Silicon Valley quoted in chapter 6, could insist that contemporary women in the United States who choose, as she does, to submit to their husbands are not doormats.

Cabrera and the Christian feminist who offended her by proclaiming submissive wives to be fearful of divorce, like all of the women portrayed in this book, are grappling with the contradictory character of women's postmodern family options. Freed from the restrictions and protections of the modern family system, women remain institutionally disadvantaged. From that position, however, we make our own choices and develop our own strategies, including patriarchal marriage and religious orthodoxy. Although the nominal ideologies of contemporary revivalist religious movements are patriarchal, many, like Global Ministries, enable women actively to reshape family life in postmodern and postfeminist directions.[33] Generated partly as a backlash against feminism, postfeminist evangelical gender ideology also selectively incorporates many feminist family reforms. There are parallel tendencies within revivalist Orthodox Judaism. "There's nothing in Judaism that says men and women can't share household responsibilities, that a man can't change a baby, or that a woman can't work," an Orthodox rabbi, echoing Eleanor Morrison and Pastor Jensen, reassures his class of recent converts, the majority of whom are single women.[34] Although we may feel troubled by its character, secular and religious feminists alike, I believe, can take credit for the extraordinary impact our ideological influence has had on even this most unlikely of constituencies.[35]

FAMILY COMPROMISES

Not so long ago feminists anticipated greater causes for self-congratulation. Now we must contend instead with the nettlesome challenges of a pervasive postfeminist milieu. In the long run, antifeminism will not prove to be the most serious barrier to democratizing intimacy. Despite the impressive victories of the profamily movement, it represents the practices and beliefs of a declining minority of Americans. Many more citizens favor feminist than antifeminist visions of family justice.[36] However, most restrict their family reform efforts to the "private" sphere and shun political activism.

Different generational and individual experiences with feminism and with postindustrial family and work conditions foster diverse postfeminist strategies for remaking family life. Pam and Dotty, like most white women of their generation, were young when they married in the 1950s and early 1960s. They entered their first marriages with conventional "Parsonsian" gender expectations about family and work responsibilities and "roles." For a significant period of time, they and their husbands conformed to the then culturally prescribed pattern of "instrumental" male breadwinner and "expressive" female homemaker. Assuming primary responsibility for rearing the children they began to bear immediately after marriage, Pam and Dotty supported their husbands' successful efforts to progress from working-class to middle- and upper-middle-class careers in the electronics industry. In the process, both men became workaholics, uninvolved with their families.

As their marriages deteriorated, Pam and Dotty, along with many of their friends, enrolled in women's reentry programs where they were profoundly stirred by feminist courses. Both women left their husbands and became welfare mothers, an experience each found to be both liberating and debilitating. Each experienced an initial "feminist high," a sense of enormous exhilaration and strength in her newfound independence. Pam divorced her husband, developed a viable social service career, experimented with the single life, but gradually became desperately unhappy. Dotty did not develop a career, lost her lover, and only then decided to take back her newly disabled husband (with his pension). Their rather different experiences with failed intimacy and their different economic and occupational resources, I believe, help explain their diverse postfeminist strategies.

262

For many women of Dotty and Pam's generation, those who married and reared children in modern families before postindustrial and feminist forces rendered these anachronistic, feminist consciousness has become as much a burden as a means of support. Where once it helped them to reform or leave unsatisfactory relationships, now it can intensify the pain and difficulty of the compromises many feel they must make to sustain intimacy and to cope with family crises under postindustrial circumstances. This, I believe, helps to account for Pam's turn to evangelical religion as well as her creative use of its surprisingly flexible patriarchal ideology to serve democratic family reform goals. It accounts also for Dotty's return to a previously unsatisfactory marriage, which feminism helped her to reform, as well as her shift from political engagement to paid work, organized religion, and mysticism. In a general social climate and stage of their lives characterized by diminished expectations and heightened vulnerability to personal loss, both seek support for the compromises with, and commitments to, family and work they have chosen to make, rather than for greater achievement or autonomy. Without repudiating feminism, Dotty and Pam, as well as their close friends Marilyn and Lorraine, have retreated somewhat from feminist identity and activism. They read feminism as an autonomy text.

Jan, the most steadfast, unflinching feminist in this book, may be the exception who shores up the rule. As a lesbian, she has little incentive to indulge in nostalgia for the modern family or to resist the progress of a democratic gender and kinship order. While Jan too craves intimacy, community, and spirituality, she has no choice but to seek these outside mainstream institutional forms. By affirming women's capacity for self-reliance and solidarity, feminism continues to meet Jan's needs, just as she, in turn, tries to meet other women's needs through feminist means. Collectivity and autonomy intermingle in Jan's reading of feminist morality.

Pam's and Dotty's five daughters—children of modern families that were disrupted by postindustrial developments and feminist challenges—come to their disparate postfeminist strategies more spontaneously than their mothers. To varying degrees, all have distanced themselves from feminist identity and ideology, in some cases in conscious reaction against what they regard as the excesses of their mothers' earlier feminist views. At the same time, however, all have semiconsciously incorporated feminist principles into their gender and kinship expectations and practices. They take for granted and at times eschew the gains in women's work opportunities, sexual autonomy, and male participation in childrearing and domestic work for which feminists of their mothers' generation struggled. Ignorant or disdainful of the political efforts feminists expended to secure such gains, they are preoccupied instead coping with the expanded opportunities and burdens women now encounter.[37] Although they have come of age in a period in which a successful woman is expected to combine marriage to a communicative, egalitarian man with motherhood and an engaging, rewarding career, none of these daughters of successful white working-class fathers has attained such a pattern.

Kristina and Lanny, both firstborn daughters with strong achievement drives and marketable postindustrial skills, still struggle quixotically to secure both handles of the postfeminist grail. Lanny has achieved an impressive grasp on its familial goals while Kristina frantically grips its slippery occupational rewards. Both seem oblivious to the impact of feminism on their gender expectations and experiences. Lanny emulated her mother by entering a youthful, modern blue-collar marriage. Unable to tolerate its isolation, boredom, and emotional deprivation, she quickly entered the work force and traded in her short-lived modern family for a postmodern "blended" one. There is an ease to her attitudes regarding the gender division of labor at home and at work and about gender norms generally. These are not political issues to Lanny, nor even conscious points of personal struggle. She actively rejected her conventionally gendered first marriage, but without conceptualizing it that way. And while she detests her current work, she has no desire to be a homemaker; she hopes fervently for a creative, satisfying career. Indeed, Lanny claims to be perfectly willing to support her husband if he wants to stay home and take care of the children, or if, as they hope, she can afford to send him back to engineering school. Lanny takes for granted the right to be flexible about family and work priorities. Her equally flexible husband, Ken, appears to be just as oblivious to feminist influences on his notably enlightened attitudes. Gender inequities in the postindustrial occupational structure, however, are proving to be less flexible. The shift from mechanical drafting to computer-aided design has slashed Lanny's employment and income opportunities, making it logical for her to assume primary domestic responsibilities, while Ken, by expanding his hours of paid work and reducing his involvement at home, has become the family's primary earner.

Dotty's firstborn, Kristina, alone among these five daughters, has resolutely rejected the terms of the modern gender agreement. Direct and indirect experiences with battering made her determined not to replicate her mother's dependence and vulnerability to abuse. Staking almost all of her "chips" on a strategy of self-reliance, Kris is the only one of these daughters who has achieved significant occupational success in the post-industrial work world. She has done so, however, at enormous cost to her familial goals as well as to her physical and mental health. Although Kristina adores the challenge and creativity of her work and appreciates the relative financial autonomy her salary allows, she labors under extraordinary pressure, inordinate and unpredictable work schedules, and the constant threat of a layoff. The demands of her career conflict directly with her needs as a single mother. There have been long periods when Kris rarely saw her son. Without the support of her extended family, her friends, and her past and present lovers, Kris would have been unable to pursue her career. Indeed, the desire for a father for Tommy fostered Kristina's brief, ill-fated marriage, just as it fueled her efforts to secure a marital commitment from her resistant, but unusually accommodating, boyfriend. Neither attempt was successful, and the death of her father and sister temporarily interrupted Kristina's efforts to combine a post-feminist marriage with her career.

None of Lanny's or Kris's younger sisters, however, found the quest feasible or worthy enough to pursue. Their lesser skills and drive, combined with unpromising experiences in the world of postindustrial employment, encouraged Katie, Polly, and Carole all to craft their postmodern gender strategies on modern family principles that their mothers and older sisters had rejected. Carole resorted to the prefeminist, modern patriarchal bargain only with great reluctance, and with the fewest compensations. Emotional deprivation and low self-esteem propelled her to marry early and poorly and to entrap herself through profligate childbearing that helped to "fry" her fervent wish to combine motherhood with paid work. When rising child care expenses coincided with cutbacks in production jobs, Carole lost her precarious foothold in the expendable postindustrial work force. She never repudiated democratic family or work ideals, but personal and social forces kept both of these well beyond her reach. Forced into an undesired full-time home-maker role with scant prospects that she would receive the customary compensations to which the prefeminist patriarchal bargain entitled

265

women, only a tragic, premature death released Carole from her oppressive circumstances.

Carole's more fortunate sister, Polly, embraced modern family principles more instrumentally, in self-conscious reaction to her experiences with discriminatory, exploitative work and to her mother's feminist convictions. Reaping the unacknowledged benefits of feminist labors, Polly experimented sexually and deferred marriage and childbearing until she was able to negotiate a marriage whose domestic labor arrangements represented a distinct improvement over those of the conventional modern family.

Pam's younger daughter, Katie, on the other hand, was never even tempted to experiment with an alternative to modern family life. Finding revivalist Christianity an effective refuge from the disruptions of parental divorce and adolescent drug culture that threatened her more rebellious siblings, Katie retreated from the arena of postmodern gender and family reform. How ironic, therefore, that her involvement in evangelical religion led her to practice the most alternative family arrangement of all. And as the unlikely source of the chain of conversions she fostered among her natal and marital kin, Katie wielded a profound, cross-generational influence over their postmodern gender strategies.

Beneficiaries and victims of the modern family's disarray, all of Pam's and Dotty's daughters craft their gender and kinship relationships on unsettled, postmodern terrain. Although their family experiences, convictions, and desires differ widely, not even the most "traditional" among them inhabits an unrevised modern family. Feminist family reforms, such as those that expanded abortion rights, campaigned against battering, and increased social respectability for divorce, for unwed mothering, and for male participation in housework and child care enabled all but Carole to avoid the unhappy modern gender arrangements that once constrained their mothers. Preoccupied coping with postindustrial instabilities, however, the daughters do not conceptualize their family and work problems in political terms. Feminism and politics appear irrelevant or threatening.

I have less to say, and less confidence in what I do have to say, about postmodern family strategies among men. Despite my concerted efforts to study gender relationally by defining this study in gender-inclusive terms, the men in these families remained comparatively marginal to my research. In part, this is an unavoidable outcome for any one individual who attempts to study gender in a gendered world. Being a woman inhibited my access to, and likely my empathy with, as full a range of male family experience as that which I enjoyed among their female kin. Still, the relative marginality of men in this book is not due simply to methodological deficiencies. It also accurately reflects their more marginal participation in contemporary family life. Most of these men narrate gender and kinship stories that are relatively inarticulate and undeveloped, I believe, because they have less experience, investment, or interest in the work of sustaining kin ties.[38]

While economic pressures have always encouraged expansionary kin work among working-class women, these have often weakened men's family ties. Men's muted family voices whisper of a masculinity crisis among blue-collar men. As their access to breadwinner status recedes, so too does confidence in their masculinity. The decline of the family wage and the escalation of women's involvement in paid work seems to generate profound ambivalence about the eroding breadwinner ethic. Young postfeminist men like Jimmy, Danny, and Frank appear uncertain whether a man who provides sole support to his family is a hero or a chump. Like Frank, some avoid domestic commitments entirely, while others, like Eric, Ken, and Polly's husband, Paul, embrace these wholeheartedly. Some, like Jimmy and Danny, vacillate between romantic engagements and the unencumbered single life. Many, like Danny, Bobby, Loujoo, Lanny's first husband, Kristina's ex-husband, and Polly's abusive boyfriend, express their masculinity in antisocial, self-destructive, and violent forms.

Women strive, meanwhile, as they always have, to buttress and reform their male kin. Responding to the extraordinary diffusion of feminist ideology as well as to sheer overwork, working-class women, like middle-class women, have struggled to transfer some of their domestic burdens to men. My fieldwork leads me to believe that they have achieved more success in the daily trenches than much of the research on the "politics of housework" yet indicates—more success, I suspect, than have most middle-class women.[39] While only a few of the women in this study expected, or desired, men to perform an equal share of housework and child care, none were willing to exempt men from domestic labor. Almost all of the men I observed or heard about routinely performed tasks that my own blue-collar father and his friends never deigned to contemplate. Some, like Al, Don Franklin, and especially Bobby, did so with reluctance

267

and resentment; but most, like Lou, Ken, Frank, Eric, Jimmy, and Paul, did so willingly. Although the division of household labor remains profoundly inequitable, I am convinced that a major gender norm has shifted here.

WHOSE FAMILY CRISIS?

Ironically, while women are becoming the new proletariat and some men are increasing their participation in housework and childwork, the postmodern family, even more than the modern family it is replacing, is proving to be a woman-tended domain. There is some empirical basis for the enlightened father imagery celebrated by films like "Kramer versus Kramer." Indeed my fieldwork corroborates evidence that the determined efforts by many working women and feminists to reintegrate men into family life have had some success. There are data, for example, indicating that increasing numbers of men would sacrifice occupational gains in order to have more time with their families, just as there are data documenting actual increases in male involvement in child care.[40] The excessive media attention which the faintest signs of new paternity enjoy, however, may be symptomatic of a deeper, far less comforting reality it so effectively obscures. We are experiencing, as demographer Andrew Cherlin aptly puts it, "the feminization of kinship."[41] Demographers report a drastic decline in the average numbers of years that men live in households with young children.[42] Few of the women who assume responsibility for their children in 90 percent of divorce cases in the United States today had to wage a custody battle for this privilege.[43] We hear few proposals for a "daddy track." And few of the adults providing care to sick and elderly relatives are male.[44] Yet ironically, most of the alarmist, nostalgic literature about contemporary family decline impugns women's abandonment of domesticity, the flipside of our tardy entry into modernity. Rarely do the anxious outcries over the destructive effects on families of working mothers, high divorce rates, institutionalized child care, or sexual liberalization scrutinize the family behaviors of men. Anguished voices, emanating from all bands on the political spectrum, lament state and market interventions that are weakening "the family."[45] But whose family bonds are fraying? Women have amply demonstrated our continuing commitment to sustaining kin ties. If there is a family crisis, it is a male family crisis.

The crisis cannot be resolved by reviving the modern family system. While nostalgia for an idealized world of *Ozzie and Harriet* and *Archie Bunker* families abounds, little evidence suggests that most Americans genuinely wish to return to the gender order these symbolize. On the contrary, the vast majority, like the people in this book, are actively remaking family life. Indeed a 1989 survey conducted by *The New York Times* found more than two-thirds of women, including a substantial majority of even those living in "traditional"—that is to say, "modern"— households, as well as a majority of men agreeing that "the United States continues to need a strong women's movement to push for changes that benefit women."[46] Yet many seem reluctant to own their family preferences. Like Shirley Moskowitz, they cling to images of themselves as "back from the old days," while venturing ambivalently but courageously into the new.[47]

Responding to new economic and social insecurities as well as to feminism, higher percentages of families in almost all income groups have adopted a multiple-earner strategy.[48] Thus, the household form that has come closer than any other to replacing the modern family with a new cultural and statistical norm consists of a two-earner, heterosexual married couple with children.[49] It is not likely, however, that any single household type will soon achieve the measure of normalcy that the modern family long enjoyed. Indeed, the postmodern success of the voluntary principle of the modern family system precludes this. The routinization of divorce and remarriage generates a diversity of family patterns even greater than was characteristic of the premodern period when death prevented family stability or household homogeneity. Even cautious demographers judge the new family diversity to be "an intrinsic feature . . . rather than a temporary aberration" of contemporary family life.[50]

"The family" is *not* "here to stay." Nor should we wish it were. On the contrary, I believe that all democratic people, whatever their kinship preferences, should work to hasten its demise. An ideological concept that imposes mythical homogeneity on the diverse means by which people organize their intimate relationships, "the family" distorts and devalues this rich variety of kinship stories. And, along with the class, racial, and heterosexual prejudices it promulgates, this sentimental fictional plot

authorizes gender hierarchy. Because the postmodern family crisis rup-
tures this seamless modern family script, it provides a democratic opportunity. Efforts to expand and redefine the definition of family by
feminists and gay liberation activists and by many minority rights organizations are responses to this opportunity, seeking to extend social
legitimacy and institutional support to the diverse patterns of intimacy
that Americans have already forged.

If feminist identity threatens many and seems out of fashion, struggles
to reconstitute gender and kinship on a just and democratic basis are
more popular than ever.[51] If only a minority of citizens are willing to
grant family legitimacy to gay domestic partners, an overwhelming majority subscribe to the postmodern definition of a family by which the
New York Supreme Court validated a gay man's right to retain his
deceased lover's apartment. "By a ratio of 3-to-1" people surveyed in a
Yale University study defined the family as "a group of people who love
and care for each other." And while a majority of those surveyed gave
negative ratings to the quality of American family life in general, 71
percent declared themselves "at least very satisfied" with their own family
lives.[52]

There is bad faith in the popular lament over family decline. Family
nostalgia deflects social criticism from the social sources of most "personal
troubles." Supply-side economics, governmental deregulation, and the
right-wing assault on social welfare programs have intensified the destabilizing effects of recent occupational upheavals on flagging modern
families and emergent postmodern ones alike. This book is not the first
to expose the bitter irony of right-wing politicians manipulating nostalgia
for eroding working-class families while instituting policies that deepened
their distress. Indeed, the ability to provide financial security was the
chief family concern of most surveyed in the Yale study. If the postmodern
family crisis represents a democratic opportunity, contemporary economic and political conditions enable only a minority to realize its tantalizing potential.

The bad faith revealed in the discrepant data reported in the Yale
study indicates how reluctant most Americans are to fully own the genuine
ambivalence we feel about family and social change. Yet ambivalence,
as sociologist Alan Wolfe suggests, is an underappreciated but responsible
moral stance, and one well suited for democratic citizenship: "Given the
paradoxes of modernity, there is little wrong, and perhaps a great deal

right, with being ambivalent—especially when there is so much to be ambivalent about."[53]

Certainly, as most of the stories in this ethnography indicate, there are good grounds for ambivalence about postmodern family conditions. Even were a feminist family revolution to succeed, it could never eliminate all family distress. At best, it would foster a social order that could invert Tolstoy's aphorism by granting happy families the freedom to differ, and even to suffer. Truly postfeminist families, however, would suffer only the "common unhappiness" endemic to intimate human relationships; they would be liberated from the "hysterical misery" generated by social injustice.[54] No nostaligic movement to restore the modern family can offer as much. For better and/or worse, the postmodern family revolution is here to stay.

Epilogue

Taking Women at Their Word

For the most part, anthropologists have taken the job of reflecting back upon ourselves much less seriously than that of probing other cultures.
—George E. Marcus and Michael M. J. Fischer, *Anthropology as Cultural Critique*

But as the Fijian said to the New Ethnographer, "that's enough talking about you; let's talk about me."
—Marshall Sahlins, "The Return of the Event, Again . . ."

Along with my readings of the lives of others, the ethnographic stories in this book record a feminist "Bildungsroman"—my personal coming to consciousness and acceptance of the complexity of women's contemporary gender and kinship strategies. There too I have attempted to convey my gradual loss of naïveté about the ethical character of ethnographic research methods, which, as I have noted elsewhere, I discovered to be far less benign or feminist than I had anticipated.[1] Others have discussed the ahistorical "timeless present" character of most ethnographies.[2] I was also forced to recognize, and surrender to, the equally distorting effects of the arbitrary temporality of ethnographic research. Conducting commuter fieldwork in my own society exposed and compounded the capriciousness of my point of ethnographic entry (intrusion) into the lives of those I studied and my equally arbitrary moments of exit (abandonment). Geographic proximity allowed me to maintain contact with Pam and Dotty and their kin even as I wrote, an ethnographic "opportunity" with decidedly confusing and humbling effects.

Ever since I began writing the ethnographic stories in this book in the spring of 1987, I have been forced to watch these narratives overtaken by the truly timeless present. In January 1988, for example, Pam and Al left Global Ministries and joined an evangelical Methodist church. Later that year, failing health led Eleanor and Paul Garrett to retire and leave the Silicon Valley. With their exit, the ministry disbanded and Pastor Leonetti's pentecostal congregation absorbed Katie, Eric, and other Global disciples. While I wrote and rewrote this book, the Reagan regime retired, Jim Bakker went to prison, the Cold War collapsed, the Supreme Court's Webster decision galvanized a reinvigorated grassroots feminist activism. In Pam's and Dotty's kin sets and my own, major family changes continued. We rejoiced and suffered as kin and friends died, fought, fell in and out of love, married, divorced, gave birth, moved away. Jobs were begun, lost, and switched. Residences and household compositions changed. Many more accidents happened.

By the time Dotty and Pam read the chapters I had written about their families, the unavoidable distortions in my crafting of their stories had been severely mocked by time. Both were right to say that this is not their book, but mine. Out of gratitude for their having granted me permission and the wherewithal to write it, out of concern for the book's potentially hurtful effects on them and their kin, and in the dialogic spirit, I granted Dotty and Pam the right to control its closing words. Just before this book went to press in late November 1989 I tape-recorded interviews with each about her responses to what I had written and offered each an opportunity to edit and revise a transcript of the conversation as she wished.

Dotty unenthusiastically indulged my "noble" impulse, but claimed few grievances with my rendition of her family. She found my portraits of Danny and Kristina overly generous, but "I think, unfortunately," she acknowledged, "you were right-on with most of the rest of it." Reading my account had been painful. "Sometimes living it is easier than reading it, 'cause reading it you see it all over again and you see how hard and horrible it really was. And when you're going through it, it isn't that bad." Dotty had "mixed feelings" about placing her family's travail in the public record—uncomfortable about the exposure, but comforted by "the thought that maybe there's something in there that can steer people

273

in an entirely different direction than we ended up going." She voiced
no desire for me to fictionalize more details in order to further reduce
the risks of public exposure. "Nobody's going to know me. And if they
do, too bad. There's nothing in there that's not real." Nor did she concede
any regrets about her participation in my research. On the contrary,
Dotty claimed to deeply value my involvement in her life. "I couldn't
believe how much a part of my life you became. Wow, when something
would happen, I'd think, God, I wonder what Judy's gonna think of this
one! In the beginning you were right there in front of my face all the
time, and then afterwards you just became part of us. It was like—you
were just with us."

Pam's response to what I have written about her is much less flattering.
It is also, I believe, an eloquent contribution to postmodern meditations
on the impossibilty of "writing culture." I close this book, therefore, with
Pam's edited and revised version of a transcript of the conversation recorded on November 16, 1989.

Pam: After reading the chapters you wrote about me, I thought that
one of my big problems, and one of a lot of people's problems,
is that I'm alienated from myself. And in one sense reading
about my life, that's more alienation. Because if you read about
yourself and you're removed from yourself, it's just one more
level of alienation. And I remembered something I've read or
heard—that we go through life being terrified that we'll be taken
at our word. So when I look at the book, it's one of the rare
instances where I'm being taken at my word, and over a period
of years. It's scary to establish the impression of completeness
that print does.

Well, at first it frightened me, it disturbed me, because I
thought, is this me? You know, here I am being taken at my
word, is this the real me? And it took me awhile to realize that,
yes, it is me, but it is only a part of me. But the real solid core
of me—that isn't. The core me isn't being, doing, or saying
anything. The core me is just okay. It doesn't have performance
standards. It doesn't have to fit into a picture, it doesn't have—
it's just a very—a spiritual thing. It doesn't need to be explained. It just is. To me that's Christ—that given. That's love,
that's the pearly gate Christ or whatever, it just is. I'll want the

capturing of Pamela to include the caveat "God isn't finished with me yet." But I also have the pressure to find the definitive me because it means I've arrived, and the rest is downhill. So those problems create tension for me. The irony is that the process is me, not the pictures. If God wasn't trying to show me this, then the Bible would be a pamphlet.

Judy: So then no story, I mean, there wouldn't be any way to portray someone that way?

Pam: I don't believe so. I think it would be impossible to portray anyone, unless someone was seriously mentally ill or something. I guess what's important there, Judy, is we believe that if you can define it, or if, like an illness, if you can label it, or if you can set it up, and by "it" I mean Pamela, next to some other people that are enough alike, that if the commonality shows, then it's okay, then you can go, whewwww. We go crazy with anything that doesn't fit one of those. If we can't define it, if we can't give it a label, if we can't stack two of them together, you know, there's something wrong. And we all have ideas about what that label or definition or what little group we want to be standing in. And somebody comes along like you and puts them in another group, or makes it unclear whether we should be in that group—do you see how scary that could be? Well, all that hit me. It was very bizarre. But then I realized that I didn't have to be in the group that you— I can be in those groups, I can be out of those groups. You know, it's okay. I wish I could feel that way all of the time.

Judy: What group did I put you in, or did I put you in any groups that seemed surprising or wrong?

Pam: The group I felt like I was in there is *Diary of a Mad Housewife*— you know that picture—"Tell me what you want me to be and I'll be it"? No values, nothing but a need to be accepted, with changes coming so fast, how could I keep up if I were in that group? But you see, my okay group has got to play to whatever audience I happen to be at the time. Remember what you said a minute ago about how we all change from one minute to the next? Well, I'm reading about myself and I'm that ever-changing audience. I didn't sit down in one day and read it all. So, therefore, that audience of Pamela reading the drafts of Pamela

275

was a different audience on different days. I mean at one point, I told you I had to put it down. I was in a very deep, deeply, disturbing, depressed week when I went at it first. So I was reading and changing, always changing. You know what it's like? It would be like—re-creating any moment in that point would be like trying to find a design in one of those things that you turn—

Judy: A kaleidoscope?

Pam: Yeah, and saying "Oh, I like that design, let me go back to it." I mean, can you? Give me a break! And the value of the thing too, because, is one more beautiful than the other? Probably not. We all try to go back and recapture a picture of ourselves and our feelings, but it never works. That's control. Control is fitting the definition and protection against the big surprise, a fortress against fear. We're trying to control the kaleidoscope.

Judy: You know, you're an intuitive "postmodern" anthropologist. Anthropologists are discussing the impossibility of reporting data about the "other," about how it's always also about yourself and the dialogue between different cultures. You're a spontaneous, intuitive theorist of the postmodern period! Was there anything else that you really felt you wanted to say?

Pam: Well, the only part is like—that you left out chunks of me, you know. Real important chunks of me. You know, that's a big deal. Like, Jimmy is such a big part of my life, and he's hardly there. I spent ten years as a single mother, and that's not there. And those were the formative years for my kids. My disability isn't there, and that's a central part of my life. I never knew if I was really handicapped. I looked so normal, but parts of me just refused to behave normal and always misbehaved when exposure to others was sure and humiliation was swift. It was a problem for others also to understand, so I began to be responsible for protecting them and their need to fit me into a definition. Handicaps aren't always visible or definable. How do you explain something that is physically different at different times? Also adults aren't handicapped, only poster kids. (Except if everyone lives long enough, they're going to be handicapped too.) Like look at that period of time when I was looking for any unskilled job in the whole world. And you know why I never did assembly, even though everybody and their dog could get assembly work? Because I couldn't do it. You know why I didn't get a clerical job in electronics too? I can't do it. It requires dexterity skills that I didn't have. Plus I have learning disabilities. I don't know if I ever told you that. You know why I cleaned houses? I couldn't do most other entry-level jobs for women. You left out a lot of things.

Judy: Well then, if you knew now, I mean, if you knew then what you know now—

Pam: About what you're writing?

Judy: —would you have done this?

Pam: Probably. I don't know if I would have been as unself-conscious about what I said. I probably would have tried to plan what I intended discussing, because I probably would have not left the things out that I know are big parts of me.

Judy: One of my reservations about including all kinds of things, and one thing that I never worked out entirely was how many facts to change for disguising purposes. And your disability fell into that ambiguous category to me, because, you know, I don't know who's going to read this book or whatever and how visible to make you to people you might not want to tell about the book. You know the way I changed brothers into sisters, and changed facts here and there, not as much as most anthropologists do, but I don't know what your feelings are. Do you want more changes, or fewer?

Pam: I don't know how I feel about it. I think, with one exception— that time I said "Hands off!"—the rest of it, I don't really care. Of course, I'm not going to be running out and buying it for all my friends.

Judy: Well, I don't think it's going to be staring at you in the drug-stores. But people in some of your circles might stumble across it.

Pam: There's nothing there that would be bothersome to me that I can think of. If somebody laid their hands on this and said, "Pamela, is that yours?" I wouldn't have trouble owning it at all. Even though it wasn't my picture, there were parts of it that I think you painted an unrealistically good picture of me.

So I don't feel like you just put out this negative thing on me, at all. It's just different from my picture.

And I was thinking, if Christ is more important than his teaching, which is something that the pastor was saying in church Sunday—that the words of Christ are important, the teachings of Christ, but Christ was more important than his teaching. So I was thinking, are we more important than our words or deeds? Are we more than the sum of them? And that kind of led me to believe, yeah, we are. And that's that part of ourselves that we're not in touch with half enough, that real solid place in ourselves, the thing that's not trying to be or to do or to achieve anything else. We are more important than that. So therefore, if we're more important, just like Christ was more important, I'm in a way, no matter what you ever painted about me, I would be more important than that, and I would be different than that. You know. You know, you could never capture me.

Notes

Chapter 1

1. "When 'Families' Will Have a New Definition," 9 May, 1983.
2. Writing the majority opinion in the New York ruling, Judge Vito Titone elaborated four judicial criteria for determining what constitutes a family: (1) "exclusivity and longevity of a relationship"; (2) the "level of emotional and financial commitment"; (3) how a couple has "conducted their everyday lives and held themselves out to society"; (4) the "reliance placed upon one another for daily family services." Gutis, "Court Widens Family Definition."
3. Bodovitz, "Referendum Petitions Block S.F. Domestic Partners Law"; and Lattin, "How Religious Groups Stopped Partners Law."
4. For pessimistic assessments of family decline, see Lasch, *Haven in a Heartless World;* Davis, "Meaning and Significance of Marriage in Contemporary Society"; and Berger and Berger, *The War Over the Family.* For optimistic appraisals of "the family," see Bane, *Here to Stay: American Families in the Twentieth Century;* Caplow et al., *Middletown Families: Fifty Years of Change and Continuity;* and Collins, *Sociology of Marriage and the Family: Gender, Love, and Property.* More centrist but still somewhat anxious evaluations of the state of "the family" include Wolfe, *Whose Keeper? Social Science and Moral Obligation;* Bellah et al., *Habits of the Heart;* and Cherlin, "Marriage, Divorce, Remarriage: From the 1950s to the 1980s."
5. Gordon, *Heroes of Their Own Lives,* p. 3.
6. Anthropologists draw an important distinction between households, the residential units of daily life, and families, the more ambiguous, symbolic

279

terrain in which kinship is represented. See, for example, Collier, Rosaldo, and Yanagisako, "Is There a Family? New Anthropological Views." Moore, *Feminism and Anthropology*, provides a concise and useful discussion of the relevant anthropological literature.

7. Historians differ somewhat in periodizing the emergence of the modern American family, but most agree that its full flowering among "native" white Americans occurred in the late nineteenth century. Among the best sources are Degler, *At Odds: Women and the Family in America from the Revolution to the Present;* Mintz and Kellogg, *Domestic Revolutions: A Social History of American Family Life;* Evans, *Born for Liberty: A History of Women in America;* Van Horn, *Women, Work, and Fertility, 1900–1986;* Coontz, *The Social Origins of Private Life: A History of American Families 1600–1900.*

8. Mintz and Kellogg, *Domestic Revolutions.* See also Demos, *A Little Commonwealth: Family Life in Plymouth Colony;* and Coontz, *Social Origins of Private Life.*

9. According to Kingsley Davis, only 2.3 percent of native-born white wives were in the paid labor force in the 1890s. "Wives and Work: A Theory of the Sex-Role Revolution and Its Consequences," p. 75. See also Degler, *At Odds,* chap. 15.

10. Engels, *Condition of the Working Class in England.*

11. Kessler-Harris and Sacks, "Demise of Domesticity." Also see Mintz and Kellogg, *Domestic Revolutions,* chap. 5.

12. For the intertwined histories of the nineteenth-century cult of domesticity and American feminism, see Cott, *Bonds of Womanhood: Women's Sphere in New England, 1700–1835;* Ryan, *Cradle of the Middle Class: The Family in Oneida County, New York, 1790–1865;* Degler, *At Odds;* Evans, *Born for Liberty.* Ginsburg, *Contested Lives: The Abortion Debate in an American Community,* provides a useful synthetic interpretation of U.S. feminism and the politics of domesticity through the contemporary period.

13. See Degler, *At Odds,* pp. 165–77; Levitan, Belous, and Gallo, *What's Happening to the American Family? Tensions, Hopes, Realities,* p. 30; Davis, "Wives and Work," p. 79; and Stone, "The Road to Polygamy." The first "modern" American divorce case that included "alienation of affection" as one of its complaints occurred in 1776. Evans, *Born for Liberty,* p. 42.

14. Davis, "Wives and Work," p. 72. Fertility rates rose significantly during the aberrant 1950s, peaking in 1957 when women of childbearing age bore on average slightly more than three children each, before fertility resumed its long-term pattern of decline. Recent statistics indicate an average of 1.8 children per woman of childbearing age. Census Bureau data reported in Barringer, "Waiting Is Over: Births Near 50s Levels." Her title refers to aggregate births, which rose in the late 1980s as the childbearing years of the baby boom cohort ended.

15. May, *Homeward Bound: American Families in the Cold War Era.*
16. Gerson, *Hard Choices: How Women Decide About Work, Career, and Motherhood,* p. 237. Van Horn, *Women, Work, and Fertility,* p. 44, identifies 1940 as the date when the modern family had become the norm among all social classes, but she does not specify class data concerning access to a male family wage or the percentage of women serving as full-time homemakers then. Kessler-Harris and Sacks, however, consider it doubtful that a majority of working-class males ever earned a family wage adequate to unilaterally support their households. "Demise of Domesticity," p. 67. It is crucial to underscore that the 3/5 figure of "modern" households in 1950 includes childless married couples.
17. Bellah, "Modernity in Question."
18. Average marriage ages dropped to 22.6 for men and 20.2 for women in 1955. Levitan, Belous, and Gallo, *What's Happening to the American Family?* p. 21.
19. In 1960, 17.3 percent of women and 23.2 percent of men over the age of fifteen had never married; by 1983 these figures rose to 22.9 percent of women and 30 percent of men. Bianchi and Spain, *American Women in Transition,* p. 12. By 1960 as many Americans lived in suburbs as in cities; Mintz and Kellogg, *Domestic Revolutions,* p. 183. Evans, *Born for Liberty,* p. 246, reports that by 1960 nearly 70 percent of Americans had become homeowners, but a recent government study places peak homeownership rates at 65.6 percent of the population in 1980. Joint Economic Committee of Congress study reported in Dixon, "Senator Bentsen Says Home Ownership Has Declined." For an excellent history of suburbanization in the United States, see Jackson, *Crabgrass Frontier: The Suburbanization of the United States.* For a study of a suburb populated primarily by auto workers in what was soon to become the Silicon Valley, see Berger, *Working-Class Suburb: A Study of Auto Workers in Suburbia.*
20. Particularly Parsons and Bales et al., *Family, Socialization, and Interaction Process.*
21. See Breines, "The 1950s: Gender and Some Social Science," for a discussion of the particular myopia of sociological views of gender during that decade.
22. For an astute political and cultural reading of shifts in the television industry's portrayal of families from the 1950s to the 1980s, see Taylor, *Prime-Time Families: Television Culture in Postwar America.*
23. Levitan, Belous, and Gallo, *What's Happening to the American Family?* pp. 28–29.
24. Mills, *Sociological Imagination,* p. 166.
25. M. May, "Bread Before Roses: American Workingmen, Labor Unions and the Family Wage." May argues that the demand for a family wage was primarily a class-based demand made by labor unions on behalf of

281

working-class men and their wives in the nineteenth century, but it was achieved in the twentieth century through a cross-class gender alliance between capitalists and unionized men. This analysis helps to resolve a theoretical and political debate among feminist and socialist labor historians concerning the class and gender character of the family wage struggle. Hartmann, "Capitalism, Patriarchy, and Job Segregation by Sex," criticized the sexist character of the struggle, while Humphries, "The Working-Class Family, Women's Liberation and Class Struggle: The Case of Nineteenth-century British History," defended the struggle as a form of class and family resistance.

26. After a sharp postwar spurt, divorce rates stabilized only temporarily during the 1950s, and above prewar levels. Levitan, Belous, and Gallo, *What's Happening to American Families?* p. 27. The proportion of women entering college climbed slowly throughout the 1950s, before escalating sharply since the mid-1960s: in 1950, 12 percent of women ages twenty-four to twenty-nine had completed one year of college; this figure rose to 22 percent in 1965 and reached 43 percent by 1984. McLaughlin et al., *Changing Lives of American Women*, pp. 33–34. Van Horn, *Women, Work, and Fertility*, p. 194, makes the interesting, provocative argument that a disjuncture between the limited kinds of jobs available to women and the increasing numbers of educated women seeking jobs during the 1960s helped to regenerate feminism. For additional discussions of the rise of working wives, see Davis, "Wives and Work"; Gerson, *Hard Choices;* Degler, *At Odds*, chap. 17; E. May, *Homeward Bound;* and Evans, *Born for Liberty*, chap. 11.

27. See *Evans, Born for Liberty*, pp. 253–54; Van Horn, *Women, Work, and Fertility*, chap. 12; Kessler-Harris and Sacks, "Demise of Domesticity."

28. Ortner, "Virgin and the State."

29. Ehrenreich, *Hearts of Men: American Dreams and the Flight from Commitment.*

30. Ehrenreich, Hess, and Jacobs, *Re-Making Love: The Feminization of Sex*, argue that the sexual revolution was a women's revolution because the sexual behavior of men did not change much. More critical of this development, Lawson, *Adultery: An Analysis of Love and Betrayal*, adopts the view that women "masculinized" their sexual behavior to conform to male-defined standards.

31. The "first wave" of American feminism refers to the nineteenth-century women's rights movement, publicy initiated at Seneca Falls in 1848, which culminated in the suffrage movement. Organized feminist activity declined after the suffrage victory until a renewed movement for women's liberation emerged in the 1960s.

32. Bernard, *Future of Marriage*, p. 53.

33. See Hartmann, "Changes in Women's Economic and Family Roles," for an optimistic overview of women's recent gains.

34. A study that attempted to operationalize Marxist criteria for assigning class categories to workers in the United States (and which excluded housewives from its sample) found "that the majority of the working class in the United States consists of women (53.6%)." Wright et al., "American Class Structure," p. 22. Between 1979 and 1984 job growth in middle-income occupations dropped almost 20 percent while the growth of low-income jobs soared. More than 20 percent of the year-round, full-time jobs created paid less than $7,000 (1984 dollars). In the same period white men suffered a net loss of one million jobs in the above-$28,000 bracket, while 97 percent of net employment gain for white men was in the below $7,000 bracket. Newman, *Falling From Grace: The Experience of Downward Mobility in the American Middle Class*, p. 31. See also Harrison and Bluestone, *Great U-Turn*.

35. The much-publicized findings from Lenore Weitzman's study of no-fault divorce in California underscore this fact. In the first year after divorce women and their minor children suffered a 73 percent decline in their standard of living, while husbands enjoyed a 42 percent gain. Weitzman, *The Divorce Revolution: The Unexpected Social and Economic Consequences for Women and Children in America*. See also Arendell, *Mothers and Divorce: Legal, Economic and Social Dilemmas;* and Newman, *Falling from Grace*, chap. 7.

36. In 1980 households headed by fully employed women had a poverty rate almost three times greater than husband-wife households and twice that of households headed by unmarried men. For the relationship between female employment and poverty, see Smith, "The Paradox of Women's Poverty: Wage-Earning Women and Economic Tranformation." The concept "feminization of poverty," however, misrepresents significant features of contemporary poverty, particulary the worsening conditions for minority men. See Sparr, "Reevaluating Feminist Economics: 'Feminization of Poverty' Ignores Key Issues," and Burnham, "Has Poverty Been Feminized in Black America?"

37. In 1960 households with working wives had 25 percent more income than those with only husbands working. By 1983 the former had 47 percent more income than the latter. Van Horn, *Women, Work, and Fertility*, p. 173. The lower a family's annual income, the higher the proportion contributed by women. Paradoxically, however, there is now an inverse relationship between family income and the percentage of wives in the labor force. See Reskin and Hartmann, *Women's Work, Men's Work: Sex Segregation on the Job*, p. 4. Families with unemployed wives have been losing economic ground both in absolute terms and relative to two-earner

families. Between 1975 and 1983, the median income of married-couple households with employed wives rose by 0.6 percent while that of married-couple households without employed wives fell by 7.3 percent. Newman, *Falling from Grace,* p. 38.

38. There are recent indications, however, of more substantial reductions in the persistent earnings gap between women and men. Although between 1960 and 1980 the average hourly wages of full-time women workers remained near 60 percent of male hourly wages, by 1986 the ratio based on weekly earnings of full-time workers had increased to 70 percent. McLaughlin et al., *Changing Lives of American Women,* p. 113. However, a portion of this gain was caused by a decline in earnings for blue-collar men.

39. Marshner, *The New Traditional Woman,* p. 1. Ginsburg, *Contested Lives,* an ethnographic study of activists on both sides of the abortion struggle in North Dakota, documents the widespread perception of feminists as antinurturant.

40. Moynihan, *The Negro Family: The Case for National Action.*

41. For comprehensive documentation of the background and response to the report, see Rainwater and Yancey, *The Moynihan Report and the Politics of Controversy.* As this book went to press a new Gallup Poll surveyed public views on the impact of the women's movement on American lives. Although a majority (56%) claimed women's lives were more satisfying than 20 years ago, far larger majorities thought the women's movement had made it harder for marriages to succeed (76%), harder for parents to raise children (82%), and harder for women to combine jobs and family responsibilities (66%). Destafano and Colasanto, "Most Believe U.S. Men Have a Better Life," p. 85.

42. Ephron, "Teflon Daddy."

43. "The Daughter Who Begs to Differ."

44. Congressional report, "U.S. Children and Their Families: Current Traditions and Recent Trends," quoted in Liebert, "Gloomy Statistics on the Future of Poor Children." See also Levitan, Belous, and Gallo, *What's Happening to the American Family?*

45. Skold, "Interests of Feminists and Children in Child Care," p. 119. Also note that a sharp increase in the use of formal child care occurred during Reagan's first term, from 16 percent in 1982 to 25 percent in 1985. Levitan, Belous, and Gallo, *What's Happening to American Families?* p. 102.

46. Bumpass and Castro, "Recent Trends and Differentials in Marital Disruption"; they project that two-thirds of recent marriages will dissolve before death. Levitan, Belous, and Gallo, writing earlier, projected that 54 percent will divorce. *What's Happening to the American Family?* p. 12. The temporary decline in divorce rates was due to "cohort effects"—a

decline in the proportion of the population currently in the age and marital status categories that place them "at risk" for divorce.

47. In 1987 there were 1.8 births per woman. Levitan, Belous, and Gallo, *What's Happening to the American Family?* p. 42. As indicated in note 14 above, however, the absolute number of births rose during the late 1980s as the baby boom generation completed its childbearing years. Marriage rates during peak marriage ages dropped by 50 percent between 1975 and 1985. Bumpass and Castro, "Recent Trends," p. 24. A study for the Joint Economic Committee of Congress found that homeownership, which had been rising throughout the post–World War II period, peaked at 65.6 percent of the population in 1980 and then began falling, hitting 63.9 percent in 1988. Reported in Dixon, "Senator Bentsen Says Home Ownership Has Declined." See also Ehrenreich, *Fear of Falling: The Inner Life of the Middle Class,* p. 205.

48. There has been a two-thirds increase in nonmarital fertility among whites since the mid-1970s. Bumpass and Castro, "Recent Trends," p. 27. Forty percent of children of women who gave birth for the first time between 1985 and 1988 were conceived out of wedlock—33 percent among white women, 79 percent among Black women. Berke, "Late Childbirth is Found on Rise."

49. In 1985 only 7 percent fit the pattern of a breadwinning father, a full-time, homemaking mother and one to four children under the age of eighteen. Van Horn, *Women, Work, and Fertility,* p. 152. This understates the percentage of households that pass through a life cycle stage with this pattern.

50. For the rightward drift of the discourse about the declining family, see literature cited in note 4 above. I discuss the family backlash literature among feminists in Stacey, "Are Feminists Afraid to Leave Home? The Challenge of Profamily Feminism."

51. Data reported in a three-part *New York Times* series published 20–22 August 1989 on women's changing lives. See Belkin, "Bars to Equality of Sexes Seen as Eroding, Slowly"; Cowan, "Poll Finds Women's Gains Take Personal Toll"; Dionne, "Struggle for Work and Family Fueling Women's Movement." For further evidence of broad, increasing support for feminist goals, see Fleming, "Public Opinion on Change in Women's Rights and Roles"; Mason and Lu, "Attitudes Towards Women's Familial Roles: Changes in the United States, 1977–1985"; Wallis, "Onward, Women!"; Destafano and Colesanto, "Most Believe U.S. Men Have Better Life."

52. Dilnot, "What is the Post-Modern?"

53. Ibid., pp. 245, 249.

54. Tolstoy, *Anna Karenina* (p. 17).

55. The postmodern condition emerges, Jean-Francois Lyotard argues in *The Postmodern Condition: A Report on Knowledge,* when legitimation through grand historical narratives has broken down. I sidestep here the debate over whether the postmodern represents a clear break with the modern, or, as Nancy Scheper-Hughes argued during a conference on "Anthropology and Modernity" held at the University of California, Berkeley in April 1989, is simply "capitalism on speed." Mascia-Lees, Sharpe, and Cohen, "The Postmodernist Turn in Anthropology: Cautions From a Feminist Perspective," discuss feminist concerns that the rejection of grand narratives coincides with new attempts by women and other subordinated groups to write their own. For additional useful discussions of feminism, modernism, and postmodernism, see Wolff, *Feminine Sentences: Essays on Women and Culture.*

56. Block, *Postindustrial Possibilities: A Critique of Economic Discourse.* Like Block, I use the term to designate a form and period of capitalist social organization rather than to signal the end of capitalism. Because Daniel Bell's original formulation of the concept implied the latter, it incited considerable resistance among Marxists. See Bell's *Coming of Post-Industrial Society: A Venture in Social Forecasting.*

57. Newman, *Falling from Grace,* pp. 30–31. Ehrenreich, *Fear of Falling,* makes the crucial point that it is secure, well-paid, blue-collar jobs which have declined most severely, removing increasing numbers of working-class people from middle-income ranks. Several challenge the accuracy of labeling the United States as a service economy. See R. Walker, "Is There a Service Economy? The Changing Division of Labor." Few deny, however, that significant occupational changes have occurred in the past few decades that involve the decline of "basic" manufacturing industries. For an astute critique of the androcentric and ethnocentric premises of the discourse on the loss of jobs for white male blue-collar workers, see di Leonardo, "Deindustrialization as a Folk Model."

58. Overholser, "What 'Post-Feminism' Really Means," p. 30. Likewise, Eleanor Smeal, president of Fund for a Feminist Majority and former president of NOW, reportedly "worries that some would use it [the term, postfeminism] to bury feminism." Quoted in Dionne, "Struggle for Work and Family," p. A14. Rayna Rapp adds to this her quite appropriate concern that the term, like most media fads, emphasizes the experience of privileged, white professionals while ignoring the continuing activism of women of color and women trade unionists. See her "Is the Legacy of Second-Wave Feminism Postfeminism?" which was a response to my earlier essay, " 'Sexism by a Subtler Name?' Postindustrial Conditions and Postfeminist Consciousness in the Silicon Valley."

59. Quoted in Dionne, "Struggle for Work and Family," p. A14.

60. For compatible discussions of postfeminism in novels and in television

sitcoms, see Rosenfelt, "Feminism, 'Postfeminism' and Contemporary Women's Fictions"; and Press and Strathman, "Reconstructing the Family: Situation Comedy and the Construction of Postfeminism." Two studies of undergraduate students in the 1980s, one at the University of California, Berkeley, the second at Rutgers University, report precisely the attitudes toward feminism, sexuality, family, and work that I identify as postfeminist. See Machung, "Talking Careers, Thinking Jobs," and Moffatt, *Coming of Age in New Jersey: College and American Culture.* Rapp, "Is the Legacy of Second-Wave Feminism Postfeminism?" provides a critique of the race and class biases implicit in most discussions of post-feminism and a discussion of the depoliticizing tendencies of the term.

Chapter 2

1. One of the best sources for data on the occupational transformation of Santa Clara County and a superb ethnographic study of the electronics industry is Keller, "The Production Worker in Electronics: Industrialization and Labor Development in California's Santa Clara Valley." See also R. Gordon and Kimball, "High Technology, Employment and the Challenges to Education"; Hayes, *Behind the Silicon Curtain: The Seductions of Work in a Lonely Era;* Saxenian, "Silicon Chips and Spatial Structure: The Industrial Basis of Urbanization in Santa Clara County, California"; Siegel and Markoff, *The High Cost of High Tech: The Dark Side of the Chip;* Malone, *The Big Score.* For a more congratulatory portrait of the Valley, see Rogers and Larsen, *Silicon Valley Fever: Growth of High-Technology Culture.*

2. Eisenscher, "Chasing the High Tech Rainbow: Reality and Fantasy in the Valley of the Silicon Giants."

3. U.S. Bureau of the Census, *Census of Population: 1950, 1980.* Official estimates projected that in 1990 the county population would be 1,518,000. United Way of Santa Clara County, "A Community Challenged: A Public Report on Human Needs in Santa Clara County," p. 3.

4. Keller, "Production Worker in Electronics," p. iv; Howard, "Second Class in Silicon Valley," p. 22.

5. Employment Development Department, "Future of Silicon Valley," p. 2.

6. See, for example, Rogers and Larsen, *Silicon Valley Fever,* and Johnston, "High Tech, High Risk and High Life in Silicon Valley." Hayes discusses additional examples of this celebratory literature in *Behind the Silicon Curtain,* chap. 1. According to Siegel and Markoff, *High Cost of High Tech,* p. 5, as recently as 1984 delegations of economic development officials

287

headed by the king of Sweden and the presidents of Austria and France visited the Silicon Valley.

7. For data on the occupational structure of the electronics industry, see Keller, "The Production Worker in Electronics"; Gordon and Kimball, "High Technology, Employment"; Axelrad, *Profile of the Electronics Workforce in the Santa Clara Valley;* Siegel and Borock, "Background Report on Silicon Valley."

8. Gordon and Kimball, "High Technology, Employment," pp. 34–35. For data on the declining middle in the Silicon Valley, see the Association of Bay Area Governments, cited in Hossfeld, "Divisions of Labor, Divisions of Lives: Immigrant Women Workers in Silicon Valley," pp. 39–40. See also sources cited in note 7.

9. Official estimates suggest that between 1980 and 1990 the white population declined from 71 percent to 62 percent, while the nonwhite population rose to 38 percent. The Hispanic population grew from 17.5 percent to 20.6 percent, while the influx of Southeast Asian refugees rose from 8 to 14 percent of the total. United Way of Santa Clara County, "A Community Challenged," pp. 3–4.

10. Eisenscher, "Chasing the High Tech Rainbow." According to Gordon and Kimball, "High Technology, Employment," p. 32, in 1984 the average starting hourly wage for unskilled electronics workers was between $3.50 and $5.50; that same year the average hourly wage for all production workers in electronics was $8.89 compared with $13.28 in petroleum and coal, $13.09 in steel, and $12.64 in the auto industry. Keller, "Production Worker in Electronics," argues persuasively that the largely unorganized character of the county work force was a significant factor in its attractiveness to electronics corporate developers and that union-prevention policies have been an important priority of the industry.

11. Eisenscher, "Chasing the High Tech Rainbow"; Hayes, *Behind the Silicon Curtain,* p. 65.

12. Gordon and Kimball, "High Technology, Employment," p. 58. Also see Beers, "Temps—High-Tech's Ace in the Hole," and Beers, "Tomorrowland."

13. Employment Development Department, "Annual Planning Information, San Jose Metropolitan Statistical Area 1987 to 1988," p. 1.

14. Eisenscher, "Chasing the High Tech Rainbow"; Malone, *Big Score,* pp. 411–23. Carcinogens increase cancer rates, mutagens increase genetic defects, and teratogens increase birth defects.

15. Saxenian, "Silicon Chips and Spatial Structure." Between 1970 and 1975 national housing costs rose 68 percent, while in the Silicon Valley they rose 92 percent. Rising housing costs outpaced earnings; between 1970 and 1976 family income rose 42.5 percent, but home costs rose 150 percent. See Bernstein et al., "Silicon Valley: Paradise or Paradox?" p.

43. As an example, Malone notes that four-bedroom homes bought new in 1965 for $15,000 were sold in 1980 for $200,000. *Big Score*, p. 335.

16. While it is not possible to compile an accurate count of the homeless, the Santa Clara County Office of Human Relations estimated that there were at least 13,495 homeless individuals residing in the county in 1985, 18,956 homeless in 1986, and 19,600 in 1989. United Way of Santa Clara County, "A Community Challenged," p. 17.

17. Tessler, "Churches' Holy War on Drugs"; Hayes, *Behind the Silicon Curtain*, p. 22.

18. Malone, *Big Score*, p. 398. Also see Malone for accounts of drug use in the electronics industry.

19. See Carey and Gathright, "By Work Obsessed. The Silicon Valley Ethics." According to the *Mercury* survey, 35.3 percent of electronics employees reported using narcotics while at work, while 43.6 percent reported alcohol consumption; the comparable figures for employees in nonhigh-tech jobs was 23.5 percent for narcotics and 30.8 percent for alcohol. For personal testimony on the extensive use of drugs on electronics production lines, see Malone, *Big Score*, pp. 5–6, 403–11.

20. Tessler, "Churches' Holy War on Drugs." In 1989, when the total Santa Clara County population numbered approximately 1.5 million people (of all ages), the County Bureau of Drug Abuse Services estimated that approximately 112,000 were drug users. Of these, 52,640 were daily users and 14,213 were using heroin. United Way, "A Community Challenged," p. 18.

21. Between 1980 and 1986, the region grew at a rate of 8 percent compared with 14 percent for the state; 85 percent of the region's growth was due to natural increase. See Employment Development Department, "Annual Planning Information," p. 1. The Bay area regional "popularity" poll is reported in Nolte, "The North Bay Is Where Most Folks Want to Live."

22. Schneidawind, "New Flight From Silicon Valley's High Costs."

23. Flammang, "Filling the Party Vacuum: Women at the Grassroots Level in Local Politics," "Female Officials in the Feminist Capital: The Case of Santa Clara County," and "Women Made a Difference: Comparable Worth in San Jose"; Linda Blum, *Between Feminism and Labor: The Significance of the Comparable Worth Movement*. Ironically, the San Jose comparable worth strike was called when the feminist mayor and the city council—on which women held the majority of seats—failed to meet the city employees' demand to proceed on a proposed job study prerequisite to evaluating pay equity. For attitudes of Silicon Valley working-class women toward feminism, see Hossfeld, "Divisions of Labor," pp. 356–63.

24. For data on divorce rates and household composition for Santa Clara

County in comparison with California and the United States as a whole, see U.S. Bureau of the Census, *Census of Population* for 1960, 1970, and 1980. During the 1970s the county recorded 660 abortions for every 1,000 live births, compared with a statewide average of 489.5 and a ratio of less than 400 for the nation. See U.S. Bureau of the Census, *Statistical Abstract of the United States, 1981.* Also see Malone, *Big Score,* p. 395.

25. Hollands, *Silicon Syndrome: A Survival Handbook for Couples.*
26. Malone, "Family in Crisis."
27. For literature describing working-class families as favoring "traditional" gender arrangements, see Komarovsky with Philips, *Blue-Collar Marriage;* Rubin, *Worlds of Pain: Life in a Working Class Family;* Van Horn, *Women, Work and Fertility;* Caplow et al., *Middletown Families;* and Coles and Coles, *Women of Crisis: Lives of Struggle and Hope.* In *Fear of Falling,* Barbara Ehrenreich argues that the media constructed this stereotype of the blue-collar working class after it briefly "discovered" this class in 1969. I discuss this issue in chapter 11.
28. Howell's *Hard Living on Clay Street: Portraits of Blue Collar Families,* the last ethnographic book about blue-collar white families in the United States that I know of, now is seventeen years old. Rubin's *Worlds of Pain,* a widely used interview study of working-class families, appeared in 1976. A recent invaluable ethnography of blue-collar men, however, makes a crucial contribution to an analysis of contemporary working-class family life. In *America's Working Man,* Halle recognizes the inadequacy of conventional formulations of working-class families and the methods employed by studies of these which fail to address the fluidity and ambiguity of family class positions, particularly in a period when more women are in the paid labor force than not. For these reasons, Halle scrupulously restricts his book title to designate its actual subject, working-class men. Unfortunately, he often fails to honor his own critique, because he identifies working-class homes, neighborhoods, and so on, on the basis of husbands' occupations alone.
29. Barbara Epstein and Judith Stacey, "Working-Class Family Life and the Growth of Scientific Industry in the Silicon Valley, California, 1950 to the Present." Grant proposal submitted to National Endowment for the Humanities. June 1984.
30. For "representative" examples of the literature on critical ethnography, see Clifford and Marcus, *Writing Culture: The Poetics and Politics of Ethnograpy;* Clifford, *The Predicament of Culture: Twentieth-Century Ethnography, Literature, and Art;* Marcus and Fischer, *Anthropology as Cultural Critique: An Experimental Moment in the Human Sciences;* and Marcus, "Requirements for Ethnographies of Late Twentieth Century Modernity Worldwide."
31. Feminists have pointed out the parallels between the postmodern critique of conventional ethnography and feminist critiques of conventional social

science that rarely receive recognition in the postmodern literature. A sampler of feminist epistemological and methodological criticism appears in Harding, *Feminism and Methodology: Social Science Issues.* Also see Stanley and Wise, *Breaking Out: Feminist Consciousness and Feminist Research.* For ambivalent appraisals of postmodern ethnography evaluated from feminist perspectives, see Strathern, "An Awkward Relationship: The Case of Feminism and Anthropology"; Stacey, "Can There Be a Feminist Ethnography?"; D. Gordon, "Writing Culture, Writing Feminism: The Poetics and Politics of Experimental Ethnography"; and Mascia-Lees, Sharpe, and Cohen, "Postmodernist Turn in Anthropology."

32. However, numerous feminists have expressed well-founded suspicions about the postmodern rejection of grand narratives coinciding, as it does, with the historical moment when women, the colonized, and other subordinated groups are first beginning to authorize their own. Hence, the greater tension and ambivalence in many feminist responses to the decentering moves of postmodernism. A nuanced discussion of this problem appears in Mascia-Lees, Sharpe, and Cohen, "Postmodernist Turn in Anthropology."

Chapter 3

1 For data and analyses of the meagerness of customary child support awards and the infrequency with which women actually receive the full amounts awarded, see Weitzman, *Divorce Revolution: The Unexpected Social and Economic Consequences for Women and Children in America;* Arendell, *Mothers and Divorce: Legal, Economic and Social Dilemmas;* and Newman, *Falling from Grace: The Experience of Downward Mobility in the American Middle Class,* chap. 7.

2. For a compelling ethnographic description and analysis of the rhetoric of evangelical conversion, see Harding, "Convicted by the Holy Spirit: The Rhetoric of Fundamental Baptist Conversion."

3. Many feminist scholars, of course, have explored the complexities and contradictions of formally patriarchal societies and women's informal power, influence, strategies, and compensatory rewards within them. See, for example, Rogers, "Female Forms of Power and the Myth of Male Dominance: A Model of Female-Male Interaction in Peasant Society." Like Rogers, however, the vast majority of these studies treat societies in which women have no choice but to maneuver within patriachal kinship forms. The literature on fundamentalist communities in the contemporary United States, which I was not yet familiar with, has only recently begun to explore these issues in depth. I discuss this literature in chapter 6.

4. Barbara Epstein coined this phrase during an informal conversation about this interview with Pam.

Chapter 4

1. Dobson's presidential-level influence preceded his active involvement in the Reagan administration. He was also an at-large delegate to President Carter's ill-fated White House Conference on the Family.
2. Quoted in Williford, "Addressing Problems of Home On Air."
3. The data are reported in ibid. Dobson frequently reports data indicating the growth of his ministry in *Focus on the Family*, the organization's monthly magazine.
4. Colleen Johnson found this inclusive approach to former kin at family celebrations among a minority of the divorced couples she studied in suburban San Francisco. See her "Socially Controlled Civility: The Functioning of Rituals in the Divorce Process" and *Ex-Familia: Grandparents, Parents and Children Adjust to Divorce.*
5. Newman provides a sensitive portrait of downward mobility among unionized blue-collar workers in *Falling from Grace: The Experience of Downward Mobility in the American Middle Class*, chap. 6.
6. For a particularly humorous rendition of this, see Ephron's *Funny Sauce: Us, the Ex, the Ex's New Mate, the New Mate's Ex, and the Kids*, from which I drew the epigraph for this chapter.
7. Johnson's recent study of postdivorce kin relationships among middle-class people in suburban San Francisco finds nearly one-third depending on former kin in their support systems. See *Ex-Familia*.
8. As indicated in note 4 above, a minority of the divorced people studied by Johnson behaved in a similar fashion: "They were proud of their new extended family, which had expanded by multiple marriages and divorces. For example, the fiftieth wedding anniversary celebration of the grandparents in one family was described with pride. All five children had been divorced and remarried, and all attended the celebration with their new spouses as well as their former spouses. "Socially Controlled Civility," p. 695.
9. U.S Bureau of the Census, *Statistical Abstracts*, p. 449.

Chapter 5

1. For a discussion of the relationship between development of the electronics industry and regional educational developments, see R. Gordon

and Kimball, "High Technology, Employment and the Challenges to Education."

2. Wallerstein and Blakeslee, *Second Chances: Men, Women and Children a Decade after Divorce.* As several reviewers have complained, however, because this sensitive study did not include a control group of children whose parents did not divorce, few conclusions concerning the effects of divorce on children can be drawn with confidence.

3. The terms "hard" and "settled" living come from an ethnographic study of blue-collar families in Washington, D.C. that I greatly admire, Howell, *Hard Living on Clay Street.*

4. The very concept of "temporary" employment is being reshaped by postindustrial labor practices. High-tech industries in the Silicon Valley make increasing use of temporary agencies to provide "flexible staffing" and to cut employee benefits. In 1985 one of every two hundred workers in the United States was a "temp," but one of sixty workers in the Silicon Valley held a "temporary" job. See Beers, " 'Temps'—High-Tech's Ace in the Hole."

5. Men do have an advantage when they enter characteristically female occupations. See Blum, *Between Feminism and Labor: The Significance of the Comparable Worth Movement.*

Chapter 6

1. This is a pseudonym and modified title of a manuscript written by the founder of "Global Ministries," also a pseudonym.

2. See Cancian, "Feminization of Love," and *Love in America.*

3. Cancian, "Feminization of Love," p. 692.

4. Bellah et al., *Habits of the Hearts,* pp. 94 ff.

5. The cartoon strip by Betty Lorde is called "Christian." To protect the privacy of members of "Global Ministries," I omit the name of the newsletter.

6. See Ginsburg, *Contested Lives: The Abortion Debate in an American Community,* for an analysis of the relationship between life cycle and historical stages in the paths to pro- and antiabortion activism among women in Fargo, North Dakota.

7. Fleming, "Public Opinion on Change in Women's Rights and Roles."

8. Similar feminist influences appear within the Orthodox Jewish revival. See Kaufman, "Coming Home to Jewish Orthodoxy: Reactionary or Radical Women?" and Davidman, "Women's Search for Family and Roots: A Jewish Religious Solution to a Modern Dilemma."

9. Hunter, *American Evangelicalism,* see esp. p. 50. Don Lattin, religion writer for the *San Francisco Chronicle,* reports that the World Christian Encyclo-

pedia estimates that there are 22 million Pentecostals and 43 million charismatics in North America. "Two Faces of the Spiritual Revival." Since 1965 evangelical denominations are reported to have increased their memberships at an average five-year rate of 8 percent, while membership in liberal denominations declined at an average five-year rate of 4.6 percent. Hunter, *Evangelicalism: The Coming Generation*, p. 6. For estimates of numbers of evangelicals, see also Quebedeaux, *The Worldly Evangelicals;* Warner, *New Wine in Old Wineskins;* and Pohli, "Church Closets and Back Doors: A Feminist View of Moral Majority Women." The predominance of women over men in evangelical Christianity has a long history in the U.S. dating back to the first and second Great Awakenings in the 18th and 19th centuries. See Cott, "Young Women in the Second Great Awakening in New England," and Epstein, *Politics of Domesticity: Women, Evangelism, and Temperance in Nineteenth-Century America.*

10. For discussion of the characteristics of contemporary evangelicals, see Hunter, *American Evangelicalism;* Quebedeaux, *The Worldly Evangelicals;* and Warner, *New Wine.*

11. For discussions of the political beliefs of evangelicals, see Quebedeaux, *Young Evangelicals* and *Worldly Evangelicals;* Hunter, *Evangelicalism* and *American Evangelicalism:* Ammerman, *Bible Believers: Fundamentalists in the Modern World;* and Warner, *New Wine.*

12. For historical treatments of fundamentalism and evangelicalism, see Dollar, *A History of Fundamentalism in America;* Marsden, *Evangelicalism and Modern America;* Quebedeaux, *Young Evangelicals, Worldly Evangelicals,* and *By What Authority? The Rise of Personality Cults in American Christianity.*

13. "Two Job Openings at *Sojourners.*"

14. Quebedeaux identifies Letha Scanzoni's "Women's Place: Silence or Service?" in the February 1966 issue of *Eternity* as one of the earliest of these feminist essays. *Wordly Evangelicals*, p. 121.

15. Chicago Declaration, cited in Scanzoni and Hardesty, *All We're Meant to Be: Biblical Feminism for Today*, pp. 18–19.

16. For histories of evangelical feminism, see Quebedeaux, *Worldly Evangelicals;* Scanzoni and Hardesty, *All We're Meant to Be;* and Bendroth, "The Search for 'Women's Role' in American Evangelicalism, 1930–1980." The first edition of the Scanzoni and Hardesty book is described in *Christian History* magazine as "the 1973 classic that set in motion a substantial biblical feminism." "Women in the Early Church," p. 36.

17. Virginia Mollenkott, a prominent biblical feminist, devotes one of her books to an androgynous reading of divine imagery, with such chapter titles as "God as Nursing Mother," "God as Midwife," "God as Mother Bear," "God as Female Homemaker," "God as Female Beloved," and "God as Dame Wisdom." In the chapter on God as homemaker, she

argues that "Psalm 123:2 gives us permission to see in Proverbs 31 a full-scale description of Yahweh as the perfect female homemaker, the perfect wife to a humanity which is cast by this image into a masculine role." Mollenkott, *Divine Feminine*, p. 62.

18. Mollenkott, *Women, Men and the Bible*, pp. 23–24. For other examples of this form of interpreting scripture, see Stagg and Stagg, "Jesus and Women"; Mickelsen, *Women, Authority & the Bible;* Scanzoni and Hardesty, *All We're Meant to Be;* Storkey, *What's Right with Feminism.*

19. Responding to feminist criticism of the first edition of *All We're Meant to Be,* Scanzoni and Hardesty revised their book to take a more sympathetic stand on homosexuality.

20. Scanzoni and Hardesty, *All We're Meant to Be.* p. 108.

21. About 2,000 to 3,000 women are active in chapters or on the mailing list of the Evangelical Women's Caucus, according to Quebedeaux, *Worldly Evangelicals*, p. 122. The evangelical feminist journal *Daughters of Sarah* has 3,400 paid subscribers. A study of contemporary evangelical college students identifies 9 percent of them as "strongly committed and politically oriented feminists." Hunter, *Evangelicalism*, p. 105.

22. For example, Gilbert Bilezikian, a professor of biblical studies at evangelical Wheaton College, calls for "deliberate programs of depatriarchalization" to overcome sex role socialization. See his *Beyond Sex Roles*, pp. 10–11. A conference on Evangelical Christianity and Modern America held at Billy Graham Center at Wheaton College in 1983, included a talk entitled "The Search for 'Women's Role' in American Evangelicalism." Mickelsen's *Women, Authority & the Bible* is a collection of papers from the Evangelical Colloquium on Women and the Bible held in 1984 in Oak Brook, Illinois. In 1988 *Christian History* magazine published a special issue entitled "Women in the Early Church."

23. The Gallup Poll data are reported by Hunter as evidence of the more socially conservative views of evangelicals. Hunter, *Evangelicalism*, p. 126. Susan Gerard and I, however, were more surprised by the evidence of significant resistance to such conservatism.

24. Hunter, *Evangelicalism*, esp. chap. 4.

25. An analysis of national survey data on female and male attitudes toward women's familial and work roles finds not a backlash but a continuing trend toward support for more egalitarian roles among all cohorts and sectors of the population in the United States. Not surprisingly, support is greater for female equality in paid work than for equal male responsibility for unpaid domestic and child care work. See Mason and Lu, "Attitudes Toward Women's Familial Roles: Changes in the United States, 1977–1985." Also see Destafano and Colesanto, "Most Believe Men Have Better Life."

26. Pointing out that these students' beliefs stand in sharp contrast to those

espoused by many evangelical leaders, Hunter concludes that "the Evangelical family specialists (including many ministers) advocate and defend a model of the family that is said to be traditional . . . in the name of a constituency that has largely abandoned it in favor of an androgynous/quasi-androgynous model." See his *Evangelicalism*, p. 114. Just as Mason and Lu, "Attitudes Toward Women's Familial Roles," find more egalitarian views on family issues among women than men, Hunter found women evangelical students to hold more feminist views than their male counterparts.

27. Ream, "Help!"

28. Morgan, *Total Woman*. Morgan's antifeminist best-seller advised wives to submit to their husbands and to enliven their sex lives through such means as attiring themselves in Saran Wrap to welcome their husbands home from work.

29. Carmichael, Carmichael, and Boyd, "Paving the Way to Intimacy."

30. Dobson, *Love Must Be Tough*, p. 25.

31. Streeter, *Finding Your Place after Divorce;* Strom, *Helping Women in Crisis*.

32. Dobson, *Love Must Be Tough*, pp. 191–92. When he served on the Meese Commission on Pornography, Dobson appropriated radical feminist rhetoric: "Pornography is degrading to women. . . . Pornography is the theory; rape is the practice." Quoted in Williams, *Hard Core*, p. 16.

33. Zanon, "What's New."

34. Ehrenreich, Hess, and Jacobs, *Re-Making Love*, chap. 5.

35. The 1980 Gallup Poll data reported by Hunter found 41 percent of evangelicals, compared with 29 percent of nonevangelicals, claiming to support a ban on abortion. Hunter, *Evangelicalism*, p. 126. Perhaps because of the wording of the poll, this seriously understates the sexual conservatism of evangelicals and their impact on the broader American populace. Confusingly, Wuthnow cites an essay by Hunter as his source for a 1978 Gallup poll that found 97 percent of evangelicals opposed to premarital sex, 95 percent expressing "opposition to abortion," and 89 percent opposed to homosexuality. Wuthnow interprets these data as evidence that while evangelicals "remained deeply divided in many other ways . . . on questions of morality they were unified." ("The Political Rebirth of American Evangelicals", p. 178.) Although Wuthnow, I believe, slightly overstates the case, I share his view that this is the most distinctive feature of contemporary evangelical beliefs.

36. A recent *TCW* editorial, for example, concludes: "Aborting a baby is wrong, but simply stopping an abortion is not enough. . . . And I pray that the next time someone needs help, God will give me the strength to go beyond my idealist theology and live with the realities of commitment." Dale Hanson Bourke, "Cost of Commitment." "Pro-Life" and "Pro-Choice" activists in North Dakota formed a "Pro-Dialogue" forum

to attempt to overcome some of their hostilities and to promote collaborative pro-women efforts. See Ginsburg, *Contested Lives,* pp. 222–26.

37. Hunter, *Evangelicalism,* p. 106. Similarly, Faye Ginsburg found that feminists had significantly influenced the right-to-life activists she studied in Fargo, North Dakota. *Contested Lives,* esp. pp. 194, 215.

38. Quoted in Early, "Equal Before God."

Chapter 7

1. See, for example, Rollins, *Between Women: Domestics and Their Employers;* Glenn, *Isei, Nisei, War Bride: Three Generations of Japanese American Women in Domestic Service;* and Romero, "Domestic Service in the Transition to Urban Life."

2. The term comes from the title of a book by Coser, *Greedy Institutions.*

Chapter 8

1. In his book by this title *(The Crabgrass Frontier: The Suburbanization of the United States),* Kenneth Jackson claims that by 1980 most Americans lived in the suburbs, and of these three-fourths were white working-class families. Halle, *America's Working Man,* provides ethnographic description of the significance of homeownership to white working-class people.

2. "Gifts and Gadgets" is a direct sales organization that distributes its wares in a social form akin to a Tupperware party. See Biggart, *Charismatic Capitalism: Direct Selling Organizations in America,* for a study of direct-sales organizations in the United States, and Rapping, "Tupperware and Women," for a feminist analysis of the patriarchal organizational ingenuity behind Tupperware's astonishing success.

3. Jessie Bernard coined this phrase in her critique of the gender asymmetries in experience and power that are structured into heterosexual marriages in the United States. See *Future of Marriage.*

4. This was Sylvia Yanigasako's witty characterization of the ways by which the wives of Italian businessmen she had interviewed evaded her anthropological questions. "Capital and Gendered Interest in Italian Family Firms."

5. David Halle found this pattern common among the marriages of the chemical workers he studied in New Jersey. Marriages improved as children left home and as economic conditions improved. *America's Working Man.*

6. An astute, but likely ethnocentric, observation by D. H. J. Morgan suggests that all family members have projects they attempt to realize

within the family context that "are often different from and perhaps contradictory to the ends of other members of the family." *Social Theory and the Family,* p. 219.

7. This data was reported in an *Insight* magazine item reported in *San Francisco Chronicle,* 23 August 1989.

Chapter 9

1. A recent anthropological study of undergraduate college culture conducted in the dormitories at Rutgers University reports similar apolitical attitudes among the women undergraduates. These women took for granted, and actively engaged in, recent gains in sexual freedom, and they never complained of sexist treatment. "In the opinion of most female undergraduates in the dorms, apparently," Michael Moffatt writes, "the political battles for the equality of the sexes had largely been won." *Coming of Age in New Jersey: College and American Culture,* p. 49.

2. Kathleen Gerson found situationally induced shifts between nondomestic and domestic strategies to be common among the middle-class and working-class women she interviewed for *Hard Choices: How Women Decide About Work, Career, and Motherhood.*

Chapter 10

1. The Santa Clara County Office of Human Relations estimated that nearly 19,000 homeless people resided in the county in 1986, that their numbers were increasing, and that the majority of the new homeless were families. United Way of Santa Clara County, "A Community Challenged: A Public Report on Human Needs in Santa Clara County," p. 17.

2. Bowen, *Return to Laughter. An Anthropological Novel,* p. 295.

Chapter 11

1. Alice Kessler-Harris and Karen Sacks consider it doubtful that a majority of working-class men ever earned a family wage. See "Demise of Domesticity in America."

2. Bumpass and Sweet, "Preliminary Evidence on Cohabitation," report higher cohabitation rates among those with high school education than among those with college education, and higher divorce rates among those who cohabit prior to marriage. For differential divorce rates by

income and race, see also Van Horn, *Women, Work and Fertility, 1900 to 1986;* Levitan, Belous, and Gallo, *What's Happening to the American Family? Tensions, Hopes, Realities;* and Walker, "Black-White Differences in Marriage and Family Patterns." A classic ethnography of matrilineal support systems among working-class people is Young and Wilmott, *Family and Kinship in East London.* See also Schneider and Smith, *Class Differences and Sex Roles in American Kinship and Family Structure.* Stack, *All Our Kin,* is the classic ethnographic portrayal of matrifocal cooperative kin networks among poor African-Americans. However, L. Gordon, *Heroes of Their Own Lives,* cautions against the tendency to exaggerate and romanticize the existence of extended kinship support systems among the very poor.

3. For data and discussions of noneconomic motives for paid employment among blue-collar women, see Walshok, "Occupational Values and Family Roles: Women in Blue-Collar and Service Occupations"; Gerson, *Hard Choices: How Women Decide About Work, Career, and Motherhood;* and Kessler-Harris and Sacks, "Demise of Domesticity." Even Komarovsky and Philip's early, classic study *Blue-Collar Marriage* discusses the growth of noneconomic motives for employment among the wives of blue-collar men.

4. Johnson, *Ex-Familia: Grandparents, Parents and Children Adjust to Divorce.*

5. On extended, cooperative kin ties among the poor, see references cited in note 2 above. Halle, *America's Working Man,* p. 279, takes as a premise the existence of extensive kin ties among blue-collar workers.

6. Stack, *All Our Kin;* Young and Willmott, *Family and Kinship in East London.*

7. Schnaiberg and Goldenberg, "From Empty Nest to Crowded Nest: The Dynamics of Incompletely-Launched Young Adults."

8. For example, Ehrenreich suggests that "the working class, from the moment of its discovery" by the professional middle class in 1969 "was conceived in masculine terms." (*Fear of Falling: The Inner Life of the Middle Class,* p. 108.) See also Acker, "Women and Social Stratification: A Case of Intellectual Sexism."

9. Ehrenreich, *Fear of Falling,* p. 101.

10. Ibid., p. 115.

11. Ibid., p. 223.

12. For example, Bell, *End of Ideology: On the Exhaustion of Political Ideas in the Fifties,* and Lipset, *Political Man.*

13. Employing conservative measurement techniques designed to understate the extent of income loss, a recent study of changes in family income found that 40 percent of American families lost income since 1979, and another 20 percent maintained stable incomes only because employment of wives compensated for falling wages of husbands. Rose and Fasenfest, "Family Incomes in the 1980s: New Pressure on Wives, Husbands and Young Adults." See, also Newman, *Falling From Grace: The Experience of*

Downward Mobility in the American Middle Class; Harrison and Bluestone, *The Great U-Turn;* Kuhn and Bluestone, "Economic Restructuring and Female Labor: The Impact of Industrial Change on Women"; Smith, "Marginalized Labor Forces During the Reagan Recovery"; Ehrenreich, *Fear of Falling;* Wolfe, *Whose Keeper? Social Science and Moral Obligation.*

14. Wilson, *Truly Disadvantaged,* and Smith, "Marginalized Labor Forces." One consequence of this is an increasing divergence in the family patterns of whites and African-Americans as marriage rates, in particular, plummet among the latter. See Cherlin, "Marriage, Divorce, Remarriage, 1950s–1980s," pp. 17–18.

15. Smith, "Marginalized Labor Forces," p. 1. See also *Forgotten Half.*

16. Smith, "Marginalized Labor Forces," p. 1; Levitan, Belous, and Gallo, *What's Happening to the American Family?,* p. 117. Rose and Fasenfest report a 17 percent decline in absolute earnings between 1979 and 1986 for men with high school educational levels or less. "Family Incomes in the 1980s," p. 11. See also, *The Forgotten Half;* and Harrison and Bluestone, *Great U-Turn.* As the size of the standing army has decreased, military recruiters can be much more selective. For example, the U.S. Army Corps now takes very few recruits who do not have a high school diploma. The sudden collapse of the Cold War is likely to exaggerate this trend.

17. Ehrenreich, *Fear of Falling,* p. 205.

18. Quoted in Wolfe, *Whose Keeper?* p. 65.

19. See Wright and Martin, "Tranformation of American Class Structure, 1960–1980," and Kuhn and Bluestone, "Economic Restructuring and Female Labor."

20. Ehrenreich, *Fear of Falling,* p. 202. Rose and Fasenfest, "Family Incomes in the 1980s," p. 8.

21. Ibid., p. 206. For supportive data, see Wright and Martin, "Transformation of American Class Structure."

22. Smith, "Marginalized Labor Forces"; Kuhn and Bluestone, "Economic Restructuring and Female Labor"; Kessler-Harris and Sacks, "Demise of Domesticity in America."

23. Wilson, "Losing a Generation of Children."

24. Newman, *Falling from Grace;* Ehrenreich, *Fear of Falling.*

25. Bane, *Here to Stay: American Families in the Twentieth Century;* Hacker, "Farewell to the Family: Ten Recent Books."

26. For relatively optimistic appraisals of recent gains by women, see Hartmann, "Changes in Women's Economic and Family Roles in Post-World War II United States," and Sternlieb and Baker, "Placing Deindustrialization in Perspective." So disparate have been gains registered by privileged women compared with the majority that Ehrenreich argues in *Fear of Falling* that middle-class feminism can be read as a means by

which the professional middle class consolidated its economic position in a period when two careers became necessary.

27. This useful term was coined by Deniz Kandiyoti in "Bargaining with Patriarchy."

28. Generally feminist researchers report poor progress in women's efforts to involve men in domestic work. See, for example, Hochschild with Machung, *Second Shift: Working Parents and the Revolution at Home;* Hartmann, "Family as Locus of Gender, Class, and Political Struggle: The Example of Housework." However, Spalter-Roth, "Differentiating Between the Living Standards of Husbands and Wives in Two-Wage-Earner Families, 1968 and 1979," finds employed women reducing their housework hours while their husbands increase theirs, a finding consistent with this study, as I discuss below.

29. For the unanticipated, adverse effects of divorce and custody reforms, see Weitzman, *Divorce Revolution: The Unexpected Social and Economic Consequences for Women and Children in America;* and Arendell, *Mothers and Divorce: Legal, Economic and Social Dilemmas;* for the mixed benefits of shared parenting, see Ehrensaft, *Parenting Together: Men and Women Sharing the Care of Their Children;* on sexual liberation, see Lawson, *Adultery: An Analysis of Love and Betrayal*, and Person, "Sexuality as a Mainstay of Identity: Psychoanalytic Perspectives."

30. In Kristin Luker's study of pro- and antiabortion activists, for example, most of the latter were housewives who spent at least thirty hours per week on antichoice politics, whereas most of the prochoice activists were career women, few of whom spent more than five hours per week on this issue. See her *Abortion & the Politics of Motherhood.* Although survey data on the relationship between female employment and attitudes toward feminism are somewhat inconsistent, most studies find full-time homemakers the least likely to support feminist views. An excellent summary of this literature appears in Fleming, "Public Opinion on Change in Women's Rights and Roles," esp. pp. 53–55. Studies indicate, logically enough, that women's participation in voluntary organizations has been declining as their participation in employment has risen. See Wolfe, *Whose Keeper?* pp. 89–90. It seems likely, therefore, that feminist and other progressive political causes have suffered disproportionately as a result.

31. See Fleming, "Public Opinion on Change in Women's Rights and Roles," p. 55, for data indicating higher levels of support for feminism among divorced and employed women.

32. Ammerman, *Bible Believers: Fundamentalists in the Modern World*, p. 141.

33. For Orthodox Judaism, see Kaufman, *Coming Home: Women, Jewish Orthodoxy, and Feminism* and "Coming Home to Jewish Orthodoxy: Reac-

tionary or Radical Women?" and Davidman, "Women's Search for Family and Roots: A Jewish Religious Solution to a Modern Dilemma." For Protestant evangelicalism in Colombia, see Brusco, "Colombian Evangelicalism as a Strategic Form of Women's Collective Action." For Muslims in Malaysia, see Ong, "Remaking the Malay Family: Modern Power, Islamic Resurgence, and the Body Politic in Malaysia."

34. Davidman, "Women's Search for Family and Roots," p. 20.

35. And, as I reported earlier, Faye Ginsburg even found that feminists had exerted noticeable influences on the right-to-life activists she studied in Fargo, North Dakota. *Contested Lives: The Abortion Debate in an American Community,* esp. pp. 194, 215.

36. Data provided in sources cited in note 42 below.

37. See Moffatt, *Coming of Age in New Jersey: College and American Culture,* for evidence of comparable attitudes among female undergraduates in the Rutgers University dormitories.

38. There is a great deal of empirical and theoretical support for this view, from feminist psychoanalytic analyses of mothering to time-budget studies of the domestic division of labor. For a direct discussion of women and "the work of kinship," see di Leonardo, *Varieties of Ethnic Experience: Kinship, Class, and Gender Among California Italian-Americans,* pp. 194–205. For an in-depth treatment of domestic labor, see Hochschild with Machung, *Second Shift.*

39. Patricia Zavella's research on the division of household labor among "Hispano" couples provides support for this view. See "Sunbelt Hispanics on the Line." A more comprehensive treatment of these issues among Anglo and Hispanic households will appear in Lamphere et al., *Working Mothers and Sunbelt Industrialization.* A recently released Gallup poll offers additional support; 46 percent of married men and 35 percent of married women claimed they divided household chores equally. An additional 8 percent of the men and 6 percent of the women claimed men did more than half of the chores. Destafano and Colestano, "Most Believe U.S. Men Have Better Life," p. B5.

40. The controversial *Time* cover story on the future of feminism, for example, reports a 1989 survey by Robert Half International in which 56 percent of men polled said they would forfeit one-fourth of their salaries "to have more family or personal time," and 45 percent "said they would probably refuse a promotion that involved sacrificing hours with their family." See also the Gallup poll data cited in note 39. And see Zavella, "Sun Belt Hispanics on the Line," for a discussion of the active participation in child care and housework by Hispanic husbands of women who are "mainstay providers" for their households.

41. Cherlin, "Marriage, Divorce, Remarriage," p. 17.

42. Between 1960 and 1980, a 43 percent decline among men between the

ages of twenty and forty-nine. Research by Eggebeen and Uhlenberg reported in Furstenberg, "Good Dads—Bad Dads: Two Faces of Fatherhood," p. 201.

43. The 90 percent datum is reported in Cherlin, "Changing American Family and Public Policy," p. 8. See Polikoff, "Gender and Child-Custody Determinations: Exploding the Myths," for a careful refutation of the widespread view that women retain an unfair advantage over men in child custody decisions by divorce courts.

44. Abel, "Adult Daughters and Care for the Elderly."

45. See literature cited in chapter 1, note 4. Recently, Alan Wolfe has attempted to formulate a centrist position in the debate over contemporary family change that would resist nostalgia for patriarchal family forms, while recognizing the destructive effects of state and market intrusions on "the family." *Whose Keeper?* He too worries about women's increasing involvement in the market and fails to question men's inadequate involvement in domesticity.

46. Belkin, "Bars to Equality of Sexes Seen as Eroding, Slowly." Likewise the 1990 Gallup poll reports that 57 percent of adults prefer a marriage in which both spouses work and share child care and housework. Destafano and Colestano, "Most Believe U.S. Men Have Better Life," p. B5.

47. Zavella, "Sunbelt Hispanics on the Line," finds a similar discrepancy between "traditionalist" ideology and reformist practice among Chicanas who serve as primary wage-earners in their households.

48. According to Joan Smith, low-income African-Americans provide the sole exception to this generalization because the majority contain only one possible wage-earner. "Marginalized Labor Forces," p. 1. For additional data, see Strober, "Two-Earner Families."

49. According to Myra Strober, in 1985, 42 percent of households were of this type. "Two-Earner Families," p. 161. However, Census Bureau data for 1988 report that only 27 percent of all households included two parents living with children. Quoted in Gutis, "What Makes a Family? Traditional Limits Are Challenged."

50. Bumpass and Castro, "Recent Trends and Differentials in Marital Disruption," p. 28.

51. As one of the journalists reporting the results of *The New York Times* survey reported above concluded, "Despite much talk about the decline of feminism and the women's movement, American women very much want a movement working on their behalf as they try to win equal treatment in the workplace and to balance the demands of work and family." Dionne, "Struggle for Work and Family Fueling Women's Movement." See also the *Time/CNN* survey that found 77 percent claiming the women's movement made life better for American women and

82 percent claiming it was still improving women's lives. Wallis, "Onward, Women!" p. 82. The Gallup data, however, reports smaller majorities with such views. See Destafano and Colesanto, "Most Believe U.S. Men Have Better Life," p. B5.

52. Study by Albert Solnit quoted in "Most Regard Family Highly," *New York Times* (10 October 1989), p. A18. Andrew Cherlin also reports increasing marital satisfaction rates despite popular concerns over family decline. "Economic Interdependence and Family Ties."

53. Wolfe, *Whose Keeper?* p. 211.

54. Freud's famous goal for psychoanalysis was to convert "hysterical misery into common unhappiness." Freud with Breuer, *Studies in Hysteria*.

Epilogue

1. Stacey, "Can There Be a Feminist Ethnography?"

2. See, for example, Marcus and Fischer, *Anthropology as Cultural Critique: An Experimental Moment in the Human Sciences.*

Bibliography

Abel, Emily. "Adult Daughters and Care for the Elderly." *Feminist Studies* 12, no. 3 (Fall 1986):479–97.

Acker, Joan. "Women and Social Stratification: A Case of Intellectual Sexism." *American Journal of Sociology* 78, no. 4 (1973):936–45.

Aidala, Angela A. "Social Change, Gender Roles, and New Religious Movements." *Sociological Analysis* 46, no. 3 (1985):287–314.

Ammerman, Nancy Tatom. *Bible Believers: Fundamentalists in the Modern World.* New Brunswick, NJ: Rutgers University Press, 1987.

Arendell, Terry. *Mothers and Divorce: Legal, Economic and Social Dilemmas.* Berkeley: University of California Press, 1986.

Axelrad, Marcie. *Profile of the Electronics Workforce in the Santa Clara Valley.* San Jose, CA: Project on Health and Safety in Electronics, 1979.

Baca-Zinn, Maxine, and D. Stanley Eitzen. *Diversity in American Families.* New York: Harper & Row, 1987.

Bane, Mary Jo. *Here to Stay: American Families in the Twentieth Century.* New York: Basic Books, 1976.

Barrett, Michelle, and Mary McIntosh. *The Antisocial Family.* London: New Left Books, 1982.

Barringer, Felicity. "Waiting Is Over: Births Near 50s Levels." *New York Times,* 31 October 1989, p. B1.

Beers, David. " 'Temps'—High-Tech's Ace in the Hole." *San Bernardino Sun,* 28 May 1985.

———. "Tomorrowland." *Image, San Francisco Examiner Magazine,* 18 January 1987.

Belkin, Lisa. "Bars to Equality of Sexes Seen as Eroding, Slowly," *New York Times,* 20 August 1989, pp. A1, A16.

Bell, Daniel. *The End of Ideology: On the Exhaustion of Political Ideas in the Fifties.* New York: Free Press, 1962.

————. *The Coming of Post-Industrial Society: A Venture in Social Forecasting.* New York: Basic Books, 1973.

Bellah, Robert. "Modernity in Question." Paper presented at the conference on Anthropology and Modernity, University of California-Berkeley, 9 April 1989.

Bellah, Robert N., Richard Madsen, William M. Sullivan, Ann Swidler, and Steven M. Tipton. *Habits of the Heart.* Berkeley: University of California Press, 1985.

Bendroth, Margaret L. "The Search for 'Women's Role' in American Evangelicalism, 1930–1980." In *Evangelicalism and Modern America,* edited by George Marsden, pp. 122–34. Grand Rapids, MI: William B. Eerdmans, 1984.

Beneria, Lourdes, and Catharine R. Stimpson, eds. *Women, Households, and the Economy.* New Brunswick, NJ: Rutgers University Press, 1987.

Berger, Bennett M. *Working-Class Suburb: A Study of Auto Workers in Suburbia.* Berkeley: University of California Press, 1968.

Berger, Peter, and Brigette Berger. *The War Over the Family.* Garden City, NY: Anchor Press/Doubleday, 1983.

Berke, Richard L. "Late Childbirth Is Found on Rise," *New York Times,* 22 June 1988, pp. B1, B6.

Bernard, Jessie. *The Future of Marriage.* 1972. Reprint. New York: Bantam Books, 1973.

Bernstein, Alan, Bob DeGrasse, Rachael Grossman, Chris Paine, and Lenny Siegel. "Silicon Valley: Paradise or Paradox? The Impact of High Technology Industry on Santa Clara County." Pamphlet prepared by Pacific Studies Center, Mountain View, CA, October 1987.

Bianchi, Suzanne M., and Daphne Spain. *American Women in Transition.* New York: Russell Sage, 1986.

Biggart, Nicole W. *Charismatic Capitalism: Direct Selling Organizations in America.* Chicago: University of Chicago Press, 1989.

Bilezikian, Gilbert. *Beyond Sex Roles.* Grand Rapids, MI: Baker Book House, 1985.

Block, Fred. "Postindustrial Development and the Obsolescence of Economic Categories." *Politics and Society* 14, no. 1 (1985):71–104.

————. *Postindustrial Possibilities: A Critique of Economic Discourse.* Berkeley: University of California Press, 1990.

Blum, Linda. *Between Feminism and Labor: The Significance of the Comparable Worth Movement.* Berkeley: University of Californis Press, forthcoming.

Bodovitz, Kathy. "Referendum Petitions Block S.F. Domestic Partners Law." *San Francisco Chronicle,* 7 July 1989, pp. A1, A20.

Bourke, Dale Hanson. "The Cost of Commitment." *Today's Christian Woman* 10, no. 1 (March/April 1988):7.

Bowen, Elenore Smith. *Return to Laughter. An Anthropological Novel.* 1954. Reprint. Garden City, NY: American Museum of Natural History/Doubleday, 1964.

Breines, Winifred. "The 1950s: Gender and Some Social Science." *Sociological Inquiry* 56, no. 1 (1986):69–92.

Brumberg, Joan Jacobs. *Mission for Life.* New York: Free Press, 1980.

Brusco, Elizabeth. "Colombian Evangelicalism as a Strategic Form of Women's Collective Action." *Feminist Issues* 6, no. 2 (Fall 1986):3–13.

Bumpass, Larry, and Teresa Castro. "Recent Trends and Differentials in Marital Disruption." Working Paper 87–20, Center for Demography and Ecology, University of Wisconsin-Madison, June 1987.

Bumpass, Larry, and James Sweet. "Preliminary Evidence on Cohabitation," National Survey of Families and Households Working Paper No. 2, Center for Demography and Ecology, University of Wisconsin-Madison, September 1988.

Bumpass, Larry, James Sweet, and Teresa Castro-Martin. "Changing Patterns of Remarriage." Working Paper 89–02, Center for Demography and Ecology, University of Wisconsin-Madison, 1989.

Burnham, Linda. "Has Poverty Been Feminized in Black America?" In *For Crying Out Loud: Women and Poverty in the United States,* edited by Rochelle Lefkowitz and Ann Withorn. New York: Pilgrim Press, 1986.

Bynum, Caroline Walker. *Jesus as Mother: Studies in the Spirituality of the High Middle Ages.* Berkeley: University of California Press, 1982.

Cancian, Francesca. "The Feminization of Love." *Signs* 11, no. 4 (Summer 1986):692–709.

———. *Love in America.* Cambridge: Cambridge University Press, 1987.

Caplow, Theodore, Howard Bahr, Bruce Chadwick, Reuben Hill, and Margaret Holmes Williamson. *Middletown Families: Fifty Years of Change and Continuity.* Toronto: Bantam Books, 1983.

Carey, Pete, and Alan Gathright. "By Work Obsessed. The Silicon Valley Ethic." *San Jose Mercury News,* 17–23 February 1985.

Carmichael, Bill, Nancie Carmichael, and Timothy Boyd. "Paving the Way to Intimacy." *Virtue* 10, no. 6 (1988):16–19.

Chaplin, David. "Domestic Service and the Negro." In *Blue Collar World: Studies of the American Worker,* edited by Arthur Shostak and William Gomberg. Englewood Cliffs, N.J.: Prentice-Hall, 1964.

Cherlin, Andrew. "Economic Interdependence and Family Ties." Paper presented at the annual meeting of the American Sociological Association, San Francisco, 9 September 1982.

———. "The Changing American Family and Public Policy." In *The Changing American Family and Public Policy*, edited by Andrew J. Cherlin. Washington, DC: Urban Institute Press, 1988.

———. "Marriage, Divorce, Remarriage: From the 1950s to the 1980s." Paper presented at the annual meeting of the American Sociological Association, San Francisco, 11 August 1989.

Cherlin, Andrew J., ed. *The Changing American Family and Public Policy*. Washington, DC: Urban Institute Press, 1988.

Clifford, James. *The Predicament of Culture: Twentieth-Century Ethnography, Literature, and Art*. Cambridge, MA: Harvard University Press, 1988.

Clifford, James, and George E. Marcus, eds. *Writing Culture: The Poetics and Politics of Ethnography*. Berkeley: University of California Press, 1986.

Cohen, Susan, and Mary Fainsod Katzenstein. "The War Over the Family Is Not Over the Family." In *Feminism, Children, and the New Families*, edited by Sanford M. Dornbusch and Myra H. Strober. New York: Guilford Press, 1988.

Coles, Robert, and June Hallowell Coles. *Women of Crisis: Lives of Struggle and Hope*. New York: Delacorte Press/S. Lawrence, 1978.

Collier, Jane, Michelle Rosaldo, and Sylvia Yanagisako. "Is There a Family? New Anthropological Views." In *Rethinking the Family: Some Feminist Questions*, edited by Barrie Thorne and Marilyn Yalom. New York: Longman, 1982.

Collins, Randall. *Sociology of Marriage and the Family: Gender, Love, and Property*. Chicago: Nelson-Hall, 1985.

Colson, Charles W. *Born Again*. Old Tappan, NJ: Fleming H. Revell Company, 1977.

Coontz, Stephanie. *The Social Origins of Private Life: A History of American Families 1600–1900*. London: Verso, 1988.

Coser, Lewis. *Greedy Institutions*. New York: Free Press, 1974.

Cott, Nancy F. "Young Women in the Second Great Awakening in New England." *Feminist Studies* 3, nos. 1/2 (Fall 1975):15–29.

———. *The Bonds of Womanhood: Women's Sphere in New England, 1700–1835*. New Haven: Yale University Press, 1977.

Cowan, Alison. "Poll Finds Women's Gains Have Taken Personal Toll." *New York Times*, 21 August 1989.

"The Daughter Who Begs to Differ," *San Francisco Chronicle*, 22 September 1989, p. A10.

Davidman, Lynn. "Women's Search for Family and Roots: A Jewish Religious Solution to a Modern Dilemma." In *In Gods We Trust: New Patterns of Religious Pluralism in America*, edited by Tom Robbins and Dick Anthony. New Brunswick, NJ: Transaction Books, forthcoming.

Davis, Kingsley. "The Meaning and Significance of Marriage in Contemporary Society." In *Contemporary Marriage: Comparative Perspectives on a*

Changing Institution, edited by Kingsley Davis and Amyra Grossbard-Schectman. New York: Russell Sage Foundation, 1985.

———. "Wives and Work: A Theory of the Sex-Role Revolution and Its Consequences." In *Feminism, Children, and the New Families,* edited by Sanford M. Dornbusch and Myra H. Strober, New York: Guilford Press, 1988.

Degler, Carl. *At Odds: Women and the Family in America from the Revolution to the Present.* Oxford: Oxford University Press, 1980.

Demos, John. *A Little Commonwealth: Family Life in Plymouth Colony.* New York: Oxford University Press, 1970.

Destafano, Linda and Diane Colesanto. "Most Believe U.S. Men Have a Better Life." *San Francisco Chronicle* 5 February 1990, pp. B3, 5.

di Leonardo, Micaela. "Deindustrialization as a Folk Model." *Urban Anthropology* 14, nos. 1–3 (1985):237–57.

———. *The Varieties of Ethnic Experience: Kinship, Class, and Gender Among California Italian-Americans.* Ithaca: Cornell University Press, 1984.

Dilnot, Clive. "What is the Post-Modern?" *Art History* 9, no. 2 (June 1986):245–63.

Dionne, E. J., Jr. "Struggle for Work and Family Fueling Women's Movement." *New York Times,* 22 August 1989, pp. A1, A14.

Dixon, Jennifer. "Senator Bentsen Says Home Ownership Has Declined." *San Francisco Examiner,* 22 October 1989, p. F10.

Dobson, James C. *Love Must Be Tough.* Waco, TX: Word Books, 1983.

Dollar, George W. *A History of Fundamentalism in America.* Greenville, SC: Bob Jones University Press, 1973.

Dornbusch, Sanford M., and Myra H. Strober, eds. *Feminism, Children, and the New Families.* New York: Guilford Press, 1988.

Early, David. "Equal Before God." *San Jose Mercury News,* March 1986.

Ehrenreich, Barbara. *The Hearts of Men: American Dreams and the Flight from Commitment.* Garden City, NY: Anchor Press/Doubleday, 1983.

———. *Fear of Falling: The Inner Life of the Middle Class.* New York: Pantheon, 1989.

Ehrenreich, Barbara, Elizabeth Hess, and Gloria Jacobs. *Re-Making Love: The Feminization of Sex.* New York: Doubleday, 1986.

Ehrensaft, Diane. *Parenting Together: Men and Women Sharing the Care of Their Children.* New York: Free Press, 1987.

Eisenscher, Michael. "Chasing the High Tech Rainbow: Reality and Fantasy in the Valley of the Silicon Giants." Paper presented at the Marxist Scholars Conference, University of California-Berkeley, November 1987.

Employment Development Department. "Annual Planning Information, San Jose Metropolitan Statistical Area 1987–1988." San Francisco: State of California, May 1987.

———. "The Future of Silicon Valley." San Francisco: State of California, September 1987.

Elson, Diane, and Ruth Pearson. "The Subordination of Women and the Internationalisation of Factory Production." In *Of Marriage and the Market*, edited by Kate Young, Carol Wolkowitz, and Roslyn McCullagh, pp. 144–66. London: CSE (Conference of Socialist Economics) Books, 1981.

Engels, Frederick. *The Condition of the Working Class in England.* 1845. Reprint. Chicago: Academy Chicago Publishers, 1984.

English, Deirdre. "The Fear that Feminism Will Free Men First." In *The Powers of Desire,* edited by Ann Snitow, Christine Stansell, and Sharon Thompson. New York: Monthly Review Press, 1983.

Ephron, Delia. *Funny Sauce: Us, the Ex, the Ex's New Mate, the New Mate's Ex, and the Kids.* New York: Viking Penguin, 1986.

———. "The Teflon Daddy." *New York Times Book Review,* 26 March 1989.

Epstein, Barbara Leslie. *The Politics of Domesticity: Women, Evangelism, and Temperance in Nineteenth-Century America.* Middletown, CT: Wesleyan University Press, 1981.

Evans, Sara M. *Born for Liberty: A History of Women in America.* New York: Free Press, 1989.

Fernandez-Kelly, M. Patricia. "Economic Restructuring in the United States: The Case of Hispanic Women in the Garment and Electronics Industries in Southern California." Paper presented at the annual meeting of the American Sociological Association, Chicago, August 1987.

Flammang, Janet. "Filling the Party Vacuum: Women at the Grassroots Level in Local Politics." In *Political Women: Current Roles in States and Local Government,* pp. 87–113. Beverly Hills, CA: Sage Publications, 1984.

———. "Female Officials in the Feminist Capital: The Case of Santa Clara County." *Western Political Quarterly* 38, no. 1 (March 1985):94–118.

———. "Women Made a Difference: Comparable Worth in San Jose." In *The Women's Movements of the United States and Western Europe,* edited by Ira Katznelson and Carole Mueller, pp. 290–309. Philadelphia: Temple University Press, 1987.

Fleming, Jeanne J. "Public Opinion on Change in Women's Rights and Roles." In *Feminism, Children, and the New Families,* edited by Sanford M. Dornbusch and Myra H. Strober. New York: Guilford Press, 1988.

The Forgotten Half: Pathways to Success for America's Youth and Young Families. Washington, DC: William T. Grant Foundation Commission on Work, Family and Citizenship, November 1988.

Freud, Sigmund, with Joseph Breuer. *Studies in Hysteria.* In *The Standard Edition of the Complete Psychological Works of Sigmund Freud, vol. 2,* edited and translated by James Strachey. London: Hogarth Press, 1954.

Fuchs, Victor R. "Sex Differences in Economic Well-Being." *Science* 232 (1986):459–64.

Furstenberg, Frank F., Jr. "Good Dads—Bad Dads: Two Faces of Fatherhood." In *The Changing American Family and Public Policy,* edited by Andrew J. Cherlin. Washington, DC: Urban Institute Press, 1988.

Gerson, Kathleen. *Hard Choices: How Women Decide About Work, Career, and Motherhood.* Berkeley: University of California Press, 1985.

Ginsburg, Faye. *Contested Lives: The Abortion Debate in an American Community.* Berkeley: University of California Press, 1989.

Glaphré, *When the Pieces Don't Fit God Makes the Difference.* Grand Rapids, MI: Zondervan, 1984.

Glenn, Evelyn Nakano. *Isei, Nisei, War Bride: Three Generations of Japanese American Women in Domestic Service.* Philadelphia: Temple University Press, 1986.

Glenn, Norval D., and Michael Supancic. "Social and Demographic Correlates of Divorce and Separation in the United States: An Update and Reconsideration." *Journal of Marriage and the Family* 46, no. 3 (August 1984):563–75.

Gordon, Deborah. "Writing Culture, Writing Feminism: The Poetics and Politics of Experimental Ethnography." *Inscriptions,* nos. 3/4 (1988):7–24.

Gordon, Linda. *Heroes of Their Own Lives.* New York: Viking, 1988.

Gordon, Richard, and Linda M. Kimball. "High Technology, Employment and the Challenges to Education." Silicon Valley Research Group, University of California, Santa Cruz, 1985.

———. "Industrial Structure and the Changing Global Dynamics of Location in High Technology Industry." Silicon Valley Research Group, University of California, Santa Cruz, 1986.

Green, Susan S. "Silicon Valley's Women Workers: A Theoretical Analysis of Sex-Segregation in the Electronics Industry Labor Market." In *Women, Men and the International Division of Labor,* edited by June Nash and Maria Patricia Fernandez-Kelly, pp. 273–331. Albany: State University of New York Press, 1983.

Gutis, Philip S. "Court Widens Family Definition to Gay Couples Living Together." *New York Times,* 7 July 1989, pp. A1, A13.

———. "What Makes a Family? Traditional Limits Are Challenged." *New York Times,* 31 August 1989, p. B1.

Hacker, Andrew. "Farewell to the Family: Ten Recent Books." *New York Review of Books,* 18 March 1982, pp. 37–44.

Halle, David. *America's Working Man.* Chicago: University of Chicago, 1984.

Harding, Sandra, ed. *Feminism and Methodology: Social Science Issues.* Bloomington: Indiana University Press, 1987.

Harding, Susan. "Convicted by the Holy Spirit: The Rhetoric of Fundamental Baptist Conversion." *American Ethnologist* 14, no. 1 (1987):167–81.

Harrison, Bennett, and Barry Bluestone. *The Great U-Turn.* New York: Basic Books, 1988.

311

Hartmann, Heidi. "Capitalism, Patriarchy, and Job Segregation by Sex." In *Capitalist Patriarchy and the Case for Socialist-Feminism,* edited by Zillah Eisenstein, pp. 206–47. New York: Monthly Review Press, 1979.

———. "The Family as the Locus of Gender, Class, and Political Struggle: The Example of Housework." *Signs* 6, no. 3 (1981):366–94.

———. "Changes in Women's Economic and Family Roles in Post-World War II United States." In *Women, Households and the Economy,* edited by Lourdes Beneria and Catharine R. Stimpson, New Brunswick, NJ: Rutgers University Press, 1987.

Hayes, Dennis. *Behind the Silicon Curtain: The Seductions of Work in a Lonely Era.* Boston: South End Press, 1989.

Hewlett, Sylvia Ann. *A Lesser Life. The Myth of Women's Liberation in America.* New York: William Morrow, 1986.

Hochschild, Arlie, with Anne Machung. *The Second Shift: Working Parents and the Revolution at Home.* New York: Viking Penguin, 1989.

Hollands, Jean. *The Silicon Syndrome: A Survival Handbook for Couples.* Palo Alto, CA: Coastlight Press, 1983.

Hossfeld, Karen J. "Divisions of Labor, Divisions of Lives: Immigrant Women Workers in Silicon Valley." Ph.D. diss. University of California-Santa Cruz, 1988.

Hout, Michael. "More Universalism, Less Structural Mobility: The American Occupational Structure in the 1980s." *American Journal of Sociology* 93, no. 6 (1988):1358–1400.

Howard, Robert. "Second Class in Silicon Valley." *Working Papers* (September-October 1981), p. 22.

Howe, E. Margaret. *Women and Church Leadership.* Grand Rapids, MI: Zondervan Corporation, 1982.

Howell, Joseph T. *Hard Living on Clay Street: Portraits of Blue Collar Families.* Garden City, NY: Anchor Press, 1973.

Humphries, Jane. "The Working-Class Family, Women's Liberation and Class Struggle: The Case of Nineteenth-century British History." *Review of Radical Political Economics* 9 (Fall 1977):25–41.

Hunter, James Davison. *American Evangelicalism.* New Brunswick, NJ: Rutgers University Press, 1983.

———. *Evangelicalism: The Coming Generation.* Chicago: University of Chicago Press, 1987.

Jackson, Kenneth T. *Crabgrass Frontier: The Suburbanization of the United States.* New York: Oxford University Press, 1985.

Johnson, Colleen Leahy. *Ex Familia: Grandparents, Parents and Children Adjust to Divorce.* New Brunswick, NJ: Rutgers University Press, 1988.

———. "Socially Controlled Civility: The Functioning of Rituals in the Divorce Process." *American Behavioral Scientist* 31, no. 6 (1988):685–701.

Johnson, Julie. "Two Approaches to Rebuilding the Women's Movement." *New York Times,* 14 August 1989.

Johnston, Moira. "High Tech, High Risk, and High Life in Silicon Valley." *National Geographic* 162, no. 4 (October 1982):459–76.

Kandiyoti, Deniz. "Bargaining with Patriarchy." *Gender & Society* 2, no. 3 (September 1988):274–90.

Kantor, Glenda Kaufman, and Murray A. Straus. "The 'Drunken Bum' Theory of Wife Beating." *Social Problems* 34, no. 3 (1987):213–30.

Katz, Naomi, and David S. Kemnitzer. "Fast Forward: The Internationalization of Silicon Valley." In *Women, Men and the International Division of Labor,* edited by June Nash and Maria Patricia Fernandez-Kelly, pp. 332–45. Albany: State University of New York Press, 1983.

Kaufman, Debra. "Coming Home to Jewish Orthodoxy: Reactionary or Radical Women?" *Tikkun* 2, no. 3 (1987):60–63.

———. *Women, Jewish Orthodoxy, and Feminism.* New Brunswick, NJ: Rutgers University Press, forthcoming.

Keller, John Frederick. "The Production Workers in Electronics: Industrialization and Labor Development in California's Santa Clara Valley." Ph.D. diss., University of Michigan, 1981.

———. "The Division of Labor in Electronics." In *Women, Men and the International Division of Labor,* edited by June Nash and Maria Patricia Fernandez-Kelly, pp. 346–73. Albany: State University of New York Press, 1983.

Kelly, Deirdre M. "Technology's Promise Unfulfilled: A Case Study of Women and Immigrant Production Workers in Silicon Valley's Semiconductor Industry." Master's thesis, Fletcher School of Law and Diplomacy, Tufts Unviersity, 1983.

———. "Understanding Immigrant and Minority Families in Industrial Society: The Case of Mexican Americans and Vietnamese in Silicon Valley." Unpublished paper, Stanford University, 1986.

Kessler-Harris, Alice, and Karen Brodkin Sacks. "The Demise of Domesticity in America." In *Women, Households and the Economy,* edited by Lourdes Beneria and Catharine R. Stimpson. New Brunswick, NJ: Rutgers University Press, 1987.

Komarovsky, Mirra, with Jane H. Philips. *Blue-Collar Marriage.* New York: Random House, 1962.

Krieger, Susan. "Beyond 'Subjectivity': The Use of the Self in Social Science." *Qualitative Sociology* 8, no. 4 (Winter 1985):309–24.

Kuhn, Sarah, and Barry Bluestone. "Economic Restructuring and the Female Labor Market: The Impact of Industrial Change on Women" In *Women, Households and the Economy,* edited by Lourdes Beneria and Catharine R. Stimpson. New Brunswick, NJ: Rutgers University Press, 1987.

Kushner, Harold S. *When All You've Ever Wanted Isn't Enough.* New York: Summit Books, 1986.

Lamphere, Louise, Felipe Gonzales, Patricia Zavella, and Peter Evans. *Working Mothers and Sunbelt Industrialization.* Ms. in progress.

Lasch, Christopher. *Haven in a Heartless World.* New York: Basic Books, 1977.

Lattin, Don. "How Religious Groups Stopped Partners Law," *San Francisco Chronicle,* 10 July 1989, pp. A1, A20.

————. "Two Faces of the Spiritual Revival." *San Francisco Chronicle,* 1 December 1989, p. B3.

Lawless, Elaine J. *God's Peculiar People: Women's Voices & Folk Tradition in a Pentecostal Church.* Lexington, KY: University Press of Kentucky, 1988.

Lawson, Annette. *Adultery: An Analysis of Love and Betrayal.* New York: Basic Books, 1988.

Lefkowitz, Rochelle, and Ann Withorn, eds. *For Crying Out Loud: Women and Poverty in the United States.* New York: Pilgrim Press, 1986.

Levitan, Sar A., Richard S. Belous, and Frank Gallo. *What's Happening to the American Family? Tensions, Hopes, Realities,* rev. ed. Baltimore: Johns Hopkins University Press, 1988.

Liebert, Larry. "Gloomy Statistics on the Future of Poor Children." *San Francisco Chronicle,* 2 October 1989, p. A2.

Lipset, Seymour Martin. *Political Man.* Garden City, NY: Doubleday, 1963.

Luker, Kristin. *Abortion & the Politics of Motherhood.* Berkeley: University of California Press, 1984.

Lyotard, Jean-Francois. *The Postmodern Condition: A Report on Knowledge,* translated by Geoff Bennington and Brian Massumi. 1979. Reprint. Manchester: Manchester University Press, 1984.

————. "Re-writing Modernity." *Sub-Stance* 16, no. 3 (1987):3–9.

McCrate, Elaine, June Lapidus, and Randy Albelda. "What Price Economic Independence? Women's Access to Resources in the Post-WWII Period." Paper presented at the Berkshire Women's History Conference, Wellesley College, June 1987.

Machung, Ann. "Talking Careers, Thinking Jobs." *Feminist Studies* 15, no. 1 (1989):35–58.

McLaughlin, Steven D., Barbara D. Melber, John O. G. Billy, Denise M. Zimmerle, Linda D. Winges, and Terry R. Johnson. *The Changing Lives of American Women.* Chapel Hill: University of North Carolina Press, 1988.

Malone, Michael S. *The Big Score.* Garden City, NY: Doubleday, 1985.

————. "Family in Crisis." *Santa Clara Magazine* (Spring 1989), p. 15.

Marcus, George. "Requirements for Ethnographies of Late Twentieth Century Modernity Worldwide." Paper presented at the Critical Theory Series, University of California-Davis, May 1989.

Marcus, George E., and Michael M. J. Fischer. *Anthropology as Cultural Cri-*

tique: An Experimental Moment in the Human Sciences. Chicago: University of Chicago Press, 1986.

Marsden, George M. "Preachers of Paradox: The Religious New Right in Historical Perspective." In *Religion and America*, edited by Mary Douglas and Steven Tipston, pp. 150–68. Boston: Beacon Press, 1982.

———. *Evangelicalism and Modern America.* Grand Rapids, MI: Wm. B. Eerdmans Publishing Company, 1984.

Marshner, Connaught. *The New Traditional Woman.* Washington, DC: Free Congress Research and Education Foundation, 1982.

Mascia-Lees, Frances E., Patricia Sharpe, and Colleen Ballerino Cohen. "The Postmodernist Turn in Anthropology: Cautions From a Feminist Perspective." *Signs* 15, no. 1 (Autumn 1989):7–33.

Mason, Karen Oppenheim, and Yu-hsia Lu. "Attitudes Toward Women's Familial Roles: Changes in the United States, 1977–1985." *Gender & Society* 2, no. 1 (March 1988):39–57.

Matthews, Glenna, "The Fruit Workers of the Santa Clara Valley: Alternative Paths to Union Organization during the 1930s." *Pacific Historical Review* 54 (1985):51–70.

———. "The Apricot War: A Study of the Changing Fruit Industry During the 1930s." *Agricultural History* 59 (1985):25–39.

May, Elaine Tyler. *Homeward Bound: American Families in the Cold War Era.* New York: Basic Books, 1988.

May, Martha. "Bread Before Roses: American Workingmen, Labor Unions and the Family Wage." In *Women, Work & Protest: A Century of U.S. Women's Labor History*, edited by Ruth Milkman, pp. 1–21. Boston: Routledge & Kegan Paul, 1985.

Mickelsen, Alvera. *Women, Authority & the Bible.* Downers Grove, IL: InterVarsity Press, 1986.

Mills, C. Wright. *The Sociological Imagination.* New York: Grove Press, 1959.

Mintz, Steven, and Susan Kellogg. *Domestic Revolutions: A Social History of American Family Life.* New York: Free Press, 1988.

Moffatt, Michael. *Coming of Age in New Jersey: College and American Culture.* New Brunswick, NJ: Rutgers University Press, 1989.

Mollenkott, Virginia Ramey. *Women, Men and the Bible.* Nashville, TN: Abingdon, 1977.

———. *The Divine Feminine: The Biblical Imagery of God as Female.* New York: Crossroad, 1983.

———. "An Evangelical Perspective on Interreligous Dialogue." In *Women of Faith in Dialogue*, edited by Virginia R. Mollenkott. New York: Crossroad, 1987.

Moore, Henrietta L. *Feminism and Anthropology.* Minneapolis: University of Minnesota Press, 1988.

Morgan, D. H. J. *Social Theory and the Family.* London: Routledge & Kegan Paul, 1975.

Morgan, Marabel. *The Total Woman.* Old Tappan, NJ: F. H. Revell, 1973.

Moynihan, Daniel Patrick. *The Negro Family: The Case for National Action.* Washington, DC: U.S. Department of Labor, 1965.

Nash, June, and Maria Patricia Fernandez Kelly, eds. *Women, Men and the International Division of Labor.* Albany: State University of New York Press, 1983.

Newman, Katherine S. *Falling from Grace: The Experience of Downward Mobility in the American Middle Class.* New York: Free Press, 1988.

Nolte, Carl. "The North Bay Is Where Most Folks Want to Live." *San Francisco Chronicle,* 22 February 1989, p. A6.

Ong, Aihwa. "Remaking the Malay Family: Modern Power, Islamic Resurgence, and the Body Politic in Malaysia." In *The Predicaments of Families,* edited by Aihwa Ong and Cristina Blanc-Szanton. Berkeley: University of California Press, forthcoming.

Ortner, Sherry B. "The Virgin and the State." *Feminist Studies* 4, no. 3 (October 1978):19–35.

Overholser, Geneva. "What 'Post-Feminism' Really Means." *New York Times,* 19 September 1986, p. 30.

Parsons, Talcott, and Robert Bales, in collaboration with Morris Zelditch, James Olds, and Philip Slater. *Family, Socialization, and Interaction Process.* New York: Free Press, 1953.

Person, Ethel Spector. "Sexuality as the Mainstay of Identity: Psychoanalytic Perspectives." *Signs* 5, no. 4 (1980):605–30.

Plutzer, Eric. "Work Life, Family Life, and Women's Support of Feminism." *American Sociological Review* 53, no. 4 (1988):640:49.

Pohli, Virginia. "Church Closets and Back Doors: A Feminist View of Moral Majority Women." *Feminist Studies* 9, no. 3 (Fall 1983):529–58.

Polikoff, Nancy D. "Gender and Child-Custody Determinations: Exploding the Myths." In *Families, Politics, and Public Policy: A Feminist Dialogue on Women and the State,* edited by Irene Diamond. New York: Longman, 1983.

Press, Andrea, and Terry Strathman. "Reconstructing the Family: Situation Comedy and the Construction of Postfeminism." Paper presented at the Society for the Study of Social Problems, Berkeley, California, August 1989.

Quebedeaux, Richard. *The Young Evangelicals.* New York: Harper & Row, 1974.

———. *The Worldly Evangelicals.* San Francisco: Harper & Row, 1978.

———. *By What Authority? The Rise of Personality Cults in American Christianity.* San Francisco: Harper & Row, 1982.

Rainwater, Lee, and William L. Yancey. *The Moynihan Report and the Politics of Controversy.* Cambridge, MA: MIT Press, 1967.

Rapp, Rayna. "Is the Legacy of Second Wave Feminism Postfeminism?" *Socialist Review* 18, no. 1 (January–March 1988):31–37.

Rapping, Elayne. "Tupperware and Women." *Radical America* 14, no. 6 (1980):39–49.

Ream, Jan Kiemel. "Help!" *Today's Christian Woman* 10, no. 1 (March/April 1988):70.

Reskin, Barbara F., and Heidi I. Hartmann, eds. *Women's Work, Men's Work: Sex Segregation on the Job.* Washington, DC: National Academy Press, 1986.

Rogers, Everett M., and Judith K. Larsen. *Silicon Valley Fever: Growth of High-Technology Culture.* New York: Basic Books, 1984.

Rogers, Susan Carol. "Female Forms of Power and the Myth of Male Dominance: A Model of Female-Male Interaction in Peasant Society." *American Ethnologist* 2 (1975):727–56.

Roiphe, Anne. *Lovingkindness.* New York: Summit Books, 1987.

Rollins, Judith. *Between Women: Domestics and Their Employers.* Philadelphia: Temple University Press, 1985.

Romero, Mary. "Domestic Service in the Transition to Urban Life." *Women's Studies* 13, no. 3 (1987):199–222.

"Ronald Reagan's Report Card." *Psychology Today,* October 1988, p. 10.

Rose, Phyllis. *Parallel Lives.* London: Chatto & Windus, Hogarth Press, 1983.

Rose, Stephan and David Fasenfest. "Family Incomes in the 1980s: New Pressures on Wives, Husbands and Young Adults." Working Paper No. 103. Washington, DC: Economic Policy Institute, November 1988.

Rose, Susan D. "Gender, Education and the New Christian Right." *Society* 26, no. 2 (1989):59–66.

Rosenfelt, Deborah. "Feminism, 'Postfeminism' and Contemporary Women's Fictions." In *Tradition and the Talents of Women,* edited by Florence Howe. Urbana, IL: University of Illinois Press, forthcoming 1990.

Rosenfelt, Deborah, and Judith Stacey. "Second Thoughts on the Second Wave." *Feminist Studies* 13, no. 2 (Summer 1987):341–61.

Rubin, Lillian. *Worlds of Pain: Life in the Working Class Family.* New York: Basic Books, 1976.

Ryan, Mary. *Cradle of the Middle Class: The Family in Oneida County, New York, 1790–1865.* Cambridge: Cambridge University Press, 1981.

Sahlins, Marshall. "The Return of the Event, Again; With Reflections on the Beginnings of the Great Fijian War of 1843 to 1855 between the Kingdoms of Bau and Rewa." In *Clio in Oceana,* edited by Aletta Bierseck. Washington, DC: Smithsonian Institute Press, forthcoming.

Saxenian, Anna Lee. "Silicon Chips and Spatial Structure: The Industrial Basis of Urbanization in Santa Clara County, California." Master's thesis, University of California-Berkeley, 1980.

Scanzoni, Letha Dawson, and Nancy A. Hardesty. *All We're Meant to Be: Biblical Feminism for Today,* rev. ed. Nashville, TN: Abingdon Press, 1986.

Schnaiberg, Allan, and Sheldon Goldenberg. "From Empty Nest to Crowded Nest: The Dynamics of Incompletely-Launched Young Adults." *Social Problems* 36, no. 3 (June 1989):251–69.

Schneidawind, John. "New Flight From Silicon Valley's High Costs." *San Francisco Chronicle,* 11 May 1989, p. 1.

Schneider, David M., and Raymond T. Smith. *Class Differences and Sex Roles in American Kinship and Family Structure.* Englewood Cliffs, NJ: Prentice-Hall, 1973.

Siegel, Lenny, and Herb Borock. "Background Report on Silicon Valley." Prepared for U.S. Commission on Civil Rights. Mountain View, CA: Pacific Studies Center, 1982.

Siegel, Lenny, and John Markoff. *The High Cost of High Tech: The Dark Side of the Chip.* New York: Harper & Row, 1985.

Skold, Karen. "The Interests of Feminists and Children in Child Care." In *Feminism, Children, and the New Families,* edited by Sanford M. Dornbusch and Myra H. Strober. New York: Guilford Press, 1988.

Smith, Joan. "The Paradox of Women's Poverty: Wage-Earning Women and Economic Transformation." *Signs* 10, no. 2 (1984):291–310.

———. "Marginalized Labor Forces during the Reagan Recovery." Paper Presented to the Society for the Study of Social Problems, Berkeley, California, August 1989.

Sojourners: An Independent Christian Monthly 17, no. 3 (March 1988).

Spalter-Roth, Roberta. "Differentiating between the Living Standards of Husbands and Wives in Two-Wage-Earner Families, 1968 and 1979." *Journal of Economic History* 43, no. 1 (1983):231–40.

Sparr, Pamela. "Reevaluating Feminist Economics: 'Feminization of Poverty' Ignores Key Issues." In *For Crying Out Loud: Women and Poverty in the United States,* edited by Rochelle Lefkowitz and Ann Withorn. New York: Pilgrim Press, 1986.

Stacey, Judith. "Are Feminists Afraid to Leave Home? The Challenge of Profamily Feminism." In *What Is Feminism?* edited by Juliet Mitchell and Ann Oakley, pp. 208–37. New York: Pantheon Books, 1986.

———. " 'Sexism by a Subtler Name?' Postindustrial Conditions and Postfeminist Consciousness in the Silicon Valley." *Socialist Review* 17, no. 6 (November–December 1987):7–28.

———. "Can There Be a Feminist Ethnography?" *Women's Studies International Forum* 11, no. 1 (1988):21–27.

Stacey, Judith, and Susan Elizabeth Gerard. "We Are Not Doormats": The Influence of Feminism on Contemporary Evangelicalism in the United States." In *Uncertain Terms: Negotiating Gender in American Culture,* edited by Faye Ginsburg and Anna Tsing. Boston: Beacon Press, 1990.

Stack, Carol B. *All Our Kin: Strategies for Survival in a Black Community.* New York: Harper & Row, 1974.

Stagg, Evelyn, and Frank Stagg. "Jesus and Women." *Christian History* 7, no. 1 (1988):29–31.

Stanley, Liz, and Sue Wise. *Breaking Out: Feminist Consciousness and Feminist Research*. London: Routledge & Kegan Paul, 1983.

Sternlieb, George, and Carole W. Baker. "Placing Deindustrialization in Perspective." In *Women, Households and the Economy*, edited by Lourdes Beneria and Catharine R. Stimpson, New Brunswick, NJ: Rutgers University Press, 1987.

Stone, Lawrence. "The Road to Polygamy." *New York Review of Books* 36, no. 3 (2 March 1989):12–15.

Storkey, Elaine. *What's Right with Feminism*. Grand Rapids, MI: Eerdmans Publishing, 1985.

Strathern, Marilyn. "An Awkward Relationship: The Case of Feminism and Anthropology." *Signs* 12, no. 2 (Winter 1987):276–80.

Streeter, Carole. *Finding Your Place after Divorce*. Grand Rapids, MI: Zondervan, 1986.

Strober, Myra H. "Two-Earner Families." In *Feminism, Children, and the New Families*, edited by Sanford M. Dornbusch and Myra H. Strober. New York: Guilford Press, 1988.

Strom, Kay. *Helping Women in Crisis*. Grand Rapids, MI: Zondervan, 1986.

Taylor, Ella. *Prime-Time Families: Televison Culture in Postwar America*. Berkeley: University of California Press, 1989.

Tessler, Ray. "Churches' Holy War on Drugs." *San Francisco Chronicle*, 19 May 1988.

Thurow, Lester C. "The Post-Industrial Era Is Over." *New York Times*, 4 September 1989, p. A19.

Tolstoy, Leo. *Anna Karenina*. 1877. Reprint. New York: New American Library, 1961.

"Too Late for Prince Charming?" *Newsweek*, 2 June 1986, pp. 54–62.

"Two Job Openings at *Sojourners*." *Sojourners* (March 1988), p. 25.

U.S. Bureau of the Census. *Census of Population: 1950*. Vol. 2, *Characteristics of the Population*, pt. 5, California, 1952.

————. *Census of Population: 1960*.

————. *Census of Population: 1970*.

————. *Census of the Population: 1980*. Vol. 1, *Characteristics of the Population, General Population Characeristics*, pt. 6, California, 1982.

————. *Statistical Abstract of the United States, 1981*.

United Way of Santa Clara County. "A Community Challenged: A Public Report on Human Needs in Santa Clara County." Pamphlet prepared by United Way of Santa Clara County, Santa Clara, CA, October 1989.

Van Horn, Susan Householder. *Women, Work, and Fertility, 1900–1986*. New York: New York University Press, 1988.

Wakefield, Dan. "And Now, A Word from Our Creator." *New York Times Book Review*, 12 February 1989, pp. 1, 28–29.

Walker, Henry A. "Black-White Differences in Marriage and Family Patterns." In *Feminism, Children, and the New Families*, edited by Sanford M. Dornbusch and Myra H. Strober. New York: Guilford Press, 1988.

Walker, Richard. "Is There a Service Economy? The Changing Division of Labor." *Science & Society* 49, no. 1 (1985):42–83.

Wallerstein, Judith S. "Women after Divorce: Preliminary Report from a Ten-Year Follow-Up," *American Journal of Orthopsychiatry* 56, no. 1 (January 1986):65–77.

Wallerstein, Judith S., and Sandra Blakeslee. *Second Chances: Men, Women and Children a Decade after Divorce*. New York: Ticknor & Fields, 1989.

Wallis, Claudia. "Onward, Women!" *Time*, 4 December 1989, pp. 80–89.

Walshok, Mary Lindenstein. "Occupational Values and Family Roles: Women in Blue-Collar and Service Occupations." In *Working Women and Families*, edited by Karen Wolk Feinstein, pp. 63–83. Beverly Hills, CA: Sage Publications, 1979.

Warner, R. Stephen. *New Wine in Old Wineskins: Evangelicals and Liberals in a Small-Town Church*. Berkeley: University of California Press, 1988.

Weitzman, Lenore. *The Divorce Revolution: The Unexpected Social and Economic Consequences for Women and Children in America*. New York: Free Press, 1985.

Weston, Kathleen M. "A Working Report on Women in the International Division of Labor Power of the Silicon Valley-Based Electronics Industry." Stanford University, 1982.

"When 'Families' Will Have a New Definition." *U.S. News and World Report*, 9 May 1983.

Williams, Linda. *Hard Core: Power, Pleasure, and the "Frenzy of the Visible."* Berkeley: University of California Press, 1989.

Williford, Stanley O., "Addressing Problems of Home on Air." *Los Angeles Times*, 3 January 1987, part VI, p. 10.

Willis, Paul. *Learning to Labor: How Working Class Kids Get Working Class Jobs*. New York: Columbia University Press, 1977.

Wilson, William J. "Losing a Generation of Children." Paper presented at the annual meeting of the American Sociological Association, San Francisco, 10 August 1989.

———. *The Truly Disadvantaged: The Inner City, the Underclass and Public Policy*. Chicago: University of Chicago Press, 1987.

Wolfe, Alan. *Whose Keeper? Social Science and Moral Obligation*. Berkeley: University of California Press, 1989.

Wolff, Janet. *Feminine Sentences: Essays on Women and Culture*. Berkeley: University of California Press, 1990.

"Women in the Early Church." Special issue of *Christian History* 7, no. 1, (1988).

The Working Women: A Progress Report. Washington, DC: Conference Board, 1985.

Wright, Erik Olin, and Bill Martin, "The Transformation of the American Class Structure, 1960–1980." *American Journal of Sociology* 93, no. 1 (1987):1–29.

Wright, Erik Olin, Cynthia Costello, David Hacker, and Joey Sprague. "The American Class Structure." *American Sociological Review* 47, no. 6 (1982):709–26.

Wuthnow, Robert. "The Political Rebirth of American Evangelicals." In *The New Christian Right: Mobilization and Legitimation,* edited by Robert C. Liebman and Robert Wuthnow. New York: Aldine, 1983.

Yanigasako, Sylvia. "Capital and Gendered Interest in Italian Family Firms." Colloquium presentation, Department of Anthropology, University of California-Berkeley, January 30, 1989.

Young, Michael, and Peter Willmott. *Family and Kinship in East London.* 1957. Reprint. Middlesex: Penguin, 1962.

Zanon, Lee. "What's New." *Virtue* 10, no. 6 (1988):8.

Zavella, Patricia. "The Impact of 'Sun Belt Industrialization' on Chicanas." Stanford Center for Chicano Research, Working Paper Series No. 7, n.d.

———. "Sunbelt Hispanics on the Line." paper presented at History and Theory Conference, University of California-Irvine, April 1989.

Index

Photograph by Julie Brown

Judith Stacey is the Streisand Professor of Contemporary Gender Studies and Professor of Sociology at the University of Southern California. Her publications include *In the Name of The Family: Rethinking Family Values in the Postmodern Age* and *Patriarchy and Socialist Revolution in China,* which won the 1985 Jessie Bernard Award from the American Sociological Association. *Brave New Families* was a finalist for the C. Wright Mills award in 1991. Stacey is a founding and executive committee member of the Council on Contemporary Families, a group of researchers and clinicians committed to reframing the politics of family values.

Compositor: Impressions Book and Journal Services, Inc.
      Text: Berthold Baskerville
   Display: Gill Sans
   Printer: Edwards Brothers, Inc.
    Binder: Edwards Brothers, Inc.